INTERNATIONAL STATEBUILDING IN WEST AFRICA

INTERNATIONAL STATEBUILDING IN WEST AFRICA

Civil Wars and New Humanitarianism in Sierra Leone, Liberia, and Côte d'Ivoire

—∿—

ABU BAKARR BAH

NIKOLAS EMMANUEL

INDIANA UNIVERSITY PRESS

This book is a publication of

Indiana University Press
Office of Scholarly Publishing
Herman B Wells Library 350
1320 East 10th Street
Bloomington, Indiana 47405 USA

iupress.org

Manufactured in the United States of America

First Printing 2024

Cataloging information is available from the Library of Congress.

ISBN 978-0-253-07062-3 (hardback)
ISBN 978-0-253-07063-0 (paperback)
ISBN 978-0-253-07064-7 (e-book)

CONTENTS

ACKNOWLEDGMENTS

AT A TIME WHEN THERE is so much political upheaval within African states and the international system more broadly, any work on international statebuilding, civil wars, and humanitarianism must start by acknowledging the people in war-torn countries. This book is about those people—the citizens of Sierra Leone, Liberia, and Côte d'Ivoire. Too often, they have been the victims of coloniality, civilian and military dictators, warlords, and corrupt government officials. These forces have created the conditions of state decay that result in civil wars and excessive human insecurity. This book clearly captures these problems and the plights of the people while showing the efforts to enhance human security and build better states. We stand in solidary with the victims and call out the perpetrators of structural and physical violence while recognizing all those actors, domestic and external, who have made noble efforts to enhance human security. This book is an academic work that is rooted in the firm belief that the purpose of knowledge is to change the human condition—for the better! In this way, this book is about the people, and it is to be used by those in power to improve the political, economic, and social conditions of the people.

As a scholarly work, this book emanates from our intellectual and social scientific training and growth over the past decades. Even though this book is our own work, we are grateful to mentors who shaped our earlier understanding of social and political issues. For me, Abu Bakarr Bah, that goes to the scholars at the New School for Social Research in New York, notably Andrew Arato, Jose Casanova, and David Ploke. For me, Nikolas Emmanuel, I would like to thank Donald Rothchild (University of California, Davis) and Daniel Bach (Sciences Po Bordeaux) for mentoring me and encouraging me to be the scholar and person that I have become. We should also add the colleagues and friends in our fields who have been intellectual checkpoints and go-to people for support. For me, Abu Bakarr Bah, these include Bill Zartman, Wale Adebanwi, Ebenezer Obadare, Cyril Obi, Ismail Rashid, Leonardo Villalón, Nic Cheeseman, Ismael Montana, Diane Rodgers, Susan Russell, Kurt Thurmaier, Andrew Otieno, and Teresa Wasonga, just to name a few of them. For me, Nikolas Emmanuel, I would like to thank my coauthor, Abu Bakarr Bah, for encouraging me to be a part of this book. I appreciate his friendship and his hard work. Thank you for including me. As coauthors, we must also recognize the intellectual bonds we have developed over the past decade. Our common interests have resulted in multiple coauthored works on peace and conflict issues.

The research presented here comes not only from our intellectual prowess but also the rich data that underpin the book. As such, we owe deep gratitude to all those people who helped in the collection of the data, notably at the United Nations in New York and in West Africa (Sierra Leone, Liberia, Côte d'Ivoire, and Senegal). Abu Bakarr Bah spent several months in these places and received tremendous information from scholars, government officials, diplomats, military officers, ex-combatants, officials of international organizations, civil society leaders, and people who directly experienced the civil wars. This work would not have been possible without the generosity of the respondents. We are also grateful to the research assistants for their help in the process of collecting and organizing the data. In particular, these include Dimitri Sidoine Gnamien in Côte d'Ivoire, Aloysius Nyati in Liberia, Ousmane Ba in Senegal, and graduate students at Northern Illinois University (Shay Galto, Kimberly Leifker, Justin Yates, and Greta Gustafson). We also thank Amanda Victória Souza, who worked as a research assistant while a graduate student at the School of International Peace Studies at Soka University of Japan, for her excellent work supporting the last stage of the book.

Data collection requires resources and logistical support. This research was facilitated by colleagues, friends, and extended family relations in Sierra Leone, Liberia, Côte d'Ivoire, and Senegal. Some of these include Amadu Sidi Bah, Nima Bah-Chang, Russell Chang, Amadu Tejan Bah, Ibrahim Bah, and Sulaiman Bah in Sierra Leone; Lansana Gberie and Sulaiman Bah in Liberia; Younoussa Diallo in Côte d'Ivoire; and Ousmane Sene, Abibatou Ndiaye Diallo, and Abibou Diop in Senegal. We must also acknowledge the institutional support from the West African Research Association, the Council of American Overseas Research Centers, and Northern Illinois University for funding the research. We are also very grateful to the anonymous reviewers of the work and the staff and leadership at Indiana University Press for their efforts and insightful contributions in improving the work during each phase of the publication process.

All successful works come out of institutional and personal support systems, most notably family. We are deeply grateful to our families for their support and contributions, which make our work possible and successful. For me, Abu Bakarr Bah, I must first thank Rugiatu (Rugie) Bah, my wife of over two decades. Rugie has been the backbone to my professional work and the balance in my life. Our three children—Manmadu, Ibrahim, and Aisha—are always in the mix as amplifiers of joy and points of meaning in our life. They are true blessings for me, and I am deeply grateful to all four of them. In my world, family is stretched far and deep to parents and siblings. All of these people, notably my mother (Haja Isatu Bah), father (Alhaji Mohamed Bah) and sister (Mariama Jelloh Bah), provide the inner energy that fuels my professional work and grounding in the everyday world. For Nikolas Emmanuel, I would finally like to express my immense gratitude to both my wife, Frédérique, and my daughter, Margaux. From giving feedback on ideas and drafts of the project to providing unending moral support and love throughout the entire process, they were as important to this book getting done as I was. Thanks so much, both of you. Finally, we must come back to the people upon whose social, economic, and political conditions this book rests. The real success of this work and the deepest joy for us will lie not only on the reified academic measures that we have become accustomed to but on the insights that readers, especially in the policy world, can gain from this work and use to address the causes of oppression and human insecurity in Sierra Leone, Liberia, Côte d'Ivoire, and similar countries. The actual fulfillment of our gratitude lies in how this work is used in the praxis of statebuilding. We realize our limited agency in that praxis, but our scholarship and intellectual contributions are rooted not just in seeking academic accolades but in the firm belief that knowledge must be used to improve the human condition. This book is a step in that process, as we count on those in power to put the ideas into action for the benefit of the people.

Abu Bakarr Bah
Presidential Research Professor
Northern Illinois University

Nikolas Emmanuel
Professor of Political Science
Graduate School of International Peace Studies (SIPS)
Soka University of Japan

INTERNATIONAL STATEBUILDING IN WEST AFRICA

ONE

INTRODUCTION

The Contours of Statebuilding and Humanitarian Intervention

INTRODUCTION

The civil wars in Liberia (1989–1996 and 1999–2003), Sierra Leone (1991–2002), and Côte d'Ivoire (2002–2007 and 2010–2011) attracted significant international attention that led to major peacemaking and statebuilding efforts by the international community. In Liberia and Sierra Leone, there were robust international humanitarian interventions and postwar reconstruction efforts, while in Côte d'Ivoire, the international community played a critical supportive role in ending the fighting and forging a still-shaky political solution to the conflict. These civil wars and the pursuant peacebuilding efforts of the international community raise important questions about the challenges of building states in Africa. They exposed not only the fragility of African states but also the impediments to developing reasonably stable, democratic, and prosperous states in Africa. The political instabilities and poor economic and social conditions in a number of African countries have led to them being portrayed as rife with violence and poverty. Many African states have been characterized as undemocratic, underdeveloped, least developed, weak, decayed, fragile, and failed.[1] Notwithstanding the problematic nature of labeling, these ascriptions do to some extent portray the political, economic, and social predicaments of many African states. The pathologies of African states are even more acute in war-torn countries, such as Liberia and Sierra Leone. As one of the interview respondents in this study indicated concerning Liberia, "There is considerable dissatisfaction and suffering among the people of this country."[2] Côte d'Ivoire, which was once an oasis of peace and prosperity in West Africa, has also been marred by political violence and declining economic and social conditions.

1

Yet civil wars are not necessarily the underlying problems of the African state; rather, they are manifestations of fundamental problems of statehood, most notably the lack of political freedom, social justice, and economic opportunity. Civil wars must be treated not only as crises to be quelled but as opportunities to rethink the state and build better policies and institutions. In the face of the devastation in war-torn Liberia, Sierra Leone, and Côte d'Ivoire, scholars and policymakers should be seeking ways to transform these states from oppressive political and economic apparatuses into political systems that foster freedom, social justice, and economic development. These transformations could take the form of a fundamental break with the prewar political system or significant postwar changes in the political culture and state institutions that could serve as catalysts for democracy and economic development. Such changes could be the result of homegrown political and civic awareness born out of the wars, the deployment of international forces and humanitarian agencies, or a combination of changes in domestic political culture and the impact of international intervention. The critical issue is to understand the links between state decay and civil war on the one hand and international humanitarian intervention and statebuilding on the other. These interconnections must be traced not only to the antecedent colonial and neocolonial statebuilding projects but also to the evolving nature of the international community and humanitarianism.

Some notable cases in West Africa that demonstrate the interconnections between civil war and statebuilding include Nigeria, Liberia, and Sierra Leone. Since the Biafran War (1967–1970), Nigeria has engaged in numerous efforts to redesign the state in ways that take into account the country's ethnic and regional diversity.[3] The process of redesigning the Nigerian state has largely been internally driven. In contrast, the civil wars in Liberia and Sierra Leone attracted significant international intervention in both the peace processes and postwar reconstruction efforts.[4] In Côte d'Ivoire, too, the international community played a major role in the peace process, albeit with limited success during the first half of the Ivoirian Civil War.[5] These three countries present illuminating cases for understanding the nexus between civil war and international statebuilding in West Africa and contributing to the wider body of literature on civil wars, international interventions, and neoliberal statebuilding.

Over the past few decades, there has been a huge increase in intrastate wars and international humanitarian-cum-military interventions, including in West Africa. Numerous works have been published on these events with a focus on peace and conflict, democracy, and international development. These bodies of work often evoke two critical questions that are important for statebuilding in war-torn postcolonial multiethnic states: What are the underlying causes of violent conflicts? And how can countries design institutions that create conditions for a peaceful and democratic state?[6] This study taps into these questions and expands the focus. Overall, two lines of work are relevant to our study—those that address the connections between civil wars and democratic statebuilding, especially through international intervention driven by humanitarianism and regional/international security concerns, and those that examine civil wars and the challenges of peacebuilding.

The first line of work—on civil wars, statebuilding, and the building of peaceful democratic states—finds its roots in the works of scholars such as Charles Tilly.[7] Tilly's work on war making and state making has led to a growing interest in the relation between civil wars and the making of democratic states, notably in Europe. This interest now includes developing countries, especially through international humanitarian interventions. Reyko Huang, for example, has examined the connection between civil wars and democratizations in Nepal, Tajikistan, Uganda, and Mozambique.[8] In Robert Blair's study of Liberia, he examines the role of the international community in building the rule of law in postwar settings, which is critical for building a democratic state.[9] Similar issues of liberalism are addressed by Roland Paris's work on peacebuilding.[10] Paris examined the efforts to build market democracies in numerous war-torn countries in Africa, Latin America, and Asia. The critical issue is how to consolidate peace, and this often involves issues of economic and political liberalization along the lines of liberal peace. Paris argues that neoliberal political and economic reform packages make sense but warns that reforms are pushed much too quickly by the United Nations (UN), donors, and other international actors, potentially undermining postwar peacebuilding and leading the belligerents back into war.

Another important strand in this line of work examines the root causes of civil wars, notably in Africa. Key among these are the works that focus on corruption and authoritarianism. William Reno's work on Sierra Leone, for example, shows how the country became ripe for civil war.[11] Abu Bah and Ibrahim Bangura further show how patrimonialism persisted even after the civil war.[12] Robert Bates provides a panoramic analysis of the effects of corruption across several African countries.[13] Notably, he examines the impact of elite political behavior, as the elite increasingly lack incentives to promote the public good over the long term. This has led to high levels of corruption across a wide swath of African countries. Theft of public resources became a clear strategy to ensure the political survival of the elite, but that undermined legitimacy, the economy, and the political system as a whole. As financial security diminishes in such systems, various groups (regional, religious, ethnic, etc.) compete for scarce resources, bringing them into violent conflict with each other. Essentially, civil wars are attributed to ethnicity and oppressive and corrupt rule, as evidenced by the greed-versus-grievance thesis.[14] In this line of thought, the main cause of civil wars is seen to be the absence of liberal democracy.[15] However, our understanding of what appropriate institutional designs to foster thriving multiethnic democracies would look like is limited.

Other research on war-making and statebuilding focuses more on human development. For example, Ashraf Ghani and Clare Lockhart focus on the practical domestic and international problems that impede the transformation of states plagued by war and terrorism warfare, most notably in Afghanistan, Sudan, Kosovo, and Nepal.[16] In their work, the processes by which fragile states become stable depend jointly on human security and human development and international development assistance. Ghani and Lockhart argue that peacebuilding efforts and the rehabilitation of failed states generally do not succeed due to the fact that there is often no comprehensive framework for coordinated action that takes on a citizen-based approach. Tanja Schümer takes up the issue of international aid and human development in Sierra Leone during the time of its civil war.[17]

There are also works on postwar statebuilding issues particularly focusing on the area of social justice. A notable example is Peace Medie's work on violence against women.[18] Medie examines the implementation of international norms and postwar reforms with regard to violence against women in Liberia and Côte d'Ivoire. Studies focused on transitional justice and postwar reconstruction address broader issues of human development and peacebuilding. However, they are more concerned with human rights and postwar human development than addressing structural challenges to democracy and the institutional arrangement of the state. Transitional justice studies also focus on war crimes.[19] To its credit, the postwar reconstruction literature has sometimes addressed institutional reforms, especially in the security sector.[20] A key part of the postwar reconstruction studies rests on analysis of the peace dividend associated with generous international development assistance and the promotion of good governance and human development.[21] However, institutional reforms in the postwar reconstruction literature generally limit their focus to enhancing the implementation of current programs and effectiveness of extant institutions. The studies focus on good governance and human development without addressing core questions about the state and its institutional choices and designs.

A second critical line of work examines the challenges of peacebuilding in the context of civil wars, especially though international peacekeeping and peace mediation efforts. Some of the earlier works in this track relate to the ethics of international interventions, especially in relation to human security, state sovereignty, and the responsibility to protect (R2P). While the works tend to differ in their assessment of the motivations for and implications of international military intervention, they all address the interconnections between civil wars and security (human, state, regional, and international) and the ethical and practical dilemmas of international interventions. Neta Crawford, for example, covers the ethical dilemmas of international interventions through the frame of decolonization.[22] Once international intervention is initiated, there are also a host of challenges to peacebuilding. Séverine Autesserre discusses the challenges of international intervention and why peacebuilding has failed in the Congo and elsewhere.[23] Autesserre follows up on this in *Peaceland*, which examines ground-level problems that impede the success of international peace builders.[24]

There are also significant works that focus on the nature of the civil wars and the regional-cum-international interventions in West Africa.[25] Adekeye Adebajo's *Building Peace in West Africa* provides a sobering read, underlining the reality that Africa as a continent has been increasingly marginalized in the international system.[26] Adebajo focuses his research on a cluster of neighboring countries (Liberia, Sierra Leone, and Guinea-Bissau) devastated by civil war. All three countries witnessed a wide variety of initiatives to help end the violence, but Adebajo argues that the various interventions of the international community (e.g., Great Britain in Sierra Leone or France in Côte d'Ivoire) have primarily been based on the security interests of the Western intervenors. Few works researching ways to maintain security in Africa explore the links between the state and the structural conditions for peace. Instead, structural factors are framed within the political economy of war discourse.[27]

This book is about statebuilding in war-torn African countries, using Sierra Leone, Liberia, and Côte d'Ivoire as case studies. Beyond shedding light on these three critical cases in West Africa, we seek to further our understanding of the problematic nature of the postcolonial state and its effects on the well-being of its people. Our work explores both the challenges and opportunities for building peaceful and democratic postcolonial states in Africa and addresses critical factors affecting the stability of states: their vulnerabilities, the roles of the international actors in the development of states, the mechanics of statebuilding, and the nature of institutional design. This study tackles an overarching question: How can a multiethnic postcolonial war-torn country be transformed into a peaceful and democratic state? This question provokes other related questions about the case countries and broader issues of international relations: What are the causes of state collapse and civil wars? How does the international community respond to state collapse and civil wars? How are the causes of the civil wars addressed? What kinds of institutional arrangements have been established to ensure durable peace and inclusive democracy? This book examines the reasons for the problematic nature of the state in Sierra Leone, Liberia, and Côte d'Ivoire; suggests pathways for building peaceful and democratic states; and looks at the role of the international community in statebuilding.

METHODOLOGY AND DATA COLLECTION

This book is based on qualitative research that combines the comparative-historical methodology with expert interviews rooted in grounded theory. At its core, the work is a comparative and historical study of civil wars, international humanitarian interventions, and statebuilding in three West African countries: Sierra Leone, Liberia, and Côte d'Ivoire. The data collection and analysis followed established methodological traditions in the social sciences, most notably political science, sociology, and anthropology.[28] Data was collected from rich archival materials on primary documents during the fieldwork and supplemented with secondary sources from the academic literature, policy documents, and established media sources. In addition, expert interviews were conducted, and deep insights were gathered from field observations and insider knowledge of the African political experiences derived from extensive involvement with African diaspora communities and lived experiences. Such data-collection methods have deep roots in the study of political and social issues in the modern world going back to the works of Auguste Comte, Karl Marx, Max Weber, Emile Durkheim, and Bronislaw Malinowski, who are among the classical founders of modern social science rooted in comparative and historical study of social reality.[29] As Theda Skocpol and Margaret Somers rightly note, "Comparative history is not new. As long as people have investigated social life, there has been recurrent fascination with juxtaposing historical patterns from two or more times or places. Part of the appeal comes from the general usefulness of looking at historical trajectories in order to study social change. Indeed, practitioners of comparative history from Alexis de Tocqueville and Max Weber to Marc Bloch, Reinhard Bendix, and Barrington Moore, Jr. have typically been concerned with understanding societal dynamics and epochal transformations of cultures and social structures. Attention to historical sequences is indispensable to such understanding."[30] While the geographic focus and histories of the places studied vary significantly, the common methodological point here is that modern social sciences have relied heavily on observations, interviews, historical records, and comparisons to not only catalog and explain political, economic, and social realities but also to construct theories and conceptual insights into the development and trajectory of the modern state and the conditions of its citizens. As James Mahoney argued, there has been "a significant and growing literature concerning comparative-historical methods. This literature offers methodological tools for causal and descriptive inference that go beyond the techniques currently available in mainstream statistical analysis."[31]

This method of comparative-historical research geared toward causal explanations and theory building began with the classical founders of modern social sciences and continues in groundbreaking modern works currently paving a path for social science. Pioneering works of scholars such as Moore Jr., Skocpol, Tilly, and Immanuel Wallerstein have not only expanded on the issues and geographical scope of the works of the classical theorists but also provided further insights into the collection and analysis of comparative-historical data, especially in relation to the development of political and economic systems.[32] More recently, scholars such as Mahoney, Andrew Arato, Nic Cheeseman, Michael Bratton, Nicolas Van de Walle, and Bah have applied comparative and historical research methods to analysis of democracy and governance.[33] Other scholars, such as Crawford, Paris, and Mohammed Ayoob, have also used comparative and historical approaches to research peace and conflict.[34] While the works of these scholars have greatly contributed to theoretical and methodological developments in political science and related fields, discussion of the African experience in relation to mainstream theory has remained marginalized despite important comparative and historical works on African politics from such scholars as Ali Mazrui, Mahmood Mamdani, and Gilbert Khadiagala.[35] This book uses comparative-historical data from African states not only to explain core political issues in these countries but also to contribute to our theoretical knowledge of international statebuilding. We also seek to bridge some of the gaps between African case studies and theory building in comparative-historical research elsewhere, especially in the area of international relations.

A key feature of comparative-historical research is its contribution to theory. As Mahoney rightly notes, "Comparative-historical analysis has been a leading site for both the development of new concepts and the creation of new methodologies regarding the use of concepts. In terms of conceptual innovation, comparative-historical researchers have offered leading definitions for many of the most important social science concepts. An incomplete list would include authoritarianism, capitalism, corporatism, democracy, development, feudalism, ideology, informal economy, liberalism, nationalism, revolution, socialism, and the welfare state."[36] This work employs comparative-historical methodology to provide insights into the complexities of war, international intervention, and statebuilding in the three case countries but also, more importantly, to contribute the theoretical and conceptual framing of peace and conflict, international intervention, and statebuilding in the context of war-torn postcolonial multiethnic countries. As such, the three countries in this work are not mere case studies; collectively, they form the basis of a comparative analysis of historically grounded data that explains the civil wars, shows patterns in the trajectory of the state, and contributes to the conceptualization of civil wars in relation to humanitarian intervention and international statebuilding.

The comparative-historical method entails thick descriptions of historical events and processes with the goal of gaining a deeper understanding of the context of events and identifying patterns that show causality. This requires, as Weber would argue, probing the subjective meanings associated with actions and processes through a deep and detailed documentation and analysis.[37] Comparative-historical research collects and presents detailed and in-depth granular data on complex events and processes, which is very important for the advancement of social science. As Charles Ragin and Lisa Amoroso note, "Many theoretical advances come from detailed, in-depth examination of cases."[38] Moreover, historical events can be compared and traced across time and space to draw lessons and extrapolate hidden meanings and patterns. As with other methods in the social sciences, in comparative-historical research significant amount of data is collected and analyzed through an analytical frame to create a representation of social reality, answer research questions, and provide plausible explanations for events and historical outcomes. As Ragin and Amoroso rightly point out, "Much of the work of social science centers on debating, clarifying, and using analytical frames to represent social life. These frames make it possible for social researchers to see social phenomena in ways that enhance their relevance to social theory."[39]

The comparative-historical method has great value for researching historically and culturally complex phenomena that are intertwined with multiple aspects of society, such as civil wars and statebuilding. To make sense of such phenomena, which are macro in scope, the comparative-historical method requires not only detailed data but also a robust analytical frame through which data can be analyzed, leading to a plausible representation of the factors connected to the historical events. As Ragin and Amoroso note, "Researchers make sense of their evidence by constructing images of their cases from the data they have collected. In effect, an image is constructed by the investigator when he or she brings together, or synthesizes, evidence. Images often imply motives or say something about causation."[40] Ultimately, such images are the bases of the concepts that emerge from comparative-historical research. According to Mahoney, "The close examination of cases in comparative-historical research stimulates this conceptual development. Because analysts study cases in great detail, they almost inevitably match background understandings of concepts with fine-grained evidence from their cases. After many rounds of iteration, this process can lead to new conceptual understandings and perhaps the formation of entirely new concepts."[41]

With regard to the selection and use of cases in comparative-historical research, Skocpol and Somers identified three kinds of approaches: parallel comparative history, contrast-oriented comparative history, and macro-analytic comparative history. They argue that the parallel comparative-history approach is used to juxtapose case histories in order to show that "a given, explicitly delineated hypothesis or theory can repeatedly demonstrate its fruitfulness."[42] This approach is good for making generalities and showing that a given theory holds well, but the cases tend to be shallow, as the focus is more on controlling for variables in a way that is akin to quantitative methodology. In the contrast-oriented comparative-history approach, the juxtaposition of cases shows how a theory holds generally from case to case. In this approach, "differences among the cases are primarily contextual particularities against which to highlight the generality of the processes with which . . . theories are basically concerned."[43] This approach provides details and nuances that not only speak to the general theory but also to the peculiarities of the cases in a way that is holistic. As Skocpol and Somers note, "Practitioners of Contrast-oriented comparative history stand squarely in the middle between the characteristic disciplinary concerns of social scientists and historians. These comparativists actually care about general issues that cross-cut particular times and places."[44] The macro-analytic comparative-history approach is mainly used for the "purpose of making causal inferences about macro-level structures and processes."[45] Its strength lies in the possibility of showing causal relations in complex macro-phenomena. While each of these approaches tends to be used distinctively, they can sometimes be combined complementarily to address the various angles of the research question. According to Skocpol and Somers, "It is important to recognize that works of comparative history sometimes combine (especially in pairs) the major logics we have reviewed."[46]

This work follows the contrast-oriented comparative history and the macro-analytic comparative-history approaches. The contrast-oriented comparative history is the primary approach used to address the core research question about how war-torn postcolonial multiethnic states transform into peaceful and democratic states. The approach allowed us to examine the effects of international intervention and the postwar statebuilding processes. We used the macro-analytic comparative-history approach to delve into the causes of the civil wars and show the connections between these wars and state decay. We used thick descriptions to show how dictatorship and poor governance led to civil war and to provide new conceptual insights into statebuilding through international humanitarian intervention.

To address the questions raised in this book, we conducted rich comparative-historical research based on established methodological practices. We used three kinds of data: archival material, secondary sources, and expert interviews. Archival materials are the primary source documents pertaining to the civil wars and postwar reconstructions, such as the peace agreements, resolutions adopted by intergovernmental bodies, and reports by government commissions and international agencies. Most of these were collected through online archives, at the Dag Hammarskjöld Library at the UN in New York or at the personal libraries of colleagues in Sierra Leone, Liberia, Côte d'Ivoire, and Senegal. Until recently, historical archives were typically delicate pieces of paper kept in boxes at a physical location, where researchers spent an extensive amount of time taking notes and making photocopies when feasible. At the time of our initial data collection, this was certainly the case at the UN's Dag Hammarskjöld Library in New York. During the summer of 2005, data was collected at the Dag Hammarskjöld Library using orthodox practices established for collecting archival material. Similar practices were also used to collect archival materials in West Africa, in particular at the archives at the Sierra Leone Library in the summer of 2008.[47] Archival materials were also gathered from the personal libraries of colleagues, friends, and acquaintances in Sierra Leone, Liberia, and Côte d'Ivoire during the summer of 2008 and in Senegal during the summer of 2012. Archival data collection through these networks was mostly informal and based on personal or professional relations and referrals by other colleagues and friends. Most of the data collection was limited to making photocopies of original documents in their possession.

We were also able to access a lot of primary source documents through online archives. There has been a huge increase in the size and number of online archives that has resulted from both the digitalization of traditional archives and the electronic generation and storage of new documents.[48] As Bill Tally and Lauren Goldenberg observe in their study of historical thinking among students, "The growth of online archives of primary sources (such as those maintained by the Library of Congress, the National Archives, and countless universities, museums, and libraries) has made rich documentary materials widely available, and provided an extensive laboratory for teacher and curriculum development."[49] Our research greatly benefited from the vast array of primary documents stored in online archives. In particular, we accessed primary documents through the online archives of organizations such as the UN, World Bank, International Monetary Fund, UN country offices, UN Peacekeeping, United States Institute of Peace, African Union, and European Union. We also accessed the online archives of national agencies such as government ministries, special courts, and truth and reconciliation commissions. Collectively, these online archives gave us access to original documents including peace agreements, reports of commissions, binding international resolutions, testimonies, development plans, funding programs, progress reports, and policy documents, which enabled us to gain accurate and detailed accounts of historical events and processes. We complemented these primary sources with such secondary sources as reports from civil society organizations, media reports, and academic works.

In addition, expert interviews were conducted during fieldwork in New York, Sierra Leone, Liberia, Côte d'Ivoire, and Senegal. The fieldwork was primarily funded through grants from Northern Illinois University, the West African Research Association, and the Council of American Overseas Research Centers. Fieldwork in Sierra Leone, Liberia, and Côte d'Ivoire was central to the data collection, particularly in terms of accessing archival material, conducting expert interviews, and making general observations about statebuilding and the sentiments of the citizens about the civil wars and the postwar reconstruction process. New York and Senegal were also selected for fieldwork because of the huge presence of diplomats and international security and development experts at intergovernmental agencies and international organizations there. Respondents for the expert interviews included government officials, diplomats, international development experts, security experts, civil society and religious leaders, members of the political opposition, and academics.

In New York, fieldwork was conducted at the UN headquarters during the summer of 2005. Fourteen experts were interviewed, including African diplomats, a European diplomat, a US State Department official, and officials from various departments of the UN. In the summer of 2008, fieldwork was conducted in Sierra Leone, Liberia, and Côte d'Ivoire; twenty-one experts were interviewed in Sierra Leone, seventeen in Liberia, and fifteen in Côte d'Ivoire. The respondents included members of the clergy, government officials, members of opposition political parties, diplomats, staff of international agencies, leaders of civil society organizations, and academics. All of these people had firsthand knowledge of some aspects of the civil war, the peace process, and/or postwar reconstruction in their country. In the summer of 2012, fieldwork was conducted in Senegal because a lot of the international organizations operating in the region are based there, and the country has been central to the peace processes. Twenty-one people were interviewed in Senegal. The respondents included members of the Senegalese military, diplomats, and officials of international organizations. All the respondents had extensive knowledge of the interventions in Sierra Leone, Liberia, and/ or Côte d'Ivoire.

Respondents for the expert interviews were recruited via a snowballing technique using extant professional networks.[50] Paid research assistants were used to help with the logistics of copying archival materials and arranging meetings with respondents in Sierra Leone, Liberia, Côte d'Ivoire, and Senegal.[51] Typically, interviews lasted for about fifty minutes, were conducted in English, and took place at the offices or homes of the respondents. All interviews were recorded, and respondents were assigned a code and given a consent form and the option to keep their name confidential.[52] None of the recordings have the names of the respondents; a log with the names, codes, contact information, and institutional affiliation of each person is maintained on a computer file. Before the start of each interview, the code assigned to the respondent was first recorded before the first question was asked. The interviews included open-ended and standard prompt questions. Follow-up questions were asked as needed. Generally, the questions related to the respondents' professional background and involvement with certain aspects of the civil wars, the international interventions, and/or the postwar reconstruction. Respondents were also asked to share their views on core social, political, and economic problems. Before the interview date, they were sent a letter that described the research and its goal and a consent form requesting permission to record the interview and use the data for the research. Respondents' preferences for confidentiality were recorded on the consent form. Most interviews were preceded by short informal introductory conversations between the researcher and respondent. The interviews followed best practices in the collection and preservation of data. All the interview tapes and files are securely preserved.

The research yielded an enormous amount of data that was then organized and mapped out. All the interviews were transcribed by research assistants who were graduate students at Northern Illinois University and were trained in basic research ethics as part of their studies. These assistants were given access to the computer files with the interviews but not to the log of respondents. Each transcript was identified by the code assigned to the respondents, and all transcripts are saved on the same computers with the audio recordings of the interviews. The archival materials were also organized into computer files based on country and theme.

A critical element of qualitative methods is the organization and mapping of the data in a way that shows patterns and relations among events. To accomplish this, we developed conceptual categories and rubrics.[53] We went through the archival material and took notes and also inserted notes and highlights on the documents. Also, we color coded the interviews based on themes. Through repeated readings, we coded the key themes, facts, and arguments that emerged. We used both deductive and inductive approaches rooted in grounded theory to map out and analyze the data.[54] By creating categories based on the literature review, we were able to discern some themes that were largely evident in both the archival material and the interviews. The inductive approach allowed us to map out events and facts that were not very apparent during the interviews but provided critical insights into the causes of the wars, nature of international interventions, and trajectories of statebuilding. We used various coding techniques, including vivo coding, descriptive coding, structural coding, and value coding.[55] This allowed us to group information and do thematic analysis and pattern coding. Moreover, we used tables and rubrics to enter summarized text and keep track of page numbers on the original sources.

The data analysis yielded very useful concepts that allowed us to theorize statebuilding processes by showing the link between state decay and the civil wars and the context and implications of the international humanitarian interventions. We developed concepts that add further theoretical and policy insights into the problems of international statebuilding in war-torn postcolonial multiethnic states. In particular, we expanded the debates on the causes of the civil wars from the notion of failed state to that of state decay and added contextual depth to the discussions on new wars and humanitarian interventions through the notion of new humanitarianism. We also developed the idea of people-centered liberalism as an emerging mode of international statebuilding. We incorporated the issues of democracy and good governance into the notion of institutional design.[56]

STATEBUILDING: A HISTORICAL BACKGROUND

Statebuilding in Africa has been fragmented and undermined by contradicting agendas. In West Africa, the precolonial empires such as Ghana, Mali, Ashanti, Sokoto, Shongai, Oyo, Sokoto, and Futa Jallon represented the early indigenous efforts of statebuilding. They amassed vast territories, established formidable political machineries for governance, engaged in trade, and developed solid cultural institutions.[57] However, they failed to evolve into modern states, remained trapped in feudal structures, and suffered from rivalry and stagnation. Those that survived were eventually destroyed by colonialism,[58] which aborted indigenous statebuilding and initiated a new and externally driven process that was characterized by contradictory statebuilding logics. The colonial powers carved out territories, drew political boundaries, established central governments, and built some infrastructure to promote trade, forming the foundation of the states that emerged after independence.[59] These essential ingredients of statehood were developed to promote the colonial enterprise rather than to build countries that were culturally cohesive and ruled by governments that had legitimacy with the people. The key elements of statehood—defined territorial boundaries, a central government and security apparatus, and so on—were established during colonial rule. However, these states were not conceived as cohesive cultural units that could be transformed into nations. Instead of promoting nationhood, the colonial agenda undermined it. The territories continued to be amalgamations of people of diverse cultures who were pitted against one another for access to state resources. A sense of nationhood did not really emerge until the rise of the nationalist movement during the 1930s. Such movements created opportunities for forging nations within African states. However, the opportunities evaporated as indigenous political leaders started to vie for power.[60] The struggles continued after independence and frequently degenerated into political repression and dictatorships, which further undermined the state and created conditions for civil war in a wide number of cases.

The development of the state in Sierra Leone can be traced back to the establishment of the colony of Freetown in 1808 and the protectorate in 1896.[61] The two territories had separate political systems until the creation of a single legislature in 1948 under the Stevenson Constitution.[62] Since the end of colonial rule in 1961, the country's key challenges have been to transform colonial institutional structures into political and economic institutions suitable for a modern African state and foster a nation. The cultivation of a national identity has largely been tied to the nationalist movement and struggle to build the state.[63] However, this nascent identity has been superficial and fragmented.[64] The earlier part of Sierra Leone's identity and nationalism were interwoven with those of other British West African territories, most notably through the National Congress of British West Africa (NCBW).[65] The relatively decentralized nature of the British colonial administration and the decline of the NCBW provided the people of Sierra Leone the opportunity to develop their own nationalist movement, led mainly by Isaac Wallace-John and Milton Margai.[66] These leaders had a common goal of ending British rule and building an independent state but differed in their political interests and visions for the country. The development of a common national identity was hampered by the bifurcated political structure of colony and protectorate and the wider ethnic and regional divisions in the country. The colony, inhabited mainly by the Creoles, maintained a separate political system from the protectorate, which was inhabited by a variety of indigenous ethnic groups.[67] By 1961, there were intense divisions and power struggles among the various groups. While independence marked the establishment of a sovereign state, there was very little sense of nationhood. The politics of ethnicity and regionalism that followed led to violence and dictatorship, which further undermined a sense of unity and the chances of transforming the state into a nation. By 1990, political oppression and bad governance had made the country ripe for a civil war.[68]

In Côte d'Ivoire, the development of an independent state and national identity was limited by the French colonial policies of assimilation and association.[69] In principle, Côte d'Ivoire was simply an extension of the French state and nation until independence in 1960.[70] Côte d'Ivoire became a French colony in 1893. From 1904 to 1958, it was part of the French Federation of West Africa, which was comprised of eight colonies in the region. Within the wider colonial frame, Côte d'Ivoire was part of the French Union established in 1946. When the union collapsed in 1958, Côte d'Ivoire opted for membership in the French Community instead of becoming an independent country as Guinea had.[71] The centralized nature of French colonial rule made the Ivoirian state and national identity deeply intertwined with those of other French colonies in the region. This was reflected in the colonial administrative structure and the pan-African nationalism championed by the Rassemblement Démocratique Africain (African Democratic Rally, or RDA).[72] The RDA was established by Félix Houphouët-Boigny and leaders across the French Federation of West Africa who met in Bamako in 1946.[73] Côte d'Ivoire's first major step in carving out an independent national identity could be traced back to Houphouët-Boigny's break from the pan-Africanist vision of the RDA in 1958.[74] As the country moved away from pan-Africanism, it increasingly allied itself with France, which hindered the formation of a truly indigenous national identity.[75] Moreover, Côte d'Ivoire's subordinate status within the colonial administrative structure and position as a key base of French economic interest weakened the possibilities for an autonomous national identity. However, as a result, Côte d'Ivoire attracted not only French capital but also workers from neighboring French colonies who *assumed* Ivoirian citizenship.[76]

Côte d'Ivoire's colonial legacies had mixed effects on the development of the state. While technically it was just a subunit of the French Federation of West Africa, it had its own political boundaries, bureaucracy, internal politics, and economic infrastructure, which are key elements of a state.[77] When it became independent in 1960, it had all the institutional trappings of postcolonial states. In fact, its relative economic development made Ivoirian state institutions more efficient as compared to other countries in the regions.[78] Its strong political and economic ties with France helped the country develop relatively efficient state institutions. However, the Ivoirian state as a whole remained trapped in the vestiges of the political, economic, and social structures of colonial rule. This problem came to light shortly after the death of Houphouët-Boigny, when Ivoirian nationality became politicized.[79] The conflict over citizenship exposed the deep penetration of the Ivoirian economy, politics, and culture by people from the former French colonial empire. The attempt to distinguish Ivoirians who claimed autochthony from other Ivoirians whose ancestors came from neighboring parts of the former French colonial empire and deny the latter full citizenship resulted in a civil war that exposed the fragility of the state.[80] The conflict in Côte d'Ivoire "raised so many questions . . . of ethnocentrism, xenophobia, tribalism . . . and these things . . . worked as a means to break social cohesion" in the country, undermining national unity and leading to the outbreak of civil war.[81]

The Liberian state had a slightly different colonial path but faced similar predicaments of statebuilding as other countries in the region.[82] Unlike Sierra Leone and Côte d'Ivoire, Liberia was not formally colonized by Western powers. The country was founded in the early 1820s as a home for emancipated Blacks in America, who became known as Americo-Liberians.[83] Despite this aura of freedom, Liberia developed its own pedigree of colonialism. Internally, the settler Americo-Liberians exercised a form of political and economic hegemony over the natives that was reminiscent of the subordination of the native Africans by European colonizers.[84] Externally, Liberia depended heavily on the United States and maintained a virtual neocolonial relation despite its status as an independent country.[85] These two forms of quasicolonialism became the hallmark of the Liberian state and posed major impediments to building a stable and integrated nation. As one Islamic scholar and community leader in Liberia noted: "If you look at [Liberia], if you go deeply into the history of Liberia; particularly the birth of Liberia was built on the foundation of suspicions and mistrusts. . . . The pioneers, the American Liberians, the free slaves felt in America that they were sold by their people in Africa and taken into slavery. When they came to Liberia. . . . But at the same time, they tried to convince our people to accept then that they are now coming back to their homes."[86]

Liberia was ruled by the minority Americo-Liberians until 1980. In the late 1870s, they established the True Whig Party (TWP), which became the de facto sole party until 1980. The majority of people belonging to the sixteen major native ethnic groups occupied a subordinate political and economic position.[87] The natives, commonly referred to as "up-country" people, resented this.[88] Under the TWP, the Liberian state marginalized the natives and increasingly became authoritarian, despite claiming to embrace democracy. The Americo-Liberian hegemony over the state ended with the bloody April 12, 1980, coup led by Master Sergeant Samuel Kanyon Doe, who belonged to the Krahn ethnic group. Like other countries in the region, Liberia had a defined territory, state bureaucracy, and security apparatus; however, it, too, failed to foster a cohesive nation. The marginalization of the natives undermined the legitimacy of the state and created a bifurcated society. Dictatorship and ethnic oppression worsened under the Doe regime, creating conditions for the civil war.

Despite their distinct colonial experiences, Liberia, Sierra Leone, and Côte d'Ivoire had similar issues with statebuilding. In all three cases, the state was an alien political and economic structure that was imposed on the natives. They adopted models of Western state institutions but failed to foster the common national identity needed to transform a state into a nation. All three countries fell into the thorny path of dictatorship, which undermined the legitimacy of the state and intensified ethnic and regional animosities. In the case of Sierra Leone and Liberia, dictatorship led to colossal forms of bad governance and economic retardation that rendered many state institutions dysfunctional. The political and economic failures of these states were exacerbated by bloody civil wars that brought them to near collapse.[89] Though Côte d'Ivoire did not suffer from significant economic retardation and dysfunctional state institutions, the development of the state has been hampered by the north-south divide and excessive dependence on foreign capital and labor. The political tolerance for foreign input into the economic development of Côte d'Ivoire, which Houphouët-Boigny skillfully nurtured, ruptured after his death in 1993. The chaos that ensued led to significant economic decline, political violence, and civil war. The origins of the war can be traced back to years before the outbreak of violence, as an interview respondent indicated: The war "started . . . when the former president [Houphouët-Boigny] died."[90] Accordingly, some have argued that "the first president did not really prepare his . . . people successfully . . . before . . . he died in 1993."[91]

STATEBUILDING AND CIVIL WAR: SIERRA LEONE, LIBERIA, AND CÔTE D'IVOIRE

Since the outbreak of the civil wars in Liberia, Sierra Leone, and Côte d'Ivoire, there has been significant international intervention in all three countries that is critical to the future development of the state. In Liberia, "the international community was very instrumental in . . . peace, bringing an end to the war, restoring some stability."[92] Furthermore, specifically in regard to Sierra Leone, another person interviewed for this study simply argued that "the participation of the international community during the war is quite interesting. Their pressure ended the war."[93] In Liberia and Sierra Leone, the dire security and humanitarian conditions led to massive international interventions to restore order and ameliorate the humanitarian condition.[94]

Furthermore, the international community has been deeply involved in post-war reconstruction aimed at restoring state capacity and laying the foundation for democracy and economic development.[95] These interventions have been largely viewed as necessary in order to restore security in the region and fulfill the moral obligations of the international community to the peoples of these countries. Since intervening in Liberia and Sierra Leone, the international community has been involved in statebuilding. In many instances, the international intervention forces and aid agencies provided critical services on behalf of the state. In contrast, Côte d'Ivoire points to both the possibilities for and limitations of international statebuilding. During the first civil war, the external intervention in Côte d'Ivoire was largely limited to securing the buffer zone, mediating a political solution to the conflict, and supporting the implementation of the peace agreements. International intervention was viewed with some skepticism, and its results have been at best mixed.[96] The international community repeatedly failed to properly address the underlying cause of the conflict in the peace process. Ivoirians eventually sidestepped the international community and negotiated a fairly successful peace agreement. The minimal nature of the intervention in Côte d'Ivoire is largely due to the fact that the civil war was contained; additionally, the state was functional in the south, while in the north, the rebels established a fairly stable administration. Even during the second Ivoirian intervention, international involvement was largely limited to providing military support to the rebel forces to capture President Laurent Gbagbo. International intervention in Côte d'Ivoire assumed a different form of statebuilding role, which has been limited to creating an environment for Ivoirians to address the fundamental citizenship issue and to ousting Gbagbo after his refusal to accept the UN-certified election result. Economically, statebuilding in prewar-Côte d'Ivoire benefited from foreign capital. The critical issue in postwar Côte d'Ivoire was whether the international community would inject capital to promote the economic development and consolidate peace or support a truly inclusive democratic process. The country presents real opportunities for pursuing an investment approach, rather than an aid-driven approach, to international statebuilding in Africa.

STATES AND HUMANITARIAN INTERVENTION: WHAT IS INTERNATIONAL STATEBUILDING?

The notion of international statebuilding raises conceptual and policy questions about modern states and humanitarian interventions. The modern state has a defined territory, often referred to as a country, with a sovereign authority that exercises control within its territorial boundaries. Membership in the state is based on citizenship. The critical features of a state are its territorial boundaries, bureaucratic and security apparatuses for exercising authority, sense of citizenship and national identity, and relationship with other states in the international system.[97] The modern state is both a political space and a fluidly defined social and economic space and typically emerges out of the remnant of old empires or through colonial conquests.[98] States born out of empires such as France, Germany, Russia, Turkey, and Japan have often emerged as national states.[99] The vast majority are the products of colonial encounters. Some of the most notable examples are the countries in the Western Hemisphere, including the United States. In Asia, too, countries such as India, Pakistan, Indonesia, and Malaysia are products of colonialism. With the exception of Ethiopia and Liberia, all the countries in Africa are the direct product of colonialism.[100] Colonialism laid the critical first step in the establishment of modern African states by defining their external boundaries and imposing some form of sovereign authority over the territories and their inhabitants. The Berlin Conference of 1884–1885 was a critical moment in the establishment of modern states in Africa; the whole continent was carved into distinct colonial territories that later became independent states.

As Weber noted, modern states have a distinct bureaucratic form of exercising control over their territory and people. They are characterized by a political apparatus that claims the legitimate and exclusive right to make and enforce laws and to use force to maintain order within the boundaries of the state. This political apparatus is built around a government that controls the state's administrative and security institutions.[101] The critical element of the claim to authority is the basis of legitimacy, which may emanate from tradition, democracy, popular sentiments, or the application of force. States that rely exclusively on force tend to lack legitimacy and be inherently unstable. The specific form of authority over a state ranges from democracy, where the mandate of the government is derived from free and fair multiparty elections, to various forms of nondemocratic rule, such as aristocratic, colonial, one-party, military, and sultanistic regimes.[102] African states have mostly experienced nondemocratic forms of rule. The colonial regimes exercised virtual control without a mandate from the people. In most cases, the application of force and divide-and-rule stratagems were used. Around the period of independence, African states experimented with multiparty democracy, but this did not last for long; nearly all of them fell into the destructive path of one-party or military dictatorship, which undermined legitimacy, ruined the economy, and created the conditions for civil war.[103] During the 1990s, most African countries began reverting back to multiparty democracy. Democracy has been viewed as the best chance for promoting good governance and economic development, two critical elements of statebuilding.[104] While there has been major progress on this front, there are some disturbing trends in antidemocratic practices, including the improper prolongation of the presidential mandate.

States are not just defined by bare territories but, more importantly, by the people who inhabit them. In this sense, the modern state is a community of citizens who share some sentimental and cultural affinity and bear membership rights and obligations in a specific country. States define citizenship criteria and the corresponding rights and obligations of citizenship,[105] and this definition delineates members of the state from nonmembers. Furthermore, states often try to foster a common national identity and culture among the people who live there.[106] While citizenship is largely based on legal membership in the state, the nation evolves out of subjective and objective ties to the state embedded in such factors as shared culture, history, values, and political destiny.[107] Developing a sense of citizenship and nationhood is one of the most critical challenges for the establishment of a modern state. Citizenship can be complicated by contestations over civil, political, and economic rights often resulting from the acquisition of new territories or mass movement of people into a state.[108] Contested citizenship claims by a substantial category of people can result in oppression and violence.[109] The problem of nationhood lies in its fluidity and the inevitable diversity of people. While a state without some form of shared identity and culture among its people is difficult to maintain, in reality, modern states are comprised of people with diverse cultures, histories, values, and identities. Thus, modern state crafting tends to be a delicate balance between accepting diversity and promoting the necessary common culture to sustain the state. The suppression of cultural rights and ambitious homogenization projects, which in worst cases result in genocide, can destabilize the state. The modern state needs to foster a nation, but it need not be a monocultural nation. In fact, modern states are pluralistic nations with diverse cultures, ethnic groups, and religions.[110] African states are emblems of pluralistic nations characterized by a high degree of ethnic diversity.[111] Sierra Leone and Liberia each have sixteen ethnic groups. Côte d'Ivoire is divided into five major cultural groups, which are further divided into more than sixty ethnic groups. No single ethnic group is a majority in any of these countries. In many cases, members of the same ethnic groups are spread across two or more neighboring countries. This fragmentation of African states and cultural groups is a result of the artificial political boundaries imposed on the continent by the colonial powers. Since the imposition of these boundaries by the colonizers, the citizens of African states have been learning to live in a multiethnic postcolonial state.

Ethnic diversity has been at times a key source of political turmoil in Africa.[112] In Sierra Leone and Liberia, ethnic politics led to the dictatorships that ruined the states and sparked civil wars.[113] In Côte d'Ivoire, the civil war was a direct result of ethnic political marginalization and contested citizenship claims.[114] So far, ethnic diversity has been an impediment to the development of the state in all three countries examined here. However, there is a growing awareness about the common history and shared political destiny among the various ethnic groups in these countries. By recognizing the disastrous effects of ethnic politics, these countries have an opportunity to build better institutions to promote ethnic political harmony. In Côte d'Ivoire, for example, the peace process eventually centered on building mechanisms to resolve the citizenship dispute and promote political inclusion. In Sierra Leone, too, there was an effort to move away from the ethnic politics that marred the country during the 1960s, but that effort has not been successful so far.

While all modern states are sovereign, they are part of an international system that has critical effects on their development. This international system is a complex legal and institutional arrangement that facilitates and regulates relations among sovereign states, most notably in the areas of security, governance, trade, and the natural environment.[115] The international system, which has now grown to encompass nearly all aspects of modern life, is driven by powerful countries and institutions that have the most access to capital, weapons, and technology and a vested interest in international security largely under the banner of global liberal governance.[116] It is shaped by capitalism and the forces of globalization, while its excesses are challenged by a patchwork of international laws, humanitarian morality, and civic activism—and, more recently, the emergence of diabolical nationalism in Western countries.[117] One of the most critical aspects of the international system is the issue of sovereignty. States often concede some elements of their exclusive authority to make and enforce laws when they enter into international agreements. The international system has disproportionate impacts on developing countries that are less capable of asserting their sovereignty and interests. As Wallerstein observed, modern states vary according to their position within the international system. The capacity of the state to develop itself and assert meaningful sovereignty is contingent on its location within the global political and economic structure.[118] States with powerful militaries and economies, such as the United States, Russia, China, Japan, India and the major West European countries, are at the core of this system. In contrast, postcolonial states with poor economies and histories of dictatorships are at the margins of the international system.[119] States shift positions as their economies and political alliances adapt to the ever-changing world order. Countries such as Brazil, Nigeria, and South Africa have emerged as significant players in the international system and major regional power brokers. Poor developing countries such as Liberia, Sierra Leone, and Côte d'Ivoire occupy a subordinate role in the world capitalist economy and a dependent relationship with the powerful countries and Western-backed financial and political institutions.[120] This dependency, which began in earnest during colonial rule, has taken a variety of economic and political forms during the past century. Sierra Leone, for example, moved from being a colony to a raw material–exporting state and sponge in the ideological warfare between the West and East. Since the civil war, Sierra Leone has become a donor-driven state and a virtual UN experiment in international statebuilding.[121]

One critical aspect of the evolution of the international system is the security and moral interconnectedness of states.[122] Any significant breakdown in law and order, such as a civil war, becomes not only a political, economic, and social problem for the state but also a security and moral challenge for the international community. When such wars break out, those with strong interests in the affected country intervene to stop the fighting and find a peaceful solution. The extent of intervention varies from simple diplomacy and conflict mediation to the deployment of a peacekeeping force and, in exceptional cases, intervention forces with a strong UN Chapter VII mandate.[123] The security interests of other countries and the moral obligation to ordinary people have led to serious debates about the limits of sovereignty and the right to intervene.[124] Sierra Leone and Liberia clearly exemplify the kinds of security and humanitarian conditions that evoked robust international interventions even without the consent of the government or other parties vying to rule the state. In Côte d'Ivoire, the international intervention took a minimal form that was largely limited to peace mediation and monitoring the buffer zone and later to efforts to simply capture Gbagbo after he refused to accept the UN-certified election result.

In the scholarly and policy discourses, states are categorized based on such factors as their genesis, cultural composition, economic development, political system, and level of security and control. States that emerged out of empires, typically in Europe, have been characterized as old states. Most of them were industrialized by the end of the nineteenth century.[125] Conversely, the states that emerged out of colonial rule in the eighteenth and twentieth centuries are referred to as new states; they are mostly in Africa, Asia, and the Americas. New states have also emerged in Eurasia after the fall of the Soviet Union; they are typically referred to as postcolonial states.[126] States have also been characterized according to their level of cultural diversity. Those with significant ethnic or religious minority groups are referred to as multicultural states, while those with a relatively homogenous culture tend to be characterized as monocultural states.[127] However, homogeneity is not a stable factor in the life of a state. Truly monocultural states have rarely existed, and if they do emerge, they are difficult to sustain.[128] In reality, most states only aspire to create a nation out of their diverse people. States that succeeded in creating a relatively high degree of common national identity are characterized as national states, while those that remain fragmented along ethnic or religious lines tend to be multiethnic states.[129]

Apart from their historical and cultural peculiarities, states are most significantly classified according to their level of economic development, political system, and level of stability. Traditionally, industrialized countries have been labeled developed countries, while poor countries with economies that are mostly based on agriculture and the extraction of raw materials have been referred to as underdeveloped countries. This categorization has been refined to consider global economic changes, especially since the fall of communism. The UN, for example, uses four classifications: developed economies, economies in transition, developing economies, and least developed countries.[130] The World Bank has classified states, according to their Gross National Income per capita, into high-income ($12,196 or more), upper-middle-income ($3,946–$12,195), lower-middle-income ($996–$3,945), and low-income ($995 or less) economies.[131] Most African states fall into the last two categories of the UN and World Bank classifications. Too often, they are at the bottom of the UN Human Development Index.[132]

Politically, states are classified as either democratic or nondemocratic. States that meet the minimum standards for regular free and fair multiparty elections and guarantee core democratic values, such as rule of law, freedom of expression, and civil liberties, are considered democracies. Nondemocratic states include those with authoritarian, totalitarian, post-totalitarian, and sultanist regimes.[133] After the end of the Cold War, there was a growing trend toward democratization, including among African countries that were mostly military or one-party regimes. Unstable and undemocratic states are often categorized based on the extent of fragility of the states and their ability to deliver political and social goods. Typically, they have been classified as weak, fragile, failed, or collapsed states.[134] While failed and collapsed states are those that lack any credible authority capable of ruling, weak states are characterized by governments that are ineffective and unable to deliver positive political and social goods.[135] According to Robert I. Rotberg, "Weak states include a broad continuum of states that are: inherently weak because of geographical, physical, or fundamental economic constraints; basically strong, but temporarily or situationally weak because of internal antagonisms, management flaws, greed, despotism, or external attacks; and a mixture of the two."[136] The most problematic states are failed and collapsed states. Jean-Germain Gros defined failed states as those in which "public authorities are either unable or unwilling to carry out their end of what Hobbes long ago called the social contract, but which now includes more than maintaining the peace among society's many factions and interests."[137] Similarly, Zartman defined state collapse as "the situation where the structure, authority (legitimate power), law, and political order have fallen apart and must be reconstituted in some form, old or new."[138] In essence, a "collapsed state is a rare and extreme version of a failed state."[139] State failure often results from chronic conditions of state decay.[140] Africa has a disproportionate number of weak, failed, and collapsed states.[141] According to the 2010 Failed States Index, for example, more than half of the forty states classified in the critical or danger categories were in Africa; in fact, no African country was in the stable category.[142] Though the index seemed a bit apocalyptic, it pointed to the comparative disadvantage of African states as measured by the critical political, economic, and social indicators of stability.[143]

Sierra Leone, Liberia, and Côte d'Ivoire were classified as failed states. According to Rotberg, Sierra Leone and Liberia were failed states for most of the civil war period. At the height of the civil wars, they teetered into the category of collapsed before recovering and moving back into the failed state status.[144] Rotberg characterized Côte d'Ivoire as a failing state: "Côte d'Ivoire slid rapidly in late 2002 from weakness to the edge of failure" and "could easily join neighboring Liberia in full failure in 2003 or 2004."[145] While Sierra Leone and Liberia became classic failed states, Côte d'Ivoire became a peculiar kind of failed state. After the end of the civil wars in Sierra Leone (2002) and Liberia (2003) and the signing of the 2007 Ouagadougou Accord in Côte d'Ivoire, all three countries significantly recovered. In the Failed States Index, for example, Sierra Leone and Liberia respectively moved from sixth and ninth place in 2005 to twenty-ninth and thirty-third in 2010. Most significantly, they moved from the critical to the "in danger" category. Côte d'Ivoire moved from third place in 2006 to twelfth in 2010. However, the country remained in the critical category, as the peace agreement had not been fully implemented.

In his seminal work on the American state, Stephen Skowronek argues that "statebuilding is most basically an exercise in reconstructing an already established organization of state power."[146] Similarly, Fukuyama observes that the core of statebuilding is the creation of a government that has a monopoly of legitimate power and is capable of enforcing rules throughout the territory.[147] However, this Weberian approach leaves out the economic and social problems that undermine states. In developing countries, statebuilding, which is sometimes referred to as nation building, also entails developing the infrastructure for economic and social development.[148] In this sense, statebuilding is the process of governing a state in a way that makes it a viable political and economic entity within the international system. This entails establishing a legitimate political system, maintaining the rule of law, and developing an economy that creates opportunities for economic and social well-being among a vast majority of the people. Similarly, Ghani and Lockhart identified ten key functions that states must fulfill, including security, administrative, financial, managerial, and a variety of public policy duties.[149] Statebuilding is a never-ending process, since both legitimacy and well-being are unstable and virtually insatiable elements of life that are contingent on the real political and economic conditions of a state. However, statebuilding can be deemed a success or a failure depending on the extent to which the state has attained the critical internationally recognized standards of stability, political freedom, economic development, and social well-being. Too often, these include the establishment of a democracy, some level of industrialization, a fairly modern infrastructure, and access to basic social services such as health care, education, proper housing, and clean drinking water. Yet, in the case of international statebuilding, what is also needed is a lasting commitment on the part of the international community. As one international development expert in Liberia noted, "These benchmarks cut across the big issues of security, peace, and then of course the state . . . reconstruction, which is utterly the mandate of . . . the UN mission, but it is more importantly . . . a longer term engagement."[150] Essentially, statebuilding is measured by the extent to which citizens enjoy civil, political, social, and economic rights.[151] While the notions of civil and political rights are universally accepted, economic and social rights still remain ambiguous and contested by proponents of neoliberal and welfare state models. Statebuilding does not mean that citizens have the right to a set of economic and social privileges that the government must provide them for free; rather, statebuilding assumes that the state will create the conditions to provide affordable essential services and ensure the social and economic well-being of its citizens or foster an economy in which the vast majority of citizens have a realistic chance of securing their own economic and social well-being. The success of statebuilding in Africa can be best gauged by the political, economic, and social indicators used by the UN to measure development, especially among developing countries. These indicators were embodied in the UN Millennium Development Goals and the subsequent Sustainable Development Goals.[152] Given the fact that African countries fall at the bottom end of the UN Human Development Index and are classified as either the least developed counties or developing countries, statebuilding in Africa is essentially the political and economic process of realizing key development goals, which are shared by the UN and African organizations (e.g., African Union [AU], Economic Community of West African States [ECOWAS], and New Partnership for Africa's Development [NEPAD]).

Statebuilding is not a new venture in Africa. It began in earnest at the dawn of independence.[153] African nationalist leaders repeatedly pointed to the political and economic oppression of colonial rule and promised to liberate their people and create better conditions.[154] They set goals to enhance education, build infrastructure, provide health care, and generally improve the living conditions of their citizens. One of the first challenges of statebuilding in postcolonial Africa was establishing a legitimate political system that would maintain order and promote economic and social development. The nascent democracies were soon deemed unsuitable for achieving Africa's development goals. They were seen as the sources of political chaos and unnecessary impediments to progress. Nearly all African countries abandoned multiparty democracy and fell into military or one-party rule.[155]

By the late 1980s, one-party and military dictatorships had proved to be far more detrimental to economic development and the very stability of the state. African countries were forced to abandon these dictatorships and adopt democratic and neoliberal economic reforms. Some countries made significant progress, while many others took modest steps toward democracy and more open economies.[156] The net result was the end of one-party regimes and a reduction in the number of military regimes. In most cases, the democratization exercise led to significant political improvements. Some of the most notable examples include Benin, Ghana, Mozambique, and South Africa. However, the consolidation of democracy remains a problem.[157] Democratization has also exposed the vulnerability of the state in Africa. In some countries, democratization turned into political violence, which led to the breakdown of law and order and civil wars.[158] While democracy in and of itself is not the problem, there are serious questions about its feasibility and the conditions it requires to achieve stability in African states. In Nigeria, for example, manipulation of the democratization process by the power elite and ethnic grievances led to nearly a decade of political violence that brought the state to a virtual collapse. In countries such as Guinea and Guinea-Bissau, the failure to undertake meaningful democratic reforms perpetuated dictatorship and rendered the state highly vulnerable to civil war. In the Democratic Republic of Congo, Côte d'Ivoire, Liberia, and Sierra Leone, manipulation of the democratic process and the preexisting political and economic grievances led to civil wars. The democratic transitions there not only failed, they led to the near collapse of these states, creating serious humanitarian and security challenges for the international community. The civil wars exposed the failure of statebuilding and ruined the scanty infrastructure that was available. In West Africa, the damage was most acute in Sierra Leone and Liberia, where the crises led to significant international humanitarian interventions aimed at restoring security and putting the countries on the path to democracy and economic recovery.

Humanitarian intervention has become a critical element of statebuilding in failed and collapsed states.[159] In Africa, Sierra Leone and Liberia are exemplary cases of robust humanitarian interventions by the international community to restore order and state capacity, ameliorate grave human suffering, and lay the foundation for democracy and economic development. The international community has also made important efforts to restore peace and improve living conditions in other African countries plagued by civil wars such as Côte d'Ivoire, DRC, South Sudan, and Somalia. Humanitarian intervention is the use of coercion, including military force, by states on another sovereign state in order to prevent or ameliorate the catastrophic human suffering and widespread violence associated with gross violations of human rights by the state or violent nonstate actors.[160] It is undertaken on the basis of UN authorization or the decisions of coalitions representing regional organizations or concerned states. Some of the critical activities include imposing sanctions on the perpetrators of violence, protecting civilians, negotiating and implementing cease-fire and peace agreements, disarming combatants, and postwar reconstruction.[161] In cases where the underlying cause of the turmoil is limited and clearly attributable to a rogue ruler or organization, the intervention tends to be limited in scope and duration. However, in cases where the humanitarian tragedy is the result of a fundamental breakdown in state institutions and the eruption of civil war, which is often the case in failed or collapsed states, international intervention can be profound and prolonged, given sufficient interest and goodwill. In these cases, humanitarian intervention often evolves into statebuilding, which becomes unavoidable because of the incapacity of the state to carry out normal functions and the fact that state decay is often the major cause of the security and humanitarian tragedy. Typically, resolution of the conflict becomes contingent on the ability of the international community to help establish a legitimate and stable government and improve the living conditions of the people, which is essentially statebuilding.

Humanitarian intervention has raised serious concerns about violations of sovereignty, major power domination, and double standards in the application of international norms and laws.[162] However, recent debates have juxtaposed state sovereignty with popular sovereignty and delineated state security from human security.[163] The new notion of sovereignty now encompasses the responsibility of the state to protect its citizens and the right of the citizens to receive protection from the international community, if their state is unable to prevent grave human suffering and widespread violence. This notion led to new humanitarianism, which departed from orthodox neutrality and the minimalist approach to humanitarian intervention.[164] New humanitarianism openly defends human rights and democracy, differentiates victims from victimizers, and advocates comprehensive peacebuilding approaches that address the root causes of civil wars.[165] According to the International Commissions on Intervention and State Sovereignty (ICISS) "The responsibility to protect implies the responsibility not just to prevent and react, but to follow through and rebuild. This means that if military intervention action is taken . . . there should be a genuine commitment to helping to build a durable peace, and promoting good governance and sustainable development."[166] Similarly, the Humanitarian Policy Group observed: "International expectations of the role of humanitarian action have evolved. No longer seen as simply a palliative for the worst excesses of man and for the impact of natural hazards, many see humanitarian action as part of a wider agenda of conflict management and development."[167] New humanitarianism dovetails neatly with the international statebuilding efforts associated with humanitarian interventions.

In his study of international administration in Bosnia and Herzegovina, Richard Caplan distinguished indigenous statebuilding from third-party statebuilding. Caplan's notion of third-party statebuilding includes not only the international administration of war-torn territories but also the US-led Allied reconstruction of Germany and Japan and colonial regimes on the verge of withdrawal.[168] International statebuilding is a form of third-party statebuilding; unlike colonial statebuilding, it is rooted in new humanitarianism and collective security. International statebuilding is the active and sustained involvement of the international community in comprehensive peacebuilding and the reconstruction of a war-torn country in a way that is geared toward establishing a stable and democratic state that will not undermine regional or international security.[169] It is often spearheaded by the UN and international development agencies with the active support of at least one major world power with vested security, political, economic, or moral interests in the affected country. International statebuilding is different from orthodox peacekeeping or aid regimes precisely because the former relates to war-torn countries and entails significant short- and long-term development projects aimed at combating the root causes of violence.

Though international statebuilding does not occur too often and its success is often uncertain, it has been a critical strategy for maintaining international and regional security.[170] Following World War II, the United States and its allies committed to rebuilding Germany and Japan as a way to maintain international security. Both countries later became prosperous democratic states that have maintained a pacifist policy. Most recently, the United States was engaged in statebuilding in Iraq and Afghanistan as part of its strategy to combat terrorism.[171] The statebuilding mishaps of the United States in Iraq and Afghanistan underscore the security risks of failed states and the moral imperatives of international statebuilding. In Africa, Liberia, Sierra Leone, and Côte d'Ivoire are illuminating cases of international statebuilding. Both Sierra Leone and Liberia were failed states in which the international humanitarian intervention evolved into statebuilding. Unlike many other cases in Africa, these countries attracted enormous international interest and goodwill.[172] Sierra Leone, in particular, became a virtual UN experiment in statebuilding in Africa.[173] In Sierra Leone and Liberia, the international interventions have been credited with restoring the state and promoting democracy and development. Côte d'Ivoire did not degenerate into a collapsed state, but it faced formidable security, political, economic, and social challenges that attracted significant international intervention.[174] The real challenge for the intervention there was to preempt state collapse and lay the foundation of peace and democracy.[175] However, this could not be achieved without reworking the state, which has been undermined by the conflict over citizenship and efforts to monopolize power. International statebuilding in Côte d'Ivoire had a much more political angle aimed at building a peaceful, inclusive, and democratic state. The country's economic and social conditions, which worsened during the war, also provided room for a financial angle to statebuilding. Though the intervention in Côte d'Ivoire did not entail major postwar reconstruction on the scales of Sierra Leone or Liberia, the Ivoirian state was shielded from complete failure, thanks to improvements to the economy and social services. Because of its relatively developed infrastructure, significant investment in Côte d'Ivoire had the potential to provide an alternative to the typical aid-driven approach to statebuilding in Africa. The exceptional experiences of these three countries serve as critical lessons for understanding the potentials and limitations of international statebuilding in war-torn countries. Yet, a question remains: Where were these countries' neighbors and other members of the international community?

On this point, it is important to clarify the situation and point out the rather limited agency of African regional and subregional organizations as intervenors. Although clearly present in Liberia and Sierra Leone throughout most of the conflicts in the form of ECOWAS Monitoring Groups better known as ECOMOG, they lacked the ability to impose a definitive solution to the fighting in either of the countries. Nonetheless, as with other external actors, they, too, were unable to stop the internal conflicts there. Additionally, it is important not to provide a simple one-sided story of international intervention that places all of the blame on the internal or domestic problems of the affected states.

SCOPE AND ORGANIZATION

This book is about the nature and prospects of the postcolonial state in Africa through the lens of three war-torn countries: Sierra Leone, Liberia, and Côte d'Ivoire. It focuses on states that were failing and losing the capacity to maintain themselves and had become threats to regional security. In these countries, international statebuilding became the most probable path for restoring order and developing the state. The study does not seek to negate the importance of indigenous statebuilding and domestic ownership of political and economic processes.[176] As Jens Meierhenrich rightly noted, a truly unstable state can be erected only from the inside.[177] However, international efforts at renewal may play an important role in facilitating statebuilding from within. This study simply asserts the external dimension of statebuilding in Africa. It examines the conditions that led to state failure and the subsequent international efforts to rebuild. Such an endeavor has the risk of devolving into a grandiose discourse of the political, economic, and social problems of African states—indeed, the state cannot be devoid of such issues. However, this study is premised on the notion that a holistic understanding of these problems requires a discourse on the state. As both an actor and object of action, the state is at the core of the problems. Thus, a discourse on the states becomes a necessary step toward a holistic understanding of the issues African countries face.

The myriad problems of African states have featured prominently in the peacebuilding, security, democracy, and development literatures,[178] but the state itself has hardly been studied. The studies that do exist mostly focus on the dysfunctions of political institutions, resources distribution, ethnic conflicts, bad governance, and civil wars.[179] The inadequate conceptualization and analysis of the state have not only hampered a holistic discourse of the conditions in Africa but also made it difficult to gauge the future direction of African countries. This problem is best exemplified by the tragedy of Côte d'Ivoire, which was once a beacon of peace and prosperity in the region. This study seeks to put the state at the center of Africa's problems and bridge the isolated discourses on security, democracy, and development. By focusing on the state, the study provides a frame for examining the conditions that have led to civil wars and the efforts to change these conditions. We argue that the state is both the embodiment of the pathologies in African countries and the vehicle for their development. Moreover, the state is an actor and object of action. It has often acted as an oppressive political force, a predatory regime, and a patronage system. At the same time, domestic and external stakeholders use the state as a tool to realize their objectives— malevolent or benevolent. A critical question emerges: How can the state be transformed from an inefficient, predatory, and oppressive force into an instrument of political freedom and economic and social development? Mamdani's seminal work captured both the oppressive character of the African state and its potential as a vehicle for emancipation.[180] However, his discourse of the state is largely in the realm of politics and centers on the struggle for citizenship and control of the state and the legacies of late colonialism. The modern state is not only a political and cultural space but also an economic space that shapes the material well-being of its citizens. The problems of the African state have shifted a bit from foreign rule to domestic political oppression and poor economic and social conditions. Thus, the discourse of the African state needs to capture its political tribulations as well as its economic and social conundrums.

Similarly, this study seeks to shift the discourse on civil wars from their pathologies to the opportunities to rework failing states. The causes of civil wars and their tremendous humanitarian and security implications have been well examined in the governance, security, and migration literatures.[181] However, studies often fail to examine the link between civil wars and the transformation of the state. Notwithstanding the deplorable humanitarian tragedy of civil wars, such conflicts can be catalysts for ending state decay and reworking failed states. The success of these states depends on the manner in which civil wars are resolved, the kinds of political and institutional arrangements that are put in place to address the underlying cause of conflict, and the extent and nature of postwar reconstruction.[182] By focusing on the fundamental nature of the state, local actors and international partners can create opportunities to build a democratic regime, address corruption and fundamental injustices, and promote economic and social development.

Finally, this study seeks to shift the discourse on African states from their colonial and neocolonial legacies to their moral and security connectedness to the international community. Africa's relations with Western governments and financial institutions have mostly been tainted by the excesses of the capitalist and Cold War expansions.[183] The legacies of these excesses, which date back to slavery and the early colonial encounters, continue to perforate African states. However, the end of the Cold War led to significant transformation in the relation between African regimes and Western powers.[184] The failure of a number of African states coupled with domestic budget cuts and moral outrage over Africa's debt crisis during the late 1980s led Western powers to redefine their relation with African dictatorships.[185] Western governments and financial institutions abandoned longtime allies and demanded political and economic reforms as preconditions for economic assistance. Most importantly, Western powers tacitly acknowledged their role in supporting bad governments in Africa. While the actual economic and political gains of Western austerity measures against African dictatorships remained questionable, they did initiate a new relationship between Africa and Western countries that seems to emphasize good governance, democracy, investment and trade opportunities, and security, which are all consistent with new humanitarianism and people-centered liberalism.

The threats to international and regional security from failed states raised critical questions about Africa's relation with Western powers. Failing states in Africa were seen as push factors for unwelcome migration to Western countries, fertile grounds for terrorists and international criminal cartels, and recipes for regional destabilization and humanitarian tragedies.[186] Dictatorship and bad governance have been recognized as major contributors to state failure and insecurity. This situation led to critical discourses about early intervention in vulnerable states and the promotion of democracy and good governance. Africa and the Western powers seemed to embrace their shared security and moral interests in managing conflicts and addressing the political and economic roots of conflict. When civil wars break out, they draw increased attention to the problems of state failure and the need to maintain regional security. This is a significant shift from the colonial and neocolonial policies of exploitation that characterized Africa's relation with the West before the end of the Cold War. Though most war-torn African countries have not seen robust international intervention to end their conflicts, Sierra Leone, Liberia, and Côte d'Ivoire received significant international attention. In the case of Sierra Leone and Liberia, the international community deployed an unprecedented number of peacekeeping forces and civilian agencies to enforce peace and help restore state capacity. By examining the civil wars and the peacebuilding role of the international community in these three West African countries, this study points to the ways humanitarian intervention evolves into international statebuilding and addresses the often-neglected external aspect of statebuilding. The growing role of international agencies in Africa's development raises critical questions about their impact on the state and Africa's relation with the rest of the world. Most importantly, it points to the potentials and limitations of international statebuilding, which is envisioned in new humanitarianism and people-centered liberalism.

To address the research questions and conceptual issues raised in this study, the book is organized into six chapters, including this introduction chapter (chap. 1) and the conclusion chapter (chap. 6). In chapter 2, we address the issue of state decay and the civil wars in Sierra Leone, Liberia, and Côte d'Ivoire. We delve into the problematic nature of the state in the years leading to civil war through the notion of state decay. We use this notion to discuss the range of problems that created conditions for civil war. We also examine the civil wars and the security and humanitarian problems that prompted the international military interventions by regional and international powers.

In chapter 3, we address the issues of international humanitarian intervention and the peacekeeping mission. We examine both the broader moral and international security drivers and the mechanics of peacekeeping and negotiating peace agreements. Through the notion of new humanitarianism, we show how the international interventions evolved from weak observer missions to robust peace-enforcement missions under the doctrine of R2P. The chapter shows how new humanitarianism led to international statebuilding, which is largely anchored in the neoliberal multiparty election path to peace and democracy. In many ways, the peace agreements exposed both the possibilities and the missed opportunities to rethink the state and pursue creative institutional design options to address the root cause of state decay and the civil wars.

In chapter 4, we address the essence of and the ideological and policy drivers of international statebuilding. We use the notion of people-centered liberalism to examine both the neoliberal and human development approaches to statebuilding and international development programs. We examine the core postwar reconstruction frameworks for each of the countries and the roles of international and national actors in shaping the state. Through the lens of human security, we analyze both the human development and democracy aspects of international statebuilding. A critical question for us is whether the programs are mostly directed at restoring the prewar order or resolving the prewar pathologies that led to state decay. We also examine the costs of statebuilding and various avenues for funding robust programs.

In chapter 5, we look at various postwar reforms directed at consolidating peace, sustaining democracy, and inculcating good governance, all ingredients of statebuilding. The ultimate goal of these programs is to bring stability, durable peace, and democracy and boost economic development. As in the previous chapter, a critical question here is whether the programs simply restore the prewar conditions of the state or are fundamentally transforming the state in ways that avoid backsliding into decay and resolve the core causes of the civil wars. This chapter examines the core elements of the postwar reconstruction, notably security-sector reforms, human rights and justice issues, and good-governance issues.

Collectively, the chapters answer the core questions posed in this book and point to insightful lessons about the state, civil wars, international community, and statebuilding in a typical postcolonial African country. These lessons come together in chapter 6, which accentuates the conceptual and policy contributions of the book. Overall, the book provides novel ways to conceptualize international statebuilding, deep historical insights into state decay and the civil wars in the case countries, and a rich analysis of the mechanics of peacekeeping, peace mediation, and postwar reconstruction.

STATE DECAY AND CIVIL WAR

INTRODUCTION

Civil wars are most often remembered for their destruction and the manner in which they are resolved. However, beneath the stories of tragedy and triumph are the most critical questions pertaining to the causes and objectives of these wars. Understanding such causes and objectives is critical for both resolving conflicts and building stable and democratic states. As Bishop Joseph Humper noted, for example, the report of the Sierra Leone Truth and Reconciliation Commission (TRC) "is intended to enable Sierra Leoneans to understand the conflict and to come to grips with the problems which gave rise to it, many of which continue to plague Sierra Leone today. In this way, the Commission hopes the Report will serve as a roadmap towards the building of a new society in which all Sierra Leoneans can walk unafraid with pride and dignity."[1] Indeed, the TRCs of both Sierra Leone and Liberia examined the causes of their civil wars.[2] Unfortunately, the lessons about the causes of the civil wars have often been neglected as the push for justice and reconciliation became paramount. There is always the urge to leave the past behind as a way to consolidate peace. However, the prewar nature of the state is difficult to leave behind given the fact that the main objectives of the protagonists of civil wars are to control the state and shape its character. The civil wars and emergent postwar states can hardly be understood without questioning the prewar conditions of the state. As numerous studies have shown, the civil wars that erupted in West Africa are not simply the result of chance; rather, they are rooted in the fundamental problems of the state.[3] When civil war broke out in Liberia in 1989, the state had already failed. The Liberian state was plagued by chronic political, economic, and administrative problems that led to further deterioration. In 1990, Sierra Leone was in a similar predicament. The one-party regime had long lost its legitimacy, and economic and social conditions had severely worsened. The state had not only failed; it was continuously deteriorating. By 1990, Côte d'Ivoire was also experiencing an economic and political crisis that weakened the state. The state fell into deep turmoil following the death of President Félix Houphouët-Boigny in 1993, and a civil war ensued in 2002. Notwithstanding their unique realities, all three countries were in a state of decay during the period leading up to civil war.[4]

The conditions that typify state decay are similar to those in failing and failed states.[5] In his discourse on the temporality of states, Christopher Clapham sees state decay as part of a continuum of vulnerability that may end in state collapse.[6] Stephen Holmes employed the notion of state decay to describe the crumbling of the system of power and the emergence of a modern version of the state of nature in the former Soviet republics. Holmes's central concern was the erosion of the constitutional order that underpins modern democracy and superpower security relations.[7] The term *state decay* has been used loosely in the literature on Africa. In his study of corporate military intervention in Sierra Leone, for example, Abdel-Fatau Musah alluded to state decay in his description of the gradual deterioration of the security, political, and economic situation of the state.[8] Similarly, Georges Nzongola-Ntalaja referred to state decay in his analysis of Mobutu's misrule of the former Zaire, which eventually led to the collapse of the state.[9] In fact, most of the studies of state failure in Africa rest on analyses of the deteriorated political, economic, and security conditions of African states. However, these studies tend to emphasize the outcome of such conditions rather than the process of deterioration. As such, state failure and collapse, which are the cumulative results of state decay, remain the central analytical categories of the African states. The task of statebuilding requires not only a proper analysis of the notions of failed and collapsed states, however, but also a thorough examination and conceptualization of the condition of state decay. And it is important to point out that there exists a dialectical relationship between state decay and civil wars; while state decay can trigger a civil war, it can also be caused by civil war. We acknowledge this point and clarify that our approach rests on the dialectical nature of civil wars and state decay rather than on the language of variables associated with quantitative and some qualitative works influenced by scholars like Gary King, Robert O. Keohane, and Sidney Verba.[10]

State decay is the process of significant deterioration of the state's capacity to deliver positive political and social goods. It is also a transformation of the state into an oppressive political force and an impediment to economic and social development (note that both weak and strong states can be highly oppressive). It is both a manifestation of the chronically poor political, economic, and social conditions of the state and the continuous worsening of such conditions. State decay differs from temporal decline in that it is a dramatic shift in the political, economic, and social trajectory of the state in a way that undermines the stability of the country and the well-being of its citizens.[11] Moreover, it is triggered by malevolent attempts by political leaders to monopolize power, resulting in a systemic abuse of power and inefficiency of state institutions. State decay is a precursor to state failure that is manifested in increased political oppression, a breakdown of the rule of law, severe economic decline, and the dilapidation of state institutions and infrastructure. State decay has three synergetic dimensions: political, economic, and social. Politically, state decay is the erosion of civil rights and the increased use of coercion to achieve certain objectives. It is marked by an entrenchment of dictatorship, a loss of legitimacy, the suppression of civil society and the media, and the lack of a fair and transparent process for a peaceful change of government. Economically, state decay is the bankrupting of the state and the forestalling of the production of goods and service as a result of high-level state mismanagement and corruption, which may be compounded by adverse international fiscal conditions. As one interview respondent clearly indicated for this study, "Any country becomes ripe for rebellion when there's endemic corruption."[12] This problem is characterized by prebendalism, huge budget deficits and debts, hyperinflation, and a shrinking economy. On the social level, state decay is a generalized despair emanating from the state's inability to deliver basic social goods due to poor political leadership and economic mismanagement. This state of affairs is typified by declining standards of living, inadequate basic services (education, transportation, health care, etc.), and high rates of chronic unemployment and underemployment. The political and economic aspects of state decay feed into its social dimension and frequently produce a strong desire for revolutionary change that can be exploited by people seeking to gain power by force.

THE EMERGENCE AND DECADENCE OF THE STATE

The state in Sierra Leone, Liberia, and Côte d'Ivoire came into being in earnest at the time of independence. In Sierra Leone, this was marked by the formal recognition of the country as an independent state on April 27, 1961, by the British government. Côte d'Ivoire gained independence from France on August 7, 1960, after the French Union in West Africa collapsed. On July 16, 1847, the Americo-Liberians severed themselves from the American Colonization Society and declared "a free, sovereign, and independent state, by the name and title of the Republic of Liberia."[13] These states, whose foundations were laid by the colonial powers, faced a series of challenges that culminated in civil wars. The states' development climaxed shortly after the decolonization of Africa around the 1960s and reached its lowest ebb during a series of civil wars. For most of the postindependence period, the conditions in these countries hardly improved significantly, and in many cases, they actually regressed. As such, these countries never developed into stable democracies or fairly industrialized countries. State decay in Sierra Leone, Liberia, and Côte d'Ivoire can be gauged by examining their political, economic, and social development trajectories.

Statehood and Postcolonial Political Developments

The most critical element of statehood is the international legal status of a country. Since achieving independence, Sierra Leone, Liberia, and Côte d'Ivoire have emerged as sovereign members of the international community and have become full members of the United Nations (UN). The key juncture in their statehood was the recognition of their sovereignty by the former colonial powers and the superpowers.[14] In the case of Sierra Leone and Côte d'Ivoire, this recognition came as part of the decolonization of Africa around the 1960s.[15] The colonial powers had accepted their independence as a fait accompli even before the formal declarations of independence. In the case of Liberia, the United States did not recognize the country's independence until 1862. Interestingly, Liberia received early recognition from Britain, which was still acquiring colonies in Africa. While the legal status of these countries is clear, their sovereignty has arguably been compromised by neocolonialism.[16] Sierra Leone did not actually become a republic until 1971. Since then, it has remained in the British Commonwealth. Despite its status as an independent state, Côte d'Ivoire maintained strong military, political, and economic dependency on France. This dependency has been most evident in Houphouët-Boigny's pro-France African policies, the Franco-Ivoirian military pact (including an important French military base), and the French monetary control over the *franc de la Communauté financière de l'Afrique* (CFA franc), which is used in Côte d'Ivoire and most other francophone countries in the region.[17] Despite its early independence, Liberia has been under the shadow of colonialism in Africa. Between 1847 and 1960, Liberia was virtually an island of independence within a continent that was under European rule. Liberia's potential to develop as an independent state was effectively limited by the European colonial domination of the continent. The country's independence became more meaningful when the decolonization of Africa began in earnest in the 1950s. In addition to the shadow of colonialism that loomed over it, Liberia has had a dependent relationship with the United States, especially during the Cold War, which hitherto shaped its politics and economy.[18] Support from the United States has been critical for the survival of various Liberian regimes, which have mostly been undemocratic.[19] The dependency of these countries on former colonial powers extends from the political to the economic realm. Postcolonial ties to Western powers are often characterized by continued dependency and neocolonialism. Some of the most adverse effects of this dependency became evident in the debt crisis and the instability that followed the reorientation of Western policies toward Africa at the end of the Cold War. Since the outbreak of the civil wars, this dependency has increased and evolved into a new breed of humanitarianism. While independence and the overall decolonization of Africa were critical periods in the development of the state, meaningful sovereignty has been difficult to attain due to excessive dependency on aid and external debts.

Politically, most states in Africa emerged as democracies but failed to consolidate democracy. The nationalist movements that led to independence were struggles against colonial rule but also for civil and political rights. There was also a struggle for power among elites. Fundamental rights were affirmed in the constitutions of the new states, which were modeled after the democratic political structures of the metropole. The 1847 Constitutions of Liberia, for example, affirmed that "all power is inherent in the people; all free governments are instituted by their authority and for their benefit and they have the right to alter and reform the same when their safety and happiness require it" and called for an elected legislature and an elected president.[20] The preamble of the 1960 Constitution of Côte d'Ivoire commits to the principles of democracy and human rights. Article 3 asserts, *"La souveraineté appartient au peuple. Aucune section du peuple ni aucun individu ne peut s'en attribuer l'exercice."*[21] It calls for a president and a legislature elected through competitive multiparty elections. Similarly, the 1961 Constitution of Sierra Leone was modeled after a British parliamentary system of democracy.[22] The affirmation of democratic principles and the establishment of democratic institutions were significant points in the development of the state. They not only rejected colonial dictatorship but also laid a foundation for democracy.

Nevertheless, democracy did not really last long in any of the three countries. In Liberia, the True Whig Party (TWP) dominated the state from 1870 to 1980. Under the rule of William Tubman (1944–1971), Liberia effectively became a single-party state, and this continued under Tubman's successor, William Tolbert.[23] Dictatorship became more entrenched under the rule of Samuel Doe, who overthrew the TWP in 1980. In Sierra Leone, the ruling All Peoples Congress (APC) introduced a one-party system that ruled the country until 1992, when it was overthrown by the National Provisional Reformation Council (NPRC). Even before the adoption of the one-party system in 1978, there were numerous instances of electoral fraud, political oppression, and military coups.[24] Côte d'Ivoire was also a one-party state until 1990. The Parti Démocratique de Côte d'Ivoire (PDCI), led by Houphouët-Boigny, dominated Ivoirian politics until Houphouët-Boigny's death in 1993. From 1960 to 1990, it was the sole political party.[25] Despite its affirmation of democratic principles, Côte d'Ivoire failed to develop a democratic system of government. Elections under the one-party system fell short of providing opportunities for meaningful democratic participation. These three countries all abandoned multiparty democracy and instituted one-party regimes, which eroded civil and political rights. In Sierra Leone and Liberia, the political problems were worsened by the intervention of the military in politics. Instead of consolidating democracy, they substituted neopatrimonial rule for colonial rule, which further undermined the stability of the state. It is important to note that while neopatrimonialism is most frequently understood as a source of instability, as with the case of leaders like former Liberian President Doe, it can also (although more rarely) be viewed as a glue that keeps the state together, as with the case of former Ivoirian President Houphouët-Boigny and the system of hegemonic exchange he established during his rule.[26] The net results of the one-party and military dictatorships were the suppression of civil and political rights, corruption, abuse of state power, and erosion of the legitimacy of the government, all of which created the conditions for the civil wars. The regression from democracy to dictatorship led to state decay not only in the political sense but also in the economic and social realms.

Economic Trajectory of the State

Economically, Sierra Leone, Liberia, and Côte d'Ivoire failed to develop. The most telling indication of their prewar poor economic realities was their low standing in the global economy. These states had not only failed to industrialize, they had largely remained underdeveloped agricultural and mining economies.[27] As Peter Harrold, Malathi Jayawickrama, and Deepak Bhattasali candidly pointed out in their study of African and East Asian industrial and trade policies, "Africa's factor endowments and economic structures are quite similar to those found in Southeast Asia in the 1960s. The Southeast Asian countries—Indonesia, Malaysia and Thailand—have achieved rapid industrial growth over the past three decades, while Africa has struggled with adjustment, and witnessed a marginal industrial response."[28] According to a side-by-side country comparison, for example, Côte d'Ivoire's development lagged behind Malaysia's in all critical measures. Malaysia's gross domestic product (GDP) per capita increased from around $700 in 1960 to above $2,500 in the early the 1990s, while Côte d'Ivoire's GDP per capita in the early 1990s was around $800. At its prewar climax in late 1980, Côte d'Ivoire's GDP per capita was under $1,300. By 1991, the rate of manufacturing had significantly increased in Malaysia from its 1970s level, while Côte d'Ivoire saw a significant decline during the same period.[29] The failure to industrialize is most evident in the predominance of mining and agricultural goods in the exports of the three West African counties. In 1965, for example, primary commodities (excluding fuels, minerals, and metals) accounted for 93 percent of Côte d'Ivoire's exports. In 1987, they still accounted for 86 percent of the exports.[30] In Liberia, too, fuels, minerals, and metals accounted for 72 percent of exports in 1965 and 57 percent in 1987, while other primary commodities accounted for 25 percent in 1965 and 41 percent in 1987. Sierra Leone's export was also heavily based on primary commodities. Fuels, minerals, and metals accounted for 25 percent of exports in 1965 and 22 percent in 1987, while other primary goods accounted for 14 percent of exports in 1965 and 19 percent in 1987.[31]

The economies of Sierra Leone, Liberia, and Côte d'Ivoire registered their best prewar performances during the 1970s and early 1980s. However, the economic conditions were poor even at their peak performances, underscoring the underdeveloped nature of the states and their inherent economic weakness.[32] Côte d'Ivoire showed great potential for economic development before the civil war but failed to achieve solid results. The poor economic realities of these states prior to the civil wars are best illustrated by their low GDP per capita (see fig. 2.1).

Figure 2.1 shows that Sierra Leone's GDP per capita steadily grew during the first two decades of independence. It peaked in 1984 at $537.90. By the time of the outbreak of the war in 1991, however, GDP per capita had fallen to $277, which was among the twenty lowest in the world.[33] For most of the war period, GDP per capita was under $300. In 2000, it reached a mere $219. Liberia's GDP per capita also grew during the 1970s. It reached $445 in 1982 but steadily declined to $387 in 1986. It rose to a high point of $451 by the start of the war in 1989 but sharply declined to $225 in 1990, which was among the thirteen lowest in the world.[34] For most of the war period, Liberia's GDP per capita was under $200. It reached an abysmal $88 in 1994. Though Côte d'Ivoire had a significantly higher GDP per capita, it too had a problematic trajectory. Côte d'Ivoire's GDP per capita sharply increased during the first two decades of independence. It jumped from a mere $286 in 1970 to an impressive $1,209 in 1980. However, its GDP per capita sharply declined to $666 by 1985. Though this bounced back up to $943 by 1990, it was under $800 for most of the period of the political crisis (1993 to 2004). At the worst moments of the political crisis (i.e., 1994, 2000, and 2002), its GDP per capita was just around $600. Despite its strong potential, Côte d'Ivoire failed to consolidate its economic gains during its first two decades of independence; instead, the economic decline weakened the state and compounded its political crisis. Even without adjusting for inflation, the rate of decline in GDP per capita has been dramatic in all three countries. In Sierra Leone and Liberia, it is important to note that GDP per capita has always been very low.

Along with their GDP per capita, other key economic indicators showed problematic trajectories for Sierra Leone, Liberia, and Côte d'Ivoire before the civil wars.[35] These trajectories were manifested in three of the most critical moments

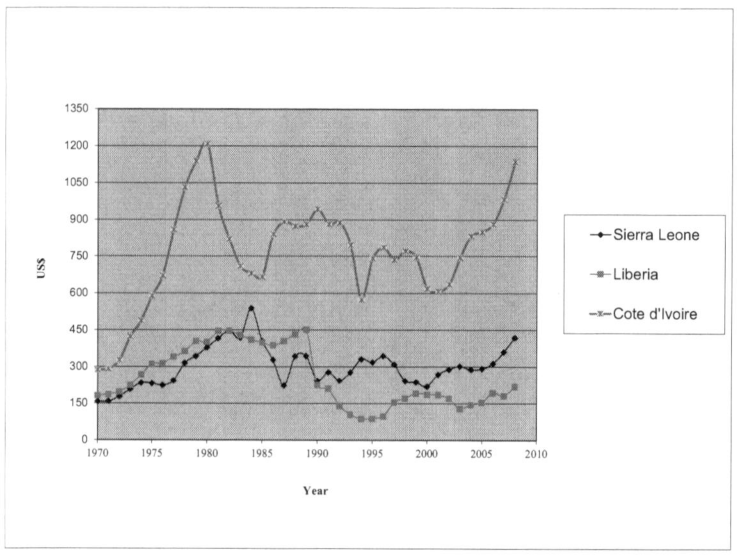

Figure 2.1. Côte d'Ivoire, Liberia, and Sierra Leone: GDP Per Capita (1970–2008).

in the development of these states (see tables 2.1, 2.2, and 2.3). In the case of Sierra Leone, the critical moments are the immediate postindependence period (1960s), the period of highest economic performance as measured by GDP per capita (1984), and the outbreak of the civil war in 1991. The critical moments in Liberia's development are also during the 1960s, when the country was just over a century old. As noted earlier, Liberia was under the shadow of colonialism until the late 1950s. As such, the decolonization of Africa is a much more useful benchmark for the economic realities of the Liberian state than the actual decade of independence. Moreover, economic data on Liberia prior to the 1960s is hardly available. Apart from the 1960s, the other critical moments for Liberia were the periods of highest economic performance as measured by GDP per capita (1982) and the outbreak of the civil war in 1989. In the case of Côte d'Ivoire, the critical moments were the immediate postindependence period (1960s), the period of highest economic performance as measured by GDP per capita (1980), the onset of the political crisis in 1993, and the escalation to civil war in 2002.[36] Unlike in Sierra Leone and Liberia, the civil war in Côte d'Ivoire was preceded by a prolonged period of severe political violence. In essence, 2002 marked the escalation into civil war rather than the outset of war. While Sierra Leone and Liberia quickly degenerated into full-scale and brutal civil wars, Côte d'Ivoire was plagued by a violent political crisis that evolved into a relatively low-key civil war.[37]

Table 2.1. Sierra Leone: Selected Economic Indicators (1964 to 1991).

Indicators	Decade of Independence		Peak Economic Period		Outbreak of Civil War Period	
	Year / Value		Year / Value		Year / Value	
Currency exchange rate (USD 1 per leones)	1964	0.71	1984	2.51	1991	295.34
Gross Domestic Product (GDP) per capita (USD)	1964	153.9	1984	537.9	1991	189.5
Gross Domestic Product (millions of leones)	1964	215.3	1984	2,729.5	1991	150,175.1
Average annual growth of GDP (%)	1960–70	4.2	1970–77	1.9	1980–90	1.2
Export of goods and services (millions of leones)	1964	66.2	1984	290.0	1991	38,123.7
Trade balance (millions of USD)	1964	−0.5	1984	−17.1	1991	−0.5
Total reserve minus gold (millions of USD)	1964	20.4	1984	7.7	1991	9.6
Government finance (millions of leones)	1964	−4	1984	−206.0	1991	−10,477.0
External public debts (millions of USD)	1970	59	1977	190.0	1990	1,151.0
External public debts as % of GNP	1970	14.3	1977	32.0	1987	54.6

Sources: International Monetary Fund, *International Financial Statistical Yearbook*, 1994 640–643.

Nation Master, "Economy > GDP > Per Capita: Countries Compared," accessed October 23, 2023, http://www.nationmaster.com/graph/eco_gdp_percap-economy-gdp-per-capita&date =1964.

United Nations, "Per Capita GDP at Current Prices—US Dollars," UN Data: A World of Information, accessed October 12, 2023, http://data.un.org/Data.aspx?q=GDP+per+capita&d =SNAAMA&f=grID%3a101%3bcurrID%3aUSD%3bpcFlag%3a1.

World Bank, *World Development Report*, 1979, 154–155; and 2000/2001, 295, 315, accessed October 12, 2023, https://openknowledge.worldbank.org/handle/10986/2124.

As indicated in table 2.1, Sierra Leone's GDP was around $303 million in 1964, while GDP per capita was at $153.90.[38] In 1984, the GDP was just above $1 billion after it fell from its peak of around $1.3 billion in 1982. By the start of the civil war in 1991, the GDP was at a meager $508 million. The GDP grew at an average rate of 4.2 percent during the 1960s but stalled at 1.9 percent (1970–1977) and 1.2 percent during the 1980s. Sierra Leone's export also showed a similar pattern of decline. It rose from $93.2 million in 1964 to a high of $256.4 million in 1981. By 1984, the value of export had fallen to $115.5 million. The value of exports remained under $150 million until the outbreak of the war in 1991, with the exception of 1989, when it spiked to $273.3 million. The fall in exports was reflected in Sierra Leone's balance-of-trade deficit, which rose from $0.5 million in 1964 to $17.2 million in 1980 before dropping again to $0.5 in 1991. At best, Sierra Leone's trade balance reached a surplus of only $11 million in 1968. Even without adjusting for inflation, Sierra Leone's economic decline was sharp. The government deficit remained low until 1974, when it was just $24.4 million. The deficit was at $82 million in 1984, $35 million in 1991, and reached its worst prewar point in 1983 at $143 million. The external public debts grew from $59 million in 1970 to $190 million in 1977 and reached an alarming $1.2 billion in 1990. In 1987, external debts amounted to 54.6 percent of the gross national product (GNP). The national reserve (excluding gold), which had grown from $20.4 million in 1964 to $54.6 million in 1974, dropped to $7.7 million by 1984. It reached its lowest prewar point of $3.7 million in 1989. In 1991, it was a paltry sum of $9.6 million. Economically, Sierra Leone was extremely underdeveloped. Even more problematic was the continuous economic deterioration of the state during the decade preceding the civil war.

Liberia reached its prewar economic peak in the early 1980s but failed to make progress during the rest of the decade. Given the country's low level of economic development, even during its best periods, stagnation was tantamount to failure.[39] This failure dramatically worsened during the civil war. Liberia's GDP had grown from $247.2 million in 1965 to $1.1 billion in 1982.[40] For most of the 1980s, GDP hovered around $1.1 billion and reached its highest point of $1.18 billion in 1989. The GDP grew at an average annual rate of 5.1 percent during the 1960s but fell to 2.7 percent (1970–1977) and -1.3 percent between 1980 and 1987. GDP per capita grew from $206.70 in 1965 to $445.30 in 1982 but had barely reached its prewar high of $450 in 1989. Similarly, the value of Liberia's exports significantly grew from $144.2 million in 1965 to a high of $613.5 million in 1980 but fell to $487.4 million in 1982. In 1989, it had increased to only $521.9 million. The trade balance fell from $104 million in 1975 to $87.2 million in 1982. It reached $166.6 million in 1985 but rapidly fell to $63.2 million in 1987. By the time of the outbreak of the war, Liberia's economy was no better than it was in 1982, even without adjusting for inflation. The stagnation in export and GDP was compounded by huge

Table 2.2. Liberia: Selected Economic Indicators (1967 to 1989).

Indicators	Century of Independence		Peak Economic Period		Outbreak of Civil War Period	
	Year/Value		Year/Value		Year/Value	
Currency exchange rate (USD 1 per LRD)	1965	1.0	1982	1.0	1989	1.0
Gross Domestic Product (GDP) per capita (USD)	1965	206.7	1982	445.3	1989	364.0
Gross Domestic Product (millions of LRD)	1965	247.2	1982	1,119.5	1989	1,182.8
Average annual growth of GDP (%)	1960–70	5.1	1970–77	2.7	1980–87	−1.3
Export of goods and services (millions of LRD)	1965	144.2	1982	487.4	1989	521.9
Trade balance (millions of USD)	1975	104.0	1982	87.2	1987	63.2
Total reserve minus gold (millions of USD)	1974	18.7	1982	6.5	1988	0.4
Government finance (millions of LRD)	1965	−18.0	1982	−116.6	1988	−91.9
External public debts (millions of USD)	1970	158.0	1977	266.0	1987	1,152.0
External public debts as % of GNP	1970	52.5	1977	37.6	1987	108.4

Note: LRD = Liberian Dollar

Sources: International Monetary Fund, *International Financial Statistical Yearbook*, 1994, 474–477.

Nation Master, "Economy > GDP > Per Capita: Countries Compared," accessed October 23, 2023, http://www.nationmaster.com/graph/eco_gdp_percap-economy-gdp-per-capita&date =1964.

United Nations, "Per Capita GDP at Current Prices—US Dollars," UN Data: A World of Information, accessed October 12, 2023, http://data.un.org/Data.aspx?q=GDP+per+capita&d =SNAAMA&f=grID%3a101%3bcurrID%3aUSD%3bpcFlag%3a1.

World Bank, *World Development Report*, 1979, 154–155; and 2000/2001, 295, 315, accessed October 12, 2023, https://openknowledge.worldbank.org/handle/10986/2124.

government deficits and external debts. The government balance, which was at a deficit of $18 million in 1965, improved to a surplus of $13.2 million in 1972. By 1982, however, the deficit was at $116.6 million after reaching a high of $141.2 million in 1979. External public debts grew from $158 million in 1970 to $266 million in 1977 and $1.2 billion in 1987. The national reserve (excluding gold) dramatically fell from $81.7 million in 1974 to $6.5 million in 1982 and a meager $0.4 million in 1989. By the time of the outbreak of the war, Liberia's economy was very weak. The long and brutal war compounded the economic and political decay of the state and led to state collapse.

While Côte d'Ivoire's economic trajectory was better than that of Sierra Leone and Liberia, the country experienced major setbacks before the war.[41] As shown in table 2.3, Côte d'Ivoire's GDP dramatically increased from $1 billion in 1964 to an impressive $10.2 billion in 1980, while the GDP per capita jumped from $223.4 to $1,208.60 during the same period.[42] The GDP grew at an annual average rate of 8 percent during the 1960s and 6.5 percent between 1970 and 1977. The value of exports also significantly increased from $0.3 billion in 1964 to $3.6 billion in 1980. While the external public debts grew from $256 million in 1970 to almost $2 billion in 1977, the debts were still under 35 percent of the GNP. Despite its huge debts, Côte d'Ivoire's prewar economic development looked promising until 1980. The country had made significant progress, which could have been a foundation for major economic development. Since the 1980s, however, Côte d'Ivoire had not made major prewar economic gains. The GDP fell to $6.8 billion in 1983 before climbing again to $10.3 billion in 1988. At the outset of the political crisis in 1993, the GDP was at $10.4 billion. Between 1995 and 2002, the GDP fluctuated between $10 and $12 billion. The GDP increased by only 0.7 percent during the 1980s. Throughout the early 1990s, the value of exports hardly reached their 1980 level of $3.6 billion. At the outset of the political crisis in 1993, the value was $3 billion. Between 1995 and 2002, it fluctuated between $4 and $5 billion. Côte d'Ivoire had consistently maintained a positive trade balance. Its surplus grew from $68.1 million in 1964 to $399 million in 1980, after reaching $573.8 million in 1976. It reached $1.5 billion in 1986 before falling to $748.3 million in 1993. After 1994, it steadily grew to $2.7 billion in 2002. In addition to its trade surpluses, Côte d'Ivoire maintained a reasonable level of liquidity. Its reserve (excluding gold) grew from $40.1 million in 1964 to $448 million in 1978. It dropped to $19.7 million in 1980 and a mere $2.3 million in 1993. After 1994, it increased to $1.86 billion in 2002. Despite some of these gains, Côte d'Ivoire's prewar economic potentials were not fully materialized. While its trade balance and liquidity significantly grew, the growths in GDP and exports from their 1980 levels were modest, even without adjusting for inflation. Moreover, the growth was not steady. In contrast, external debts grew at an alarming rate, reaching $17.2

Table 2.3. Côte d'Ivoire: Selected Economic Indicators (1964 to 2002).

Indicators	Decade of Independence Year/Value		Peak Economic Period Year/Value		Outbreak of the Political Crisis Year/Value		Escalation to Civil War Period Year/Value	
Currency exchange rate (USD 1 per francs)	1964	245.0	1980	211.28	1993	283.1	2002	696.99
Gross Domestic Product (GDP) per capita (USD)	1964	223.4	1980	1,208.6	1993	795.5	2002	662.3
Gross Domestic Product (billions of francs)	1964	239.7	1980	2,149.9	1993	2,946.2	2002	8,166.9
Average annual growth of GDP (%)	1960–70	8.0	1970–77	6.5	1980–1990	0.7	1990–2003	2.4
Export of goods and services (billions of francs)	1964	81.4	1980	752.5	1993	847.0	2002	3,390.8
Trade balance (millions of USD)	1964	68.1	1980	399.0	1993	748.3	2002	2,734.5
Total reserve minus gold (millions of USD)	1964	40.1	1980	19.7	1993	2.3	2002	1,863.3

(Continued)

Table 2.3 (*continued*)

Indicators	Decade of Independence Year/Value		Peak Economic Period Year/Value		Outbreak of the Political Crisis Year/Value		Escalation to Civil War Period Year/Value	
Government finance (millions of francs)	1979	−168.3	1980	−233,189.0	1994	−280,100.0	1999	−11,000.0
External public debts (millions of USD)	1970	256.0	1977	1,973.0	1990	17,251.0	2002	11,816.0
External public debts as % of GNP	1970	18.2	1977	34.6	1987	89.5	1998	122

Note: Francs refers to CFA francs.

Sources: International Monetary Fund, *International Financial Statistical Yearbook*, 1994, 302–305; and 2003, 243–245.

Nation Master, "Economy > GDP > Per Capita: Countries Compared," accessed October 23, 2023, http://www.nationmaster.com/graph/eco_gdp _percap-economy-gdp-per-capita&date=1964.

United Nations, "Per Capita GDP at Current Prices—US Dollars," UN Data: A World of Information, accessed October 12, 2023, http://data.un.org /Data.aspx?q=GDP+per+capita&d=SNAAMA&f=grID%3a101%3bcurrID%3aUSD%3bpcFlag%3a1.

World Bank, *World Development Report*, 1979, 128–129, 154–155; 1989, table 2, table 24; 2000–2001, 294, 314, table 21, table 11; 2005, 260, 262, accessed October 12, 2023, https://openknowledge.worldbank.org/handle/10986/2124.

billion in 1990 before dropping to $11.8 billion in 2002. As a proportion of GNP, external debts grew from 89.5 percent in 1987 to 122 percent in 1998. Similarly, the government deficit grew from $0.8 million in 1979 to $1.1 billion in 1980 before slightly dropping to just under $1 billion in 1994. While Côte d'Ivoire was on a path to economic development during the first two decades of independence, its economic development essentially stalled before the war.

Social Development and Well-Being of the Citizens

The development of the states in Sierra Leone, Liberia, and Côte d'Ivoire must also be gauged by the level of social development and the associated well-being of their citizens.[43] As noted in the introductory chapter, the state does not necessarily have to be the primary provider of the services that ensure the well-being of its citizens. However, the modern state must create the conditions for its citizens to have reasonable access to basic services such as education, health care, clean drinking water, and transportation. The absence of such services creates poor living conditions and increases the level of political and social discontent, which can undermine the stability of the state. As such, social development is critical. States that are economically and politically progressing tend to have favorable living conditions, while those that are decaying tend to exhibit poor living conditions. One of the most prominent measures of well-being is the United Nations Development Program's (UNDP) Human Development Index (HDI), which gauges and ranks the performance of countries on critical indicators of economic and social well-being. The UN Millennium Development Goals reports also provide valuable measures of the progress toward economic and social well-being in developing countries. Some of the most critical indicators of well-being include the level of poverty; life expectancy, infant and maternal mortality, and literacy rates; access to clean water; employment opportunities; and the availability of proper roads. Since social well-being is contingent on the economic and political conditions of the state, the trajectory of the state's social development will be linked to three critical moments: the immediate postindependence and decolonization period of the 1960s, the period of peak economic performance as measured by GDP per capita, and the outbreak of civil wars. In the case of Côte d'Ivoire, there is an additional category—the outbreak of the political crisis that escalated into civil war. Côte d'Ivoire has been in a precarious peace situation, as peace and democracy have not really been consolidated. In fact, the 2016 changes to the constitution to allow Alassane Ouattara to stand for a third presidential term seriously risks reversal into civil war.[44] The opposition boycotted the dubious election, and Ouattara installed himself as president and positioned himself to stay in power for an excessively long time. In the cases of Liberia and Sierra Leone, there is an additional category for the civil war and the immediate postwar period. These trajectories are illustrated in tables 2.4, 2.5, and 2.6.[45]

Table 2.4. Sierra Leone: Selected Social Development Indicators (1960 to 2004).

Indicators	Decade of Independence Year/Value		Peak Economic Period Year/Value		Outbreak of Civil War Year/Value		Civil War/ Postwar Periods Year/Value	
Proportion of population below $1 (PPP) per day	..	..	..	..	1990	62.8	2003	53.4
Life expectancy at birth (years)	1960	37	1980	41.6	1985–90	41.7	2002	44.7
Infant mortality rate (per 1,000 live births)	1965	210	1987	151	1990	169	2000	162
Maternal mortality (per 100,000 live births)	..	..	1980	450	1990–98	..	2005	2,100
Adult literacy rate	1960	7	1974	15			2004	34.8
Population with access to safe/ improved drinking water (%)	..	..	1975	..	1995	57	2000	55
Employment-to-population ratio, both sexes, percentage	..	..	..	..	1991	63.6	2002	64.4
Paved road (% of total roads)					1991	10.8	2002	8.0
Human Development Index (value)	1970	...	1985	...	1990	0.048	2002	0.273
Human Development Index (rank)	1970	..	1985	..	1990	160	2002	173

Table 2.4 (*continued*)

Note: Pre-1990 data unavailable for some of the indicators.

Sources: United Nations, "Millennium Development Goals Indicators," https://www. developmentgoals.org/About_the_goals.html. (May 15, 2017).

United Nations, "Explorer," accessed October 23, 2023, http://data.un.org/Explorer.aspx.

United Nations, "Life Expectancy," accessed October 23, 2023, http://data.un.org/Data.aspx?q =life+expectancy&d=PopDiv&f=variableID%3a68.

United Nations, "Infant Mortality Rate," accessed October 23, 2023, http://data.un.org/Data .aspx?q=infant+mortality&d=WHO&f=MEASURE_CODE%3aimr.

United Nations, "Population Using Improved Drinking-Water Sources (%)," accessed October 23, 2023, http://data.un.org/Data.aspx?q=drinking+water&d=WHO&f=MEAS URE_CODE%3aWHS5_122.

UNDP, *Human Development Reports*, 1991, 1993, 2002, 2004, 2009, accessed October 23, 2023, http://hdr.undp.org/en/reports.

UNESCO, "Data Browser," Institute for Statistics, accessed October 23, 2023, http://stats.uis .unesco.org.

UNMDG, "Employment-to-Population Ratio, Both Sexes, Percentage," https://data.un.org.

World Bank, World Bank Open Data, accessed October 23, 2023, https://data.worldbank.org.

World Bank, *World Development Report*, 1978, 108; 1979, 166, 168; 1989, 226; 2000/2001, 286, accessed October 12, 2023, https://openknowledge.worldbank.org/handle/10986/2124.

Sierra Leone's low level of social development before the civil war was poignantly reflected in its mortality rates, which were among the worst in the world.[46] In 1960, for example, life expectancy was 37 years. By the late 1980s, it had increased to only 41.7 years. In 2002, it had barely increased to 44.7 years. The infant mortality rate, which was at 210 per thousand live births in 1965, had fallen to 151 per thousand in 1987, but increased to 169 per thousand in 1990, and fell down to only 162 per thousand in 2000. In 1980, the maternal mortality rate was 450 per hundred thousand live births. By 2005, the rate was at an alarming 2,100 per hundred thousand. In 2000, only 55 percent of the population had access to safe drinking water. In 2004 the adult literacy rate was 34.8 percent. The transportation infrastructure was also poor: only 10.8 percent of the available roads were paved in 1991, and in 2002, the figure was 8 percent. These poor social conditions were also reflected in people's precarious economic situations. In 1991 and 2002, around 64 percent of the people were unemployed. In 1990, 62.8 percent of the people lived on less than one dollar per day; in 2003, that figure was still 53.4 percent. Sierra Leone had not only failed to improve the well-being of its citizens but had actually regressed in some areas. This low level of social development was amply illustrated by the HDI. Sierra Leone's HDI score was 0.048 in 1990 and 0.273 in 2002. In 1990 and 2002, the country was ranked last in the world on the HDI.

Table 2.5. Liberia: Selected Social Development Indicators (1964 to 2002).

Indicators	Decade of Independence Year/Value		Peak Economic Period Year/Value		Outbreak of Civil War Period Year/Value		Civil War and Postwar Periods Year/Value	
Proportion of population below $1 (PPP) per day	..		..		..		2007	83.7
Life expectancy at birth (years)	1960	40	1980	47.5	1985–90	47.5	2002	55.8
Infant mortality rate (per 1,000 live births)	1965	139	1975	159	1990	157	2000	157
maternal mortality (per 100,000 live births)	..		1980	173	..		2005	1,200
Adult literacy rate (%)	1960	9	1974	15	1984	32.1	2004	53.9
Population with access to safe/ improved drinking water (%)	..		1975	..	1990	58	2000	65
Employment-to-population ratio, both sexes, percentage	..		..		1991	65.7	2003	65.5
Paved road (% of total roads)	..		..		1990	5.5	2001	6.2
Human Development Index (value)	..		..		1990	0.220	2006	0.434
Human Development Index (rank)	..		..		1990	132	2009	169

Notes: Pre-1990 data unavailable for some of the indicators.

Liberia's HDI could not be computed in 2002 during the height of the war (2002–2004).

Countries in the HDI (1990, 160 countries; 1993 and 2002, 173 countries; 2009, 182 countries).

Sources: United Nations, "Millennium Development Goals Indicators," https://unstats.un.org/sdgs/dataportal.

United Nations, "Explorer," accessed October 23, 2023, http://data.un.org/Explorer.aspx.

United Nations, "Life Expectancy," accessed October 23, 2023, http://data.un.org/Data.aspx?q=life+expectancy&d=PopDiv&f=variableID%3a68.

United Nations, "Infant Mortality Rate," accessed October 23, 2023, http://data.un.org/Data.aspx?q=infant+mortality&d=WHO&f=MEASURE_CODE%3aimr.

United Nations, "Population Using Improved Drinking-Water Sources (%)," accessed October 23, 2023, http://data.un.org/Data.aspx?q=drinking+water&d=WHO&f=MEASURE_CODE%3aWHS5_122.

UNDP, *Human Development Reports*, 1991, 1993, 2002, 2004, 2009, accessed October 23, 2023, http://hdr.undp.org/en/reports.

UNESCO, "Data Browser," Institute for Statistics, accessed October 23, 2023, http://stats.uis.unesco.org.

UNMDG, "Employment-to-Population Ratio, Both Sexes, Percentage," https://data.un.org.

World Bank, World Bank Open Data, accessed October 23, 2023, https://data.worldbank.org.

World Bank *World Development Report*, 1978, 108; 1979, 166, 168; 1989, 226; 2000/2001, 286, accessed October 12, 2023, https://openknowledge.worldbank.org/handle/10986/2124.

Table 2.6. Côte d'Ivoire: Selected Social Development Indicators (1964 to 2002).

Indicators	Decade of Independence Year/Value		Peak Economic Period Year/Value		Outbreak of the Political Crisis Year/Value		Escalation to Civil War Period Year/Value	
Proportion of population below $1 (PPP) per day	..	..	..	..	1993	17.8	2002	23.31
Life expectancy at birth (years)	1960	37	1980	55.7	1990–95	57.3	2002	55.4
Infant mortality rate (per 1,000 live births)	1965	150	1987	96	1990	106	2000	95
maternal mortality (per 100,000 live births)		..	1980	..	1990–98	600	2005	810
Adult literacy rate	1960	9	1974	20	1988	34.1	2000	48.7
Pop. with access to safe/improved drinking water (%)		..	1975	19	1990	76	2000	78
Employment-to-population ratio (%)					1993	62.3	2002	61.4
Paved road (% of total roads)	..	..	..	..	1993	9.2	2000	9.7
Human Development Index (value)	..	...	..	..	1993	0.357	2002	0.399
Human Development Index (rank)	...	..	..	..	1993	136	2002	156

Notes: Pre-1990 data unavailable for some of the indicators.

Countries in the HDI (1990, 160 countries; 1993 and 2002, 173 countries; 2009, 182 countries).

Sources: United Nations, "Millennium Development Goals Indicators," https://www.developmentgoals.org/About_the_goals.html.

United Nations, "Explorer," accessed October 23, 2023, http://data.un.org/Explorer.aspx.

United Nations, "Life Expectancy," accessed October 23, 2023, http://data.un.org/Data.aspx?q=life+expectancy&d=PopDiv&f=variableID%3a68.

United Nations, "Infant Mortality Rate," accessed October 23, 2023, http://data.un.org/Data.aspx?q=infant+mortality&d=WHO&f=MEASURE_CODE%3aimr.

United Nations, "Population Using Improved Drinking-Water Sources (%)," accessed October 23, 2023, http://data.un.org/Data.aspx?q=drinking+water&d=WHO&f=MEASURE_CODE%3aWHS5_122.

UNDP, *Human Development Reports*, 1991, 1993, 2002, 2004, 2009, accessed October 23, 2023, http://hdr.undp.org/en/reports.

UNESCO, "Data Browser," Institute for Statistics, accessed October 23, 2023, http://stats.uis.unesco.org.

UNMDG, "Employment-to-Population Ratio, Both Sexes, Percentage," https://data.un.org.

World Bank, World Bank Open Data, accessed October 23, 2023, https://data.worldbank.org.

World Bank, *World Development Report*, 1978, 108; 1979, 166, 168; 1989, 226; 2000/2001, 286, accessed October 12, 2023, https://openknowledge.worldbank.org/handle/10986/2124.

Liberia also had a low level of social development before the civil war and even regressed in some areas.[47] Life expectancy increased from 40 years in 1960 to a mere 47.5 during the 1980s. In 2002, it was still at 55.8 years. Infant mortality went up from 139 per thousand live births in 1965 to 159 in 1975. In 1990 and 2000, the rate was still an appalling 157. Maternal mortality increased from 173 per hundred thousand live births in 1980 to 1,200 in 2005. Access to clean drinking water barely increased from 58 percent in 1990 to 65 percent in 2000. Only slightly more than half of adults were literate in 2004. The adult literacy rate only increased from 9 percent in 1960 to 15 percent in 1975 and 32.1 percent in 1984. In terms of infrastructure, only 5.5 percent (1990) and 6.2 percent (2001) of the available roads were paved. These conditions were compounded by poverty. Only 65 percent of the people were employed in 1991 and 2003. In 2007, 83.7 percent of the people lived on less than one dollar per day. Liberia's social and economic conditions were among some of the worst in the world. It ranked 132 out of 160 countries in 1990 and 169 out of 182 in 2009 on the HDI. For most of the war and immediate postwar periods, Liberia was not even featured on the HDI; its HDI score was 0.220 in 1990 and 0.434 in 2006.

Côte d'Ivoire presented a slightly better level of prewar social development, but it did experience stagnation and in some areas regressed. As in the economic realm, Côte d'Ivoire failed to maintain its social development gains or significantly improve the well-being of its citizens.[48] Life expectancy significantly increased from 37 years in 1960 to 55.7 in 1980. For most of the 1990s, however, it stagnated at around 57.3 years and fell to 55.4 in 2002. Infant mortality dipped from 150 per thousand live births in 1965 to 96 in 1987. However, it rose again to 106 in 1990 before dropping to 95 in 2000. For most of the 1990s, maternal mortality was at 600 per hundred thousand live births. It increased to 810 in 2005. The proportion of people with access to clean drinking water only increased from 76 percent in 1990 to 78 percent in 2000. Though the adult literacy rate steadily increased from 9 percent in 1960 to 20 percent in 1974 and 34.1 percent in 1988, half of the adult population was not literate in 2000. The proportion of paved roads barely changed, going from 9.2 percent in 1993 to 9.7 percent in 2000. Côte d'Ivoire's stagnation and failure to significantly improve the well-being of its citizens was reflected in its HDI ranking and score. It fell from 122 out of 160 countries in 1990 to 136 out of 173 in 1993 and 156 out of 173 in 2002. Its HDI was 0.357 in 1993 and barely increased to 0.399 in 2002.

THE CAUSES OF STATE DECAY

The deterioration of political, economic, and social conditions that characterized state decay in Sierra Leone, Liberia, and Côte d'Ivoire is not the result of accidental factors. Rather, state decay in these countries can best be understood through the prisms of structure and agency. Aristide Zolberg made one of the earliest attempts to interject structure and agency into the African political discourse by examining the processes that shape African regimes and conflicts. As he argued, "To understand political life in Africa, instead of viewing political disturbances as the shapeless ground surrounding institutions and processes which define the regimes of the new states, we must try to view them as characteristic processes which themselves constitute an important aspect of the regime in certain types of political systems."[49] Many studies of Africa have focused on the nature of the one-party and military regimes and the structure of African economies, especially with respect to mineral dependency.[50] These studies not only point out the political and economic challenges in African states but also attribute the problems to structural factors and leadership issues.[51] Though these studies rightly point to fundamental problems, they do not frame the discourse in terms of state decay. Instead, the discourse has mostly revolved around issues of democracy, economic failure, mineral resources, and civil wars.[52] In contrast, this study sees these problems not simply as distinct pathological aspects of the African state. Rather, it views these structural and leadership issues as chronic problems that account for the gradual deterioration of the state as a whole. In particular, state decay in Sierra Leone, Liberia, and Côte d'Ivoire is the result of the domestic political structures, the failure of political leadership, and the residual effects of the international environment.[53] These problems led to major political crises and the dilapidation of the economies and fueled the violent conflicts that characterized state failure. However, poor leadership cannot be blamed for everything. Deep structural problems can confront even the best of leaders, making their job at times virtually impossible. Plus, as some argue, benign and enlightened leaders are few and far between.[54]

In terms of political structure, states range from democracies to a variety of nondemocratic regimes, not to mention the so-called hybrid regimes that fall somewhere between democracy and authoritarianism. Democracies are typified by elected governments that have legitimacy with the people and an environment in which citizens enjoy civil and political rights. Nondemocratic regimes tend to be lacking in both legitimacy and freedom.[55] By design, nondemocratic regimes, such as the one-party and military regimes in the three West African countries examined here, do not provide meaningful political choice or accountable governments. This structural limitation to political freedom and accountability tends to breed irresponsive governments and a system of patronage that rests on state corruption and oppression, which are the hallmarks of state decay.[56] One-party and military regimes emerged very early in the three West African countries and shifted the political structures toward authoritarianism.[57] This trajectory was seen similarly in most African cases shortly after independence. The political environment gradually became more oppressive as the democratic mechanism for accountability eroded. Because the authoritarian political structures that emerged shortly after independence foreclosed meaningful political opposition, regime change happened only through military coup or violent revolt, which further contributed to state decay.

The TWP in Liberia, for example, stayed in power until it was overthrown. In Sierra Leone, the APC regime, which was resisting the prodemocracy campaign and battling an armed rebellion, was eventually overthrown in a military coup. In Côte d'Ivoire, a popular revolt forced the PDCI to introduce multiparty democracy, which it barely survived through the savvy politics of Houphouët-Boigny and outright political oppression under Henri Konan Bédié. The PDCI was eventually overthrown in 2000 by a military coup. Both of these methods of regime change carried the risk of degenerating into further political oppression and violence and thereby contributed to more state decay. In Liberia, the military regime of Doe turned into the worst dictatorship out of the three cases examined here. It resisted popular demands for democracy, rigged the 1985 elections, and eventually plunged the country into civil war. The antidemocratic nature of the regime not only hastened state decay but also contributed to state collapse. In Côte d'Ivoire, the rigged democratic transition and military dictatorship paralyzed the state and pushed it into a civil war after a prolonged period of massive political violence. Similarly, the APC's suppression of the prodemocracy campaign and military intervention in politics in Sierra Leone aggravated state decay and the nascent civil war, which eventually led to state collapse.

In addition to the antidemocratic political structures, African states have been plagued by poor leadership. The general trend has been to concentrate power in the hands of a president who nurtures a system of political patronage in order to stay in power indefinitely.[58] This poor form of political leadership has resulted in the development of personal rule, the entrenchment of a dictatorship, and the internalization of state corruption.[59] Not surprisingly, African presidents and their anointed successors have tended to stay in power for too long even when the economic and social conditions of their countries continue to deteriorate. Until the push for democracy in Africa that started in the late 1980s and early 1990s, military coups were the only viable means of removing dictators. Unfortunately, the military rulers themselves turned out to be poor leaders and dictators.[60] Poor political leadership has dovetailed with the antidemocratic structures to produce colossal forms of corruption that simultaneously breed and thrive on state decay. Corruption is so ingrained in many Africa countries that it has become an integral feature of failing and failed states.[61] This dialectical relation between corruption and state decay has made the fight against corruption nearly impossible without a fundamental transformation of the state. The critical question is whether the civil wars would serve as catalysts for fundamental transformation of the state.

Poor political leadership and the dialectical relation between corruption and state decay are amply manifested in all three countries, especially Sierra Leone, where the state virtually failed even before the outbreak of the civil war. The conditions that led to state decay there can largely be attributed to the corrupt leadership of Siaka Stevens, who introduced postcolonial dictatorship and pre-bendalism.[62] Since the time of independence, Stevens manipulated the political system to advance his personal quest for power. He transformed the country into a one-party state and nurtured a form of personal rule built on corruption, patronage, and ethnic loyalty. He passed the same system to a hand-picked military successor who proved to be incapable of managing the dilapidated political and economic system. Joseph Saidu Momoh failed to halt the economic decline, condoned corruption, increased nepotism in government, and resisted popular demands for democracy.[63]

In Liberia, too, poor political leadership under the TWP perpetuated the division of the state, increased alienation, and nurtured corruption.[64] Tubman, who ruled the country from 1944 until his death in 1971, drifted toward authoritarianism despite some of his earlier efforts to expand the inner circle of the TWP.[65] His successor, Tolbert, continued the status quo, albeit with some modest reform to expand beyond the Americo-Liberian circle that had dominated Liberia.[66] The failures of Tubman and Tolbert to undertake meaningful political reforms underscore their penchant for authoritarian rule but also the failure of leadership. They missed critical opportunities to revive democracy and seriously address the division of the state, which had marginalized the natives for too long. The poor leadership became even more acute during the rule of Doe, who was a sergeant in the military with no meaningful political or administrative experiences. He executed political opponents, increased state corruption, and manipulated the democratization process in order to stay in power.[67] The political brutality coupled with old political grudges from the Americo-Liberians led to an armed struggle to remove Doe from power and eventually resulted in state collapse.

In Côte d'Ivoire, Houphouët-Boigny's leadership produced mixed results.[68] To his credit, he managed to advance the Ivoirian economy and maintain stability without using the excessive force against opponents typical of most African countries.[69] In many ways, he developed domestic and foreign policies that provided meaningful economic advantages for Côte d'Ivoire. His economic achievements earned him a reasonable level of legitimacy and support to temper the discontent over the lack of democracy. However, his leadership was largely based on political survival rather than a long-term democratic vision for his country.[70] As such, he nurtured a neopatrimonial regime and failed to use his political capital to build democratic institutions that would survive after his departure from office. He relied on expedient ethnic political alliances, the massive immigrant population, the dominant foreign entrepreneurs, and France to maintain support. The net effect of these political survival stratagems was an emergence of personality cult in politics, ambiguous citizenship policies, xenophobia, and excessive dependency on France and foreign capital, which undermined the cohesion of the state. Shortly after his death in 1993, the political system he had managed with dexterity crumbled. Côte d'Ivoire fell into political violence that escalated into a civil war. In retrospect, Houphouët-Boigny missed the opportunity to turn the 1990 democratization exercise into a fundamental democratic reform that would address issues of ethnic and economic marginalization as well as the citizenship question. Instead, he relied on political manipulation and the weaknesses of the opposition parties to salvage his rule. While it is difficult to lump Houphouët-Boigny with other dictators in Africa, it is clear that he missed the opportunity to be a great leader for Côte d'Ivoire. The situation there was made worse by the outright manipulation of ethnicity and nationalism under the rule of Bédié and the intervention of the military in politics.[71]

While state decay has largely been the result of domestic factors, it is also important to recognize the constraints placed on African states by wider global forces. Most notably, the political and economic development of African states has been impeded by the legacies of colonial rule, the Cold War ideological and geopolitical struggles in Africa, and the capitalist world economy.[72] While these elements alone could not account for all the factors that led to state decay, they do provide an important context for understanding the structural and leadership problems that contributed. As noted earlier and argued succinctly in a recent book by Catherine Gegout, colonialism created states that were difficult to maintain.[73] The issue of the colonial legacy (borders, etc.) had an enormous impact on state formation in postindependence Africa, as most evident in the relationship between colonialism and external intervention since independence and the over-reliance on the intervention of former colonial powers.

The states were fragmented along ethnic lines and built around the authoritarian political institutions and culture of colonialism.[74] The ethnic divisions and the authoritarian notion of power to which African leaders have been accustomed made multiparty democracy difficult to consolidate. Accordingly, our main task is not to provide a blueprint on how to solve these shortcomings but to problematize the issues and provide insights for scholars and policymakers based on rich historical cases and comparisons. The unfavorable colonial legacy for the development of democracy was exacerbated by the struggle for dominance during the Cold War between the Western and Eastern bloc countries. African leaders exploited the international divisions to form expedient alliances to gain weapons and some form of economic aid, which they used to consolidate their own power and to pacify political opposition in their home countries.[75] Moreover, they cherry-picked elements of capitalist and socialist ideologies to serve their ambitions for power. While many African leaders espoused the socialist doctrine of a one-party state, they failed to embrace socialist ideals of economic justice. Instead, they operated economies that were tied to the capitalist world economy, albeit peripherally, and relied on capitalist institutions such as the International Monetary Fund (IMF) and mining corporations. At the same time, they failed to adhere to capitalist values of freedom and choice in the political sphere. In many ways, African leaders combined the oppressive elements of socialism with the exploitative elements of Western capitalism. In the process, they left out the virtues of democracy and freedom associated with Western capitalism and the noble goals of economic justice in socialism.[76] As a result, African leaders failed to fundamentally transform their countries into modern socialist or capitalist states. These countries remained trapped in the authoritarian rule and mining and agricultural economies that came out of colonialism. Their ambiguous position within the international political and economic system left them at the margins of the international system and relegated them to the bottom of the international division of labor and to donor dependency. By the end of the Cold War, a vast number of African countries were in a state of decay, including Sierra Leone, Liberia, and Côte d'Ivoire. But, as Gegout argues, why would the major world powers in the international system allow these states (among others) to decay to the point of failure instead of intervening in a proper manner when the evidence shows they could have stopped or even prevented war from starting in the first place?[77] This question is critical, and we return to it later.

African leaders' ability to exploit the international political structures was significantly reduced after the end of the Cold War. When communism failed, they had no option but to agree to the IMF and World Bank demands for political and economic liberalization.[78] The changes in Western policies toward African governments contributed to the democratic changes and decline in authoritarian rule in several countries. However, the economic rise of China opened a new avenue for African leaders in the global economy.[79] Many have increasingly turned to China and Russia, both of which have shown no interest in promoting democracy in Africa and do not ask for the political or economic reforms that the major Organization for Economic Cooperation and Development (OECD) donors demand in the form of conditionality in exchange for economic assistance and trade. In the meantime, Western countries are softening their stance on human rights, good governance, and free and fair elections in Africa and turning more attention to security issues and the struggle to control mineral resources. The struggle for economic dominance in Africa has critical political implications for African countries that largely rely on rents from minerals. The governments in those countries could gain access to resources that enable them to support the political and military apparatus of the state without conceding to international or domestic pressures for democracy and good governance. Such a situation not only impedes democracy but actually leads to state decay.

FROM STATE DECAY TO STATE FAILURE: THE DIALECTICS OF CIVIL WAR AND STATEBUILDING

The outbreak of civil war in Liberia, Sierra Leone, and Côte d'Ivoire hardly came as a surprise, as state decay had already created the conditions. However, the way the wars were conducted and their implications could hardly have been fully anticipated. One of the most intriguing questions from the three cases is the potential impact of the civil wars on the future development of the state. All three wars have been viewed as both the result of and potential remedy for state decay. In that sense, the civil wars are dialectically tied to both the prewar and postwar state. They could mark either the climax of state decay and the restoration of the prewar status quo or the end of state decay and the dawn of progress toward democracy and economic development. Paradoxically, while the civil wars were intended to halt state decay, they actually led to state collapse.

In Sierra Leone and Liberia, civil war became the instrument of eventual destruction of the state, which could not be resurrected without massive international intervention. In Côte d'Ivoire, the civil war not only brought the state to near collapse but also exposed its underdeveloped notion of citizenship and its inherent vulnerabilities to nationalist and regional-cum-ethnic politics. The other part of the paradox is whether these destructive civil wars could serve as a catalyst for the development of a democratic and economically successful state. This is the challenge of statebuilding. In Liberia and Sierra Leone, the international community started the process by undertaking massive postwar reconstruction with the aim of consolidating democracy and addressing the economic and social causes of the wars. This started with the enforcement of the peace agreements. As one respondent noted: "By and large, the international community came and ensured that there was an agreement [in Sierra Leone], we call it the peace accord."[80] In Côte d'Ivoire, Ivoirians agreed on a mechanism to rectify the citizenship problem. However, they also needed to build a democratic system and ensure even development. While the process was largely driven by Ivoirians, there was some significant international support to organize elections and remove Laurent Gbagbo from power. As one respondent noted, "We need to be grateful at the international community because . . . they began to put a stop to the war. . . . This was something good."[81]

In Liberia, the civil war quickly shifted from a struggle to end the dictatorial regime of Doe to anarchy and a criminal war enterprise driven by power-hungry warlords.[82] The war, which occurred in two phases, started in 1989 with the invasion of Nimba County by the National Patriotic Front of Liberia (NPLF), led by Charles Taylor. Taylor's purported goal was to remove Doe and establish democracy. Though the war ended shortly after the warring factions signed the Abuja Peace Agreement in 1995, it quickly erupted again in 1999. Peace only returned to the country after the international community forced Taylor into exile in 2003. The departure of Taylor, who was the main figure behind the war, paved the way for the 2003 Accra Peace Accord and the establishment of a transitional government. The international community deployed a massive intervention force and steered the country toward multiparty elections in 2005. The NPLF was at the center of the Liberian war. It began as a rebel movement against Doe and metamorphosed into the National Patriotic Party (NPP), which dubiously won the 1997 elections. Prior to 1997, the NPFL fought to seize control of the government. When it came to power in 1997, it continued to brutalize opponents and wage war against the other factions in the Liberian war in order to stay in power. In addition, Taylor supported the Revolutionary United Front (RUF) in the Sierra Leone civil war and engaged in the trade of blood diamonds. Even though Doe was assassinated in 1990 by a splinter group of the NPFL led by Prince Yormie Johnson (the Independent National Patriotic Front of Liberia, or INPFL), Taylor showed no interest in ending the war. As early as 1990, it became clear that his primary goal was to take power by any means possible. In 1991, the NPFL established an alternative government, the National Patriotic Reconstruction Assembly Government which was based in the town of Gbarnga. However, this government failed to gain international recognition or popular domestic legitimacy.

The Liberian war had numerous Liberian factions that frequently overlapped and changed.[83] One of the problematic aspects of ending the war was the proliferation of splinter groups and warlords. Though it is difficult to identify clear and consistent factional alliances, three loose clusters of Liberian forces remained prominent throughout the war. The first cluster was the NPFL led by Taylor, which was at the center of the fighting throughout the war. The NPFL had splinter groups, with the main ones being the INPLF, led by Prince Johnson, and the National Patriotic Front of Liberia–Central Revolutionary Council, led by Sam Dokie and Tom Woewiyu. These two splinter groups emerged largely due to leadership disputes within the NPFL. While they shared the NPFL's goal of taking power, they were also bent on stopping Taylor from becoming president. The Lofa Defence Force later emerged as an ally of the NPFL. The second cluster consisted of the Armed Forces of Liberia (AFL), which supported Doe, and its militia allies, such as the Liberian Peace Council, which emerged in 1993. They fought to stop the NPFL from taking over the government and defended the interest of the Krahn people. The AFL crumbled after the assassination of Doe and increasingly became a smaller force in the conflict. The third cluster was comprised of groups that emerged after the assassination of Doe and were largely independent of the AFL. While some of them were sympathizers of Doe, they mostly included people, especially from the Krahn and Madingo ethnic groups, who strongly opposed the NPFL because they saw Taylor as a major threat to their personal and collective ethnic interests. Their ambition to take over the state evolved with the war. Unlike the NPFL, which was created with the goal of taking power, this cluster of forces was more interested in stopping Taylor from taking over the state or removing him from power than actually governing the state.[84] Taking over the state would not only mean gaining power but more importantly would indicate success in their effort to defeat Taylor. During the initial phase of the war, the main group in this cluster was the United Liberation Movement of Liberia for Democracy (ULIMO).[85] ULIMO was formed by Liberian exiles in Sierra Leone. They began fighting for the government of Sierra Leone against RUF and then entered Liberia to fight the NPFL. Ethnic conflicts between the Krahn and the Mandingo resulted in the split of ULIMO into two groups: ULIMO–J and ULIMO–K. ULIMO–J was a dominated by the Krahn and led by Major General Roosevelt Johnson, while ULIMO–K became a predominantly Mandingo group led by Alhaji Kromah. ULIMO disappeared after the 1997 elections, but its members reemerged in 1999. They combined with other factions opposed to Taylor to form Liberians United for Reconciliation and Democracy (LURD). In 2000, LURD launched a massive offensive against the NPP government of Taylor. In 2003, a majority of the Krahn broke away from LURD and formed the Movement for Democracy in Liberia (MODEL).[86]

In the midst of factional chaos and the divergence of war motives, the central rationale of the Liberian civil war was the struggle for power. In practical terms, this meant that the war was largely a struggle by Taylor to take over the government and maintain his stay in power on one hand and a struggle by a variety of forces to stop Taylor from taking power or remove him from power on the other. This is not to neglect the underlying political, economic, and social grievances associated with state decay that led to war.[87] Rather, it is to underscore how the war became a struggle for power instead of a struggle for democracy and good governance. While state decay was the cause of the war, the struggle for political power and control of the war economy built around illicit trade in timber, minerals, and weapons became the fuel that sustained the war. This shifted the war from a struggle to end state decay to a struggle that ruined the state. Despite this unfortunate shift, the implications of state decay cannot be underestimated. Indeed, the challenge for Liberia is not only to address the factors that fueled the war but also to understand and rectify the problems of state decay that led to the war in the first place.

In addition to the three clusters of Liberian factions, international intervention forces were an important category of military force in the Liberian war. This was mostly comprised of members of the Economic Community of West African States Monitoring Group (ECOMOG), which was deployed in 1990 as a peacekeeping force. However, it quickly became a party to the war as it tried to stop Taylor from taking over the government. After the assassination of Doe, ECOMOG installed an Interim Government of Nation Unity (IGNU) headed by Amos Sawyer and became heavily involved in defending the IGNU against the various rebel groups. In 1993, the UN established the UN Observer Mission in Liberia (UNOMIL) to support ECOMOG in implementing the Cotonou Accord. UNOMIL was later transformed into the UN Peacebuilding Support Office in Liberia. In 1996, the US military was briefly deployed to halt the anarchy as part of Operation Assured Response. It is important to note that the primary objective of the American military operation was to evacuate US citizens trapped in Liberia.

The peacekeeping role of the UN significantly increased during the second half of the war and evolved from traditional peacekeeping to a comprehensive peacebuilding mission. After the signing of the 2003 Accra Accord, the UN established the UN Mission in Liberia (UNMIL). The force had a UN Chapter VII mandate and was made up of around fifteen thousand troops. UNMIL was a multidimensional force tasked with supporting the national transitional government and implementing the Accra Accord. It took over the peacekeeping role of ECOMOG and incorporated some of the ECOMOG troops.[88] UNMIL moved the country through the 2005 elections and took a lead role in the postwar reconstruction efforts. An interview respondent for this research indicated that it was "very commendable, in the sense that the international community did provide support both financially and logistically to raise the attainment of general peace and stability" in Liberia.[89]

During Liberia's fourteen-year civil war, 800,000 Liberians were displaced and an estimated 270,000 were killed.[90] An estimated 250,000 Liberians died during the war. At least half of the victims were civilian noncombatants.[91] Many more were forced out of their homes. Between 1993 and 1996, the Liberian refugee population stood above 700,000, reaching a high of 797,800 in 1994.[92] In 2003, there were over 350,000 Liberian refugees and an estimated half-million people displaced within Liberia. Seventy-eight percent of the refugees were between the ages of five and fifty-nine. Women accounted for 53 percent of the refugees. Nearly half of the refugees were in Guinea, while most of the others were in Côte d'Ivoire (74,200), Sierra Leone (61,200), Ghana (42,500), and Nigeria (3,700).[93] For most of the war period, Liberia was without a functioning government. During the first part of the war, the IGNU hardly functioned as a real body. Sawyer, who became chairman when the body was formed by Economic Community of West African States (ECOWAS) in 1990, was a powerless figurehead of an interim government that was falling apart and being held hostage by warlords. When Sawyer resigned in March 1994, the IGNU became even more dysfunctional and constantly changed leaders.[94] Though some level of peace returned after the 1997 elections, the Liberian state barely functioned due to Taylor's lack of legitimacy at home and within the international community. The Liberian state was further weakened by international sanctions for Taylor's dubious role in fueling the war in Sierra Leone and the threat of insurgency by rival warlords. Not surprisingly, the state quickly collapsed again during the second part of the civil war, which erupted in 2000.

The Sierra Lone civil war was started in March 1991 by RUF, which was supported by combatants belonging to the NPFL and commonly referred to as rebels.[95] The declared goal of RUF was to overthrow the corrupt APC government of Momoh and implement a revolutionary change for economic progress, social justice, and democracy.[96] The war, which was officially declared over in January 2002, was very brutal. The TRC of Sierra Leone documented 40,242 violations that occurred between 1991 and 2000. The violations included forced displacement, abduction, arbitrary detention, killing, torture, forced labor, rape, amputation, sexual abuse, drugging, extortion, and destruction of property. The commission also identified 14,995 victims. It is estimated that there were around a hundred thousand amputations and over twenty thousand people killed during the course of the war.[97] At the height of the war in 1999, nearly half a million Sierra Leoneans were refugees and over half a million people in Sierra Leone were listed as persons of concern by the UNHCR.[98] By the end of the war in 2002, there were still 141,400 Sierra Leoneans listed as refugees.[99] The bulk of the refugees were in Guinea and Liberia. The war shattered more than three thousand towns and villages and destroyed the scanty infrastructure.[100] The TRC attributed 59.2 percent of the documented violations to RUF, 9.8 percent to the Armed Forces Revolutionary Council (AFRC), 6.7 percent to the Sierra Leone Army, 5.9 percent to the pro-government Civil Defence Forces (CDF), and 0.7 percent to ECOMOG.[101]

The civil war in Sierra Leone became largely a struggle for power between the RUF and successive civilian and military governments. The RUF, which was supported by Taylor, was formed by Sierra Leonean dissidents in Libya and led by Foday Sankoh.[102] It fought the APC government and continued to fight the NPRC military government of Valentine Strasser, which overthrew the APC in 1992. The RUF refused to participate in the 1996 elections and continued to fight the elected Sierra Leone People's Party (SLPP) government led by Ahmed Tejan Kabbah. Initially, the Armed Forces of the Republic of Sierra Leone (AFRSL), supported by Nigerian and Guinean troops, mercenaries, and ULIMO, fought the rebels on behalf of the successive governments. The government, especially the SLPP government of Kabbah, allied itself with the CDF, commonly referred to as Kamajos, created by local communities to defend themselves against the rebels and renegade soldiers of the AFRSL. As the war evolved, a significant fraction of the AFRSL began working with the RUF and formed the AFRC, which overthrew the SLPP government of Kabbah in 1997. The exiled government of Kabbah, supported by ECOMOG, CDF, and mercenaries, fought the RUF and the AFRC. In March 1998, ECOMOG deposed the AFRC and restored Kabbah to power.[103]

The Sierra Leone civil war was born out of state decay but quickly became a struggle for power between the leaders of the various fighting factions.[104] The RUF claimed to be fighting to end corruption and dictatorship and promote economic development and democracy. However, it continued to fight even after the overthrow of the APC regime and refused to participate in the 1996 multiparty elections, in which there was no incumbent government. On an abstract idealistic level, the RUF saw its mission as a revolutionary agenda that should not be restricted by the mechanisms of democratic politics. On a practical level, however, the RUF failed to fight for the interest of the people. To the contrary, it committed grave human rights abuses against civilians and engaged in the illicit exploitation of minerals. By assuming that it alone had the solutions to the economic and social problems of the country, insisting on taking power by force, and using civilians as instruments of war, the RUF delegitimized its very vision of restoring power to the people and promoting economic and social progress. The RUF's lack of legitimacy with the people further strengthened popular skepticism that it was simply another group of people hungry for power and wealth.[105] The RUF rebellion raised major concerns about how to reconcile the legitimacy of their grievances with their lack of a credible agenda.

Similarly, the ruling elite of the one-party and military regimes were mostly interested in salvaging their power. The APC's claim to legitimacy and sovereign responsibility to protect the people was clearly contradicted by the corrupt and dictatorial nature of the regime; this led to state decay, undermined the well-being of the people, and contributed to the continuation of the civil war. These factors (state decay, bad leadership/corruption, and civil war) all interact in a dialectical manner, and it is difficult to parse out the order of the relationship between them. All three develop in a complex manner (see discussion in the beginning of this chapter). Notably, the APC refused to recognize the legitimacy of the war grievances or concede to the popular demands for democracy. As such, its military campaign against the RUF was no more than a struggle to hold onto power.

Despite the aura of change, the NPRC did not differ much from the APC regime. The NPRC brought high hopes for change and enjoyed initial popular support. Unfortunately, it, too, was corrupt, brutal, and reluctant to restore democracy. Popular support for the NPRC campaign against the RUF gave way to popular discontent with military rule and doubts about the loyalty of the military. Military officers formed alliances with local RUF commanders, engaged in illicit diamond exploitation, and victimized civilians.[106] The dubious role of the military became apparent in the emergence of the category of *sobel* in the war— military personnel who doubled as soldiers during the day and rebels during the night. The military's lack of discipline and loyalty culminated in the AFRC coup that overthrew the elected government in 1997. The AFRC became a significant player in the conflict because of its brief rule (1997–1998), alliance with the RUF, and participation in the blood diamond trade. Unlike the RUF, it had no ideological vision or articulated grievances. The AFRC's only argument for staying in power rested on its claim to have the ability to restore peace by working with the RUF, but this claim was questionable, as its alliance with the RUF was often tenuous. The RUF never gave up its ambition of taking power by force, as evidenced by the clashes between the AFRC and RUF. In reality, the AFRC further escalated the violence, abuse of civilians, and illicit exploitation of minerals.

Though the elected SLPP government had a legitimate claim to power and enjoyed significant popular support, it was deeply involved in the struggle for power. To its credit, the SLPP government made a significant concession to the RUF in the Abidjan Accord by agreeing to withdraw foreign mercenaries. However, the agreement insisted too much on the government's legitimacy at the expense of addressing the genuine grievances that led to the war. After the RUF failed to honor the 1996 Abidjan Accord and used the cease-fire to rebuild its forces, the government took an even more hard-line stance in its claim to legitimacy and became extremely suspicious of the RUF.[107] This attitude made it even more difficult to peacefully solve the conflict and address the underlying causes of the war. In the process, the SLPP government became complacent with its legitimacy and failed to make meaningful reforms in governance. Corruption continued unabated as economic and social conditions further deteriorated. The SLPP government's insistence on its democratic mandate became a cover for its desire to stay in power. In the process, it became more obsessed with its struggle for political survival than with addressing the root causes of the war and working with the RUF to end the conflict.[108] The SLPP government's struggle for political survival became more intense after the 1997 coup. The government in exile engaged in a robust campaign to gain international support for its restoration. After it was restored in 1998, it became overtly focused on maintaining the international support that kept it in power at the expense of pursuing a peaceful solution to the conflict. In fact, the government reluctantly signed the Lomé Peace Agreement only after it became clear that ECOMOG was incapable of delivering a decisive military victory over the RUF and Nigeria signaled its desire to withdraw its forces from Sierra Leone.[109] The SLPP government had a precarious approach to the war and governance. While it had well-founded claims to legitimacy and mistrust of the RUF, it confounded democracy with peace and economic development. It wrongly assumed that its democratic mandate was to simply maintain the state as a democracy, instead of fundamentally transforming it and thereby addressing the root causes of the war.

As in Liberia, international forces were critical players in the Sierra Leone civil war. International military involvement occurred in the forms of ECOWAS and UN interventions, not to mention support from mercenaries and allied countries. The latter category included government and RUF mercenaries from countries such as Liberia, Burkina Faso, South Africa, and Ukraine and the intervention of Guinean, Nigerian, and British forces in support of the government. The most significant international military involvements were the ECOMOG and UN interventions. ECOMOG was deployed at the outset of the war to prevent cross-border attacks from Liberia. It quickly grew in size and reached around fifteen thousand troops, comprised of nearly twelve thousand Nigerians, six hundred Ghanaians, six hundred Guineans, and five hundred Malians.[110] ECOMOG became the main defender of the government against the RUF as the Sierra Leone military became increasingly incapable and disloyal. When AFRC deposed the elected government, ECOMOG drove the junta out of Freetown and restored the elected government in March 1998. It continued to defend the government until the deployment of UN Mission in Sierra Leone (UNAMSIL) forces in 2002. The UN military intervention began in 1998 with the established of the UN Observer Mission in Sierra Leone (UNOMSIL). However, UNOMSIL was an unarmed team mainly charged with monitoring the conduct of the war.[111] UN military intervention significantly increased with the establishment of UNAMSIL in 1999. UNAMSIL was established in the wake of Nigerian fatigue with the Sierra Leone war, the growing realization of ECOMOG's inability to defeat RUF, and the signing of the Lomé Peace Agreement. UNAMSIL's mandate was to implement the Lomé Peace Agreement. It was later given a Chapter VII mandate, and its size significantly increased.[112] By March 2001, UNAMSIL's troop size had increased to 17,500, and its role had significantly expanded beyond traditional peacekeeping.[113] Its overall objectives became "to assist the efforts of the Government of Sierra Leone to extend its authority, restore law and order and stabilize the situation progressively throughout the entire country, and to assist in the promotion of a political process which should lead to a renewed disarmament, demobilization and reintegration programme and the holding, in due course, of free and fair elections."[114] UNAMSIL suffered significant initial setbacks. It had a difficult relation with ECOMOG, while the RUF saw it as a pro-government force. The RUF humiliated UNAMSIL by kidnapping over three hundred of its troops and seizing their equipment in May 2000. However, with the help of a British military intervention, the strengthened force was able to meet the challenges posed by the RUF and AFRC and steer the country through the 2002 elections.[115] UNAM-SIL's mission ended in 2005 with the establishment of the UN Integrated Office for Sierra Leone (UNIOSIL) to consolidate peace and democracy and help the country address the root causes of the war.[116]

The civil war in Côte d'Ivoire was the culmination of the violent political conflict that had been taking place since the death of Houphouët-Boigny in December of 1993.[117] The conflict began as a power struggle within the ruling PDCI and between the PDCI and the opposition Front Populaire Ivoirien (FPI) to succeed Houphouët-Boigny. The power struggle between Henri Bédié and his opponents within the PDCI led to the formation of the Rassemblement Des Républicains (RDR) by PDCI dissidents who opposed Bédié's ascension to the presidency. The RDR, which was mostly supported by northerners, invited former Prime Minister Ouattara to be its presidential candidate in the 1995 elections. At the same time, the opposition FPI and its veteran opposition leader, Gbagbo, tried to oust the PDCI from power. The tripartite PDCI-RDR-FPI power struggle took a dangerous turn when Bédié started to restrict political freedoms and exploit the highly divisive doctrine of Ivoirité in order to win the 1995 presidential election.[118] The antidemocratic tactics of Bédié forced the RDR and FPI to boycott the 1995 presidential election. The doctrine of Ivoirité was introduced into politics as a nationalist-qua-ethnic political stratagem disguised as patriotism. It rested on a controversial distinction between "indigenous Ivoirians" and "Ivoirians of immigrant ancestry" that weaved together antiforeigner and antinortherner sentiments.[119] The tacit goal of Ivoirité was to marginalize northerners, who were lumped together with immigrants from Burkina Faso and other neighboring countries as foreigners or at best Ivoirians of immigrant ancestry, and facilitate a victory for PDCI, which was controlled by southern political elites.[120] The conflict increasingly became a north-south divide as the military government of General Robert Guéï and the FPI government of Gbagbo embraced the Ivoirité policies initiated by the PDCI.

Successive post-Houphouët-Boigny governments applied the doctrine of Ivoirité in the political arena in order to disqualify Ouattara from seeking the presidency. In the process, they denied Ivoirian citizenship to many people from the north of the country. In 1994, Bédié's government passed a law requiring candidates for the presidency and legislature to prove that they and their parents were Ivoirians by origin.[121] The law was later incorporated into the 2000 Constitution, which stated that a candidate for the presidency "must be Ivoirian by birth, born of a father and of a mother themselves Ivoirians by birth. He must never have renounced the Ivoirian nationality. He must never have had another nationality. He must have resided in Côte d'Ivoire continuously during the five years preceding the date of the elections and have totaled ten years of effective presence."[122] The restrictions in the laws were tacitly tailored to disqualify northern political leader Ouattara from running for the presidency. Southern political leaders alleged that Ouattara's father was from Burkina Faso, while Ouattara argued that his parents were from Côte d'Ivoire.[123] The dispute over Ouattara's ancestry evoked three key issues surrounding citizenship in Côte d'Ivoire, the first of which was the huge immigrant population from neighboring countries such as Burkina Faso. While some of these were recent immigrants, many others had been in Côte d'Ivoire for several generations going back to the colonial era. The second issue was rooted in French colonial policies and Houphouët-Boigny's policies that facilitated the flow of immigrant labor and their participation in Ivoirian politics and the economy. The policies of the colonial administration and Houphouët-Boigny's government blurred the line between Ivoirian and non-Ivoirian and promoted a loose notion of Ivoirian citizenship. The third problem was the cultural and ethnic affinity between indigenous Ivoirians in the north and the immigrants from some of the neighboring countries.[124] Collectively, these three factors made it difficult to differentiate an indigenous Ivoirian from an Ivoirian of immigrant ancestry in the absence of a long, accurate, and rich record of births and deaths.

As the conflict over citizenship expanded from the political elites to the voters, it became clear that the lack of proper birth and death records would complicate the implementation of a narrowly defined citizenship policy. The question of Ivoirian citizenship became less of a disagreement over the extant citizenship law, which was mostly based on the principle of jus sanguinis, and more of a dispute over the intent of the law and policies of the government and how to prove one's claim to Ivoirian citizenship. The government insinuated that many people from the north were falsely claiming Ivoirian citizenship, while northerners accused the government of deliberately refusing to issue certificates of nationality to qualified Ivoirian citizens from the north. The successive post-Houphouët-Boigny governments applied Ivoirité policies to national identification, land tenure, and public sector employment policies. They refused to issue certificates of nationality to many people from the north on the grounds that they were not Ivoirians because they did not have proper documents to prove that their parents were Ivoirians. According to the 2001 identification policies of the FPI government, for example, "Anyone requesting an identity document was required to prove their nationality by obtaining a statement of origin issued by a committee from their village of origin."[125] Under these policies, Ivoirian citizenship was based on proof of autochthony to an Ivoirian village. The controversial Ivoirité policies were adopted even though it was clear that the chasms in birth records would make it difficult to provide documentary evidence of ancestry.

As Daniel Chirot observed, a large number of "genuine" Ivoirians from the north found themselves in a precarious situation. Many did not have complete documents because of missing records, family relocation, or the confiscation of their documents by security agents.[126] Some of the southern leaders that were interviewed in this study insisted on applying the laws and placed the burden of proof of Ivoirian ancestry on the individuals. In their view, all genuine Ivoirians could obtain the necessary records to prove their Ivoirian ancestry. However, some agreed that the records were not perfect.[127] In addition, they understood that urbanization had weakened ties to ancestral villages. The wrongful denial of citizenship and exclusion for contesting the presidency were epitomized in Ouattara's struggle with successive post-Houphouët-Boigny governments. Bédié claimed that Ouattara's father was from Burkina Faso and was therefore not a genuine Ivoirian. Ouattara insisted that his parents were born in Côte d'Ivoire. When Judge Zoro Ballo issued Ouattara a certificate of nationality in September 1999, the government investigated the judge and forced him to resign. The Bédié government accused Ouattara of falsifying his documents and revoked the certificate in October 1999.[128]

Ivoirité made northerners feel politically marginalized and see themselves as victims of state-sponsored discrimination in the application of citizenship policies. This sense of being wrongfully denied citizenship became the bedrock of the violent political protests that had marred Côte d'Ivoire since the death of Houphouët-Boigny and the civil war. The political and social crisis was exacerbated by the December 1999 coup that brought General Guéï to power.[129] Popular resistance to military rule dovetailed with the tripartite power struggle and vehement RDR-led campaign to end Ivoirité. Like the PDCI, Guéï suppressed political freedom, promoted Ivoirité, and prevented Ouattara from contesting the October 2000 presidential election. The PDCI and RDR boycotted the presidential election. Guéï manipulated the election results and arbitrarily declared himself the winner, which led to a massive street protest by the FPI. Guéï was forced to flee, paving the way for Gbagbo to be installed as president.[130] Violent clashes between the pro-FPI Young Patriots (YP) and RDR continued, and the RDR demanded a new election based on inclusive citizenship policies that would not disenfranchise northerners.[131] Gbagbo insisted on his electoral mandate and continued to support Ivoirité. The RDR and disgruntled northerners dismissed the FPI government as illegitimate, while Gbagbo continued to insinuate that Ouattara was not an indigenous Ivoirian and was unqualified to be president.[132]

The political and social crisis surrounding Ivoirité and democracy degenerated into a civil war after the September 19, 2002, coup-cum-rebellion. The mutiny in Abidjan was instigated by reports of an imminent involuntary demobilization program believed to be part of the Ivoirité purge against northerners. Rebel forces of the Mouvement Patriotique de Côte d'Ivoire (MPCI) attacked Abidjan and cities in the north.[133] The rebels retreated to their bases in the north after loyalist forces repelled the attack on Abidjan. The stated goals of the MPCI were to overthrow the government of Gbagbo, hold inclusive elections, and reinstate all disbanded soldiers. By the end of 2002, two smaller rebel groups had emerged. Both the Mouvement pour la Justice et la Paix and the Mouvement Populaire Ivoirien du Grand Ouest expressed similar intentions to overthrow Gbagbo.[134] The rebels regrouped into a new movement called Forces Nouvelles (FN) under the leadership of Guillaume Soro.[135] By the end of 2002, Côte d'Ivoire's political crisis had degenerated into a civil war. The government had lost control of the north, while hostility continued to brew between northerners and southerners.

The fight to end Ivoirité was masked as a struggle for democracy. By seeking to oust Gbagbo and hold inclusive elections, the rebels were fighting to stop the marginalization of northerners. As Soro himself confessed, the rebellion was instigated by dissatisfaction with the 2000 elections and Ivoirité, which he characterized as *"n'est ni plus ni moins qu'un concept xénophobe. L'ivoirité est un mot dont le vrai sens ne signifie rien d'autre que: «la Côte d'Ivoire aux Ivoiriens», c'est-à-dire, en clair, à ceux qui sont originaires du Sud, les Nordistes étant considérés comme étrangers dans leur propre pays."*[136] The rebels wanted to ensure that northerners were issued their citizenship documents and allowed equal participation in politics. Evidently, peace never started until the citizenship issue was properly addressed in the Ouagadougou Agreement. Despite the resolution of the citizenship issue, the north-south power struggle continues to fuel violence, especially around presidential elections.

In addition to the rebel attacks, violent demonstrations preceded Côte d'Ivoire's civil war, especially in Abidjan. Most of the violence erupted during planned demonstrations by pro-government YP and opposition supporters. On October 22, 2002, for example, there was a violent anti-French protest by supporters of Gbagbo, which paralyzed the city of Abidjan. The protesters were angry with France for sheltering opposition leader Ouattara. In January 2006, supporters of Gbagbo attacked UN peacekeepers and staff when UN-backed mediators recommended dissolving parliament after the country failed to hold elections scheduled for the end of 2005. One of the worst violent demonstrations occurred on Mach 25, 2004, during an opposition rally in Abidjan. The demonstration left 120 people dead and many more wounded.[137]

The initial phase of the conflict in Côte d'Ivoire left around three thousand people dead and up to seven hundred thousand displaced. At the height of the war in 2004, more than thirty-three thousand Ivoirians were listed as refugees, mostly in Liberia and Guinea. A huge number of West African immigrants were forced to leave the country. An additional five hundred thousand Ivoirians were displaced from their homes.[138] The conflict also led to serious human rights violations including extortion, arbitrary tax collection, forceful abduction, and summary execution. The disruption of basic services, especially in the north, led to major humanitarian problems. Numerous schools, hospitals, courts, and administrative institutions were forced to close. According to UN reports, in the areas controlled by the FN, up to 85 percent of the medical staff fled. The conflict contributed to an increase in malnutrition and such diseases as cholera, yellow fever, meningitis, and measles. The UN estimates that in 2004, seven hundred thousand children were out of school as a result of the war.[139] The war also took a heavy toll on the Ivoirian economy. After the violence in November 2004, 125 out of 500 foreign-owned businesses closed, leaving about thirty thousand people unemployed. Between 1999 and 2003, the GDP declined by around 7.4 percent. In November 2004, the country slipped into nonaccrual status after failing to service its debts with the World Bank.[140]

While Côte d'Ivoire did not descend into the kind of prolonged and brutal war experienced in Sierra Leone and Liberia, it suffered significantly. In addition to the casualties and human rights violations, the country experienced significant economic decline that not only worsened state decay but also had tremendous negative impacts in the region. The escalation to civil war in 2002 brought significant international attention to the political crisis in Côte d'Ivoire. The international community was particularly concerned about the deteriorating political situation there because of its potential regional impact. As soon as the war erupted in 2002, ECOWAS began mediating the conflict and began plans to send an interposition force. France immediately deployed its troops to protect its interests and support the international peace mediation efforts of ECOWAS and the UN. However, the French forces were viewed with suspicion by the FPI government. ECOWAS brokered the October 17, 2002, cease-fire between MPCI and the government and organized peace talks in Lomé. The ECOWAS talks were followed by peace talks in France, resulting in the 2003 Linas-Marcoussis Agreement. In May 2003, the UN established the UN Mission in Côte d'Ivoire to facilitate the implementation of the Linas-Marcoussis Agreement in collaboration with French and ECOWAS forces. Despite the deployment of international forces and the international mediations, the war continued. Further peace agreements were brokered by the international community during peace talks in Ghana (2003, 2004) and Pretoria (2005). Unfortunately, all of these agreements failed to properly address the core issue of citizenship and end the conflict.[141] The critical break in the conflict came in 2007, when the Ivoirians took ownership of the peace process and directly negotiated the Ouagadougou Peace Agreement. The agreement resulted in the formation of a power-sharing government led by Gbagbo and Soro, stipulated a mechanism for resolving the dispute over citizenship, and called for an election. Though implementation of the agreement was painfully slow, the country largely maintained a delicate peace that was dubbed *ni paix, ni guerre* (no peace, no war). That peace lasted until the 2010 presidential election, when both candidates claimed victory and declared themselves president. The UN eventually certified the victory of Ouattara. Renewed fighting erupted between the forces supporting Ouattara and those supporting Gbagbo. International forces eventually backed the pro-Ouattara forces, leading to the capture of Gbagbo and the pacification of the pro-Gbagbo forces. Since the 2010 defeat of Gbagbo and his allies, Ouattara has entrenched his rule and even extended his term in office to a third term. Ouattara's pacification of southerners and grip on power has again placed Côte d'Ivoire in a precarious situation that is making the country ripe for renewed violence.

CONCLUSION

The three countries in this study present contrasting, albeit equally bitter, realities of civil war and statebuilding. The wars in Liberia and Sierra Leone were driven by warlords and the illicit trading of natural resources and weapons and used civilians as instruments of war. Unlike ideologically driven wars fought by disciplined and well-structured forces, the wars in Sierra Leone and Liberia became emblematic cases of *new wars,* which often degenerate into a criminal enterprise that victimizes civilians and lacks any clear agenda for addressing the legitimate political and social grievances that lead to conflict.[142] The states collapsed, and the countries were unable to resolve any differences and rebuild without enormous international intervention driven by the doctrine of *new humanitarianism.* In Côte d'Ivoire, the conflict did not degenerate into the kind of anarchy and criminal war enterprise that developed in Sierra Leone and Liberia. Though there were serious accusations that the FN was supported by foreign governments, most notably Burkina Faso, and that Liberian combatants were recruited in Côte d'Ivoire, the war was largely fought by Ivoirians and fueled by domestic grievances.[143] The war itself lasted for a relatively shorter period of time and produced fewer casualties; this was true for both the 2002 fighting and the fighting that erupted after the 2010 elections. However, Côte d'Ivoire, too, was characterized by gross violations of human rights and a war economy in the northern part of the country under the control of the FN. The Ivoirian war was contained partly because it had a clear and legitimate political grievance that centered on citizenship and partly because the state did not crumble, even though it was split into two halves. The state remained largely functional in the south, while in the north, the FN successfully established an administration that maintained quasi state authority. Most significantly, Ivoirians took ownership of the peace process and negotiated a mechanism for solving the citizenship aspect of the conflict, as evidenced by the Ouagadougou Accord. Thus, while the Ivoirian civil war was not a conventional conflict between two state actors, it did not degenerate into a typical case of *new war*. In fact, international intervention in Côte d'Ivoire was mostly limited to a supportive role for Ivoirians to resolve their conflict. The international peacekeeping missions fell short of undertaking comprehensive peacebuilding and reconstructions roles. This limited role of international peacekeeping is in stark contrast to the comprehensive statebuilding role that the international community assumed in Liberia and Sierra Leone. Côte d'Ivoire's mixed results with state decay and the conduct of the war, which teetered between stability and breakdown, impart important lessons about the vulnerabilities and potentials of African states.

THREE

—⚏—

HUMANITARIAN INTERVENTION AND PEACEBUILDING

INTRODUCTION

The destabilization of the West African region that occurred at the end of the twentieth century created tremendous security and humanitarian challenges for the international community. The destabilization took the form of highly charged political violence and civil war across the subregion. The most notorious cases were the civil wars in Liberia, Sierra Leone, and Côte d'Ivoire. The insecurity within these three adjacent countries was compounded by the volatile regional political and security situations in neighboring Guinea and Guinea-Bissau, both of which came close to full-scale civil war on a number of occasions. There were also significant levels of political violence in other West African countries, such as Nigeria, Mali, and Togo.[1] In all of these countries, civil wars and political violence tended to coincide with attempted democratic transitions. In Côte d'Ivoire, for example, the political violence that marred the democratization process eventually escalated into a civil war. In Nigeria, the political violence that erupted during the democratic transition subsided, but the campaign for environmental and social justice in the Niger Delta and the north lingered in the form of an armed insurgency and Boko Haram terrorism.[2]

The conflicts in West Africa not only led to serious internal crises but also caused major regional security and humanitarian problems, such as massive refugee flows, tensions among West African leaders, and the illicit trafficking of minerals and weapons. During the democratization process of the 1990s, these problems were epitomized in the civil wars in Liberia, Sierra Leone, and Côte d'Ivoire. In particular, the wars in Liberia and Sierra Leone were typified by gross human rights violations against civilians, anarchy, state collapse, and the

75

notorious exploitation and trade of blood diamonds. The destabilization in the West African region followed a long history of catastrophic civil wars in other parts of Africa that the international community either failed or had been unable to resolve. These include the genocide in Rwanda and the tragic conflicts in Democratic Republic of Congo (DRC), Somalia, and Sudan.[3] In West Africa, however, the international community eventually acted to successfully end the civil wars in Liberia and Sierra Leone and, to a large extent, in Côte d'Ivoire. The three case countries provide important lessons for the international community about dealing with violent conflicts that result from the struggles against military and one-party dictatorships in Africa. While it is often assumed that the international community will come to the aid of countries in trouble, there are fundamental questions about the objectives, nature, and impact of humanitarian interventions.

The humanitarian interventions in Sierra Leone, Liberia, and Côte d'Ivoire were spearheaded by a variety of countries and organizations collectively referred to as the *international community*. However, the notion of international community is ambiguous. Arguably, the international community is a broad yet compartmentalized political and legal entity that supposedly includes all countries of the world and covers a wide range of issues of global significance, including security, the environment, human rights, health, trade, communication, transportation, and sports.[4] Such a broad notion of international community tends to miss the realities of humanitarian military interventions, which are often driven by a few countries and organizations operating within fluidly defined international norms in order to achieve specific interests.[5] A much more useful understanding of international community narrows the focus to the activities of those countries and organizations that are engaged in a specific issue or event with international implications due to historical, political, economic, legal, or moral considerations. With respect to the humanitarian interventions in West Africa, the international community essentially consisted of former colonial powers, regional powers, neighboring countries, and the international organizations that had a mandate to deal with security and humanitarian issues in the area. In particular, they include the United Nations (UN), African Union (AU), Economic Community of West African States (ECOWAS), Nigeria, Ghana, Togo, Senegal, Burkina Faso, Guinea, South Africa, Morocco, Libya, Britain, France, the United States, and a variety of nongovernmental humanitarian agencies, such as the Red Cross, Doctors without Borders, and Action Aid. Though each of these actors had unique interests and ties to the region, they formed an ad hoc international group of concerned states and organizations that acted to protect their interests and simultaneously promote shared international values of human rights, humanitarianism, democracy, and security.

NEW HUMANITARIANISM AND THE LIMITS
OF TRADITIONAL PEACEKEEPING

Humanitarian intervention is a contentious issue that revolves around morality and sovereignty in the legal and political discourses of international security. As noted in the previous chapters, humanitarian intervention is the use of coercion, including the minimal necessary military means, in a sovereign state, even without its consent, to avert or ameliorate grave human suffering and widespread violence resulting from gross violations of human rights by either the state or violent nonstate actors.[6] Humanitarian intervention is most often based on a UN authorization or the collective decisions of coalitions representing concerned states or a regional organization. The extent and nature of humanitarian intervention can range from short-term and narrowly defined peacekeeping missions to more prolonged and profound peacebuilding-cum-statebuilding efforts to enforce peace and rebuild a collapsed state.[7] Some of the most common activities include creating safe havens for civilians, providing safe transportation corridors, peace mediation, disarming combatants, and postwar reconstruction.[8]

In his critique of military humanitarianism, Robert Johansen makes a distinction between narrowly defined humanitarian interventions and interventions motivated by concerns about human rights violations or collective security. Johansen argues for conflict mitigation and peacebuilding strategies and nonmilitary coercive instruments as "a third path between doing nothing and sending the troops."[9] While this third path can be a model for preventing the need for military humanitarianism, it begs the question of how to respond to catastrophic civil wars that the international community has been unable to prevent. As the International Commission on Intervention and State Sovereignty (ICISS) noted, "Millions of human beings remain at the mercy of civil wars, insurgencies, state repression and state collapse.... What is at stake here is not making the world safe for big powers, or trampling over the sovereign rights of small ones, but delivering practical protection for ordinary people, at risk of their lives, because their states are unwilling or unable to protect them."[10] The most pertinent question in humanitarian intervention is not whether military force should be used but when should it be deployed and what the implications of military humanitarianism are.[11] Following the logic of natural law, Terry Nardin anchors humanitarian intervention in the moral imperative to rectify wrongs and protect the innocent.[12] Similarly, the ICISS points out that the real issue in humanitarian intervention is how to use minimal military force, when nonmilitary options have been reasonably exhausted, to fulfill the international moral responsibly to avert or halt large-scale loss of life or ethnic cleansing.[13]

Skepticism about humanitarian intervention is not necessarily based on rejection of the moral imperative to protect vulnerable populations. Rather, it is rooted in the uneasiness about violations of sovereignty and the reinforcement of the vestiges of colonialism, which undermine the principles of equality of rights of states and noninterference in the domestic affairs of a state.[14] This skepticism is articulated by the Non-Aligned Movement, which states: "We stress the need to maintain a clear distinction between humanitarian assistance and other activities of the United Nations. We reject the so-called 'right' of humanitarian intervention, which has no legal basis in the United Nations Charter or in the general principles of international law."[15] Furthermore, as Neta Crawford points out, colonialism has always been masked in aggressive and reformist humanitarianisms.[16] Skepticism is also fueled by the morally indefensible selectivity in humanitarian interventions and lack of clear criteria and consensus in the authorization process.[17] Abu Bakarr Bah also notes similar problems with military humanitarianism, especially in cases where the interests of the intervening powers override the interests of the locals.[18]

Proponents of humanitarian intervention question orthodox notions of sovereignty that privilege the independence of the state over the natural rights of its citizens.[19] This has led to critical discourses that distinguish state security from human security and disaggregate state sovereignty from popular sovereignty.[20] As the Commission on Human Security notes, "Human security is concerned with safeguarding and expanding people's vital freedoms. It requires both shielding people from acute threats and empowering people to take charge of their own lives."[21] The decoupling of the security interests of the state and its power elite from the human rights and safety of the citizenry has undercut traditional notions of state sovereignty and redefined sovereignty as a responsibility on the part of the state to protect its citizens.[22] Thus, when states are unable to protect their citizens, they are expected to seek and accept international humanitarian help.

The evolving meaning of sovereignty and expanding scope of humanitarian action has led to *new humanitarianism*, which is necessitated by *new wars*, such as the civil wars in Sierra Leone and Liberia.[23] New wars, which do not neatly coincide with state borders, deliberately victimize civilians and use them as instruments of war. These wars are waged by state and violent nonstate actors and are funded through the illicit exploitation of minerals.[24] New wars "challenge the traditional operating principles of humanitarians—consent, impartiality, and neutrality"— and necessitate a political stance that draws a moral boundary between victims and victimizers, peace seekers and war makers, promoters of democracy and warlords.[25] New humanitarianism is openly political in defending human rights and democracy and stretches intervention beyond traditional peacekeeping and relief work to building peace and addressing root causes of wars.[26] The interventions in West Africa present illuminating cases for understanding the prospects and limitations of new humanitarianism.

The key components of the interventions include the deployment of military forces to protect civilians and maintain the rule of law, peace mediation and enforcement intended to result in a successful multiparty election, and postwar reconstruction.[27] While these are all fluidly interconnected activities that overlap, humanitarian interventions tend to begin with an international promise of an interposition force and ad hoc peace mediation intended to secure an immediate cease-fire. Actual military deployment tends to evolve with the peace processes, which are frequently protracted in nature. Substantial postwar reconstruction often comes after the end of combat activities. However, this is a fluid activity that can begin with basic humanitarian assistance to displaced people and evolve into the rehabilitation of communities and long-term national programs to promote democracy and economic development.

INTERVENTION FORCES: HUMAN SECURITY AND THE RULE OF LAW

The military components of the humanitarian interventions in Liberia, Sierra Leone, and Côte d'Ivoire began immediately at the start of each of these civil wars. In Liberia and Sierra Leone, the interventions evolved from traditional peace-keeping missions to robust military and civilian missions aimed at enforcing peace and promoting postwar reconstruction.[28] In Côte d'Ivoire, the intervention largely remained a traditional peacekeeping mission that was mostly tasked with manning the demarcation lines between the belligerents and supporting the Ivoirian government in implementing the peace agreement. However, during the 2010 presidential election debacle in which both Alassane Ouattara and Laurent Gbagbo claimed victory and swore themselves in as president, the international community took a more proactive position in favor of Ouattara, whom the UN believed was the actual winner of the election.[29] Despite their differences, all three interventions had a common goal of protecting civilians and restoring the rule of law in line with a neoliberal model of democracy. In Liberia and Sierra Leone, the intervention forces had to take over security control of the country in order to achieve these goals, while in Côte d'Ivoire, they had to delicately collaborate with the belligerents.

International Military Intervention in Sierra Leone

The intervention in Sierra Leone had two interconnected phases. The first phase began at the outset of the war and continued until the 1997 Armed Forces Revolutionary Council (AFRC) coup, which toppled the elected government. The initial peacekeeping operation in Sierra Leone was essentially an expansion of the ECOWAS peacekeeping mission in Liberia, namely ECOMOG. During that period, the international community treated the war largely as a power struggle between the RUF and successive governments.[30] Even though there were outside forces supporting the government and the RUF, ECOMOG was the only international peacekeeping-cum-intervention force in the country. ECOMOG in Sierra Leone had the tacit support of key regional and international powers and organizations. Its main mission was to prevent cross-border attacks from Liberia.[31] When the Abidjan Accord was signed in 1996, ECOMOG was charged with assisting the Government of Sierra Leone and the RUF to disarm and demobilize ex-combatants. Under the Abidjan Accord, the government and the RUF were responsible for implementing the agreement. The international community was only expected to provide resources and a supportive environment and serve as a neutral arbiter. As such, ECOMOG's role was to assist the Commission for the Consolidation of Peace and the Demobilization and Resettlement Committee, which were both comprised of Sierra Leoneans.

The Nigerian-led ECOWAS intervention in Sierra Leone fundamentally changed after the 1997 coup. ECOMOG's campaign to restore the elected government marked the beginning of the second phase of the military aspect of the intervention. During this period, ECOMOG in Sierra Leone became a distinct mission, and its size significantly increased to around fifteen thousand troops. The June 26, 1997, ECOWAS communiqué and the October 1997 Conakry Accord empowered ECOMOG to use force, if necessary, to restore the elected government and disarm AFRC and RUF combatants. The ECOWAS communiqué specifically called on the international community to "restore the lawful government by a combination of three measures, i.e.: the use of dialogue; the application of sanctions, including an embargo; and the use of force."[32] ECOWAS's policy to restore the elected government was supported by the AU, the Commonwealth, the UN, and the British government.[33] Under the Conakry Accord between ECOWAS and the AFRC junta, ECOMOG was to supervise the disarmament and demobilization of combatants and facilitate the flow of humanitarian assistance. It was also understood that if the junta failed to relinquish power to the elected government by May 22, 1998, ECOMOG would use force to restore the elected government. ECOMOG, in collaboration with the UN, was to implement the terms of the agreement. The Conakry Accord fundamentally transformed ECOMOG's mission from peacekeeping to peace enforcement. When the junta refused to faithfully implement the agreement, ECOMOG fought the AFRC and RUF and restored the elected government in March 1998. ECOMOG continued to defend the government against the RUF and AFRC until its mission was withdrawn in April 2000 and some of its troops were absorbed into UN Mission in Sierra Leone (UNAMSIL).[34]

Similarly, the UN mission evolved from a simple observer group to a robust mission charged with enforcing peace and rebuilding the country. The UN military involvement began with the establishment of the UN Observer Mission in Sierra Leone (UNOMSIL) in July 1998. This was a long-delayed effort to provide the international support envisioned in the 1996 Abidjan Accord. The deployment of a neutral UN force became even more imperative as ECOMOG became entangled in the fighting. UNOMSIL was a modest unarmed team with a very limited mandate. Its main duty was to monitor the security situation, disarmament process, conduct of ECOMOG, and compliance with international humanitarian law.[35] The role of the UN mission drastically increased after the July 1999 Lomé Peace Agreement between the government and the RUF. By then, it was clear that the alarming escalation of atrocities and the limited capacity of Nigeria, and ECOWAS as whole, to defeat the RUF would require the UN to take a lead role in ending the war.[36] In October 1999, UNOMSIL was replaced with the UNAMSIL, which was given a mandate to implement the Lomé Peace Agreement. Its duties were later expanded, and troop level increased from 6,000 to 11,100. Most significantly, UMAMSIL had a Chapter VII mandate that empowered it to "take the necessary action to ensure the security and freedom of movement of its personnel and, within its capabilities and areas of deployment, afford protection to civilians under imminent threat of physical violence."[37] By March 2001, UNAMSIL's troop size had been increased to 17,500 and its role significantly expanded beyond traditional peacekeeping.[38] Its overall objectives became "to assist the efforts of the Government of Sierra Leone to extend its authority, restore law and order and stabilize the situation progressively throughout the entire country, and to assist in the promotion of a political process which should lead to a renewed disarmament, demobilization and reintegration programme and the holding, in due course, of free and fair elections."[39]

The strengthened force successfully implemented the terms of the Lomé and the subsequent Abuja peace agreements. The RUF's reluctance to faithfully abide by the terms of the Lomé Peace Agreement increasingly eroded the international community's tolerance for the RUF and its leader, Foday Sankoh.[40] The efforts to implement peace took an unexpected turn in May 2000, when Sankoh was arrested by a mob after RUF guards opened fire on civilians protesting at Sankoh's Freetown residence against his reluctance to abide by the Lomé Peace Agreement. Sankoh was handed over to the government and British forces. The government, in concert with the international community, refused to release him. Instead, the RUF was asked to replace Sankoh with new leadership committed to peace.[41] The RUF named its field commander, General Issa Sesay, as interim leader and negotiated the Abuja Ceasefire Agreements. In the meantime, the AFRC was also becoming defunct. In 2000, Johnny Koroma reportedly disbanded the AFRC, declared loyalty to the elected government, and went into hiding.[42] Koroma, who was indicted for war crimes on March 7, 2003, is believed to have died in Liberia. The notorious Westside Boys remnants of the AFRC were eventually defeated by British forces.[43] The strengthening of UNAMSIL, presence of British forces, strong sanctions imposed by the UN in 2001 (Resolution 1343) against President Charles Taylor of Liberia for his support of the RUF, change in RUF leadership, and ECOWAS outreach to RUF leaders created a real opportunity for peace. After the May 2001 Abuja Agreement, disarmament began. By the end of 2001, around 75,000 former combatants had been disarmed and demobilized and the RUF had formed a political party.[44] On January 18, 2002, President Ahmad Tejan Kabbah declared the war officially over, paving way for the May 2002 elections. The Revolutionary United Front Party (RUFP) did poorly in the elections. It clearly lost the presidential election and failed to meet the threshold for representation in parliament, which effectively led to the demise of the moribund RUF movement.

The ECOWAS and UN military interventions in Sierra Leone are largely tied to the security and humanitarian interests of the international community there. The international community viewed military intervention as a means to fulfill its regional security responsibilities and its humanitarian obligation to the people of Sierra Leone, whose legitimate government was incapable of protecting them.[45] Arguably, the initial deployment of ECOMOG was motivated by the desires of some ECOWAS leaders, most notably Nigeria, to stop Taylor from taking over the government in Liberia. Because Sierra Leone was used as a base for ECOMOG operations in Liberia, it became necessary to support the government of Sierra Leone against attacks from the NPFL and RUF. As the war evolved, however, the objectives of several international actors aligned neatly to generate a moral and political consensus for military intervention to protect civilians and restore the rule of law.[46] The overthrow of the elected government and the images of heinous crimes against civilians galvanized international support for the robust military intervention to end the war.[47] ECOWAS wanted to restore regional security and demonstrate its commitment to democracy. Most significantly, General Sani Abacha saw the crisis as a chance to assert Nigerian leadership in the region and repair the tarnished reputation of his pariah regime.[48] The AU used the coup to initiate a zero-tolerance policy for coups, while the Commonwealth asserted its principles on democracy enshrined in the 1991 Harare Declaration.[49] At the UN, Kofi Annan's advocacy for protecting vulnerable populations and Kabbah's long UN career generated further interest in the crisis in Sierra Leone.[50] The international political and moral consensus on Sierra Leone, which tended to see the RUF as the obstacle to peace, was strengthened by the RUF's refusal to participate in the 1996 elections, connivance with the AFRC to overthrow the elected government, reluctance to disarm, attacks on UN troops, gruesome tactics of maiming civilians, and exploitation of blood diamonds.

Apart from the ECOMOG campaign to restore the elected government in 1998, there were numerous incidents during the course of the war that pitted the international forces against the RUF and AFRC. The RUF viewed ECOMOG as an enemy force instead of as a peacekeeping mission and repeatedly clashed with it. In June 1997, for example, the AFRC and RUF repelled an ECOMOG attack in Freetown and captured a significant number of Nigerian soldiers. UNAMSIL also clashed with the RUF and AFRC. In May 2000, the RUF kidnapped over three hundred UNAMSIL troops and seized their equipment.[51] Some of the UNAMSIL troops were not rescued until after the British intervened in support of the government and UNAMSIL.[52] The confrontations between the RUF and the international forces attest to the distrust between them. In contrast, the international community sympathized with the government, which it considered legitimate and representative of a majority of the people.

International Military Intervention in Liberia

Like the war itself, the international intervention in Liberia occurred in two interconnected phases. The first phase began in August 1990 with the establishment of the Nigerian-dominated ECOMOG by the Standing Mediation Committee of ECOWAS and continued until the election of Taylor in 1997. ECOMOG's mission formally ended in February 1998.[53] The second phase of the intervention started in August 2003 with the deployment of the ECOWAS Military Mission in Liberia (ECOMIL) and its subsequent replacement with UNAMSIL in October 2003. ECOMOG was the main intervention force during the first phase of the war. The UN force took charge of the second phase of the intervention. Despite their peculiarities, ECOWAS and the UN closely collaborated to ensure security and promote peace in Liberia. ECOMOG was created by Nigeria and the other anglophone countries in ECOWAS as a peacekeeping force to stabilize the situation in Liberia.[54] Guinea was the only francophone country in ECOWAS to support the creation of ECOMOG. In retrospect, the ECOWAS intervention in Liberia was based on reasonable concerns for security in the region. Some of the regional leaders also saw the rebellion in Liberia as a potential threat to their dictatorial regimes. The countries that supported the initial interventions were ruled by dictators who were unwilling to undertake genuine democratic reforms. These countries included Nigeria, Sierra Leone, Ghana, the Gambia, and Guinea. Nigeria's involvement was also instigated by the close relation between Samuel Doe and Nigerian President Ibrahim Babangida and Nigeria's desire to establish itself as a regional power.[55] The country's position was also intended to undermine the positions of Côte d'Ivoire and Burkina Faso, which were believed to support Taylor.[56]

ECOMOG began as a small peacekeeping force of around four thousand troops from Nigeria, Sierra Leone, Ghana, the Gambia, and Guinea. It grew into a large intervention force that supported the Interim Government of National Unity (IGNU) and tried to enforce peace. ECOMOG became heavily involved in the fighting as the NPFL, which opposed its deployment, and other factions saw it as a biased force preventing them from taking power. ECOMOG was charged with restoring law and order and implementing the peace agreements, most notably the Yamoussoukro IV (1991), Cotonou (1993), and Akosombo (1994) agreements. Despite ECOMOG's ambiguous position in the war, it was given a critical role in ending the conflict. As stated in Article 3.1 of the Cotonou Agreement, "ECOMOG and the United Nations Observer Mission shall supervise and monitor the implementation of this Agreement. The Parties . . . expressly recognize the neutrality and authority of the Economic Community of West Africa States (ECOWAS) Military Observer Group (ECOMOG) and the United Nations Observer Mission. . . . Accordingly, the ECOMOG and United Nations observers shall enjoy complete freedom of movement throughout Liberia."[57] At its peak in 1997, ECOMOG had around eleven thousand troops in Liberia.[58] While the vast majority were from Nigeria, there were modest contributions from the other four countries that supported the original deployment. Uganda, Tanzania, Senegal, and Mali also contributed troops, albeit in small numbers and for a short period.

ECOMOG's operations were complemented by the UN Observer Mission in Liberia (UNOMIL). UNOMIL was created by the UN Security Council in September 1993 as a small military force and civilian staff with a limited mandate. Initially, UNOMSIL was to include around 300 military observers. The number of military observers was reduced to 160 in November 1995 and 92 in November 1996.[59] Its main duties were to monitor compliance with the Cotonou Peace Agreement, investigate cease-fire violations, observe the election process, assist the humanitarian efforts, report on violations of international humanitarian law, and train ECOMOG engineers in mine clearance.[60] In November 1995, UNOMIL's mandate was adjusted to include supporting ECOWAS and the interim government, monitoring compliance with the cease-fire and other military provisions of the peace agreements, and verifying the disarmament and demobilization of combatants.[61] UNOMIL began deploying military personnel in October 1993 and reached its authorized strength of 303 military observers in January 1994. It established four regional headquarters in Monrovia and in the western, northern, and eastern regions of the country and deployed in twenty-seven out of the projected thirty-nine sites. However, by January 1997, UNOMIL was reduced to seventy-eight observers on the ground. The reduced UNOMIL force reached its full authorized strength of ninety-two military observers in March 1997. By June 1997, it was deployed in sixteen sites across the country. The mission ended after the installation of the elected government in 1997. By September 1997, most of the UNOMIL staff had been repatriated. In November 1997, the UN Security Council established the UN Peacebuilding Support Office in Liberia to promote the postwar reconstruction effort.

Because of the incoherent nature of the Liberian conflict, frequent breakdown of agreements, and proliferation of armed factions, the peacekeeping activities of ECOMOG and UNOMIL were often ad hoc and dispersed. However, ECO-MOG's main activities included providing security, enforcing the arms embargo, ensuring the implementation of cease-fires and peace agreements, and disarming combatants. Most of these activities were to be undertaken in collaboration with UNOMIL. The overall responsibilities of ECOMOG and UNOMIL were spelled out in the peace agreements. According to Article 6 of the Cotonou Agreement, "the Parties hereto agree and express their intent and willingness to disarm to and under the supervision of ECOMOG, monitored and verified by the United Nations Observer Mission." It further stated that "ECOMOG shall have the authority to disarm any combatant or non-combatant in possession of weapons and warlike materials. The United Nations observers shall monitor all such activities."[62] Article 4 of the agreement empowered ECOMOG to enforce the arms embargo imposed by ECOWAS and the UN. It stated that "ECOMOG shall create zones or otherwise seal the borders, whichever is militarily feasible, of Liberia-Guinea, Liberia-Sierra Leone and Liberia-Côte d'Ivoire to prevent cross-border attacks, infiltration or importation of arms. There shall be deployed United Nations observers in all of such zones to monitor, verify and report on any and all of the foregoing and the implementation thereof." Furthermore, "All points of entry including seaports, airfields and roads shall be monitored and supervised by ECOMOG. There shall be deployed United Nations observers to monitor, verify and report on the implementation of the foregoing activities."[63]

Though ECOMOG was not able to properly secure the country for most of the war, it deployed in some critical areas in order to protect the IGNU and key Liberian and international actors involved in the peace process. During the period leading to the 1997 elections, ECOMOG was deployed in forty-eight different locations across the country.[64] It provided security for the UN observer mission and created safe havens for civilians and safe corridors for humanitarian agencies during some of the most chaotic periods of the war. During the intense fighting that occurred in early 1995, for example, ECOMOG had around 8,430 troops deployed in the central region and some parts of the western region, including Monrovia.[65] However, ECOMOG's capacity to provide security was undermined by its limited resources, including well-trained troops. In some instances, ECOMOG could hardly defend itself against attacks. During the fighting that occurred in April 1994, for example, its troops were abducted by ULIMO and LPC fighters. In December 1995, United Liberation Movement of Liberia for Democracy – Johnson (ULIMO-J) attacked ECOMOG at Tunmanburg, which resulted in heavy fighting. On numerous occasions, UN observers could not carry out their duties because ECOMOG was unable to provide the necessary security. UN offices and warehouses were looted, and in some cases, UN staff had to be evacuated. In mid-1994, UNOMIL had to withdraw from the western region due to a lack of security. In September 1994, the NPFL detained forty-three UNOMIL observers and six NGO workers for nearly a week. ECOMOG was also unable to secure Monrovia during the fighting that broke out in April and May 1996, leaving about three thousand people dead and driving out half of the city's population. ECOMOG's limited ability to protect civilians was epitomized in the massacre of nearly six hundred Liberians on June 6, 1993, near the town of Harbel by units of the AFL.[66] ECOMOG's failure to enforce the arms embargo was evident in the continued fighting, use of heavy weaponry by the belligerents, and flow of combatants and weapons across Liberia's land borders.

The implementation of the cease-fires and the critical terms of the peace agreements, especially disarmament, also proved to be problematic. While the cease-fires were intended to ease humanitarian crises and provide room for substantive negotiations, the peace agreements were supposed to end the fighting and lead to the establishment of an elected government. Unfortunately, most of the cease-fires and peace agreements did not really take hold. ECOMOG and UNOMIL had very limited capacity to enforce the agreements. In most cases, they simply reported violations and tried to negotiate with local commanders and faction leaders. One of the earliest efforts to implement a cease-fire occurred in late 1990. Despite repeated international pleas, the fighting, which had been raging for most of the year, continued well into 1991. A temporary Joint Ceasefire Monitoring Committee (JCMC) was created after the Cotonou Peace Agreement (1993) to monitor and investigate cease-fire violations. The JCMC was replaced with the Violation Committee envisioned in the Cotonou Agreement. The Violation Committee was comprised of the belligerents and ECOMOG and chaired by the UN. Both of these committees faced enormous difficulties in implementing the August 1, 1993, cease-fire and the plethora of subsequent cease-fire arrangements. The April 19, 1996, cease-fire agreement was one of the few notable successes. ECOMOG established checkpoints and patrolled central Monrovia, which facilitated the withdrawal of combatants from the city and enabled UNOMIL to organize security escorts for participants in peace consultations. When the cease-fire collapsed on April 29, 1996, ECOMOG concentrated its forces in order to protect against attacks. The cease-fire in Monrovia was restored on May 26, 1996, and most of the combatants left the city.[67]

Two of the most critical tasks of the international intervention were to disarm the combatants and hold elections. It is estimated that between fifty thousand and sixty thousand combatants participated in the first half of the civil war. Twenty-five percent of the combatants are believed to have been children.[68] Despite the numerous commitments to the disarmament and demobilization of combatants, most notably in the Cotonou Peace Agreement, the belligerents repeatedly failed to comply with the timetable for the disarmament, encampment, and demobilization. The failure to disarm allowed the fighting to continue and made elections impossible. The most notable progress occurred in late 1996. The dormant Task Force on Demobilization and Reintegration was reactivated, and ECOMOG and UNOMIL established fifteen disarmament and demobilization sites. Official disarmament began on November 22, 1996, and continued until February 7, 1997. During this period, 20,332 fighters were disarmed under the supervision of UNOMIL. The UN Humanitarian Assistance Coordination Office, which had been providing humanitarian relief since the war began, also demobilized 21,315 fighters. The combatants turned in nearly ten thousand weapons and over a million pieces of ammunition during the official disarmament period. An additional 132 combatants disarmed voluntarily in Rivercess, Grand Kru, and Grand Gedeh counties after the official end of disarmament. By June 1997, UNOMIL had verified the surrender of 10,036 weapons and more than 1.24 million pieces of ammunition. In additions, around 3,750 weapons were surrendered to ECOMOG outside of the official disarmament sites. ECOMOG also seized around 3,500 weapons and 150,000 pieces of ammunition.[69] The disarmament operation significantly improved security in the country and created conditions for elections. ECOMOG was able to handle the security situation leading to the 1997 elections.

By the end of 1996, there was broad consensus that elections would be held in 1997. The electoral commission and the reconstituted Supreme Court were installed in April 1997. Elections were set for July 19, 1997. The new government was to be inaugurated on August 16, 1997. The elections were successfully held by the Liberian Independent Elections Commission with the strong assistance of ECOMOG and UNOMIL. Thirteen political parties contested the presidential and legislative elections. Taylor presumably won the presidential election, while his National Patriotic Party (NPP) won the legislative elections. Despite accusations of voter intimidation, especially by Taylor's NPFL, the results were accepted, albeit temporarily. Taylor's government was installed, and peace returned to the country. However, the war erupted again in 1999, after Taylor's opponents regrouped and launched new attacks to remove him from power. There was some discontent with the results of the 1997 elections, and Taylor was accused of suppressing political opposition and undermining democracy and national security.[70] He was also heavily implicated in fueling the war in Sierra Leone, which tarnished his reputation within the international community.[71] The war quickly escalated and caused renewed security and humanitarian problems. By 2003, Liberia was again in a state of total anarchy.

The international intervention in Liberia significantly changed during the second phase of the war that began in 1999. By 2003, the UN, which was heavily involved in Sierra Leone, was far more willing to significantly intervene in Liberia. Peace in Liberia was seen as essential to ensuring regional stability. Moreover, there was a broad consensus that Taylor was the main impediment to peace.[72] As such, the second international intervention was a far more robust campaign, driven by principles of new humanitarianism. The international community became more determined to avert further humanitarian tragedy and regional insecurity and to take a firm stance against those believed to impede peace. Some of the most significant actions of the international community were the decisions to indict Taylor for war crimes and to force him into exile in Nigeria just before the Accra Accord was signed in August 2003. Taylor was arrested in March 2006 by the Nigerian government and handed to the Special Court for Sierra Leone, which sentenced him to fifty years in prison for war crimes. The second military intervention began with the deployment of ECOMIL in August 2003 as a vanguard force. ECOMIL consisted of around 3,500 troops charged with immediately stabilizing the country following the intensification of the bitter fighting that broke out in 2002. The United States deployed troops to support ECOMIL.[73] The precarious security and humanitarian situation in Liberia, which had the potential to destabilize the neighboring countries, generated significant international attention.

Unlike the first intervention, this time, the UN and the major powers, most notably the United States, immediately recognized the limited capacity of ECOWAS and gravity of the crisis and agreed to be more involved. ECOMIL was replaced by the UN Mission in Liberia (UNMIL) on October 1, 2003, following the signing of the Accra Peace Agreement in August 2003. UNMIL was established in September 2003. It was envisioned as a multidimensional force that would work in collaboration with ECOWAS, AU, UNAMSIL, MINUCI, and the UN Office for West Africa.[74] UNMIL was given broad responsibilities to protect UN staff, facilities, and civilians, support the implementation of the cease-fire and peace process, facilitate humanitarian assistance, monitor human rights, and help the National Transitional Government of Liberia (NTGL). In particular, it was given the power to investigate cease-fire violations, monitor the disengagement and cantonment of combatants, carry out voluntary disarmament, destroy weapons in line with the disarmament, demobilization, rehabilitation, and reintegration

(DDRR) program, provide security at key government installations, assist the NTGL in restructuring the police and Liberian military and establishing national authority throughout the country, and help organize the scheduled 2005 elections.[75] In November 2005, UNMIL was given the authority "to apprehend and detain former President Charles Taylor in the event of a return to Liberia and to transfer him or facilitate his transfer to Sierra Leone for prosecution before the Special Court for Sierra Leone and to keep the Liberian Government, the Sierra Leonean Government and the Council fully informed."[76]

UNMIL was to be comprised of 15,000 military personnel and 1,115 civilian police officers operating under a UN Chapter VII authority.[77] Its deployment started in October 2003 with the "re-hatting" of ECOMIL soldiers as UN peacekeepers. Some of the UN troops in Sierra Leone, most notably Bangladeshi and Pakistani, were transferred to UNMIL, which allowed it to rapidly deploy beyond Monrovia. By June 2004, UNMIL was fully deployed. In March 2006, it had 15,071 military troops from forty-eight countries and over a thousand police personnel from thirty-five countries.[78] The mandate, size, diversity, and rapid deployments of ECOMIL and UNMIL were in stark contrast to the previous ECOWAS and UN forces that trickled into Liberia during the first part of the war.

UNMIL successfully accomplished its mission of implementing the peace process, which culminated with the installment of an elected government in November 2005. In particular, it established a new Liberian security force, disarmed the combatants, and ensured the proper conduct of elections. In May 2004, recruitment for the new police force commenced. By June 1, 2004, at least 712 cadets had graduated from the Police Service Training Academy. At the same time, around five hundred seaport police and Special Security Service personnel had been trained.[79] The first phase of the disarmament program, which mostly focused on Monrovia, began in December 2003. The program was extended to the areas close to Monrovia in April 2004. The final phase of disarmament began in July 2004 and targeted the remote areas of the country. By February 2005, around 101,495 combatants had been disarmed and demobilized, including 8,523 boys and 2,440 girls. UNMIL collected over 61,000 weapons and nearly 6.5 million rounds of small arms ammunitions.[80] Starting in 2005, the program focused on reintegrating and rehabilitating ex-combatants. The demobilization of former AFL soldiers was completed in December 2005, paving the way for the creation of a new army. By March 2006, at least 1,525 applicants were successfully screened.[81] Similarly, the elections were well conducted. Twenty-two political parties contested the October 2005 elections. In November 2005, Ellen Johnson Sirleaf was sworn in as president after winning the runoff election. UNMIL continued to promote postwar reconstruction, most notably in the area of security reform, until the mission was ended on March 30, 2016, in accordance with Resolution

2239 (adopted on September 17, 2015), which called for the transfer of power to Liberian authorities.[82]

International Military Intervention in Côte d'Ivoire

The international intervention in Côte d'Ivoire was a joint collaboration of ECOWAS, the AU, the UN, and France. As compared to Sierra Leone and Liberia, the scope of the intervention here was limited and was the result of a convergence of the security and economic interests of ECOWAS and France.[83] While French interest was tied to its huge economic investments and long-standing alliance with Côte d'Ivoire, ECOWAS's interest was rooted in the country's economic centrality in the region and the need to minimize the instability there. The intervention, which was spearheaded by ECOWAS and France, began shortly after the political conflict escalated into a civil war in September 2002. ECOWAS immediately established a contact group to promote dialogue and decided to arrange for the deployment of an ECOWAS force. The force was to monitor a proposed cease-fire and ensure disengagement and disarmament.[84] A cease-fire agreement was signed on October 17, 2002. France, which already had troops in the country under its long-standing bilateral defense agreement with Côte d'Ivoire, was asked to assign forces to monitor the cease-fire in advance of the deployment of ECOWAS forces. In the meantime, ECOWAS continued to promote the Lomé peace talks and decided to deploy the ECOWAS Peace Force for Côte d'Ivoire (ECOFORCE), also known as the ECOWAS Mission in Côte d'Ivoire (ECOMICI), at the end of December 2002. ECOWAS urged the AU and UN to be more involved in settling the conflict. While the Lomé talks continued, France made a fresh effort to broker an agreement. In January 2003, the parties signed the Linas-Marcoussis Agreement. However, the international peace meditation efforts did not end the conflict. Fighting continued as the government and rebels failed to implement the terms of the agreement. In January 2003, ECOFORCE started deploying the first batch of its proposed 1,300 troops.[85] In March 2003, ECOWAS decided to increase ECOFORCE's strength to 3,411 troops.[86] However, the deployment of ECOWAS forces proceeded slowly.[87] Despite the deployment of French Licorne and ECOWAS forces, which the UN endorsed, the fighting did not stop. The belligerents signed a new cease-fire agreement on May 3, 2003, as peace mediation efforts for a durable solution to the conflict continued.

On May 13, 2003, the UN Mission in Côte d'Ivoire (MINUCI) was established. MINUCI was a political mission comprised of a modest civilian staff to support the work of the Special Representative of the Secretary General (SRSG) and a small military liaison group. MINUCI initially had twenty-six military liaison officers, who were deployed in June 2003. MINUCI's mandate was to assist the Ivoirian parties to the Linas-Marcoussis Agreement with implementing the terms of the agreement, complement the work of French and ECOWAS forces, and advise the SRCG. In particular, the military liaison group was to monitor the security situation, work with the international intervention forces and the government and rebel forces, and advise on the disarmament and demobilization process.[88]

Given MINUCI's weak mandate and the limited capacity of ECOMICI, ECOWAS pressured the UN to transform MINUCI into a peacekeeping force that would incorporate the ECOWAS force. In February 2004, the UN created the UN Operations in Côte d'Ivoire (UNOCI), which was to replace MINUCI and ECOFORCE on April 4, 2004, and work in coordination with the French Force. UNOCI was created on the basis of UN Chapter VII authority, which gave it more power to carry out its mandate.[89] Moreover, French forces were given the authority to use all necessary means to support UNOCI as needed. UNOCI's mandate was to monitor the cease-fire and the armed groups, assist in the implementation of the peace process, and support the humanitarian work of the international community.[90] In particular, UNOCI was empowered to prevent hostile actions and investigate cease-fire violations, promote trust among the belligerents, help the government monitor the borders and reestablish state authority across the country, support the government in implementing the disarmament process (including securing and destroying weapons and ammunitions surrendered by combatants), help provide security and technical assistance for the identification process and elections, assist in the restructuring of the defense and security forces, protect UN interests, civilians, and members of the government, confiscate arms and ammunitions that violated the arms embargo,[91] and monitor the media for incitement to hatred and violence. UNOCI started with 6,240 military personnel but later grew to 9,105 uniformed personnel in November 2010. However, given the size of the country and the strength of the government and rebel forces, the size of the UN force was still too small to undertake any significant peace enforcement role. The limited capacity of the UN force became more evident after the 2010 election debacle. Though UN troops were protecting Ouattara, they were unable to provide comprehensive security or oust Gbagbo, whom the international community had asked to concede defeat in the 2010 presidential election. In January 2011, the UN decided to increase the size of UNOCI by two thousand more troops.[92]

The actual fighting in Côte d'Ivoire's civil war did not really last for a long time in comparison to other civil wars in the region. This was partly due to the nature of the underlying cause of the conflict, the deployment of international forces, the division of the country between the north under the control of the Forces Nouvelles (FN) and the south under the control of the government, and the peace process. However, the conflict and the sporadic violence persisted for too long. Since the conflict erupted in the late 1990s, Côte d'Ivoire has been in a state of *no war, no peace*. The low intensity of the fighting and the fact that Ivoirians have been primarily responsible for implementing the peace agreements made it less likely for the international forces to engage in robust peace enforcement activities. Instead, the intervention forces were mostly manning the buffer zone and ensuring that Forces Armées Nationales de Côte d'Ivoire (FANCI) and Forces Armées des Forces Nouvelles (FAFN) troops did not cross the demarcation line. At the same time, there were numerous peace agreements that failed to end the conflict. The only agreement that significantly calmed the conflict and moved the peace process forward was the 2007 Ouagadougou Peace Accord negotiated by Ivoirians themselves.[93] The agreement led to a fairly stable power-sharing government, a successful identification program that issued citizenship papers to a significant number of people who did not previously have their documents, some notable progress in the disarmament process, and the long-awaited 2010 presidential election.[94] The election was supposed to definitively end the conflict. Unfortunately, it ended in a stalemate in which incumbent Gbagbo of La Majorité Presidentielle (LMP) and Ouattara of the Rassemblement des Républicains (RDR) both claimed victory and declared themselves president, though the international community endorsed Ouattara as the winner. This precarious situation left the international community in a critical position wherein it had to take a clear and open stance on the war. The international community publicly named Gbagbo as the key Ivoirian actor impeding the restoration of peace and imposed sanctions against him and his allies. The international intervention moved from its orthodox peacekeeping role into a more robust enforcement role driven by the principle of new humanitarianism, although it proved to be a relatively short, robust intervention that was limited to ousting Gbagbo. In fact, UNOCI's mandate ended on June 30, 2017.

As in Sierra Leone, the intervention rested on the principle of ensuring democracy and respecting the rule of law. Unlike in Sierra Leone, where the All People's Congress (APC) conceded to the Sierrra Leone People's Party (SLPP) after the 2002 elections, in Côte d'Ivoire, the result of the 2010 presidential election was contested. A salient fact in the Ivoirian civil war is that though the actual violent war was short and sporadic, peace has still not been consolidated because the north-south divide continues to linger in Ivoirian elections. After the 2010 election, Gbagbo and his allies were defeated, and the citizenship issue was resolved. However, since 2010, Ouattara has governed as a victor, which has shattered democracy and opened the country to renewed risk of political violence and even civil war. Ouattara's decision to alter the constitution and run for a third consecutive presidential term in 2020 further incited southern bitterness about political marginalization. Since the start of the political crisis in 1993, Côte d'Ivoire has mostly been in this state of no war, no peace.

PEACE AGREEMENTS AND THE
ELECTIONS PATH TO PEACE

The primary objective of the UN and other members of the international community in countries plagued by civil war is to peacefully and quickly resolve the conflicts. This is often done in the interest of maintaining regional and international security and fulfilling the humanitarian obligations of the international community. The primary strategy to achieve this goal is mediation aimed at reaching an immediate cease-fire and a long-term peace agreement that culminates in a multiparty election. Like international military intervention, peace mediation is a complicated process that demands significant international attention in order for it to be successful. As noted earlier, the civil wars in West Africa attracted international attention, though it was either too little or came a bit late. In Sierra Leone and Liberia, most of the initial international peace mediation efforts and military interventions were undertaken by ECOWAS, as the UN and other key members of the international community were slow in responding to the conflict. However, as the wars escalated and the atrocities increased, other members of the international community became more involved. Robust international involvement became a critical factor in ending the wars. In Côte d'Ivoire, the war generated rapid international attention, especially from ECOWAS and France, but the involvement was not strong enough to decisively end the conflict. During the earlier phase of the conflict, the international involvement failed to focus on the core issue of citizenship or take decisive action. At the same time, the intervention was viewed with skepticism by Ivoirians from the south.

The international community's approach to solving the wars in West Africa provides intriguing insights into the potentials and limitations of international peacebuilding in Africa. While there were notable successes in Sierra Leone and Liberia, it is also true that it took the international community too long to resolve the conflicts. Despite some of the shortcomings, the UN saw those countries as candidates for robust international intervention and statebuilding under Responsibility to Protect (R2P) that would require long-term commitment. As some respondents noted, "The UN wants to continue to remain in those places [i.e., being innovative in its peacebuilding efforts] and continue to deal with those root causes of the [Sierra Leonean] conflict on a much longer term basis to see the country out of the woods."[95] Furthermore, in a "postwar situation, you understand the reason why [it] . . . is critical so when you talk about the international community you cannot ignore their presence. . . . They make a critical contribution to this process, but my fear is that in their absence, are we going to be able to sustain the peace?"[96] This issue of long-term commitment—that is to say, how long they will remain committed to building states and establishing peace—underlies all interventions by the international community.[97]

The inability of the international community to quickly resolve the civil wars in Sierra Leone, Liberia, and Côte Ivoire raises important questions about the nature of international peace mediation. In Côte d'Ivoire, for example, the international community repeatedly failed to broker a viable peace agreement. One notable problem is the issue of power. International peace mediation, especially in Africa, seems to be focused on multiparty elections as a panacea for civil wars. Perhaps this is partly because civil wars are often presented by the belligerents as a fight for democracy. However, democracy can be an open-ended idea that masks a variety of social, economic, and political grievances in a state. As such, a fight for democracy is not always a fight for free and fair multiparty elections. Indeed, this was the case in all three countries, where the democratic elections failed to end the civil wars, even though all the belligerents claimed to be fighting for democracy. The mantra of democracy has been misappropriated by lumpen revolutionaries, promoters of regional-cum-ethnic interests, and power-hungry warlords.[98] In the meantime, the international community uncritically assumed that a reasonably free and fair election would end a civil war. In all three countries, multiparty elections became the central focus of the peace process, and the mediation efforts and peace agreements failed to focus on the central reasons for the war. In Liberia and Sierra Leone, issues of ethnicity and the power ambitions of the warlords, especially Taylor and Sankoh, and their clear lack of commitment to multiparty elections were ignored for too long. In Côte d'Ivoire, the issue of citizenship and the north-south divide were not properly factored into the internationally driven peace process. As a result, the belligerents signed numerous peace agreements that they failed to honor. Even when elections were held, long-term peace and democracy have been undermined by the very institutional and leadership problems that led to state decay and the continuation of the civil wars. Perhaps the peace processes should have been not only an opportunity to promote multiparty democracy but also a chance to redesign the institutional arrangement of the states in a way that addressed some of the core grievances of the wars. The international community could have also made a more timely delineation between those leaders who were committed to democracy and peace and those who were seeking power at all costs. This would have allowed it to take more appropriate and timely actions in relation to those people impeding peace. Even more, it could have insisted that mechanisms be established for addressing core ethnic and regional grievances. Instead, international mediation simply followed the neoliberal playbook on simple winner-takes-all multiparty elections.

Peace Agreements in the Sierra Leone Civil War

Major international peace mediation in the Sierra Leone civil war began in late 1995, after International Alert and the Organization of African Unity (OAU) established contacts with the RUF.[99] In December 1995, International Alert facilitated a meeting between the RUF and OAU officials in Abidjan. At the same time, the military government, which was under domestic and international pressure to hand over power to an elected government, became eager to negotiate a peaceful end to the conflict. In January 1996, Julius Maada Bio offered to meet Sankoh without any precondition. Sankoh responded favorably, but in a radio communication facilitated by the Red Cross, he told Bio that the scheduled elections must be postponed before talks could proceed. The peace talks leading to the Abidjan Accord were largely facilitated by Côte d'Ivoire, whose foreign minister, Amara Essy, met with Sankoh in RUF territory in Eastern Sierra Leone in early February 1996. Other notable actors included the UN and Commonwealth. Representatives of the RUF and the Sierra Leone government met in Abidjan on February 25, 1996, for their first formal peace talks. In late March 1996, Sankoh and Bio met in Yamoussoukro and promised to stop military actions and to continue the negotiation. Kabbah continued the peace negotiation initiated by his predecessor. The peace talks lasted until the end of November 1996, when the Abidjan Peace Agreement was signed. The sticky issues in the meetings between the RUF and the Sierra Leone government held in Côte d'Ivoire were the RUF's opposition to the 1996 elections and refusal to accept the legitimacy of the elected government, the presence of Executive Outcomes, and the formula for power sharing.[100] The RUF wanted the government to expel Executive Outcomes mercenaries and offer Sankoh the position of vice president.[101] The government rejected these demands and insisted on its democratic legitimacy. It offered the RUF amnesty and promises of reforms and inclusion in the government. The domestic and international pressures on the elected government to end the war and the military pressure mounted on the RUF by the pro-government CDFs and Executive Outcome created a favorable environment for a peace agreement. The RUF tacitly recognized the legitimacy of the government, and the government agreed to withdraw Executive Outcomes from Sierra Leone and absorb some RUF members into the military and government positions, most notably in the diplomatic service.[102]

The Abidjan Accord, signed on November 30, 1996, largely focused on disarmament and the causes of the war. The key elements of the accord included ceasefire, amnesty, disarmament, and reforms to hold the government accountable and promote economic development.[103] The international community, in conjunction with the belligerents, was to supervise the disarmament program. The accord called for the transformation of the RUF into a political party, electoral reform, the establishment of a human rights commission and an office of an ombudsman, and reform of the judiciary and police. It acknowledged that "there is a socio-economic dimension to the conflict which must also be addressed in order to consolidate the foundation of peace."[104] The agreement was to be implemented by the Commission for the Consolidation of Peace, comprised of the government and the RUF, while the international community was expected to provide financial and technical support. The UN was to immediately deploy international observers to supervise the disarmament process and the implementation of the agreement.

The Abidjan Accord led to a temporary lull in the fighting but failed to end the war. In retrospect, the intermittent cease-fires following the Abidjan Accord only gave the RUF an opportunity to reorganize and rearm. Though the government terminated its contract with Executive Outcome, most of the provisions of the agreement were not properly implemented. The disarmament process failed to proceed as planned, and the RUF continued to be a military organization instead of transforming into a political party. As such, members of the RUF were not integrated into the military and government as envisioned in the agreement. Moreover, the promised international support failed to be delivered, which hampered the disarmament process and transformation of the RUF into a political party. Apart from the logistical problems, Sankoh was reluctant to disarm, which led to growing internal and international skepticism about his commitment to peace. In March 1997, Sankoh was arrested in Nigeria on weapons-related charges and transferred to Sierra Leone in July 1998. He was charged with treason and remained in detention until 1999. His detention became a political ploy to destroy the RUF and force it to implement the peace agreement. However, his arrest caused some friction within the RUF and inadvertently strengthened his supporters and his mythical image of being a revolutionary leader within the RUF. Shortly after his arrest, a group of senior RUF members who were suspicious of his commitment to the peace process tried to replace him. The plan was thwarted by Sam Bockarie, the RUF's battlefield commander, who arrested some of the people plotting to replace Sankoh and reaffirmed the RUF's loyalty to him.[105] The Abidjan agreement was finally shattered by the military overthrow of the elected government by the AFRC, which changed the discourse in the peace process from reconciliation with the RUF to restoration of the elected government.

ECOWAS embarked on a diplomatic and military campaign to restore the elected government and defeat the AFRC and RUF. It successfully drove the AFRC and RUF from Freetown and restored the elected government but failed to defeat the RUF and AFRC, both of which retreated to the interior of the country and waged a bitter war against the government. The RUF vowed to avenge the detention of its leader and increased its brutal campaign against civilians, which climaxed with the January 1999 invasion of Freetown. The inability of ECOMOG to defeat the RUF and AFRC, the RUF's near success in taking over Freetown, and the alarming atrocities against civilians led to renewed and vigorous diplomatic efforts to negotiate a peaceful end to the conflict. The intensive international peace mediation effort, which began in February 1999, was led by ECOWAS and the UN with the support of the OAU, the Commonwealth, and the United States. Sankoh became a critical player in getting the RUF to negotiate with the government. During the crisis, Kabbah and international mediators regularly met with Sankoh and promised to release him in exchange for a cease-fire and genuine peace. Sankoh's calls for a cease-fire and peace negotiations were aired on the radio, but RUF commanders insisted on his release as a precondition for any cease-fire. In March 1999, Sankoh was taken to Lomé to meet with key RUF members and promote a peaceful solution to the conflict. Sankoh and other RUF members stayed in Lomé and participated in the peace talks, which resulted in the July 7, 1999, Lomé Peace Agreement, signed by Kabbah and Sankoh.

Unlike the Abidjan Accord, the Lomé Peace Agreement was largely about the distribution of power between the government and RUF and the election of a new government. The key parts of the agreement dealt with cease-fire, disarmament, restructuring of the military, inclusion of the RUF in the government, and transformation of the RUF into a political party.[106] While the government was desperate for a cease-fire and total disarmament, the RUF insisted on holding key positions in a broad-based government of national unity. The RUF was given four ministerial positions, including one senior position, and four deputy ministerial positions in an eighteen-member cabinet. In addition, RUF members were to be appointed to various parastatal, diplomatic, and civil service positions. Sankoh was named chairman of the powerful Commission for Management of Strategic Resources, National Reconstruction, and Development and accorded the status of vice president. This was a significant concession to the RUF, given the importance of diamonds in the war and economy at large. The cease-fire was to be monitored by the Cease-fire Monitoring Committee at the local level and the Joint Monitoring Commission at the national level, which would be chaired by UNOMSIL. A neutral peacekeeping force comprised of UNOMSIL and ECO-MOG was to disarm "all combatants of the RUF/SL, CDF, SLA and paramilitary groups."[107] The agreement also addressed practical political and social issues underlying the war. It gave a blanket amnesty to members of the RUF, AFRC, CDF, and ex-SLA and called for the release of all war prisoners and abductees. However, the UN representative signed the agreement with a disclaimer: "'The United Nations does not recognize amnesty for genocide, crimes against humanity, war crimes and other serious violations of international humanitarian law.'"[108] The parties agreed to review the constitution, establish a new impartial National

Electoral Commission, and create a human rights commission and a truth and reconciliation commission. The implementation of the agreement was to culminate with free and fair presidential and parliamentary elections.

The implementation of the agreement was to be monitored by the belligerents, international partners, and civil society. The last was viewed by some as being critical; one Ivoirian respondent noted, "We cannot have a national solution . . . without civil society" being involved.[109] The Commission for the Consolidation of Peace, comprised of two representatives of civil society and one representative each for the government, RUF, and parliament, was charged with implementing the agreement and promoting national reconciliation. Any discord about interpreting the agreement was to be resolved by the Council of Elders and Religious Leaders, made up of two members from the Inter-Religious Council of Sierra Leone and one member each for the government, RUF, and ECOWAS. At the international level, the Joint Implementation Committee, chaired by ECOWAS, was to periodically review the agreement's implementation and make recommendations to move the process forward. The international community was expected to provide generous financial and technical support for the implementation and postwar reconstruction.[110]

The implementation of the Lomé Peace Agreement was marred by extensive delays and mistrust. The biggest problem was disarmament, which the RUF was reluctant to do. Disarmament did not begin until late October 1999, and only 24,042 combatants (4,949 RUF, 10,055 AFRC/ex-SLA, and 9,038 CDF) were disarmed by May 15, 2000. Only 10,840 weapons were surrendered, and they were of low quality.[111] The unity government was not formed until November 1999. In the meantime, the alliance between the RUF and AFRC ruptured. Violations of the cease-fire and atrocities against civilians continued as the belligerents battled for strategic towns. UN peacekeepers continued to face serious difficulties and were attacked by the RUF and remnants of the disbanded AFRC. UNAMSIL became increasingly drawn into fighting the rebels in order to protect itself, the government, and civilians. The crisis took an unexpected turn on May 7, 2000, when RUF guards opened fired on civilians protesting at Sankoh's Freetown residence against his reluctance to abide by the Lomé Peace Agreement. Sankoh was finally captured by a mob on May 17, 2000, near his Freetown residence and handed over to the government and British forces. The international community refused to release him as the RUF demanded; instead, it asked the RUF to replace Sankoh with new leaders committed to peace. The RUF named Sesay, its field commander, as interim leader and negotiated the Abuja Ceasefire Agreements.[112] Another important development in the RUF leadership was the ousting of Bockarie, the notorious field commander. Reports indicate that he fell into disagreement with Sakoh, and ECOWAS leaders pushed for his removal from Sierra

Leone. Bockarie left Sierra Leone before Sankoh's arrest in May 2000. Numerous reports indicate that he stayed in Liberia with the consent of Taylor. Bockarie was indicted for war crimes in March 2003 and is presumed to have been killed in Liberia on the orders of Taylor shortly after being indicted.[113]

The November 2000 Abuja Ceasefire Agreement between the government and RUF was spearheaded by the ECOWAS Committee of Six on Sierra Leone. The agreement was essentially a public endorsement of the new RUF leadership and a recommitment to implement the Lomé Peace Agreement.[114] The RUF promised to return all items seized from UNAMSIL, while the government pledged to accelerate the restructuring of the military.[115] The agreement led to a significant reduction in fighting, but there was not much progress on disarmament and the transformation of the RUF into a political party. In May 2001, ECOWAS and the UN brokered the Abuja Ceasefire Review Agreement; this required the government to control the CDF, which had been violating the cease-fire, remove all impediments to the transformation of the RUF into a political party, and immediately and simultaneously disarm CDF and RUF combatants. The RUF promised not to impede the deployment of UNAMSIL and government structures.[116]

The change in RUF leadership, strengthening of UNAMSIL, presence of British forces, strong sanctions imposed by the UN in 2001 (Resolution 1343) against President Taylor of Liberia for his support of RUF, and ECOWAS outreach to RUF leaders created a real opportunity for peace. After the May 2001 agreement, disarmament significantly progressed. Around 75,000 former combatants were disarmed and demobilized by the end of 2001. Also, the RUF formed its political party.[117] All of these positive developments paved the way for the January 18, 2002 declaration of the end of the war and for the May 2002 elections to be held.

Peace Agreements in the Liberia Civil War

The international effort to build peace in Liberia effectively began with the deployment of ECOMOG on August 24, 1990. Prior to the deployment of troops, the anglophone-dominated Standing Mediation Committee of ECOWAS met in Banjul on August 7, 1990, and created the ECOWAS Peace Plan, which adopted the proposals of the Liberian Inter-Faith Mediation Committee and called for an immediate cease-fire, an ECOWAS intervention force (ECOMOG), a Liberian National Conference to set up an interim government, and legislative and presidential elections in June 1991. ECOMOG was created to restore security in Liberia at a time when the government of Doe was on the verge of collapse due to mounting military pressure from the NPFL. The intervention was opposed by the governments of Côte d'Ivoire and Burkina Faso, which supported the NPFL, and other francophone countries that preferred negotiation.[118] Several countries contributed troops, including Ghana, Guinea, Sierra Leone, and Gambia, but the majority of the four thousand troops were from Nigeria. The mandate of ECOMOG was to restore law and order and create conditions favorable for humanitarian operations and cease-fire negotiations. Upon its arrival, ECOMOG quickly secured the Freeport of Monrovia, a vital commercial and transportation facility. Doe and Prince Yormie Johnson saw the intervention as an opportunity to relieve the military pressure on their respective forces. In contrast, Taylor was strongly opposed to ECOMOG and saw it as impeding him from a military victory.[119] Despite the intervention and the establishment of an ECOWAS-backed IGNU headed by Amos Sawyer, the fighting continued, and the ECOWAS Peace Plan remained largely unfulfilled. One of the key problems was the refusal of the NPFL to participate in the formation of the IGNU. Instead, it established an alternative government, the National Patriotic Reconstruction Assembly Government (NPRAG), in its areas of control.

The protracted peace process in Liberia produced over a dozen agreements that quickly collapsed.[120] The first significant agreement to end the war was the Yamoussoukro IV Accord, signed by the IGNU, NPFL, and several West African states on October 30, 1991. It was engineered by ECOWAS under the auspices of the president of Côte d'Ivoire. Building on the previous agreements, it called for a cease-fire, encampment and disarmament of combatants, elections within six months, the formation of an elections commission and an ad hoc Supreme Court, and the restoration of normalcy in the border area of Sierra Leone and Liberia. It also renewed the mission of ECOMOG and charged it with disarming the combatants and supervising the implementation of the agreement. However, the agreement quickly collapsed, as the belligerents failed to respect the cease-fire or disarm. ULIMO was not a party to the agreement, creating further mistrust and impeding the disarmament process. The confrontation between ECOMOG and the NPFL over disarmament and ECOMOG's alleged bias toward ULIMO and the AFL continued to grow, while the fighting between the NPFL and ULIMO increased. In October 1992, the NPFL launched a major attack on Monrovia, Operation Octopus, which further embroiled ECOMOG in the fighting. Despite the UN arms embargo and the increase in ECOMOG troops, the flow of arms and fighting continued. In June 1993, around six hundred civilians were massacred near the town of Harbel. The deteriorating situation led to renewed diplomatic effort to end the conflict. In July 1993, ECOWAS and the UN convened peace talks in Geneva, leading to a cease-fire agreement and the Cotonou Peace Agreement.

The July 1993 Cotonou Accord between the IGNU, NPFL, and ULIMO was the most comprehensive peace agreement during the first phase of the Liberian civil war. Its implementation was to be supervised and monitored by ECOMOG and the UN Observer Mission (UNOM). ECOMOG was to be expanded to include African troops from outside the West African region. Moreover, the UN and the international community were expected to fund the full implementation of the peace agreement, especially the DDR, elections, and return of refugees and internally displaced persons (IDPs). The agreement called for a cease-fire starting on the seventh day after the signing of the agreement and granted general amnesty to all those involved in the conflict. The warring parties agreed to end the displacement of people, facilitate the delivery of humanitarian assistance and return of IDPs and refugees, release all detainees and prisoners of war, repatriate their foreign fighters, maintain their position, surrender their weapons, encamp their combatants in facilities established by ECOWAS, and disclose their combatants and weapons to ECOMOG and UNOM. Under the agreement, ECOMOG was given peace enforcement powers. In particular, it was empowered to disarm combatants and noncombatants, search for lost or hidden weapons, and defend itself. In addition, ECOMOG was asked to create buffer zones around Liberia's borders (or seal them if necessary) and supervise all ports of entry to prevent cross-border attacks, infiltrations, or importation of arms. UNOM was to monitor and supervise the disarmament and the encampment process. Cease-fire violations were to be reported to UNOM, which would investigate and rectify the matter or submit its investigative findings to the Violation Committee. A temporary JCMC was created to monitor the cease-fire until the arrival of the full contingents of UNOM and the expanded ECOMOG force.

On the political front, the Cotonou Agreement called for the establishment of a new transitional government within thirty days to replace the IGNU and the NPRAG. The transitional government was primarily charged with providing essential services and conducting general and presidential elections within six months, in accordance with the ECOWAS Peace Plan. The transitional government would consist of three organs: executive, legislative, and judiciary. Executive power was vested in the Council of State, which included one member each from the IGNU, NPFL, and ULIMO and two members selected from a pool of nine eminent Liberians evenly nominated by the three parties. The five-member council was to select a chairman and two vice chairmen. All decisions of the council were to be made by consensus. Cabinet posts were to be determined by the parties in consultation with one another. The extant structure of the Supreme Court was maintained, with ULIMO given the right to nominate a qualified person to fill the fifth seat, which was vacant at the time. The Transitional Legislative Assembly was to consist of thirty-five members (thirteen from IGNU, thirteen from NPFL, and nine from ULIMO). One of the ULIMO members was to be nominated as speaker. The critical part of the agreement was the general and presidential elections, which were to be held approximately seven months from the signing of the agreement. To ensure a free and fair election, people in leadership positions in the transitional government were disqualified from contesting the elections.[121] The Elections Commission was expanded to seven members, with ULIMO given the right to nominate the two new members.

Despite the expansion of ECOMOG, the deployment of UNOMIL, and the creation of the Liberia National Transitional Government (LNTG), the crisis continued. The belligerents disagreed over the composition of the LNTG and violated the cease-fire. Even when the LNTG was installed, its members remained under the control of their respective factions. At the same time, new and splinter armed factions emerged.[122] Given the impasse in implementing the Cotonou Agreement and the precarious political and military situation, Ghana spearheaded a renewed effort to revive the peace process. This effort led to the Akosombo Agreement, which supplemented and amended the Cotonou Agreement.

The September 1994 Akosombo Agreement was signed in Ghana by the NPFL, United Liberation Movement of Liberia for Democracy - Kromah (ULIMO-K), and Armed Forces of Liberia (AFL). The agreement prohibited parties from creating new or splinter groups and addressed the structural problems that rendered the LNTG ineffective. It strengthened the powers of the LNTG by giving it an active role in disarmament and encampment issues, monitoring the ports of entry, enforcing the peace agreement, and rebuilding the new Liberian army. It also gave the LNTG greater flexibility in making decisions and modified the composition of the government. In particular, each party was to have one member in the Council of State, which was vested with executive powers during the transitional period. The remaining two members, representing unarmed Liberians, were to be prominent Liberians. The Liberian National Conference (LNC) was to appoint one of the two members, and the NPFL and ULIMO would appoint the second.[123] The council was to elect its chairman and two vice chairmen within seven days of the signing of the agreement. All decisions of the council were to be made by a simple majority. The agreement called for the executive head and the deputies of ministries, autonomous agencies, and public corporations to come from different parties. The agreement allowed the parties to review the status of their appointees. The TLA was expanded by thirteen members appointed by the Council of States. These individuals were to be eminent Liberians selected through the Ministry of Internal Affairs from each of the thirteen counties. The transitional government was to last for about sixteen months, and general and presidential elections were scheduled for October 10, 1995.

As with previous agreements, the Akosombo Agreement did not end the conflict. Renewed fighting erupted between NPFL and ULIMO-K, while friction within the NPFL led to the formation of the National Patriotic Front of Liberia-Central Revolutionary Council (NPFL-CRC). The agreement languished as the factions formed new alliances and continued to fight and attack civilians and international humanitarian personnel. Following the failure to implement the Akosombo Agreement and the emergence of a new factional alignment in the war, renewed efforts were made to bring peace to Liberia. Acting in his capacity as chairman of ECOWAS, Jerry Rawlings made another effort to resolve the conflict. On December 21, 1994, eight parties to the conflict signed two agreements in Accra, which on one hand clarified and expanded some provisions of the Akosombo Agreement and on the other hand committed the parties that were not involved in the agreement to its terms and its subsequent clarification. The Agreement on the Clarification of the Akosombo Agreement was signed by the AFL, NPFL, and ULIMO-K, while the Lofa Defense Force (LDF), LPC, National Patriotic Front of Liberia-Central Revolutionary Council (NPFL-CRC), ULIMO-J, and LNC signed the Acceptance and Accession Agreement. Despite the renewed commitments, the fighting continued as the various faction leaders sought to strengthen their positions. West African leaders again struggled to keep the framework of the Cotonou Agreement alive by embarking on a series of deals with the warlords and clarifying and amending the Cotonou Agreement.

The Abuja Accord was spearheaded by Nigeria and Ghana and signed by leaders of the NPFL, ULIMO-K, LPC, AFL, ULIMO-J, LDF, NPFL-CRC, and LNC on August 19, 1995. It was largely an effort by West African states to bring the leaders of the various factions into the defunct LNTG. The parties to the conflict agreed to a cease-fire and the composition of the LNTG. Executive power was vested in a six-member Council of State comprised of leaders of the major armed groups and civil society (Charles Ghankay Taylor, Alhaji G. V. Kromah, George E. S. Boley Sr., Oscar Jaryee Quiah, Chief Tamba Tailor, and Wilton Sankawulo). Sankawulo was designated chairman, while the others were vice chairmen of equal status. The agreement maintained the allocation of executive positions established under the Cotonou Agreement. Given the new military reality on the ground, the allocations of the former IGNU were given to the LPC/COALITION. Also, members of the smaller armed factions were given ministerial or senior government positions. ULIMO-J was specifically given the top positions in three ministries and four public corporations/autonomous agencies and one additional minister of state without portfolio position. It was also allocated the deputy positions in four ministries and eight public corporations and autonomous agencies. The reconfigured LNTG was to last for twelve months and be replaced with a duly elected government. ECOWAS, OAU, and the UN were to monitor the operations of the Elections Commission. Members of the transitional government wishing to contest the elections were required to step down from office three months before the elections. The chairman of the Council of State was not allowed to contest the first presidential and parliamentary elections.

Despite the efforts to include the faction leaders in the transitional government, the agreement was not properly implemented, and some of the factions were not happy with the way it had been negotiated. In addition, implementation of the agreement was hampered by a lack of resources and international support. Factions clashed as they tried to guard their territories and consolidate their powers within the transitional government. The volatile security situation and lack of cooperation delayed the elections until July 1997. The elections were also marred by intimidation. Taylor and his NPP won the elections but failed to unite the country and build trust. Aside from the problem of election irregularities, it is widely believed that Liberians deliberately voted for Taylor out of fear that he would not accept defeat.[124] By voting for him, they were taking a gamble that other warlords would accept defeat and trusting Taylor to act responsibly and end the war. Others have argued that the elections were rigged in favor of Taylor. Clearly, the elections failed to bring peace to Liberia.

Though the elections brought some sense of calm and gave Taylor international recognition as a head of state, he continued to undermine peace in Liberia and its neighbors. At the same time, the war in Sierra Leone was intensifying. Taylor's support of the RUF became increasingly annoying to the international community, which had been working hard to bring peace to Sierra Leone. His forces were also accused of intruding into Guinea. At home, he terrorized opponents and suppressed democracy. Taylor lost credibility as a peace partner within the international community and among his former opponents during the Liberian civil war. Soon, it became apparent that he was the main obstacle to peace. The international community imposed sanctions and embargoes on Liberia in order to put pressure on Taylor. By 2000, some of the rebel groups in the Liberian civil war and Taylor's opponents within the NPFL had regrouped and formed Liberians United for Reconciliation and Democracy (LURD). From their bases in Guinea, Taylor's opponent launched attacks on Liberia with the aim of overthrowing him. The LURD attack on the NPP government of Taylor marked the beginning of the second phase of the Liberian civil war. As the fighting intensified, a section of the LURD broke away and formed Movement for Democracy in Liberia (MODEL). By March 2003, rebel forces opposed to Taylor were within ten kilometers of Monrovia.

It was within this deteriorating political, military, and humanitarian situation that the international community stepped up its peace mission in Liberia. One major development was the establishment of the International Contact Group on Liberia (ICGL) in 2002, which was a critical step in building solid support for a robust international peace mediation and enforcement in Liberia that went beyond the efforts of ECOWAS.[125] The invigorated peace process aimed to immediately halt the fighting and forge a comprehensive political settlement that would lead to democracy. Moreover, peace in Liberia was also widely seen as critical to securing the nascent peace in Sierra Leone. ECOWAS, with the support of the UN, the AU, and the ICGL, spearheaded the peace initiative. The Liberian peace talks were held in Ghana from June 4 to August 18, 2003, and mediated by former Nigerian President General Abdulsalami Abubakar, who had skillfully managed the Nigerian transition from a brutal dictatorship to democracy. The international community was now willing to take a firm stance against those believed to be impeding peace and deploy a strong international force. The new strategy was built on the lessons of the international intervention in Sierra Leone. Militarily, ECOWAS and the United States were willing to deploy forces to stabilize the situation. At the same time, the UN had capable troops in Sierra Leone that were readily transferred to Liberia. Politically, there was a growing agreement within the international community on the need to force Taylor out of Liberia and eventually try him for war crimes, practically in the same way Sankoh was removed from the Sierra Leone peace process. Taylor was indicted for war crimes and sent into exile during the peace talks. This unprecedented action against Taylor, who was a sitting president, sent a clear message of international resolve to the other warlords. Members of the Liberian civil society were also determined to resist the warlords.[126] Most notably, women's groups, who were not invited to the peace talks, defiantly traveled to the Accra. They informally partook in the negotiations and exerted cultural, moral, and psychological pressures on the leaders of the armed groups to reach a meaningful peace agreement.[127] The tough stance of the international community in the Liberian peace process and the war fatigue among Liberians created a conducive environment for the adoption and enforcement of an agreement. The talks led to a cease-fire agreement, which was followed by a comprehensive peace agreement. Unlike previous deals, the 2003 peace agreement ended the war and was implemented as generally envisioned. Sufficient international forces were quickly deployed, and the international community provided the critical technical and financial support. Elections were held, and a new government was installed in 2005 according to the timetable stipulated in the agreement. The UN and other international agencies engaged in postwar reconstruction until the end of the international intervention mission in 2018.

The cease-fire agreement was signed by the Government of Liberia (GOL, i.e., Taylor's NPP government), LURD, and MODEL on June 17, 2003. The belligerents agreed "to refrain from committing any act that might constitute or facilitate a violation of the ceasefire" and committed to an inclusive dialogue that would result in a peace agreement within thirty days.[128] In addition, they pledged security guarantees to allow humanitarian assistance and free movement of people. The cease-fire agreement called for the deployment of an International Stabilisation Force (ISF) and the creation of a Joint Verification Team (JVT) and a Joint Monitoring Committee (JMC). The JVT and JMC were to be led by ECOWAS and include an equal number of representatives of the warring factions as well as representatives of the UN, AU, and ICGL. The JVT would document the locations of the various combat units and their equipment, while the JMC would supervise and monitor the cease-fire.

The Comprehensive Peace Agreement (CPA) was signed by the three warring factions (GOL, LURD, and MODEL) and eighteen political parties in Accra on August 18, 2003.[129] Several civic organizations present at the peace talks signed as witnesses.[130] The accord reaffirmed the June 17, 2003, cease-fire agreement, which had been repeatedly violated, and pledged "a total and permanent cessation of hostilities forthwith."[131] The parties agreed to release all political and war prisoners, respect international humanitarian law, and provide security guarantees for humanitarian agencies. This time, the CPA did not grant a blanket amnesty; the issue of amnesty was to be addressed by the incoming transitional government. Some, however, did not agree with the objectives of the CPA-related amnesty. As one respondent argued, "Without justice, we still have problems in this country. You know why? Those who have committed the worst crimes in this country have always moved on to become key leaders and have always been able to escape justice. It would be very difficult to achieve justice. Every time we talk about war crime code and we say no, you're not coming here, and we see war infraction leaders are the ones who call for TRC, Truth and Reconciliation Commission, because they want some sort of amnesty. Amnesty, that's what they're fighting for, you know."[132] Nonetheless, the pivotal parts of the agreement addressed the role of the international community, disarmament process, transitional government, and elections. The agreement spelled out an implementation schedule that would culminate with a multiparty election in October 2005.

The CPA gave the international community significant powers in the implementation of the agreement. It retained the JMC and called on ECOWAS and other international power brokers to establish an Implementation Monitoring Committee to "ensure effective and faithful implementation of the Peace Agreement by all the Parties."[133] The involvement of the international community was deemed critical not only for brokering the peace agreement but also for ensuring its successful implementation. As such, "The Parties call on ECOWAS, the UN, the AU and the International Contact Group on Liberia (ICGL), to use their good offices and best efforts to ensure that the spirit and content of this Peace Agreement are implemented in good faith and with integrity by the Parties."[134] In collaboration with the UN, AU, and ICGL, ECOWAS was tasked with mediating any disputes that might arise in the application and interpretation of the agreement. ECOWAS was to immediately deploy an interposition force "to secure the ceasefire, create a zone of separation between the belligerent forces and thus provide a safe corridor for the delivery of humanitarian assistance and free movement of persons."[135] The force was also tasked with ensuring the security of senior military officials, political leaders, and persons involved in the implementation of the agreement and laying the groundwork for the DDR program. The ECOWAS interposition force was to become part of the ISF operating under a UN Chapter VII mandate. The main objective of the ISF, which became known as UNMIL, was to support the transitional government and assist in the implementation of the peace agreement. Its tasks included disarming combatants, alleviating humanitarian problems, building a new Liberian army, and facilitating elections. The international community was expected to provide proper financial and technical assistance for the implementation of the agreement, especially in regard to the transitional government, DDRR program, and restructuring of the army and elections. It specifically called for the "establishment of a consolidated United Nations Mission in Liberia that will have the resources to facilitate the implementation and coordination of the Political, Social, Economic and Security assistance to be extended under this Agreement."[136]

The CPA called for the disbanding of all irregular forces and the disarmament, demobilization, rehabilitation, and reintegration of all combatants. The disarmament process was to be coordinated by the National Commission for Disarmament, Demobilization, Rehabilitation and Reintegration (NCDDRR) with the support of the ISF and other international bodies. Under the agreement, the NCDDRR would be comprised of representatives from relevant NTGL agencies, GOL, LURD, MODEL, ECOWAS, the UN, the AU, and the ICGL. The actual disarmament of combatants was to be conducted through a DDRR program. The agreement also called for the restructuring of the AFL into a professional force that would be appropriate for a democratic state. Qualified members of the warring factions were eligible to join the new AFL. To ensure long-term stability, the agreement stipulated that the new force "be composed without any political bias to ensure that it represents the national character of Liberia."[137] In addition, the National Police Force and other security agencies, such as the Immigration Force, Special Security Service, and custom security guards, were to be restructured with the help of the UN Civil Police Component and other international agencies. The DDRR and restructuring of the security forces were critical steps in the implementation of the agreement and creating the conditions for the planned October 2005 elections.

Like the previous agreements, the CPA called for a transitional government and established a framework for the composition of an all-inclusive government.[138] Unlike all the previous agreements, however, in this case, the transitional government was to be dominated by the political parties and civil society organizations instead of the armed factions in the war. It would consist of an executive (NTGL), a legislature (National Transitional Legislative Assembly or NTLA), and the judiciary.[139] The path to peace was predicated on successful legislative and presidential elections that would produce a legitimate government to replace the NTGL and NTLA. The mandate of the NTGL would run from October 14, 2003, to January 16, 2006. Its primary responsibility was to ensure the scrupulous implementation of the peace agreement. It was specifically charged with implementing the cease-fire, developing political and rehabilitation programs, contributing to the internationally supervised elections, and promoting national reconciliation.

Under the agreement, the NTGL was to be comprised of mainly technocrats from a broad section of Liberian society selected through a consultative process and headed by a transitional chairman. The critical positions were the transition chairman and vice chairman; both were allocated to the political parties and civil society, which would nominate three candidates for each position, while the warring factions would select one of the candidates for each position on the basis of consensus. The transitional chairman, transitional vice chairman, and principal cabinet ministers of the NTGL were ineligible to stand for the 2005 elections. The agreement allocated to each of the three warring factions five ministries, while the remaining six went to the political parties and civil society. Each of the warring parties would also receive two deputy ministerial positions within their five allocated ministries. Four public corporations were allocated to each of the three warring factions, and the remaining ten corporations were given to the political parties and civil society. The warring factions were each given two autonomous agencies/commissions, with the remaining sixteen allocated to the parties and civil society. The names of nominees were to be sent to the transitional chairman, who would then forward them to the NTLA for confirmation.

The agreement also spelled out the composition of the NTLA and the process for selecting members of the Supreme Court. The seventy-six-member unicameral NTLA was to include twelve members each from the GOL, LURD, and MODEL, eighteen members from the political parties, seven members from civil society and special interest groups, and one member from each of the fifteen counties selected in consultation among the various Liberian stakeholders. The speaker and deputy speakers, elected by the NTLA, would be ineligible to contest the next elections. All decisions of the NTLA would require at least 51 percent of the entire membership of the assembly. The agreement maintained the existing structure of the judiciary, but the current members of the Supreme Court were to be replaced by new appointees. New judiciary members were to be nominated by the National Bar Association and appointed by the transitional chairman subject to the approval of the NTLA. All members of the Supreme Court serving under the transitional government were ineligible to contest the 2005 elections.

The peace agreement was largely hinged on elections. A successful election would mark a real end of the war and lay the foundation for democracy and postwar reconstructions. As such, the peace process was supposed to create favorable conditions for elections and build the capacity of the elected governments. To ensure a credible election, the agreement carved a significant role for civilians and tried to minimize the power of armed groups in the operations of the transitional government and conduct of the elections. The agreement postponed the scheduled October 2003 elections to October 2005, called for the re-demarcation of constituencies, and requested the international community to "conduct, monitor, and supervise" the next elections.[140] The new National Elections Commission (NEC), appointed by the transitional chairperson with the advice and consent of the NTLA, was to be independent and operate in accordance with UN standards. In order to consolidate the peace and ensure good governance, the agreement established several independent national commissions, including the Independent National Commission on Human Rights, the TRC, the Contract and Monopolies Commission, NCDDRR, and the Governance Reform Commission.

Peace Agreements in the Ivoirian Civil War

The peace process in Côte d'Ivoire had two separate yet complementary tracks. The first was the internationally driven peace mediation, which produced five major agreements but stalled after the failure of the Pretoria Agreements.[141] The second was the Ivoirian-driven peace negotiation, which emerged in earnest after the failure of the Pretoria Peace Agreement and led to the 2007 Ouagadougou Peace Agreement. While the Ouagadougou Peace Agreement led to the cessation of violence and produced a relatively stable unity government, the dispute over the results of the 2010 presidential election shattered the peace, resulting in a renewed war that ended with the capture of Gbagbo in April 2011. The 2010 presidential election crisis undermined the Ivoirian peace process and invigorated the dormant international peace mediation and enforcement effort. Ironically, the peace that was achieved after the capture of Gbagbo has again been undermined by Ouattara's controversial third term in office. As has been the case since the conflict started in 1993, Côte d'Ivoire is again in a state of negative peace that is akin to the previous state of no war, no peace.

The international peace mediation in Côte d'Ivoire was spearheaded by ECOWAS, the UN, the AU, and France. ECOWAS and the UN saw the conflict as a serious regional security problem, especially given the speculation of foreign involvement, fragile security in neighboring countries, and economic centrality of Côte d'Ivoire in the region.[142] The AU supported the ECOWAS peace mediation efforts and often acted as a neutral mediator when ECOWAS efforts stalled.

France, which has deep-rooted economic and security interests in Côte d'Ivoire, also treated the crisis with urgency. African countries such as Togo, Mali, Angola, Nigeria, South Africa, Ghana, Senegal, and Burkina Faso also became involved in the mediation effort.

Though the internationally mediated peace agreements did not resolve the conflict, intervention contained the conflict and ameliorated the humanitarian situation. It created opportunities for dialogue and laid the groundwork for the Ouagadougou Agreement. With the collapse of the agreement, robust international intervention became even more critical in ensuring an end to the conflict. The international intervention departed from the traditional peace mediation and peacekeeping approach that had plagued the previous international effort to resolve the conflict and became a critical factor in the capture of Gbagbo. The previous effort had relied heavily on the typical ingredients of the internationally mediated agreements in African conflicts, namely cease-fire, power sharing, disarmament, human rights guarantees, and elections. The path to peace was predicated on successful democratic elections.[143] This recipe failed in Côte d'Ivoire because it did not pay sufficient attention to citizenship which was a central cause of the war, and the north-south power divide.[144] With the exception of the Linas-Marcoussis Agreement, the internationally engineered accords were often mute on citizenship and instead focused on the interim distribution of power, disarmament, and elections. The end results were successive failed peace agreements and continued violence.

As soon as the fighting erupted, ECOWAS and France took a proactive posture to end the conflict. Peace talks were hastily held in Accra, Lomé, and Paris.[145] During the January 2003 Paris Conference, the belligerents signed the Linas-Marcoussis Agreement.[146] However, the Young Patriots immediately held a demonstration against the agreement, which it saw as a French ploy against the government of Gbagbo. Ironically, this blemished agreement became the cornerstone of the subsequent agreements negotiated by the international community. Not surprisingly, Gbagbo repeatedly demonstrated distaste for international solutions to the conflict.[147] The Linas-Marcousis Agreement identified the key citizenship issues in the conflict but did not give it proper attention.[148] The main part of the agreement dealt only with the formation of a Government of National Reconciliation (GNR), comprised of representatives of each of the signatories to the agreement and a consensus prime minister. The GNR's critical mission was to restructure the security forces and organize credible elections. The annex to the agreement spelled out the agenda of the GNR, which included citizenship, electoral, land tenure, media, human rights, and economic reforms and a disarmament program. It also called for a cease-fire, amnesty, and the restoration of state authority.

The underlying citizenship issue in the war was relegated to the annex of the agreement. The Linas-Marcousis Agreement treated the issue of citizenship simply as a struggle for power and an administrative problem.[149] As a power issue, the agreement focused on the citizenship and residency eligibility criteria for the presidency, which it tried to defuse by modifying the controversial provision of the constitution. The agreement questioned the language of the 2000 Constitution, which incorporated many of the laws that were used to disqualify Ouattara from contesting presidential elections. The agreement recommended that a candidate "must have only Ivoirian citizenship and have a father or a mother born Ivoirian"[150]; this replaced the language in Article 35 of the 2000 Constitution, which required that a candidate "must be Ivoirian by birth, born of a father and of a mother themselves Ivoirians by birth."[151] It called for clarification of the conditions under which Ivoirian citizenship could be revoked to avoid ambiguity in the eligibility for the presidency. While this was intended to reconcile the two divergent notions of citizenship, the agreement inadvertently reduced the issue to a mere struggle for power. It failed to address the political and social contentions about the definition and proof of citizenship and, more broadly, the north-south divide. Similarly, the Linas-Marcoussis Agreement recognized the 1961 and 1972 Ivoirian citizenship laws as generous and well-drafted but pointed to problems in their application that led to the wrongful denial of citizenship rights. The government was asked to simplify the application of the laws, suspend its identification program, and establish a National Identification Commission to supervise a new identification system. To ease the identification problem, the agreement called for the elimination of the residency permit requirement for ECOWAS citizens. With respect to national identification, it touched on citizenship but treated it as an administrative problem that could be rectified by the proper application of extant laws. The agreement again failed to address the social construction of citizenship, provide a political solution, and more broadly address the north-south divide through creative institutional design to minimize political marginalization of northerners by southerners or vice versa.

The belligerents retreated to their own definitions of citizenship and squabbled over birth records and nationality certificates, poisoning the whole agreement.[152] The Linas-Marcoussis Agreement collapsed under the weight of conflicting understandings of citizenship. Gbagbo's government insisted on a narrow legal definition of citizenship, official birth records, and verifiable ancestral ties to Ivoirian villages. Northerners challenged the spirit of the interpretation of the laws. They saw it as insensitive to the chasms in birth records, urban roots of many Ivoirians, and social dislocations emanating from internal migration. Southerners continued to view citizenship in terms of deep-rooted ancestry dating back to at least the early colonial period—mostly along the lines of jus sanguinis.

Furthermore, they made a distinction between citizens who had deep-rooted ancestry in Côte d'Ivoire (i.e., indigenous Ivoirians) and those whose ancestors settled in Côte d'Ivoire during the late colonial period or thereafter (i.e., Ivoirians of immigrant ancestry). Northerners tied citizenship to place of birth (jus soli) and settlement, which did not necessarily go back to the precolonial era. They attacked indigeneity as an unrealistic legal or political construct in a country created out of French colonialism.[153] Northerners saw the distinctions between purported indigenous Ivoirians and Ivoirians of immigrant ancestry as state-sponsored ethnic discrimination that infringed on their citizenship and wrongly lumped them with immigrants from neighboring countries simply because they shared the same cultures.[154]

The formation of the GNR stalled despite the appointment of Seydou Diarra as prime minister.[155] Tensions grew over allocations of ministerial posts and the specific powers of the prime minister.[156] The ECOWAS Contact Group on Côte d'Ivoire tried to resolve the stalemate. In March 2003, the parties to the Linas-Marcoussis Agreement signed the Accra II Agreement,[157] ironically renewing their commitment to the flawed Linas-Marcousis Agreement. The conflict was once again treated as a mere struggle for power among the political elite. Gbagbo's authority as head of state, commander in chief, and guarantor of the constitution and republic was reaffirmed as a gesture to diffuse the legitimacy issue surrounding his controversial election. Reciprocally, he agreed to apply the terms of the Linas-Marcousis Agreement, most notably by facilitating the formation of the GNR and delegating power to the prime minister. The belligerents agreed to create a fifteen-member National Security Council comprised of the president, the prime minister, a representative of each of the signatories to the agreement, the military, the gendarmerie, and the police. The council was to oversee the contentious ministries of defense and interior.

Following the Accra II Agreement, direct talks were held between the FANCI and FAFN and the UN-deployed peacekeepers.[158] The agreement stalled as violent clashes continued between opposition and government supporters, while the rebels controlled the north. ECOWAS, the AU, and the UN spearheaded a new peace initiative. The belligerents and leaders from sixteen African states (including twelve heads of state) met in Accra at the end of July 2004 and signed the Accra III Agreement.[159] The meeting was an attempt to exert immense regional pressure on the Ivoirian factions to implement the previous agreements, but it failed to establish a new peace path, as it was bogged down by lingering references to the defunct Linas-Marcoussis Agreement. Gbagbo was emphatically asked to implement the Linas-Marcoussis provisions on eligibility for the presidency by the end of September 2004. In turn, all the factions pledged to support the adoption of the legal reforms envisioned under Linas-Marcoussis by the end of August

2004. Gbagbo agreed to issue a decree specifying the powers of the prime minister in accordance with the agreement. The belligerents committed to start the disarmament by October 15, 2004, in line with the terms of the Linas-Marcoussis Agreement and the agreements at Grand Bassam and Yamoussoukro. The GNR was asked to set a timetable for the restoration of the state administration and public services throughout the country.

After the Accra III Agreement, the National Assembly made efforts to pass the reforms envisioned in Linas-Marcoussis. However, the military situation deteriorated as government forces bombed rebel positions and inadvertently hit French military bases in November 2004. French retaliation against government forces sparked violent anti-French protests, which worsened the precarious situation. The April 2005 Pretoria Agreement, mediated by President Thabo Mbeki on behalf of the AU, brought together Gbagbo, Guillaume Soro, Henri Bédié, Ouattara, and Diarra.[160] It focused on the urgent military and electoral issues. The centerpiece of the military component was disarmament and dismantling the militia. The chiefs of staff of FANCI and FAFN were to immediately implement the National Disarmament, Demobilization and Reintegration plan and make specific recommendations for integrating the armies and restructuring the security forces in line with Linas-Marcoussis. The agreement underscored the need to hold a presidential election in October 2005, which would be followed by legislative elections. The composition of the Independent Electoral Commission (IEC) was modified. Each of the signatories to the Linas-Marcoussis Agreement would have two representatives to the Central Commission of the IEC, with the understanding that six would be from the FN. The Bureau of the Central Commission would consist of one representative of the president, the president of the National Assembly, and each of the ten parties to the Linas-Marcoussis Agreement. The predictable doom of the agreement was evident in the failure to come to a consensus on eligibility requirements for the presidency. Though Gbagbo later announced that any candidate nominated by the parties to Linas-Marcoussis would be eligible to participate in the presidential election, the underlying citizenship issue was unresolved. Like the ECOWAS-brokered agreements, the Pretoria Accord was anchored in the flawed Linas-Marcoussis Agreement and failed to pay sufficient attention to the citizenship issue or structural power imbalance between the north and south.[161]

The Pretoria Agreement languished as violence continued, disarmament stalled, elections became elusive, and the government remained dysfunctional.[162] Prime Minister Diarra was replaced with Charles Banny in December 2005. Banny, too, faced insurmountable obstacles in implementing peace agreements that barely touched the core issues in the conflict. Ivoirians were getting weary of internationally brokered agreements as mediation options waned. The

Ouagadougou Agreement was hatched within this quagmire.[163] The agreement was preceded by two key developments that altered the political calculus in Côte d'Ivoire. First, there was a clear sense of war fatigue among the masses and realization by the elite that outright military victory was illusive.[164] This reality was echoed in conciliatory remarks by Gbagbo and Soro. In his December 19, 2006, address to the nation, Gbagbo appealed for direct dialogue with the rebels. Soro responded positively in his New Year speech.[165] The other development was the adoption of UN Security Council Resolution 1721, which significantly expanded the power of the prime minister.[166] Gbagbo, whose legitimacy largely rested on UN-backed extensions of his expired electoral mandate, saw Resolution 1721 as a serious threat to his presidency. In addition to the internal dynamics, there were shifts in the attitude of President Blaise Compaoré of Burkina Faso, who was suspected of supporting the rebels. Compaoré understood that peace in Côte d'Ivoire would ensure the flow of remittances to Burkina Faso and repair his tarnished image as a supporter of warlords. The combination of a sense of vulnerability, war fatigue, the lack of a clear path to military victory, and the shifting position of Burkina Faso provided fertile ground for compromise. The Ouagadougou Agreement was predicated on assumed mutual trust among the belligerents and the facilitator, a spirit of dialogue, and parity between the government and FN.[167] This tacit power-sharing understanding between Gbagbo and Soro was buttressed in the code of conduct provisions and generous amnesty covering offenses relating to national security committed since September 17, 2000.[168]

The Ouagadougou Agreement departed from the formula devised in Linas-Marcoussis and marked a monumental shift in the peace process.[169] In contrast to all the other agreements, the Ouagadougou Agreement was spearheaded by Ivoirians; it specifically noted that Gbagbo personally asked President Compaoré in January 2007 to facilitate direct talks between his government and the FN. Most remarkably, the agreement directly addressed the underlying citizenship issue and provided a behind-the-scenes power-sharing model. From the start, the belligerents acknowledged that "the identification of the Ivoirian and foreign populations living in Côte d'Ivoire is a major concern. The absence of a clear and standard identity document and of individual administrative documents attesting to the identity and nationality of persons is a source of conflict."[170] By recognizing this bare fact, Ivoirians demonstrated a profound understanding and appreciation of the core issue of citizenship. Moreover, the agreement identified a clear mechanism for resolving the citizenship issue. However, the issue of the north-south power divided did not receive any durable institutional solution; instead, it was addressed with an informal short-term solution in the form of a national unity government that would last until elections were held. As with the citizenship issue, what could have been a more durable solution would have been a creative institutional arrangement to ensure equity and the balance of power between northerners and southerners.

To resolve the citizenship issue, the protagonists agreed to provide credentials to all Ivoirians who did not have proper documents and establish a reliable identification system.[171] Under the agreement, mobile courts (*audiences foraines*), presided over by a judge, would issue substitute birth certificates (*jugements suppletifs*) to "individuals born in Côte d'Ivoire who have never been registered in a registry office."[172] These individuals would go for a hearing at the mobile court corresponding to their place of birth during a three-month grace period. Birth registers that were lost or destroyed in registry offices were to be reconstituted. New forgery-proof identity documents were to be issued to Ivoirians and foreigners. Foreigners who had a birth certificate or substitute birth certificate and a document from their consulate affirming their nationality would be issued residence permits. Ivoirians would receive their new national identity cards through the standard identification process or "identification on the basis of the new electoral roll."[173] Under the standard identification, Ivoirians who had a certificate of nationality and a birth certificate or substitute birth certificate would be issued the new national identity card. All other Ivoirians would receive their national identity cards after they were registered on the electoral roll. Ivoirians who had reached the age of eighteen and held a birth certificate or substitute birth certificate were entitled to register on the electoral roll. National identity cards would be issued after the electoral roll was validated. The IEC, with the help of the National Institute of Statistics and a contracted technical agency, would be responsible for creating an accurate electoral roll.[174] The agreement envisioned the use of biometrical data to ensure accurate identification.

Though the agreement did not define Ivoirian citizenship, it provided a mechanism for resolving the Ivoirité citizenship grievances.[175] Articles 6 and 7 of the extant nationality law defined an Ivoirian citizen as any person born to at least one Ivoirian parent or someone born in Côte d'Ivoire to unknown parents.[176] There were provisions for the acquisition of citizenship by adoption, marriage, naturalization, or reintegration. The citizenship (i.e., Ivoirité) dimension of the Ivoirian conflict centered on two issues. First was the attempt to narrowly define eligibility for the presidency on the basis of ancestry. This change was enshrined in Article 35 of the 2000 Constitution, which required that a candidate for the presidency "must be Ivoirian by birth, born of a father and mother who themselves are Ivoirians by birth."[177] The second issue was about documentation of place of birth and ancestry in order to ascertain Ivoirian citizenship and eligibility for the presidency. Successive post-Houphouët-Boigny governments insisted that only individuals who could provide official documents, approved by the government in power, to prove their place of birth and the Ivoirian roots of at least one of their parents were eligible to receive nationality certificates. Similarly, candidates for the presidency had to provide official documents, approved by the government in power, to prove their place of birth and the Ivoirian roots of their mother and father. Northerners complained about the gaps in birth records and inherent difficulty of providing complete records about their ancestors. The governments of Bédié, Guéï, and Gbagbo insinuated that many northerners were falsely claiming Ivoirian citizenship, while northerners complained that these governments were maliciously refusing to issue certificates of nationality to qualified Ivoirian citizens from the north. Ouattara's saga with successive post–Houphouët-Boigny governments, which claimed that he was not an indigenous Ivoirian who met the strict citizenship criterion for the presidency, became an embodiment of the conflict—both the denial of citizenship to and the political marginalization of northerners.[178] Southerners viewed Ouattara as the son of an immigrant falsely posing as a native Ivoirian in order to take power from indigenous Ivoirians. In contrast, northerners saw Ouattara as a typical case of southerners' attempts to define northerners as immigrants in their own country and disenfranchise them, thereby entrenching their political marginalization in the post-Houphouët-Boigny era. Though the restrictive criteria for the presidency did not directly affect the vast majority of northerners, as very few people ever aspire to be president, the refusal to issue them nationality certificates became a serious concern to northerners in general. Moreover, the refusal to let Ouattara stand for the presidency galvanized northern support of Ouattara and made his candidacy both a symbolic and an existential fight for northerners' status as autochthones and citizens of Côte d'Ivoire with equal rights as southerners.

The Ouagadougou Agreement provided flexibility in the mechanism for proving one's citizenship, thereby resolving the citizenship dimension of the conflict in a manner that was reasonable and consistent with Ivoirian law.[179] This worked in part because northerners did not necessarily challenge the citizenship laws; their main concern was with the application of the laws and documentation that proved citizenship. Under the agreement, the mobile courts would accept documents and testimonies in their deliberations. Petitioners who did not have documented evidence could bring two witnesses to attest to their place of birth and/or the citizenship of at least one of their parents.[180] Petitioners no longer needed to go to their ancestral village; instead, they could file a petition at their place of birth. This mechanism was designed to fill gaps in the records and acknowledge the social dislocation resulting from internal migration. It provided a realistic path for Ivoirians to prove their place of birth and their parents' citizenship and thereby establish their legitimate claim to Ivoirian citizenship. This identification mechanism, coupled with the provision that extended citizenship to persons born in Côte d'Ivoire to unknown parents, resolved the problematic distinction between indigenous Ivoirians and Ivoirians of immigrant ancestry. With the implementation of the identification program, northerners were able to prove that they were Ivoirians by birth, just as southerners were.

The Ouagadougou Agreement also addressed the military issues that stalled the previous agreements and provided a means for continuous dialogue. The belligerents agreed to restructure the two armed forces and set up an Integrated Command Structure under the joint command of the chief of staff of FANCI and chief of staff of FAFN. The integrated command was charged with disarming and reintegrating combatants, ensuring free movement of people and goods, and providing security. They agreed to remove the zones of confidence manned by French and UN peacekeepers, facilitate free movement across the country, and redeploy the administration in the north. The agreement created two high-level bodies—the Permanent Consultation Framework (PCF) and the Evaluation and Monitoring Committee (EMC)—to facilitate the continuation of direct talks. The PCF, comprised of Gbagbo, Soro, Ouattara, Bédié, and Compaoré, was the organ of supervision and permanent dialogue. The EMC, which monitored implementation of the agreement, included the facilitator and three representatives each for the government and FN. The two parties could jointly extend membership to other Ivoirian political forces. The facilitator could also invite observers and members of the international community. This framework for continuous dialogue proved invaluable in adjusting the implementation schedule and keeping the agreement intact until the presidential election was held in 2010.

One critical element not mentioned in the text of the Ouagadougou Agreement was the power-sharing deal between Gbagbo and the FN. This covert part of the agreement addressed the power dimension of the conflict. The deal gave Gbagbo the presidency, while the FN got the office of prime minister. Normally, Côte d'Ivoire has a presidential system of government. Under Article 41 of the 2000 Constitution, for example, "The President is the exclusive holder of the executive power. He appoints the Prime Minister, [the] Head of Government, who is responsible to him. He terminates his functions. The Prime Minister animates and coordinates the governmental action. On the proposal of the Prime Minister, the President of the Republic appoints the other members of the Government and determines their attributions. He terminates their functions under the same conditions."[181] However, the power-sharing deal that accompanied the Ouagadougou Agreement limited the powers of the president over the prime minister and the cabinet and provided for a balanced power relation between the president and the prime minister. The prime minister was the head of a cabinet comprised of the FN, FPI, and other political parties. As agreed to in the power-sharing deal, Gbagbo nominated Soro to be prime minister shortly after signing the Ouagadougou Agreement. The arrangement not only satisfied the political egos of Gbagbo and Soro but also gave them considerable influence over the political future of the country. Gbagbo remained preseident until the 2010 election. As a powerful prime minister, Soro was in a strong position to shape the implementation of the agreement and deliver to northerners their citizenship documents. More importantly, Soro, who was too young to be eligible to be president, was seen as a formidable and reliable placeholder for northerners in the ongoing battle for the presidency.[182] While Gbagbo remained a central part of the new power-sharing arrangement, Ouattara was ostensibly on the outside. However, he remained the northern presidential candidate in waiting. Moreover, there was strong speculation that Ouattara was closely associated with the FN, though he denied any ties to the rebel group and the civil war.[183] However, the collaboration between Ouattara and the FN and the military support the FN accorded him since the disputed 2010 presidential elections pointed to the existence of strong ties between the two.[184] Even if there were no formal ties between them, their political positions and demands in the conflict were remarkably similar. The FN fought to end the Ivoirité citizenship laws and policies that disenfranchised Ouattara and other northerners and disqualified him from contesting the presidency.

The March 2007 Ouagadougou Agreement and the power-sharing deal between the government and the FN was very promising until a dispute erupted over the 2010 presidential election. After the signing of the agreement, security greatly improved, and the prospects for durable peace became real. Significant progress was made in implementing the agreement; the fighting stopped, a fairly stable government was formed, disarmament progressed, substitute birth certificates were issued to a significant number of people, the identification and voter registration process progressed, and presidential elections were eventually held in late 2010.[185] By March 2008, the mobile courts had issued 372,810 supplement birth certificates.[186] The hearings, which occurred intermittently, were relaunched in August 2008, giving more people the opportunity to receive their documents. Voter registration commenced in September 2008. By the end of the year, there were around three thousand registration sites, and approximately 2.8 million people had registered.[187] By May 14, 2009, more than six million voters had been registered.[188] The final voter list certified by the UN SRSG on September 24, 2010, had 5,725,720 people.[189] On the military side, disarmament progressed, albeit slowly. By the end of 2008, 11,769 of the 34,678 profiled FN combatants had gone through the cantonment exercise.[190] Some FN combatants were integrated into the security services, but disagreement over salaries and ranks slowed the process.[191]

Despite the major gains, the Ouagadougou Agreement was plagued by implementation delays, distrust among the belligerents, and strategic manipulation of the implementation process in order to unfairly gain or retain political power.[192]

These problems led to repeated postponement of the presidential election, which was not held until October 31, 2010.[193] During the first round, Gbagbo received the highest number of votes (38% of the votes cast), Ouattara came in second (32%), and Bédié came in third (25%). The second round of the election between Gbagbo and Ouattara was peacefully held. On December 2, 2010, the Election Commission declared Ouattara the winner with 54.1 percent of the votes, while Gbagbo received 45.9 percent. However, Gbagbo refused to accept the result and appealed to the Constitutional Court, which overturned the election results on the grounds of fraud and declared Gbagbo the winner. Ouattara refused to accept the decision on the grounds that the court was biased and controlled by Gbagbo loyalists. Both Ouattara and Gbagbo declared themselves president and formed separate administrations. Acting on its authority to certify the results of the presidential elections, the UN SRSG issued a statement on December 3, 2010, certifying the results of the second round of the election announced by the Election Commission.[194] The UN, ECOWAS, the AU, the EU, and the United States all endorsed Ouattara as the elected president of Côte d'Ivoire and called on Gbagbo to concede defeat. Côte d'Ivoire again fell into a state of turmoil. There were two competing governments, the international community imposed sanctions on Gbagbo and the country, and major financial organizations withdrew. Violence between the supporters of Gbagbo and Ouattara significantly increased.[195] The rapprochement between the FPI and the FN ended, and the Ouagadougou Agreement fell apart, reigniting the war. Sporadic fighting between the military, which was loyal to Gbagbo, and civilians supporting Ouattara continued. On February 14, 2011, fighting erupted between the army and the ex-rebels in the village of Teapleu in the western part of the country. This marked a major breach of the six-year-old cease-fire between the government and the FN, and the fighting rapidly escalated as the rebels seized control of the western town Zouan-Hounien.[196]

The Ouagadougou Agreement was a milestone in the conflict because it clearly identified the key citizenship grievance and outlined a mechanism for rectifying it. However, the agreement failed to properly deal with the north-south power dimension of the conflict in a durable way. It also missed the opportunity to redesign the state in a way that would consider the inherent ethnic and regional divisions that exacerbated the struggle for political power, provided only a temporary solution to the power struggle, and maintained the neoliberal election path to peace. The agreement was anchored in a temporary power-sharing deal between Gbagbo and the FN and the principle of free and fair multiparty presidential elections. The temporary power-sharing deal was expected to halt the fighting and provide an environment for the presidential election, which was expected to take place within ten months of the signing of the agreement.[197] The power-sharing deal was a temporary structural arrangement that balanced power between the president and the prime minister—and, in essence, between southerners represented by Gbagbo and northerners represented by Soro. As it was a solid structural arrangement, neither Gbagbo nor the FN could change the balance of power, and it brought relative peace to the country and paved the way for the 2010 presidential election. However, the deal was a temporary arrangement that was to end as soon as the election was conducted. The postwar political arrangement was anchored in a neoliberal presidential system of democracy, which was inadequate to ease the fears of political marginalization that poisoned relations between northerners and southerners. More generally, we hold that power sharing (which clearly has its pitfalls and problems) has advantages over presidential regimes. Nonetheless, it must be remembered that the various actors involved in the negotiations have a certain level of agency during the process of postwar institution building. The choices that are made are their own.[198]

Neither northerners nor southerners were willing to accept defeat in the presidential election, as both saw the outcome of the election as winner-takes-all politics. The Ouagadougou Agreement failed to carve out a creative institutional arrangement to ensure political inclusion of the two groups, irrespective of who would win the election. This problem became very clear during the violence that surrounded the 2010 presidential election and during the 2020 presidential election, when Ouattara altered the constitution so that he could continue to stay in power and exert northern domination. The irony is that northerners are now subjecting southerners to the same political oppression they suffered when southerners were in power. The challenge for Côte d'Ivoire is figuring out how to create inclusive institutional arrangements to ensure that the constituent ethnic and regional groups are adequately represented in the institutions of power, namely the executive, legislative, judiciary, and security forces.

Despite Gbagbo's apparent loss in the 2010 election, the reality is that he had significant support in the country, particularly in the south. The dichotomous support, which privileged Gbagbo among southerners and Ouattara among northerners, was evident in the results of the second round of the 2010 presidential elections. Notwithstanding the allegations of fraud and the contested nature of the results, the regional distribution of the results from the nineteen regions and the city of Abidjan showed a clear pattern of ethnic and regional voting.[199] Gbagbo won 2,107,055 votes, while Ouattara won 2,483,164 votes (4,590,219 total). In the heavily populated mosaic capital city of Abidjan (in the south), Gbagbo won 740,693 votes, while Ouattara received 686,427 votes. Seventy percent of Gbagbo's total vote came from seven core southern regions (including the city of Abidjan), while 20 percent came from four central regions (Montagnes, Haut Sassandra, Marahque, and Moyen Comoe) and the northeastern region of Zanzan.[200] Similarly, the majority of Ouattara's votes came from areas where northerners were heavily concentrated (the core north and pockets of the regions in the center, northeast, and south). Thirty percent came from the four core northern regions (Denguele, Worodougou, Savanes, and Bafing), the center-northern region of Valle Du Bandama, and the Baoule regions of Lacs and N'zi-Comoe.[201] Another 29 percent came from the central regions (Montagnes, Haut Sassandra, Marahque, and Moyen Comoe) and the northeastern region of Zanzan, while 28 percent came from Abidjan. Gbagbo won five regions (with at least 62% of the votes in those regions), which are all in the south. He won 84 percent of the votes in Agneby, 70 percent in Lagunes (excluding Abidjan), and 67 percent in Fromager. Similarly, Ouattara overwhelmingly won in all the northern regions; he received 97 percent of the votes in Denguele, 94 percent in Worodougou, 93 percent in Savanes, 85 percent in Valle Du Bandama, and 82 percent in Bafing. In the main Baoule regions, he won 80 percent in Lac and 63 percent in N'zi-Comoe.[202] The election results were only reasonably close (within the range of 43% to 57%) in the central regions of Montagnes, Haut Sassandra, Marahque, and Moyen Comoe, the northeastern region of Zanzan, the Krou-dominated region of Bas Sassandra in the southwest, and Abidjan. Interestingly, these six regions (excluding Abidjan) were the ones where Bédié or other third-party candidates got a significant amount of the votes during the first round. The pattern of ethnic and regional voting was similar in both rounds.

During the first round of the 2010 presidential election, Ouattara won a huge majority of the votes in the four core northern regions and a majority of the votes in the center-northern region of Valle du Bandama—93 percent in Denguele, 87 percent in Worodougou, 85 percent in Savanes, 73 percent in Bafin, and 50 percent in Vallee du Bandama. Similarly, Gbagbo won big majorities in six core southern states—74 percent in Agneby, 59 percent in Lagunes (excluding Abidjan), 55 percent in Sud-Comoe, 53 percent in Fromager, 53 percent in Moyen Cavally, and 47 percent in Sud-Bandama. Bédié also won big majorities in the heavily dominated Baoule regions, garnering 69 percent of the vote in Lac and 66 percent in N'zi-Comoe.[203]

After the first round, both Ouattara and Gbagbo sought the support of Bédié's Baoule people, who are mostly in the eastern and central regions. While Ouattara hoped to gain a significant share of the Baoule vote, Gbagbo counted on being the southern candidate who would gain the support of the Baoule and others in the south.[204] Not surprisingly, Gbagbo saw Ouattara's new gains outside of the core northern regions as largely the result of fraud. In essence, he refused to concede a significant portion of the southern vote to Ouattara and insisted on being the true heir of Bédié's votes. While the result of the second round of the election may affirm the fundamental principle of majority rule typical of neoliberal democracy, it risked alienating southerners, undermining the legitimacy of the democratic process, and further destabilizing the state, since the majority of southerners would not see a government headed by Ouattara and dominated by northerners as representative of them. This problem became very clear in the problematic 2020 elections. This is the dilemma of multiparty democracy in divided countries where people vote largely along ethnic and regional lines.[205] This precarious situation makes fluid political accommodations and power sharing difficult to achieve and increases the need for durable structural arrangements to maintain political balance between the north and south and among the major ethnic groups.

The peace in Côte d'Ivoire is back in limbo. The promising Ivoirian-driven peace process eventually collapsed at the very end. At the same time, the international community was caught up in a situation where it could hardly be a neutral peace mediator, given its commitment to the UN-certified election result. As the international community exhausted its traditional peace recipes, it publicly supported Ouattara and used force against Gbagbo. ECOWAS and the AU stepped up their efforts to persuade Gbagbo to concede defeat. As soon as the dispute over the election results erupted, the AU sent former South African President Mbeki to mediate and convince Gbagbo to concede defeat. The AU's mediation effort was continued by Kenyan Prime Minister Rail Odinga, who was appointed as the AU special envoy.[206] At the same time, ECOWAS dispatched a high-level delegation comprised of the presidents of Benin, Cape Verde, and Sierra Leone to offer Gbagbo a chance to peacefully step down without humiliation.[207] Most of the initial international mediation hinged on the threat of force to remove Gbagbo if he failed to peacefully relinquish power. However, this threat was resisted by countries such as Ghana and Uganda, and doubts grew over the ability of ECOWAS to muster the necessary force to take on the Ivoirian military. Most of the international effort focused on applying sanctions against Gbagbo and potentially offering him some kind of political compromise. In late January, the AU set up a panel of five heads of state drawn from each region of the continent to "come up with a legally binding settlement within a month."[208] The panel, which was comprised of the presidents of South Africa, Tanzania, Chad, Mauritania, and Burkina Faso, visited Côte d'Ivoire. However, Gbagbo's supporters opposed the inclusion of Compaoré, as they saw him as a backer of Ouattara.[209] The international peace mediation strategy banked on high-level diplomatic pressure from African heads of states and steep economic sanctions directed at Gbagbo's power base. Gbagbo offered to do a recount or fresh elections but his offers were rejected. In the end, the rebel forces, supported by the international intervention forces, captured Gbagbo and affirmed Ouattara's presidency. Gbagbo was eventually tried and acquitted for war crimes at ICC.

CONCLUSION: NEW HUMANITARIANISM
AND INSTITUTIONAL DESIGN

The insecurity in West Africa and the international response to the conflicts raise important questions about the outbreak of civil wars, their security and humanitarian implications, and international approaches to peacebuilding. In particular, the civil wars point to three important lessons.

The first lesson is about the link between stalled democratic transitions and civil wars. In all three countries, the civil wars occurred around the period of democratization. In Liberia, the war broke out shortly after the rigged democratization process, during which Doe manipulated the results of the 1985 elections and declared himself winner. In Sierra Leone, the APC government was reluctant to implement democratic reforms. In both countries, state decay and the lack of a meaningful democratic path to a regime change strengthened the case for an armed rebellion against the government. The argument for democracy became a legitimate cover for the rebellions, even though they were antithetical to democracy. In Côte d'Ivoire, the civil war was born out of the stalled democratization process that began with the prodemocracy movement in 1990. Attempts to rig multiparty elections led to the dangerous infusion of nationalism and ethnicity into politics, sparking the civil war. While democracy itself is not the problem, all three cases show the dangers of stalled democratization and the limits of winner-takes-all multiparty democracy.

The second lesson relates to the destabilizing effects of civil wars on vulnerable neighboring countries. Civil wars may not only inspire dissidents in neighboring countries under dictatorship to take up arms against their government; they can also provide some of the manpower, logistics, and networks necessary to begin an armed rebellion. This is most evident in the interconnections between the civil wars in Sierra Leone and Liberia. The flow of combatants, weapons, and blood diamonds between the RUF and the NPFL and the role of Taylor in supporting the RUF are clear indications of how Liberia became a launchpad and fuel for the Sierra Leone civil war. Rebel groups in Côte d'Ivoire have also reportedly recruited combatants from the civil wars in Liberia and Sierra Leone. The destabilization of neighboring countries also occurs through the flow of refugees and the unplanned return of immigrants. During the wars, each of the three countries saw a sudden increase in refugees that was far beyond their capacity to absorb. The huge number of refugees and IDPs created significant humanitarian challenges for the host countries and the international community.

The third lesson relates to the potential for successful international intervention driven by new humanitarianism and the limitations of international peace intervention. The international community rightly approached the conflicts in

West Africa as regional security and humanitarian problems. This allowed for not only the coordination of diplomatic efforts and peacekeeping missions but also a holistic approach to the security and humanitarian crises. This approach proved to be extremely useful in Liberia and Sierra Leone. However, Côte d'Ivoire points to the limitations of international intervention and an overcommitment to traditional peace recipes. Even more importantly, the long-term success of international intervention depends on the extent to which core causes of conflict are addressed and the nature of the solutions. This issue of creative institutional design seems to be lacking in all three cases. Hence, postwar democracy gains can quickly evaporate under the weight of corruption, poor governance, and ethnic and regional politics.

PEOPLE-CENTERED LIBERALISM AND INTERNATIONAL STATEBUILDING

INTRODUCTION

The embrace of the doctrine of new humanitarianism has to a large degree settled some debates about sovereignty, morality, and human security in the international security discourse. It has also paved the way for policy experimentation in international development and postwar politico-institutional design. New humanitarianism's insistence on the duty of the international community to address the root causes of violence in war-torn countries has elevated intervention into international statebuilding. The UN and its various agencies have been key actors in this effort. As one United Nations Development Programme (UNDP) official saw it, the "big issues of security, peace, and then of course . . . statebuilding, reconstruction . . . [are] utterly the mandate of this, the UN mission. It is more importantly that the agencies have a longer term engagement in the conflicts in the sub-region."[1] Thus, international statebuilding has become the praxis of new humanitarianism, and the real challenge is figuring out not only how to end civil wars but also how to build democratic and economically viable states in war-torn countries, maintain peace, and improve the well-being of the people. New humanitarianism's vision of political and economic development is not necessarily a new idea in international development. However, it does bring a new morality rooted in liberalism and social well-being into the discourse on development policies that sees civil wars as opportunities to build better states.[2]

The practical question that has come out of the doctrine of new humanitarianism is how to implement international statebuilding and redirect orthodox international development policies from their macroeconomic indicators and geopolitical orientations toward meaningful opportunities that impact people's well-being, enhance human security, and promote sustainable development.[3] Traditional development policies in Africa have been influenced by Cold War ideological and geopolitical struggles that tolerated dictatorship and focused on the export of raw minerals and cash crops.[4] While traditional development policies have technically been viewed as "aid" to African states, they did not meaningfully contribute to the development of these states or the well-being of the masses. The elitist and dependency-driven approach to international development failed to improve the African states' political or economic conditions; in reality, it contributed to the phenomenon of state decay. By the end of the Cold War, African states were characterized by dictatorships, huge debts, shrinking economies, high mortality rates, low levels of literacy, and poor infrastructure. This orthodox international development frame was shattered with the end of the Cold War.

PEOPLE-CENTERED LIBERALISM: THE CONCEPTUAL AND POLICY FRAME OF INTERNATIONAL STATEBUILDING

The first significant ideological and policy change in the international development frame for African countries came at the end of the Cold War, when Western powers and financial institutions demanded that African countries introduce neoliberal economic reforms to reduce government spending and open their markets to more competition.[5] In particular, the International Monetary Fund (IMF) insisted on the strict implementation of structural adjustment programs as a precondition for new loans. This change in policy not only imposed the neoliberal economic doctrine on African states but also signaled a new relation between African rulers and Western powers. Structural adjustment programs across the continent caused major social and economic hardship, which instigated the movement for democratic reforms during the early 1990s.[6] As the neoliberal policies of the IMF failed to produce the desired results, international development policies shifted toward insistence on democracy, good governance, and sustainable human development. This shift did not abandon liberalism but instead led to a *people-centered liberalism* approach to international statebuilding.[7] The World Bank, the IMF, and Western powers attributed the economic failures of Africans states to poor political leadership, a lack of democratic accountability, and restrictive economic policies. As such, democratic reforms and good governance were added to the demands for neoliberal economic reforms as preconditions for international development assistance.[8]

Neoliberalism and Human Development: UN, Work Bank, and IMF

The core international development institutions, notably, the UN, World Bank, and IMF, all tied economic development to political reforms toward free and fair multiparty elections.[9] Such elections were seen as both a way to promote economic development and as the true actualization of the 1948 Universal Declaration of Human Rights and the 1966 International Covenant on Civil and Political Rights.[10] Building on the Commission on Human Rights Resolution 1989/51 of March 7, 1989, and its own Resolution 44/146 of December 15, 1989, the UN General Assembly passed Resolution 46/137 on December 17, 1991. This resolution states that "periodic and genuine elections are a necessary and indispensable element of sustained efforts to protect the rights and interests of the governed and that, as a matter of practical experience, the right of everyone to take part in the government of his or her country is a crucial factor in the effective enjoyment by all of a wide range of other human rights and fundamental freedoms, embracing political, economic, social and cultural rights."[11] While the language of the resolution was also saliently directed at condemning apartheid, it did underscore the UN's commitment to pushing for democratic reforms and opened the door for significant UN involvement in conducting multiparty elections in developing countries. In particular, Resolution 46/137 endorsed the UN secretary general's request to "designate a senior official in the Offices of the Secretary-General to act as a focal point . . . who would assist the Secretary-General to coordinate and consider requests for electoral verification."[12] The resolution also asked the secretary general to allocate a small number of staff and other resources to support the designated senior official. This led to the establishment of the UN Electoral Assistance Unit (UNEAU) in 1992.[13] Since 1991, the UN has been very active in promoting multiparty democracy and helping organize elections in Africa and other developing countries. Between 1991 and 2002, for example, eighty-nine countries requested UN electoral assistance; sixty-eight of those (including forty in Africa) received electoral assistance from the UNDP.[14]

The UN's commitment to democracy and good governance was reinforced in the September 2000 UN Millennium Declaration, in which world leaders stated: "We will spare no effort to promote democracy and strengthen the rule of law, as well as respect for all internationally recognized human rights and fundamental freedoms, including the right to development."[15] The declaration led to the UN Millennium Development Goals (MDG), project which developed an action plan containing eight goals, also known as the MDG Indicators, "to reverse the grinding poverty, hunger and disease affecting billions of people."[16] Goal 8 of the MDG Indicators was to develop a global partnership for development. The first target of Goal 8 (Target 8A) was to "develop further an open, rule-based, predictable, nondiscriminatory trading and financial system (includes a commitment to good governance, development, and poverty reduction—both nationally and internationally)."[17] Target 8A became a critical measure of the progress toward democratic consolidation and quality of governance in developing countries.

The MDG Indicators as a whole were critical measures of the extent to which developing countries progressed toward sustainable human development and what the Institute for Economics and Peace and recent studies refer to as *positive peace*.[18]

The democracy and good-governance principle filtered deeply into the international development discourse and, along with free-market reforms, became part of the wider notion of liberalization promoted by Western powers and financial institutions.[19] Collectively, democracy, good-governance, and free-market reforms were expected to lead to sustainable human development and positive peace. On September 29, 1996, the IMF Interim Committee issued the Partnership for Sustainable Global Growth declaration, which states that the IMF "attaches particular importance to," among other neoliberal principles, "promoting good governance in all its aspects, including by ensuring the rule of law, improving the efficiency and accountability of the public sector, and tackling corruption, as essential elements of a framework within which economies can prosper."[20] In 1997, the IMF released "The Role of the IMF in Governance Issues: Guidance Note." The document specified "improving management of public resources through reforms covering public sector institutions (e.g., the treasury, central bank, public enterprises, civil service, and the official statistics function), including administrative procedures (e.g., expenditure control, budget management, and revenue collection); and supporting the development and maintenance of a transparent and stable economic and regulatory environment conducive to efficient private sector activities (e.g., price systems, exchange and trade regimes, and banking systems and their related regulations)" as two spheres in which the IMF could contribute to "good governance (including the avoidance of corrupt practices)."[21]

The World Bank's policies on liberalization and good governance were embodied in the Worldwide Governance Indicators (WGI) project (1996–2009), which reported individual and aggregate governance indicators for 213 countries. The specific indictors were voice and accountability, political stability and absence of violence, government effectiveness, regulatory quality, rule of law, and control of corruption. The first indicator in particular measured the extent to which countries were progressing toward consolidated democracies that ensure civil rights and free and fair multiparty elections. One of the key shifts in international development policies was the promise to help countries that were making meaningful reforms toward economic and political liberalism and good governance while reducing or cutting aid to countries that were failing to make such progress. Hence, the WGI and MDG Indicators became critical in shaping how individual African countries were viewed by international development agencies and donor governments. Other notable measures of governance include the Freedom House's Freedom in the World Report and the Ibrahim Index.[22]

With the shift toward economic liberalization, democracy, and good governance in the international development debate came the discourses on sustainable development and human development, which evolved into the notion of sustainable human development,[23] an idea that can be traced back to the report of the World Commission on Environment and Development, *Our Common Future*, presented to the UN in 1987. The report, which is commonly referred to as the *Brundtland Report*, made an argument for a more holistic approach to human well-being in which economic and social development policies are positively integrated with environmental policies. The report introduced the notion of *sustainable development*, which it defined as "development that meets the needs of the present without compromising the ability of future generations to meet their own needs." The definition centered on "the concept of 'needs,' in particular the essential needs of the world's poor, to which overriding priority should be given" and "the idea of limitations imposed by the state of technology and social organization on the environment's ability to meet present and future needs."[24] While most of the initial focus has been on the interconnection between economic and social development and the environment, one of the key conceptual contributions of the report is its system approach to human well-being. This approach considers environmental, technological, economic, and social factors in the development of countries and their impacts on the quality of living conditions. The broader notion of sustainable development argues that just as environmental factors are interconnected with the economic well-being of humans, so is economic well-being interconnected with the social system. As such, human well-being rests on the positive interconnection among a variety of areas, most notably the natural environment, the economy, health, education, and so on. As the report states, "The satisfaction of human needs and aspirations . . . [is] the major objective of development. The essential needs of vast numbers of people in developing countries for food, clothing, shelter, jobs are not being met, and beyond their basic needs these people have legitimate aspirations for an improved quality of life. A world in which poverty and inequity are endemic will always be prone to ecological and other crises. Sustainable development requires meeting the basic needs of all and extending to all the opportunity to satisfy their aspirations for a better life."[25]

In a similar way, the notion of human development presented a people-centered and system approach to well-being that is concerned with both basic needs satisfaction and participation. The idea of human development emerged in 1990 out of the UNDP's *Human Development Report*. The report took a more holistic approach to development that deviated from conventional approaches to economic growth and human welfare, viewing it both in terms of "the production and distribution of goods and the expansion and use of human capacities," and emphasized the availability of "choices—on what people should have, be and do to be able to ensure their own livelihood."[26] In essence, it defined human development as "a process of enlarging people's choices. The most critical ones are to lead a long and healthy life, to be educated and to enjoy a decent standard of living. Additional choices include political freedom, guaranteed human rights and self-respect."[27]

The notions of sustainable development and human development converge on their emphasis on needs and the holistic nature of human well-being. As needs satisfaction expands from the privileged class to the wider citizenry and its impacts on the environment grow, the question of sustainability becomes even more central. These two notions of human well-being have merged into what is now termed *sustainable human development*.[28] As Sudhir Anand and Amartya Sen argue, "There is, in fact, no basic difficulty in broadening the concept of human development . . . to accommodate the claims of future generations and the urgency of environmental protection."[29] The 1996 *Human Development Report* expanded the notion of human development to include "protection of the life opportunities of future generations . . . and . . . the natural systems on which all life depends."[30] However, "this safeguard of future prospects has to be done without sacrificing current efforts toward rapid human development and speedy elimination of widespread deprivation of basic human capacities."[31] Anand and Sen anchored the concept of sustainable human development in the principles of universalism and distributive equity. Sustainability, they argue, is "a matter of distributive equity, that is, of sharing the capacity for well-being between present and future generations in an acceptable way—a way that neither the present generation nor the future generations can readily reject."[32] In essence, the notion of sustainable human development states that "the promotion of human development in the contemporary world must be integrated with the safeguarding of its potential for the future. . . . The moral value of sustaining what we now have depends on the quality of what we have, and the entire approach of sustainable development directs us as much toward the present as toward the future."[33]

The economic and political discourses of the 1990s led to a unique convergence of liberalism with more holistic notions of human well-being, governance, and development that has been referred to as *people-centered liberalism*.[34] People-centered liberalism begins with firm commitments to neoliberal economic and political principles but moderates their practical excesses with distributive and social justice. Rights, which are typically attributed to the individuals, are reframed to include the categories of citizens whose rights have not been met under the individualistic conception of rights. In this sense, rights are approached from both individualistic and collectivistic perspectives. Under people-centered liberalism, free-market and multiparty liberalism dovetail with the more holistic notions of good governance and sustainable human development to produce international development policies that demand political and economic liberalization while at the same time centering the outcomes of such policies on improving the quality of life of the vast majority of people and expanding their participation in consumption and decision-making.[35] This people-centered liberalism approach is evident in the new international development assistance regime, most notably the Poverty Reduction Strategy Paper (PRSP).

People-Centered Liberalism: Aid, Governance, and Trade

The people-centered liberalism approach to international development promised to give more assistance to countries that were making meaningful efforts to liberalize their economies, adopt multiparty politics, and promote good governance while allowing them to define their own needs and priorities for development. People-centered liberalism was embodied in several initiatives aimed at helping the poorest countries in the world, especially those ravaged by civil war.[36] In 1996, the IMF and World Bank launched the Heavily Indebted Poor Countries (HIPC) Initiative. HIPC was intended "to reduce to sustainable levels the external debt burdens of the most heavily indebted poor countries."[37] In September 1999, the IMF established the Poverty Reduction and Growth Facility (PRGF) program. PRGF was replaced with the Extended Credit Facility (ECF) program. Both PRGF and ECF were intended to help countries move "toward a stable and sustainable macroeconomic position consistent with strong and durable poverty reduction and growth" and serve as a catalyst for additional foreign aid.[38] Under the Multilateral Debt Relief Initiative (MDRI) launched in 2005, the Group of 8 "proposed that three multilateral institutions—the IMF, the International Development Association (IDA) of the World Bank, and the African Development Fund (AfDF)—cancel 100 percent of their debt claims on countries that have reached, or will eventually reach, the completion point—the stage at which a country becomes eligible for full and irrevocable debt relief—under the joint IMF-World Bank enhanced Initiative for Heavily Indebted Poor Countries (HIPC Initiative)."[39] By December 16, 2010, for example, thirty-two countries had benefited from MDRI, including twenty-six sub-Saharan African countries.[40] Though the actual positive economic impact of these initiatives on Africa's development is not entirely clear, they actually set new standards for African governments seeking international development assistance from Western governments and financial institutions.

The eligibility criteria for these programs rested on neoliberal economic and political reforms and good governance. These expectations were articulated in the Poverty Reduction Strategy Papers (PRSPs) that countries were required to adopt. The PRSP concept was approved in December 1999 by the executive boards of the IMF and the World Bank as a new policy framework for funding and bank lending to poor countries. In particular, PRSP was intended to be "the basis for official external debt forgiveness under the Heavily Indebted Poor Country (HIPC) Initiative, begun in 1996, and subsequently as a pre-condition for financing from the IMF under the Poverty Reduction and Growth Facility (PRGF) and from the Bank's International Development Association (IDA) concessional lending facility. . . . [and] an instrument which all donors, including the UN, can use to plan and coordinate their own assistance strategies and budgets."[41] The same principles of liberalization and good governance in the PRSP were embodied in the UN Development Assistance Frameworks (UNDAF), which was the strategic framework for UN operational support, especially in achieving the MDGs, at the country level. As the UNDG stated, PRSP is "a crucial instrument for macro-economic and sectoral planning. As such, the PRSP will have a major impact on the work of the UN and will be critical in achieving the Millennium Development Goals (MDGs). In some cases, the PRSP will be the only national planning document on poverty reduction."[42] PRSPs and UNDAFs became the key templates for the people-centered liberalism approach to international development assistance and peacebuilding in African countries such as Sierra Leone, Liberia, and Côte d'Ivoire. PRSPs and UNDAF became the cornerstones for promoting liberalization, sustainable human development, and positive peace in these countries.

Nearly all African countries introduced economic and political reforms during the 1990s, in part to meet the new liberalization and good-governance preconditions for international development assistance. While a few countries, such as Benin, Zambia, and Ghana, quickly made meaningful reforms, many made only minimal changes and dragged the process on. In countries such as Sierra Leone, Liberia, Côte d'Ivoire, and the Democratic Republic of Congo (DRC), the lack of meaningful reforms dovetailed with salient political grievances to produce brutal civil wars. Despite the mixed approaches and results from the reforms, a new sense of African responsibility for good governance and development emerged in Africa. This sense of responsibility, which mirrored people-centered liberalism, was reflected in the New Partnership for Africa's Development (NEPAD) initiative created by the African Union (AU) in 2001. NEPAD sought to be "a radically new intervention, spearheaded by African leaders to pursue new priorities and approaches to the political and socio-economic transformation of Africa."[43] One of NEPAD's key programs was Economic and Corporate Governance.[44] NEPAD acknowledged that the delivery of high quality programmes and projects to promote Africa's development and regional integration can only be realised in an environment that permits good economic and corporate governance.[45] NEPAD focused on enhancing management, procurement processes, and accountability and creating transparent government policies. The cornerstone of NEPAD's Economic and Corporate Governance program was the African Peer Review Mechanism (APRM), which was "a mutually agreed programme, voluntarily adopted by the member states of the African Union, to promote and re-enforce high standards of governance."[46] APRM focused on four areas: democracy and political governance, economic governance, corporate governance, and socio-economic development. The underlying theme of all the areas was the promotion of democratic and accountable systems of governance and a transparent and ethical leadership that benefits the people. The review process itself is conducted by three organs of the APRM—the Country Review Mission Team, the Panel of Eminent Persons, and the Committee of Participating Heads of State and Government. Though the effectiveness of NEPD has been questioned, its existence underscored the need for people-centered liberalism in African economic development.[47]

People-centered liberalism was also reflected in the works of nongovernmental organizations. One notable actor in this effort has been the Mo Ibrahim Foundation. The foundation had two key programs aimed at directly impacting the quality of governance and leadership at the highest level of the state. First is the Ibrahim Prize, which "is awarded to a democratically elected former African Executive Head of State or Government who has served their term in office within the limits set by the country's constitution, has left office in the last three years, and has demonstrated excellence in office." The prize "consists of US$5 million over 10 years and US$200,000 annually for life thereafter."[48] It has been awarded to at least seven people (include the honorary award to Nelson Mandela) and was really intended to promote democracy by creating an incentive for African leaders to abide by the rules of free and fair multiparty elections and serve ethically. The second program was the Ibrahim Index, which measures the quality of governance based on four indicators: safety and rule of law, participation and human rights, sustainable economic opportunity, and human development.[49] The index was intended to be a tool for assessing the quality of governance in each African state and stimulating a constructive discourse on governance and development. Both programs sought to promote good governance in Africa by providing incentives to leaders and a tool for differentiating countries striving to improve governance from those not making sufficient progress.

Another aspect of people-centered liberalism in African development is the "aid" debate, which mirrors the economic liberalization and good-governance discourses. In her provocative book, *Dead Aid*, Dambisa Moyo rhetorically asks, "But has more than US$1 trillion in development assistance over the last several decades made African people better off? No. In fact, across the globe the recipients of this aid are worse off; much worse off. Aid has helped make the poor poorer, and growth slower. Yet aid remains a centerpiece of today's development policy and one of the biggest ideas of our time."[50] Moyo's critique of the aid regime and orthodox international development assistance amplifies other criticisms of the traditional approach to African development, which has left many African countries with huge debts and corrupt governments.[51] Her argument for a shift from aid to alternative development financing mechanisms that rely on financial markets, investment, trade, and microfinancing as a solution for Africa's development crisis is anchored in the belief that bad governance and overregulation are the primary impediments to development there. Notwithstanding aid's limitations, other economists continue to see its positive role, albeit with modifications.[52] As Jeffrey Sachs and John McArthur candidly point out, "Everybody that deals with aid wants to promote financial transparency and market-led growth, not aid dependency."[53] People-centered liberalism does not reject aid as a tool for promoting African development; rather, it seeks to redesign aid in a way that can promote liberalization, good governance, and sustainable human development and avoid excessive debt burdens. As such, aid has been redefined to emphasize trade and poverty reduction through entrepreneurship and strategic investment in sustainable human development.

This trade-oriented approach to aid fits well with the people-centered liberalism approach to international development assistance to Africa. The November 14, 2001, Doha Ministerial Declaration emphasized technical assistance and capacity building as "core elements of the development dimension of the multilateral trading system" and asked the World Trade Organization (WTO) "to support domestic efforts for mainstreaming trade into national plans for economic development and strategies for poverty reduction."[54] Based on this mandate, the WTO launched the Aid for Trade initiative in 2005. As the WTO and the Organization for Economic Cooperation and Development (OECD) note, "Aid for Trade is not a new global development fund, nor a new aid category. It is an integral part of normal Official Development Assistance (ODA) programmes. Aid for Trade is a holistic framework which encourages policymakers to use trade as a lever for economic growth and poverty alleviation. It encourages developing countries to write trade objectives into their development plans—and donors to respond by making resources available to meet the needs which are expressed."[55] Like other international development initiatives for Africa, the WTO program also rested on the notion of people-centered liberalism.

People-centered liberalism was also evident in the work of the Commission for Africa led by former British Prime Minister Tony Blair, which was at the forefront of boosting aid to Africa. In its 2005 report, for example, the commission called for a $25 billion annual increase in aid to Africa by 2010. It also called for another $25 billion per year by 2015 subject to a satisfactory review of the progress toward good governance. However, this new aid money was intended to develop the human capital and physical infrastructure necessary for the advancement of African trade. The commission's underlying approach to African development rested on good governance, total debt relief, grants, investment, and improved market access for African products.[56] The commission reinforced this vision in its 2010 report, which assessed the progress since 2005 and pointed to new challenges for African development.[57]

The emphasis on trade as the most appropriate way to aid sustainable human development in sub-Saharan Africa was reinforced in US and European Union (EU) trade and international development assistance policies. In 2000, the United States passed the African Growth and Opportunity Act (AGOA) in an attempt to offer "tangible incentives for [sub-Saharan] African countries to continue their efforts to open their economies and build free markets."[58] AGOA overlapped with, and expanded, the 1976 US Generalized System of Preferences (GSP) program, which provided preferential duty-free entry for up to 4,800 products from designated beneficiary countries and territories.[59] Since AGOA's initial passage, amendments to it have been made several times, including the Africa Investment Incentive Act of 2006 (commonly referred to as AGOA IV). The overall goal of AGOA was to provide "reforming [sub-Saharan] African countries with the most liberal access to the US market available to any country or region with which the United States does not have a Free Trade Agreement" and help US firms gain more access to investment opportunities in Africa.[60] Under AGOA, eligible sub-Saharan African countries could export up to 6,400 kinds of products to the United States with zero import duty, as stipulated in the US GSP. Eligibility for AGOA was determined by the US president based on the satisfactory establishment of or continual progress toward a market-based economy, rule of law and political pluralism, the elimination of barriers to US trade, poverty reduction and social well-being economic policies, proper anti-corruption mechanisms, and the protection of human and labor rights.[61] Since its establishment, more than thirty-eight sub-Saharan African countries have been designated as eligible, but the designation is subject to continuous review. Countries that falter on democracy and human rights are removed from the list of eligible countries. Overall, AGOA was part of the wider people-centered liberalism approach to international development assistance for Africa.[62] AGOA rested on the belief that enhanced trade preferences for sub-Saharan Africa would "encourage both higher levels of trade and direct investment in support of the positive economic and political developments under way throughout the region."[63]

The cornerstone of the EU's trade-oriented aid to Africa has been its GSP established in 1971 to give developing countries reduced or zero customs tariffs on imports of goods.[64] The EU GSP was modified for the post–Cold War economic and political order with the creation of the Everything But Arms (EBA) and GSP+ initiatives in 2001 and 2005, respectively. EBA gave duty-free access to imports of all products from LDCs [least developed countries], excluding arms and ammunitions, without any quantitative restrictions (with the exception of bananas, sugar and rice for a limited period).[65] GSP+ gave duty-free access for most eligible goods from developing countries that demonstrated a concrete and continuous commitment to core universal values on human rights, labor rights, environmental protection, and good governance by implementing the sustainable development and governance policies specified in the GSP+ incentive. In particular, countries were required to ratify and implement twenty-three of the core international conventions relating to human and labor rights by October 2005. In addition, they were expected to ratify and implement other international conventions on sustainable development and good governance.[66] Since most sub-Saharan African countries are classified as LDCs, EBA has become critical in the EU's development assistance to Africa. Like AGOA, the EU's African trade policies rested on people-centered liberalism. EU development assistance to African countries was anchored in the belief that more trade can "reduce poverty and promote good governance and sustainable development by helping them generate additional revenue through international trade, which can then be re-invested for the benefit of their own development."[67]

Though most of the discourse on trade and aid was driven by the nature of the economic and political ties between African countries and Western powers, it is important to note that the African trade and development path has increasingly been shifting toward Asia and Latin America. China and India, in particular, have become major trading partners and aid donors for Africa. As the *Financial Times* concluded, "it is now difficult to consider African prospects without mention of its pre-eminent foreign suitor [China], which in the past decade has increased trade with the continent 10-fold—from $10bn to more than $100bn—and has overtaken the US and Europe as the largest trading partner in some important economies."[68] Between 2000 and 2007, the annual average export from Intergovernmental Authority on Development (IGAD) countries to China was USD 2.74 billion, which was more than their exports to the EU ($1.481 billion) and US ($212.7 million).[69] Though Southern African Development Community (SADC) and Economic Community of West Africa (ECOWAS) countries had more exports to the EU and US, their exports to China and other parts of Asia had significantly increased. Between 2000 and 2007, SADC countries exported an annual average of $7.139 billion to China and $5.185 billion to other parts of Asia. ECOWAS countries exported an annual average of $616 million to China and $3.694 billion to other parts of Asia.[70] The 2010 African Export-Import Bank annual report showed similar trends. The growth rate of African exports (2009–2010) to "Developing Asia" was 19.4 percent, to the Western Hemisphere was 14 percent, and to "Advanced Economies" was 12.5 percent. Similarly, the rate of growth of African imports (2009–2010) was 22.4 percent (Developing Asia), 15.8 percent (Western Hemisphere), and 11.3 percent (Advanced Economies).[71]

In 2003, the Canadian International Development Agency started the Programme for Building African Capacity for Trade (PACT).[72] The five-year program was extended in 2008 as PACT II. Under PACT, which cost CAD 19.8 million, the International Trade Center would work with ECOWAS, the Common Market for Eastern and Southern Africa, and the Economic Community of Central African States to expand the regional market, with free movement of goods and services, and give African producers access to a large consumer base and new opportunities to build and specialize along regional supply chains. More broadly, the program sought to give regional exporters "the skills necessary to meet quality standards and to manage supply-chain operations, allowing them to achieve higher levels of competitiveness and prepare for integration into the global economy."[73] To achieve its goals, PACT focused on building pan-African networks and strategic South-South market development and promoting opportunities for information exchange through the use of new technologies and outreach to the private sector, especially networks for women in business. In addition, PACT emphasized trade development and promotion through the formulation of business plans, market analysis, and training programs. The final component of PACT's strategies was enhancing entrepreneurship, especially for women. The program called for providing support services to entrepreneurs, such as quality management, standards (including environmental standards) compliance, export training, and supply-chain management.

The biggest players in Africa's growing economic relations with Asia have clearly been China and India. The proportion of sub-Saharan Africa's export to China increased from around 1 percent in 2000 to around 10 percent in 2010. Similarly, Chinese Foreign Direct Investment (FDI) outflow to Africa increased from around $2 billion in 2003 to around $9 billion in 2008.[74] The US Congressional Research Service observed:

In 2007, China was the destination for some 13% of Africa's exports and the source of roughly 10% of Africa's imports. These figures represent a long trend of increased Chinese trade and commercial ties with Africa, particularly with countries rich in natural resources. China's trade with Africa greatly increased in recent years, reportedly growing to $74 billion in the first eight months of 2008, a 62% increase over the previous year. Even with the impact of the crisis in the second half of 2008, total Sino-African trade for the year was reportedly $106.8 billion, a significant increase from 2007. This trade has spurred Chinese investment in large infrastructure projects in Africa, which in some cases are thought to have helped alleviate constraints on economic competitiveness.[75]

In May 2011, *The Guardian* noted that annual trade between India and Africa stood at $46 billion (it had grown from $1 billion in 2001 to $50 billion by 2010). Moreover, Africa-India bilateral investments reached $90 billion in 2010.[76] In addition to the increased volume of trade, both India and China became significant aid donors to Africa. In 2011, India pledged $5 billion to help African countries meet the MDGs.[77] According to Chinese government estimates, China gave $37.7 billion in aid to Africa between 1950 and 2009.[78] In 2006, China established the Africa-China Development Fund, which was expected to reach $5 billion.[79] In 2008, Chinese ODA to Africa was around $1.2 billion.[80] Chinese aid to Africa included the $10 billion concessional loans it pledged at the 2009 China-Africa Cooperation Forum in Sharm el-Sheikh, Egypt.[81]

The shift of Africa's economic relations toward Asia did not necessarily undermine the people-centered liberalism approach to African development. As the data show, Africa's economic ties with Asia largely centered on trade instead of orthodox aid. As such, it fit the trade-oriented approach to aid and dovetailed with the principles of economic liberalization and sustainable human development that were shaping the international assistance frame for African countries. In fact, both China and India showed strong commitments to economic liberalization and sustainable human development. However, Africa's economic relation with Asia has raised concerns for democracy and good governance, which are important elements of people-centered liberalism. This is largely due to the fact that Asian countries, especially China, did not make democratic reform a precondition for economic relations with African countries. China maintained strong economic ties with states that have resisted democratic reforms and engaged in major human rights abuses. China's relations with Sudan and Zimbabwe, for example, were sharply criticized for the indifference to the gross human rights violations of the governments of those countries. Thus, a critical question is whether Africa's own commitment to good governance and democracy, its continued reliance on Western aid, and the internal political development of African countries themselves would mitigate the negative tendencies toward dictatorship and bad governance.

BLUEPRINTS FOR INTERNATIONAL STATEBUILDING: DEMOCRACY AND HUMAN DEVELOPMENT

In essence, the prevailing principles and policies of liberalization, good governance, and sustainable human development provided the framework for international support for most donors in Africa. This people-centered liberalism approach was clearly articulated in core documents from international agencies that provided the blueprints for political, economic, and social development in many African countries. As previously noted, the key goal of the international community in war-torn countries was to restore security and build peace by creating favorable conditions for the consolidation of democracy and sustainable human development. This was the focus of international statebuilding in Sierra Leone, Liberia, and Côte d'Ivoire. The plans for this people-centered liberalism approach to international statebuilding were spelled out in the UN and AU policy documents on democracy,[82] the PRSP of the IMF and World Bank, and the UNDAF developed by the UNDG. All of these policy documents reinforced the principles of political and economic liberalization and good governance as the vehicles for achieving human security, sustainable human development, and positive peace.

Democratization

Democratization was a key part of international statebuilding. At its core, it was a process rooted in political liberalization. However, democratization was also expected to lead to governments that would serve the people well. As people-centered liberalism implies, democratization must go in tandem with good governance. The basic criterion of democracy in the international discourse was regular free and fair multiparty elections. This was based on the procedure-oriented minimalist notion of democracy, which rests on freedom of association, freedom of expression, free media, universal adult suffrage, regular multiparty elections, and an independent electoral commission and judiciary.[83] This notion of democracy was articulated in UN General Assembly Resolution 46/137 (December 17, 1991) and other UN Security Council resolutions pertaining to elections in specific countries. Similarly, the AU issued a declaration on democratic elections in 2002.[84] In its declaration, AU Heads of State and Government affirmed that "Democratic elections are the basis of the authority of any representative government" and further agreed that "regular elections constitute a key element of the democratization process and therefore, are essential ingredients for good governance, the rule of law, the maintenance and promotion of peace, security, stability and development."[85] The declaration specified that democratic elections had to be conducted freely and fairly by a competent impartial and inclusive electoral body at regular intervals. In addition, a democratic constitution and an independent judiciary were required. AU democratization policies were articulated in a series of documents, including the Lomé Declaration of July 2000 on the Framework for an OAU Response to Unconstitutional Changes of Government and the 2007 African Charter on Democracy, Elections and Governance.[86]

The first major step in the democratization process is a successful multiparty election that is recognized by the international community as free and fair. Sierra Leone and Liberia achieved this with their respective 2002 and 2005 UN-supervised elections. Côte d'Ivoire's controversial 2010 presidential election can also be viewed as a significant first step, albeit an incomplete one. However, the election gained credibility because it was certified by the UN.[87] Sierra Leone successfully conducted postwar democratic elections in 2007, 2012, and 2018, resulting in two changes of power from a ruling party to an opposition party.[88] Liberia also has conducted postwar democratic elections in 2011 and 2017 that led to a significant change of power. In Côte d'Ivoire, democracy is shaky, as both the 2010 and the 2020 presidential elections were problematic. All three countries received significant assistance from the UN for their immediate postwar elections.[89] As one respondent noted, "There are these destabilizing forces in these structures, but I think the presence of the international community is serving as a deterrence to these destabilizing forces. That is . . . in the absence of the international community, these destabilizing forces or potential destabilizing forces can become heightened again."[90]

The primary role of the UN and other members of the international community in the democratization process has been to help countries conduct multiparty elections in a manner that is free, fair, secure, and consistent with the electoral laws of the country and international norms of democracy. UN General Assembly Resolution A/49/675 (November 17, 1994) outlined the guidelines for UN election assistance.[91] The guidelines stipulated that the UN would provide seven main forms of electoral assistance: organization and conduct of elections, supervision, verification, technical assistance, coordination and support for international observers, support for national observers, and observation. In order to qualify for electoral assistance, the government of the recipient country had to submit a formal written request for electoral assistance. Furthermore, the UN would conduct a needs-assessment mission to determine whether "basic conditions for a legitimate and truly democratic process are present."[92] In cases where the UN was asked to conduct, supervise, or verify an election, a formal mandate would need to be approved by the Security Council or the General Assembly. The UN rarely undertakes the complex role of conducting elections that it did in Cambodia. Supervising elections is typically handled in the context of larger

UN peacekeeping operations, such as in Namibia (1989), Sierra Leone (2002), and Liberia (2005). The role of verification requires the UN to certify whether an election has been conducted freely and fairly by the national electoral authority. This is often undertaken as part of a broader peacekeeping mission, such as in Côte d'Ivoire (2010) and Mozambique (1994).[93] The most common role of the UN has been to provide such technical assistance as capacity building for electoral institutions, designing electoral systems, human rights training, and handling logistics (computers, voter registration cards, vote counting, etc.). The UN also coordinates and supports the work of international observers invited by governments to witness the election process. In such cases, the UN provides logistical support to the observers but makes no formal statement on the electoral process. Similarly, the UN provides support for national observers by undertaking capacity-building programs for domestic organizations observing elections. In some cases, the UN may send a small team to observe an electoral process and report to the UN secretary general. However, the UN sees this role as having a negligible effect and rarely acts as an observer. The UN also provides postelection assistance to ensure the consolidation of the democratization process. In such cases, it works with other bodies of the UN system to improve governance and provide technical assistance. African countries often seek UN electoral assistance in order to gain technical and logistical support and bring credibility to the elections.

The 2002 AU declaration on democratic elections mandated the AU to observe and monitor elections in Africa in order to ensure that they meet the standards and strengthen the democratization process.[94] This led to the establishment of the Democracy and Elections Assistance Unit (DEAU) in 2006. DEAU was given "the responsibility of not only coordinating and organising the participation of the African Union in the observation of elections but also implement[ing] the African Union Commission's program for the promotion of democracy and democratic elections in the continent."[95] In addition to training and sending AU election observers, DEAU provides technical assistance and organizes a continental meeting for national electoral bodies. The AU not only observes and monitors elections but also issues a declaration on the elections to ascertain the degree to which they meet the standards for democratic elections. Under the guidelines, the AU will not monitor any election that lacks legitimacy in the process. As the 2002 declaration states, "The General Secretariat shall have the right to decline invitations to monitor elections which in its considered opinion, do not measure up to the normative standards" for democratic elections.[96] This AU mechanism, in addition to the UN electoral-assistance program, has become critical in assessing whether an African country is democratic or not. Countries whose elections are deemed by the AU and UN to meet the standards of democratic elections are recognized as democratic states. In some cases, such as the 2010 presidential election in Côte d'Ivoire, AU and UN certification of the election results has been critical in resolving disputes about them.

The underlying assumption in all of the policies on democracy in Africa is that free and fair multiparty elections would produce governments that are accountable to the people. Such elections would not only be the actualization of the right of the people to choose their rulers, it would also protect their civil liberties from abuse by the state and allow civil society to flourish. Under such conditions, governments would be constrained (by the constitution and civil society) to govern in a manner that promotes the interest of the vast majority of citizens. Thus, democracy would both affirm the liberal principles of political and civil rights and result in good governance. While democracy, in its liberal sense, rests on legal proceduralism, good governance is mostly reflected in subjectively measured outcomes. Good governance provides the critical link between the individual political and civil rights embodied in liberalism and the distributive economic and social justice implicit in sustainable human development.

Economic Liberalization and Sustainable Human Development: PRSP and UNDAF

International statebuilding in war-torn countries seeks to end the civil wars and establish democratic governments but also to promote economic and social development. The basic framework for postwar reconstruction and long-term economic and social development is rooted in principles of economic liberalization and sustainable human development, which are embodied in people-centered liberalism. These principles shape the PRSP and UNDAF development plans, which were the cornerstones of the peace-consolidation and postwar reconstruction efforts in Sierra Leone, Liberia, and Côte d'Ivoire.

The PRSPs and the UNDAFs are synergetic development plans. Each country's UNDAF is closely aligned to its PRSP, which was the core development plan. Sierra Leone's postwar development planning began with the Interim PRSP (IPRSP) in 2001. Shortly after, the government adopted the National Recovery Strategy (2002) and Vision 2025 (2003). The PRSP was adopted in 2005 for the period 2005–2007 (PRSP I) and revised in 2009 for the period of 2008–2012 (PRSP II). Liberia's postwar development planning began in 2006 with the adoption of the 150-Day Action Plan and the IPRSP. The PRSP was adopted in 2008. Côte d'Ivoire's IPRSP was approved in 2002, but the actual PRSP was not adopted until 2009. In the interim, UNDAF (2003–2007) and UNDAF (2009–2013) were adopted. In 2007, the country also signed the Post-Conflict Assistance Program with the World Bank and the Emergency Post-Conflict Assistance Program with the IMF. However, implementation of the programs lagged as the conflict lingered. The PRSPs and the UNDAFs recognized the core problems of each country, identified specific focus areas for medium- and long-term development, and laid out specific strategies to help achieve the overall development goals. Tables 4.1, 4.2, 4.3, and 4.4 provide a summary of the key features of the PRSPs and the UNDAFs.

THE CORE PROBLEMS OF DEVELOPMENT

Apart from the civil wars themselves, which undermined human security and destroyed the limited infrastructure in the countries, poverty has been the main hindrance to development. Following the UN MDGs, poverty was defined in terms of ability to meet the most basic human needs, most notably food.[97] Using 2008 as a baseline, Côte d'Ivoire defined poverty as "consumption expenditure of less than CFAF 661 per day, or CFAF 241,145 per annum."[98] In Sierra Leone, 57 percent of the population was below the food and extreme poverty line (lived on less than a dollar a day). Moreover, 70 percent of the people were below the full poverty line (lived on less than two dollars a day).[99] In Liberia, 63.8 percent of the people were below the poverty line, while 48 percent were in extreme poverty.[100] In Côte d'Ivoire, poverty increased from 10 percent in 1985 to 48.9 percent in 2008. In 2008, nearly 10.2 million people in Côte d'Ivoire were living in poverty. Poverty dovetailed with unemployment and lack of access to basic services such as health care, education, proper housing, and clean water. In all three countries, the pervasiveness of poverty was clearly reflected in low Human Development Index (HDI) and failure to meet the MDGs.

In addition to poverty, Côte d'Ivoire had two unique challenges. First was the missed opportunity to capitalize on the country's impressive economic growth during the first two decades of independence. Côte d'Ivoire saw itself as a country that should go far beyond merely meeting the MDGs. As such, its PRSP was a plan to not only meet the MDG targets by 2015 but also to establish the nation as an emerging country with rapid economic and social development. Second was the failure to peacefully resolve the conflict, which had far more of an ethnic and regional character than that in Liberia and Sierra Leone. In some ways, Côte d'Ivoire's political conflict is a bit unique in Africa, as it is a conflict over both power and citizenship. While the Ouagadougou Accord provided a durable frame for resolving the citizenship issues, political animosity between the north and south has hampered the consolidation of peace and democracy. In contrast to Côte d'Ivoire, Sierra Leone and Liberia successively implemented their peace agreements and conducted successive free and fair elections.

Poverty was largely attributed to bad governance and the civil wars. Sierra Leone's PRSP I, for example, states that "the people's assessment of the poverty

Table 4.1. Key Elements of PRSP: Sierra Leone.

Country	Pillars/ Priority Areas/ Objectives	Strategies	Cost/Funding PRSP and HIPC Status	Evolution toward PRSP/PRSP Schedule
Sierra Leone	**PRSP I Pillars:** 1) Good governance, security, and peace; 2) Pro-poor sustainable growth for food security and job creation; 3) Human development **PRSP II Priority Areas:** 1) Energy 2) Agriculture 3) Transportation 4) Sustainable human development	Good governance (fight corruption and boost transparency and management efficiency) Economic liberalization (tax reduction and rationalization, streamlining of regulation, promotion of private sector) Increase production in mining and agriculture Investment in infrastructure, human development, education, and ICT Gender equity Regional integration	**PRSP I**: Total cost of USD 1.8 billion roughly divided between the three pillars. **PRSP I:** $784.8 million budgeted in previous programs; $941 million funding gap Total donor disbursements (2005–2007) toward **PRSP I**: $975 million **PRSP II**: Total cost of $1.92 billion with a funding gap of $850.3 million Debt canceled under HIPC: $1.4 billion	IPRSP adopted 2001 National Recovery Strategy (NRS) adopted in 2002 Vision 2025 Development Plan adopted 2003 PRSP I (2005–2007) adopted 2005 PRSP II (2008–2012) adopted 2009

situation has emphasised various aspects of bad governance as one of the main causes of their deepening poverty."[101] In particular, "for almost thirty years, bad governance in Sierra Leone was characterised by an over-centralised system of administration, an over-burdened and ineffective judicial system, weak and inefficient public and local government institutions, thriving corruption, mismanagement, inappropriate fiscal policies and ill-conceived economic policies."[102] In Côte d'Ivoire, the problems were mostly attributed to the civil war and especially to the dismantling of state authority and government administration in the

Table 4.2. Key Elements of PRSP: Liberia.

Country	Pillars/ Priority Areas/ Objectives	Strategies	Cost/Funding PRSP and HIPC Status	Evolution toward PRSP/PRSP Schedule
Liberia	**PRSP (2008 to 2011) Pillars:** 1) Peace, consolidation, and security; 2) Economic revitalization; 3) Governance and the rule of law; 4) Infrastructure and basic services	Security sector reform Strengthening human rights Good governance (fight corruption and boost transparency management efficiency) Economic liberalization (tax reduction and rationalization, streamlining of regulation, promotion of private sector) Increase production in mining and agriculture Improve the delivery of basic services Investment in infrastructure, human development, education/ training, and ICT Gender equity Regional integration	PRSP total cost: USD 1.61 billion, 62% toward pillar 4 and the rest roughly divided between the other three pillars. $510 million expected government revenues toward PRSP $1.1 billion PRSP funding gap $4.6 billion of debt canceled under HIPC	150-Day Action Plan adopted April 2006 IPRS adopted December 2006 PRSP (2008 to 2011) adopted July 2008

Table 4.3. Key Elements of PRSP: Côte d'Ivoire.

Country	Pillars/Priority Areas/ Objectives	Strategies	Cost/Funding PRSP and HIPC Status	Evolution toward PRSP/PRSP Schedule
Côte d'Ivoire	**PRSP (2009–2015) Objectives:** 1) Reduce the poverty rate to 16% and thereby achieve the MDGs by 2015; 2) Achieve a 5.9% average annual rate of economic growth for 2009 to 2015 and thereby become an emerging country and a regional economic power **PRSP (2009–2015) Outcomes:** 1) Restoration and consolidation of the foundation of the republic; 2) Transformation of Côte d'Ivoire into an emerging country; 3) Ensuring social welfare for all; 4) Making Côte d'Ivoire a dynamic actor on the regional and international scene	Successful 2010 presidential election; results would be accepted Peacebuilding and restoration of state authority Rebirth of Côte d'Ivoire; country would become a regional hub that attracts investments (national and foreign) in diversified sectors Macroeconomic stabilization (reduce government spending, cut taxes, increase revenue, create incentives for private investment, improve the management of state resources) Development of transport infrastructure to serve as engine of economic growth Increase production in mining, energy, fishing, and agriculture and increase exports Investment in education/training, health care, sanitation, and ICT Gender equity Regional and international integration	PRSP 2009–2015 total cost: $37.368 billion, 52.3% toward Outcome 3 and 43% for Outcome 2 Increase Government contribution toward $571.8 million by 2010 and up to $1.356 billion in 2013 (if country receives HIPC debt cancelation by 2010) Côte d'Ivoire reached HIPC decision point in March 2009, not yet reached completion point	IPRSP adopted March 2002 UNDAF (2003–2007) adopted May 2002 Post-Conflict Assistance Program (PAPC), World Bank, July 2007 Emergency Post-Conflict Assistance Program (EPCA), IMF, August 2007 UNDAF (2009–2013) adopted July 2008 PRSP (2009–2015) adopted 2009

Table 4.4. Key Elements of UNDAF: Sierra Leone, Liberia, and Côte d'Ivoire.

Country	Focus Areas/Outcomes	Strategies	Cost/Overlaps with PRSP	Evolution toward UNDAF/ UNDAF Schedule
Sierra Leone	**UNDAF (2004–2007) Focus Areas:** 1) Poverty reduction and reintegration of victims and combatants; 2) Human rights and reconciliation; 3) good governance, peace, and stability; 4) Economic recovery **UNDAF (2006–2007) Outcomes:** 1) Transparent, accountable, democratic governance; 2) Increased production, availability, accessibility, and utilization of food with improved employment opportunities for youth; 3) Improved health; 4) HIV/AIDS prevention, care, and support; 5) Reconciliation, security, and respect for human rights	Coordinate development activities with international agencies, government, civil society Increase income generation opportunities for the poor Increase food production Promote adoption and amendment of human rights laws, human rights training, and efficient judiciary Increase local government capacity Promote public-sector reform Strengthen security institutions Promote private-sector investment	**UNDAF (2004–2007)** Total cost: $140.9 million, $116.7 million toward focus area 1 (poverty reduction and reintegration) **UNDAF (2006–2007)** Total cost: $69 million, $29.2 million toward outcome 1 (transparent, accountable, democratic governance) UNDAF cost overlaps with the PRSP	MDGs targets IPRSP adopted 2001 National Recovery Strategy (NRS) adopted in 2002 UNDAF (2004–2007) adopted in 2003 UNDAF (revised, 2006–2007) adopted 2006

(Continued)

Table 4.4 (*continued*)

Country	Focus Areas/Outcomes	Strategies	Cost/Overlaps with PRSP	Evolution toward UNDAF/ UNDAF Schedule
Liberia	**UNDAF (2008–2012) Outcomes:** 1) Peace and security; 2) Equitable socioeconomic development; 3) Good governance and the rule of law; 4) Education and health; 5) HIV/AIDS prevention and care.	Coordination of development activities with international agencies, government, civil society Rights-based and conflict-sensitive approach to development Prioritize well-being of the youth Gender equality	UNDAF cost aligned with the PRSP	MDGs targets 150-Day Action Plan adopted April 2006 IPRS adopted December 2006 PRSP (2008 to 2011) adopted July 2008 UNDAF (2008–2012) adopted September 2008
Côte d'Ivoire	**UNDAF (2003–2007) Priority Areas:** 1) Poverty reduction; 2) Good governance and human rights; 3) Health and HIV/AIDS; 4) Global and regional integration; and 5) Peace and security **UNDAF 2009–2013 Outcomes:** 1) Peace consolidation; 2) Good governance; 3) Job creation and food security; 4) Access to basic social services; and 5) Protection of the environment	Coordination of development activities with international agencies, government, civil society Peacebuilding Macroeconomic reform Private sector and rural job creation Decentralization Improved access to quality basic social services Gender equity Regional and international integration	**UNDAF 2009–2013** Total cost: $426 million, 63% going toward outcome 4 (basic social services) UNDAF cost aligned with the PRSP	MDGs targets IPRSP adopted March 2002 UNDAF (2003–2007) adopted May 2002 UNDAF (2009–2013) adopted July 2008 PRSP (2009–2015) adopted 2009

northern region, the lack of a proper mechanism for national identification, and inefficiency in the public sector.

The PRSP provided a blueprint for addressing poverty and promoting the overall development of each of the countries. Sierra Leone's PRSP I states, "To reverse this level of poverty and its underlying causes, the government is following a new strategic direction . . . aligned to and consistent with the Millennium Development Goals (MDGs). This PRSP . . . provides that framework."[103] Similarly, the PRSP was Liberia's "strategy for rapid, inclusive and sustainable growth and poverty reduction, including progress toward achieving the MDGs."[104] Côte d'Ivoire's PRSP, which was far more ambitious than those of Sierra Leone and Liberia, was described as "a commitment of the State towards the population and also a tool that enables development partners to better align their support and actions to the strategy pursued by the Government." It sought to reduce the poverty rate to 16 percent and thereby achieve the MDGs by 2015 and achieve a 5.9 percent average annual rate of economic growth for 2009 to 2015, thereby positioning the nation as an emerging country and a regional economic power. By defining the development agenda in terms of poverty reduction, the PRSP clearly incorporates the principle of sustainable human development.

Côte d'Ivoire's ambitious PRSP recognized both the opportunities and fragility of the country. It identified three possible scenarios for the country's future development: stalemate, recovery, and rebirth. These scenarios were premised on the outcome of the delayed 2010 presidential election. The stalemate scenario would be "the blockage of the peace process and the return to normalcy. The organization of general elections would not succeed or else, the result would be challenged . . . the crisis recovery process could be challenged and compromise the reunification of the country. The international community would lose every hope of the possibility of Côte d'Ivoire getting out of the socio-political and military crisis."[105] The recovery scenario assumes that "the country would recover its unity and the normal functioning of public institutions. . . . The general elections would be held without any major incidents and the government that would emerge from the ballot box would not be challenged. The development partners would actively resume their support programs and public investment would resume in earnest."[106] Côte d'Ivoire's development plan was built around the rebirth scenario, which assumed that the country would go beyond the "recovery [scenario] by adding new dimensions to it," and sought to achieve "transformation and diversification of the economy and the successful establishment of new, transparent and inclusive governance policies."[107] Moreover, "Côte d'Ivoire would become a pole of competitiveness and a regional hub that would attract a great . . . investment . . . in diversified branches. . . . New infrastructure would be built throughout the country, thus bringing the country in line with the best international standards. The country would be quoted as a new economic miracle . . . [and] resume its stabilizing role in the regional environment and become a listened[-to] actor on the international scene."[108] Based on the 2010 and 2020 elections, Côte d'Ivoire is best described as a stalemate.

Focus Areas for Promoting Sustainable Human Development

Both the PRSPs and the UNDAFs specified key focus areas, often referred to as *pillars* or *outcomes*, for development of the three countries (see tables 4.1, 4.2, 4.3, and 4.4). Sierra Leone's PRSP I (2005–2007) had three pillars: governance and security, food security and job creation, and human development. PRSP II (2008–2012) maintained these pillars but narrowed them down to four specific areas: electricity, agriculture, transportation, and human development. Similarly, Sierra Leone's UNDAF (2004–2007) had four focus areas: poverty reduction and reintegration, human rights and reconciliation, governance, and economic recovery. UNDAF (2006–2007) regrouped these into democratic governance, food security and employment opportunities for youth, health, HIV/AIDS, and reconciliation and human rights. Liberia's PRSP (2008 to 2011) had four pillars: peace and security, economic revitalization, governance, and infrastructure and basic services. Its UNDAF (2008–2012) focused on peace and security, socioeconomic development, governance, education and health, and HIV/AIDS. In Côte d'Ivoire, the PRSP (2009–2015) focused on four outcomes: restoration of state authority, transformation into an emerging country, social welfare improvements, and regional and international integration. The priority areas of UNDAF (2003–2007) were poverty reduction, governance and human rights, health and HIV/AIDS, global and regional integration, and peace and security. UNDAF (2009–2013) reformulated these into peace consolidation, good governance, job creation and food security, basic social services, and protection of the environment.

Notwithstanding their nuances, these development plans all focus on similar political, economic, and social challenges. Given the overlaps between the PRSPs and the UNDAFs and their similarities across the three countries, the focus areas of the PRSPs and the UNDAFs can be regrouped into three main categories: peace and governance, human development, and economic growth and employment. Côte d'Ivoire's PRSP uniquely saw regional and international cooperation as a focus area. However, regional and international cooperation can be viewed more as a strategy to boost Côte d'Ivoire's economic and political stability. In a similar way, both Sierra Leone and Liberia saw greater regional and international cooperation as a way to enhance security, trade, and international development assistance.

The development plans of all three countries are predicated on the consolidation of peace and inculcation of good governance. In Côte d'Ivoire, peace consolidation involved the full implementation of the Ouagadougou Peace Accord (2007). This included completion of the national identification and the disarmament, demobilization and reintegration of programs, a free and fair 2010 presidential election that would lead to a government acceptable to southerners and northerners, the redeployment of state agencies, and a meaningful national reconciliation. The PRSP clearly states that the most likely condition for Côte d'Ivoire would be a stalemate if "the general elections would not succeed or else, the result would be challenged."[109] Unfortunately for Côte d'Ivoire, the results of the 2010 election were contested, and Gbagbo was removed from power through military force, albeit with international support.[110] Though Thomas J. Bassett sees the elections as a remarkable step in forming a "winning coalition of ethnic and regional interests" that should "ultimately be remembered for their possibilities rather than for their achievements,"[111] the failure of the election to peacefully resolve the political crisis meant that Côte d'Ivoire would face a stalemate. Unfortunately, Ouattara exacerbated the problem by controversially amending the constitution in order to stay in power beyond the two-term limit.

The development plans of Sierra Leone and Liberia also emphasized peace consolidation. However, since the key term of their respective peace agreements (free and fair multiparty elections) had been implemented, the PRSPs and UNDAFs focused more on security reforms, the rule of law, and good governance. In Liberia, the security reforms sought to build gender-sensitive professional security forces under democratic civilian control, with women making up at least 20 percent of the forces and represented throughout the command structure. Given the political and social causes of the civil war, the centerpiece of long-term peace was human security, which "requires that the Government take a broad view of security that recognizes the importance of human rights, good governance and access to economic opportunity, education and health care."[112] In Sierra Leone, where most of the security-sector reforms had been implemented,[113] the emphasis was largely on the inculcation of human rights and good governance—the continuation of multiparty democracy and "rapid improvement in public sector governance . . . [to ensure] efficient, transparent and accountable delivery of services."[114]

In all three countries, good governance embodied the rule of law, democracy, efficient management of the state, ethical leadership, and citizen-centered government policies. As Liberia's PRSP rightly noted, "Improving governance necessarily entails transforming the relationship between the state and its citizens, focusing especially on those who are underrepresented or disadvantaged."[115] In Côte d'Ivoire, good governance was understood as improving the efficiency and transparency of government and delivering vital social services to the people. The strategies to achieve this were rooted in the principle of liberalization and would include devolving power to local governments and "transferring the responsibility of providing . . . services to the private sector."[116] Other strategies included decentralization, public-finance management and procurement reforms, and anticorruption campaigns. Good governance also assumed the inclusion of women in the decision-making process. In Côte d'Ivoire, the PRSP called for increasing the proportion of women in elected legislative positions at the municipal and national levels to 30 percent by 2015 from their 2008 levels, which ranged from 4.56 to 11 percent. At the national executive level, the proportion of women would be increased from 12.12 percent in 2008 to 40 percent in 2015.[117]

Given the depth of poverty, poor physical infrastructure, and lack of basic social service, human development was a major part of the overall development agenda. All three countries saw poverty reduction as a primary goal. The development plans sought to significantly increase the amount and quality of basic infrastructure and social services, which was expected to contribute to both economic growth and human development. Sierra Leone's PRSP stated: "Promoting human development is critical to the desire of the people to come out of poverty. After food security, the majority of the country's poor want to have access to basic education, health, water and sanitation as the route out of extreme poverty, and to reduce the risk of falling into poverty."[118] In addition, human development was seen as the ultimate manifestation of democracy and of making government work for the people. One critical part of this implicit social democracy was ensuring gender equity in accessing social services. The development plans in all three countries called for significant investment in basic infrastructure (roads, bridges, energy plants, communication networks, etc.) and social services (health, education, water, housing, etc.) in a way that would promote sustainable human development. In fact, roughly half of the entire budgets of the PRSPs were dedicated to this area.[119] The most critical areas were education, health, water, housing, sanitation, and transportation.

Côte d'Ivoire's PRSP had concrete targets for achieving the MDGs by 2015. In particular, it sought to increase net primary school enrollment from 56.1 percent in 2008 to 70 percent by 2015 and boost graduation rates from 39.2 percent to 60 percent during the same period.[120] By 2015, the plan also sought to have reduced the child mortality rate from 84 deaths per thousand live births in 2005 to 32 deaths; maternal mortality from 543 deaths per hundred thousand live births in 2005 to 149 deaths; and HIV/AIDS rates from 4.7 percent in 2005 to 1.8 percent.[121] The plan sought to build a vast amount of First Contact Health Establishments and thereby increase the proportion of people living within less than five kilometers from a medical facility from 44 percent in 2008 to 100 percent by 2015.[122] It envisioned universal health-care access through private and community insurance plans and subsidized medical services and drugs. Most of the focus was on maternal health care and common diseases (malaria, tuberculosis, Buruli ulcer, and HIV/AIDS). The plan also sought to increase access to potable water from 61 percent in 2008 to 82.5 percent by 2015.[123] In particular, 2,500 public standpipes would be constructed in disadvantaged urban centers and four water-production and -treatment units with a total capacity of 5,000 m3/h would be installed in Abidjan. Also, sufficient mini water-supply facilities would be installed in big rural areas, while smaller areas would get boreholes fitted with hand pumps.

In line with the principle of sustainable human development, all three countries committed to respect international environmental agreements, preserve forests, and incorporate environmental policies into mining agreements. Côte d'Ivoire's PRSP, for example, sought to increase the protected areas from 10 percent in 2008 to 20 percent of the territory by 2015.[124] All three countries sought to substantially reduce slum dwellings, improve sanitation services, especially in major urban areas, and increase access to energy. In particular, Côte d'Ivoire sought to increase access to energy from 17 percent in 2008 to 55 percent in 2015 and the proportion of households with modern cooking systems from 20 percent to 60 percent during the same period. However, most of the energy would come from traditional sources, as renewable energy would only increase from [zero] percent to a mere 5 percent in 2015.[125]

Economic growth and job creation were major macroeconomic objectives. The PRSPs saw infrastructure and social service development as engines for economic growth and the enhancement of human development. All three countries have rich mineral deposits that were expected to provide some revenue for infrastructure development and social services and create jobs—especially for youths. Additionally, the PRSPs saw macroeconomic stabilization, deregulation, private investment, and increased agricultural production and mining as key areas for promoting financial growth and jobs. Sierra Leone's PRSP, for example, called for reducing the budget deficit, liberalizing the exchange rate regime, restructuring import tariffs according to the ECOWAS Common External Tariff and the ECOWAS Trade liberalization scheme, opening the Information Communication and Technology (ICT) market to more competition, and diversifying exports. Liberia had similar neoliberal macroeconomic policies that were expected to attract private-sector investment in mining and agriculture. Liberia's PRSP expected mining to reach 12 percent of GDP by 2011 and food production and exports of timber, rubber, timber, coffee, cocoa, and seafood to significantly increase. It also sought to diversify the economy in the medium and long term by promoting manufacturing, commerce, and service industries.

Côte d'Ivoire's economic growth was predicated on massive improvements in transportation infrastructure, diversification, and macroeconomic stabilization, which were expected to significantly increase production. In the energy and mining sector, the PRSP sought to increase the production level of hydrocarbons and petroleum products. The plan called for the increased exploitation of known mineral deposits, transformation of mineral extracts, and production of geological and mining exploitation data maps to enhance the discovery of new mineral deposit. Though the PRSP sought to reduce the share of agriculture in the GDP to 19.9 percent by 2013, the overall goal was to increase agricultural production to ensure food self-sufficiency and generate more revenues for farmers through the domestic and international markets.[126] The agricultural policy primarily focused on rice production, livestock and fishing, and cash crops (coffee, cacao, cotton, and cashew). It specifically sought to significantly boost the amount of livestock and fisheries yields and increase rice production by two million tons by 2015.[127] In the service sector, Côte d'Ivoire's PRSP sought to significantly increase telecommunication, especially quality internet access, and increase tourism and artistic products.

Strategies for Promoting Development

The development plans laid out the key strategies for overall development goals. The strategies could be grouped into five major categories: peace consolidation, good governance, economic liberalization, investment in critical infrastructure and human resources, and regional and international cooperation. Though the strategies were often conterminous with some of the focus areas, they were clearly seen as a means for ensuring that the overall development goals were achieved. The synergetic nature of the development plans made some of the key elements to simultaneously be focus areas and strategies.

Peace consolidation as a strategy for achieving the development goals was most evident in Côte d'Ivoire, which was in a state of no war, no peace. The country's entire development plan was based on the assumption that the 2010 presidential election would be successfully implemented and lead to a legitimate government. Thus, the key strategy in Côte d'Ivoire was to ensure that the terms of the 2007 Ouagadougou Accord were fully implemented. This required significant international engagement to ensure that the Disarmament, Demobilization and Reintegration (DDR), national identification, voter registration, ballot counting, and installation of the elected candidate went as envisioned under the agreement. The strengthening of the mandate of the UN, which gave it the authority to verify the 2010 elections, was a critical element of the peace-consolidation strategy. As in Sierra Leone and Liberia, peace consolidation largely rested on a free and fair multiparty election strategy. Each successful democratic election would be a critical step toward peace consolidation. To ensure that democracy continued, the strategy included restructuring the security forces to keep them under civilian control and make them ethnically and regionally balanced. Peace consolidation also included transitional justice in the form of truth and reconciliation and a tribunal. The transitional justice programs were simultaneously aimed at bringing closure for victims, fostering meaningful reconciliation, and holding those most responsible for the war accountable. Both Sierra Leone and Liberia created TRCs, which documented some of the crimes committed during the wars and made recommendations for reparations. Côte d'Ivoire's was mostly a sham committee. Sierra Leone had a special war crimes court that tried key figures involved in the civil war, including Charles Taylor, who was the most notorious warlord in Liberia. In the long run, peace consolidation dovetailed with the overall effort to enhance human security through good governance and poverty reduction.

The most pervasive strategy was good governance. Implicit in the entire development agenda, good governance began with maintaining democracy and extended into the day-to-day management of public agencies and ethical leadership of the state. In all three countries, combating corruption and implementing public-finance management reforms were of central importance. Liberia's PRSP called for broadening the 2006 Public Finance Management Reform to combat corruption and improve government efficiency. Both Sierra Leone and Liberia established anticorruption commissions to enforce good governance in the management of public resources. Good governance included promoting decentralization and efficiency in the management of public resources and delivery of services. The emphasis on efficiency was most pronounced in Côte d'Ivoire, which wanted to position itself as an emerging country.

Economic liberalization was a strategy deeply rooted in the dominant free-market principles and policies of the IMF and World Bank. It rested on macroeconomic reforms and the enhancement of the private sector. By accepting IMF and World Bank support, the three countries fully committed to neoliberal economic policies. As Sierra Leone's PRSP stated, "The Government will seek to further reduce the budget deficit and money supply growth, while maintaining a flexible exchange rate regime and a liberal exchange and trade system. Structural impediments to greater factor mobility and improved resource allocation will be removed, particularly in the mining and fisheries sectors, and implementation of civil service and public enterprise reforms will continue."[128] In Côte d'Ivoire's cocoa sector, for example, the PRSP called for the reduction of the registration tax from 10 percent to 5 percent of the cost, insurance, and freight (CIF) price and refraining "from increasing any other tax and duties in the cocoa sector."[129] Moreover, "the global taxation of the cocoa sector . . . should not represent more than 22% of the CIF price by 2011."[130] Sierra Leone's PRSP called for a restructuring of the import tariffs according to the ECOWAS Common External Tariff. It warmly endorsed the fact that "the fiscal incentive framework embedded in the tariff regime is being rationalised. Import duty rates, especially for raw materials and capital goods, are now lower; export duties eliminated; and a duty drawback system introduced for exports. The income tax regime now includes a provision for a more generous depreciation schedule; and the corporate rate of tax has been progressively reduced."[131] Côte d'Ivoire's PRSP called for increasing the tax collection rate by 17 percent and reducing unproductive expenditures to less than 10 percent of the budget, excluding debt servicing, by 2011.[132] Its strategy also included an aggressive marketing campaign to attract investment and tourists.

Economic liberalization also involved promoting the private sector. As Liberia's PRSP stated, "the private sector will be the main driver of growth.... The Government will focus only on services that the private sector cannot or will not offer at an appropriate price, such as maintaining safety and security, ensuring the rule of law, providing infrastructure and other public goods, providing basic services for the poor, and establishing a regulatory environment conducive to long-term development."[133] Private investment was expected to increase in the mining sectors and in Small and Medium Enterprises (SME). Liberia's PRSP called for a restructuring of the banking system to give SMEs more access to credit. Similarly, "Côte d'Ivoire committed itself to making the private sector the engine of growth. The emergence of the private sector was accelerated with the policy of government withdrawal from the productive sectors, initiated in the 1990s."[134] Sierra Leone's PRSP reiterated that "the Government will continue to recognise the centrality of the private sector to its poverty reduction efforts in this post-conflict period. This is underscored in the Government's Vision 2025 Report of 2003, which already foresaw a leading role for the sector."[135] Côte d'Ivoire's PRSP called for the firm protection of intellectual property as a way to promote private enterprises, especially in the arts, crafts, and music sectors.

The most potent strategy and the focus of all the plans was the investment in infrastructure and human resources to unleash economic development and reduce poverty. Infrastructure as a strategy for development was most explicit in Côte d'Ivoire's PRSP, which stated that "the main pillar of the strategy for the economic emergence of Côte d'Ivoire will be built around the transport infrastructure sector."[136] In essence, "Economic growth should rely on the development of transport infrastructure as the basic link for driving other sectors of activity like agriculture, mining and energies and ICTs."[137] The PRSP called for the construction of adequate roads that could make all subprefectures and villages accessible and connected to an efficient network of paved intercity, urban, and international roads and the development of adequate airports and ports to make Côte d'Ivoire a regional and international commercial hub. In 2000, Côte d'Ivoire had 82,000 kilometers of intercity highways, around 4,000 kilometers of tarred urban road network, 327 bridges, and twenty ferries.[138] However, about

44 percent of the entire paved road networks were over twenty years old and had exceeded their degradation tolerance level. To promote rapid development, the development plan sought to construct or rehabilitate 11,703 kilometers of N1 national intercity roads (motorways of international and heavy national traffic), over 11,479 kilometers of N2 national intercity roads (national roads of regional significance), and 8,810 kilometers of urban roads (in major cities) by 2015.[139] In addition, the 630-kilometer railway line linking Côte d'Ivoire to Burkina Faso was to be improved and connected with the Port of San Pedro and the western part of the country. The plan also sought to improve the infrastructure and service delivery at the Port of Abidjan, repositioning it as the leading port in West Africa, and to expand the export capacity of the Port of San Pedro. Similarly, the safety and quality of services at the international airports were to be improved so as to meet all international standards and increase the volume of air traffic. Most notably, Abidjan Félix Houphouët-Boigny (FHB) Airport was to be upgraded to meet the requirements for the US Federal Aviation Administration certification.[140] Côte d'Ivoire's infrastructure development strategy went beyond transportation; it also sought to mechanize agriculture and integrate scientific research into its development. In particular, the Centre National de Recherche Agronomique was to serve as a vehicle for modernizing agriculture through continuous quality research. In Sierra Leone and Liberia, the development of roads, energy sources, and telecommunication services was an integral strategy for promoting development. As Sierra Leone's PRSP argued, they "have a potential to transform the economy, accelerate growth in the productive sectors and rapidly improve market access . . . [and] provide the necessary incentive for both local and foreign investment . . . and employment generation in service sectors such as tourism."[141] Though the PRSPs of Sierra Leone and Liberia did not give numerical targets, infrastructure development was a key part of their development strategies.

The other component of the investment strategy was human resources, which included plans to invest in the areas of health and education to improve the productive potential of the population. As one civil society leader stated, "the solution would come from education. . . . There is no written book or solution to [such a] crisis. People need to be creative, to find out [a] way or solution, how we want our future to be and then work towards that. . . . That's where currently our energy is working on programs that will be taught in school, peacebuilding in school, from the primary school up to the university . . . democracy cannot be obtained over one generation. It's a long term process and people need to integrate that in their mind."[142] In the short and medium terms, the plans sought to attract expatriates and provide rapid training. Both Sierra Leone and Liberia recognized the huge shortage of professionals in critical areas such as health, engineering, and management. Liberia's PRSP counted on enticing its expatriates to return and provide some of the critical skills needed for the development of the country. Moreover, it called for vocational training, restructuring the civil service (and providing salary increases), and training senior managers. Côte d'Ivoire's development called for investment in secondary and vocational education as a way to quickly boost its human resources capacity. It sought to increase collaboration between higher education and the private sector so that universities could rapidly respond to the skilled labor needs of the country. The plan called for the increased privatization, decentralization, and regionalization of universities to give them the necessary market flexibilities. While investment in human resources was critical for Sierra Leone and Liberia precisely because of their lack of qualified professionals, Côte d'Ivoire's effort to boost human resources was intrinsically tied to its desire to significantly enhance efficiency in the public and private sectors and thereby take a big step toward becoming an emerging country. In particular, Côte d'Ivoire sought to substantially increase efficiency in the delivery of health care, primary education, and public administration services.

Another notable strategy was regional and international integration and development coordination. All three countries pursued regional integration to enhance trade and security. However, Côte d'Ivoire saw regional and international integration as a way to reposition itself as the economic power of the area and become an emerging country. Côte d'Ivoire sought to go beyond the region and significantly integrate itself in the global economy. All three countries sought to take advantage of such trade agreements as the Cotonou Agreement, the EU EBA, and the US AGOA. The strategy also included increasing international development coordination, especially among international agencies, government, and civil society. This strategy was even more pivotal in UNDAF, which served as a coordinating template for all UN and other international development agencies working in these countries.

In addition to the five major strategies, there were other, more targeted ones; these were implicit in most of the major strategies but also stood out as critical for achieving the development goals and included such issues as gender equity, food production, youth employment, and mining. Liberia's UNDAF, in particular, emphasized a rights-based and conflict-sensitive approach to development. All three countries saw mining as a primary source of revenue to support long-term development. In fact, the PRSPs consistently referred to the natural resources of each of the countries and pointed to the fact that they were *not necessarily poor countries* but rich countries that had been poorly managed.

Cost and Funding

The total costs of the development plan outlined in the PRSPs of each of the three countries vastly exceed their short- and medium-term revenues. The international financial institutions, especially IMF and the World Bank, and donor countries were expected to cover the funding gaps in addition to providing debt relief under the HIPC initiative. Sierra Leone's PRSP I cost nearly USD 1.8 billion, roughly divided among the three pillars of the development plan.[143] Of the total amount, $784.8 million had already been budgeted in the medium-term expenditure framework (MTEF), which left a gap of $941 million.[144] Sierra Leone received a total of USD 975 million in donor disbursements toward PRSP I from 2005 to 2007.[145] PRSP II was estimated to cost just over $1.9 billion, with a funding gap of $850.3 million.[146] Similarly, Liberia's PRSP (2008–2011) cost around USD 1.61 billion, with a funding gap of USD 1.1 billion. Nearly 62 percent of the cost went toward infrastructure and basic services (pillar four), while the remaining cost was roughly divided between the other three pillars.[147]

Côte d'Ivoire's ambitious PRSP (2009–2015) was estimated to cost a total of $37.368 billion (17,645.05 billion CFA francs) at an average annual cost of around $5.3 billion.[148] Over half of the budget (52.3%) went to outcome three, with 43 percent toward outcome two, and 4 percent toward outcome one. More specifically, the bulk of the budget was for education and training (22.14%), transportation (15.67%), health care (14.68%), rural development and agriculture (10.13%), and energy (10.9%).[149] The government of Côte d'Ivoire was expected to contribute up to $572 million by 2010 and gradually increase its contribution to around $1.36 billion in 2013 as the country reached the completion point of the HIPC initiative.[150] Other projected domestic sources of funding included concessional home and education loans from private banks directly to citizens and various forms of levies, such as a polluter tax. The vast majority of the funding was expected to come from the international agencies and donors, most notably UN agencies and the EU, IMF, World Bank, and TICAD.

The budgets for the PRSPs included most of the costs of the programs outlined in the UNDAFs and other related developed plans. As such, the budgets for the PRSP represented the global cost of the development agenda for each of the countries. Moreover, the costs of these plans assumed that the countries would receive debt cancelation under the HIPC initiative. Sierra Leone reached the completion point of HIPC in 2006, which led to the cancelation of its debts. The debt relief included approximately USD 994 million from the enhanced HIPC initiative. As the IMF noted, "In NPV [net present value] terms, the stock of debt would be reduced from USD 1,197.6 million at end-2005 to USD 483.0 million at end-2006 after HIPC relief and to USD 110.0 million after MDRI. This assistance was estimated to correspond to approximately USD 1,603 million in nominal terms."[151] In June 2010, the World Bank and IMF decided that Liberia had "reached the 'completion point' under the Heavily Indebted Poor Countries (HIPC) Initiative and will be granted a total debt relief of US$4.6 billion."[152]

Liberia received its first HIPC debt relief in December 2007, when the World Bank and the African Development Bank reduced the country's debt by USD 400 million and USD 240 million, respectively. In September 2010, the Paris Club canceled $1.2 billion of Liberia's debts.[153] Other canceled debts included $391 million from the United States, $8 million from Norway, $194.1 million from Japan, and $90 million from Germany.[154] In April 2009, Côte d'Ivoire also met the requirements for debt relief under HIPC and received over $4 billion in debt relief.[155]

The funding and implementation of Sierra Leone's PRSP was largely based on the Country Assistance Strategy (CAS) and the Joint Assistance Strategy (JAS) programs prepared by Sierra Leone's development partners (World Bank, African Development Bank or AfDB, Department for International Development or DFID, International Finance Corporation or IFC, and European Commission or EC).[156] CAS replaced the Transitional Support Strategy (TSP), which was launched in 2002 to facilitate implementation of the IPRSP. As the World Bank noted, TSP "emphasized the decentralization of service delivery and the restoration of local government in order to reorient the allocation of resources from the capital to the rural communities."[157] In particular, TSP aimed to consolidate peace and security, resettle and reintegrate displaced persons, improve governance through institutional reform and capacity building, accelerate economic growth, expand access of the poor to basic social services and economic opportunities, and combat HIV/AIDS. By 2005, the IDA had committed $230 million to Sierra Leone under TSP.[158]

CAS was initially adopted in 2005 to cover fiscal years 2006–2009. CAS was aligned with the PRSP I to address Sierra Leone's "overriding challenge of extreme poverty, which is accentuated by high unemployment (especially of the youth), food insecurity (compounded by poor infrastructure) and dismal social sector indicators."[159] CAS focused on governance; decentralization and public financial management; sustainable growth, food security, and jobs creation; and human development as a way to meet the development goals envisioned in PRSP I. Sierra Leone received USD 117 million from the IDA during the 2005–2009 CAS period and graduated from the exceptional postconflict allocation window in fiscal years 2007.

Like CAS, JAS was adopted in 2010 to support the implementation of Sierra Leone's PRSP II. JAS continued to strengthen the series of investments in Sierra Leone's postwar economic, social, and political development. As the World Bank stated, JAS was organized around two pillars: growth and human development. The growth pillar provided financing for investments in agriculture, fisheries, energy, transport, and the financial sector. The human development pillar focused on investments to support decentralized delivery in health, education, and water supply services; to improve primary education, reproductive, and child health services; and to lower child and maternal mortality rates. In addition, JAS had two cross-cutting themes: governance and democracy. As the World Bank stated, "JAS has a focus to help strengthen governance and address governance issues. . . . Opportunities for private-sector-led growth are being sought in all sectors, including those dealing with human development."[160] The JAS partners (AfDB, IDA, and IFC) were expected to generate nearly USD 300 million to implement the development goals envisioned in PRSP II.

Liberia's CAS was jointly prepared and adopted by the World Bank and AfDB in 2008 to support the implementation of the PRSP during fiscal years 2009–2012.[161] CAS replaced the Joint Interim Strategy (mid-2007 to mid-2008), which supported implementation of the IPRS. The World Bank stated, "The CAS will pursue three strategic themes: (i) rebuilding core state functions and institutions; (ii) rehabilitating infrastructure to jump-start economic growth; and (iii) facilitating pro-poor growth. These themes are fully aligned with pillars II, III, and IV of the Poverty Reduction Strategy. The CAS will also focus on the crosscutting objective of capacity development. Gender and the environment are important elements of the strategy that will be increasingly mainstreamed into World Bank and AfDB programs."[162] Liberia was expected to receive $503 million through CAS to support the development goals envisioned in the PRSP.[163]

Côte d'Ivoire's 2010–2013 Country Partnership Strategy (CPS) was developed in 2010 by the World Bank in coordination with Côte d'Ivoire and its development partners (IMF, EU, AfDB, UN).[164] The first full CPS (I-CPS) was started in 1997, but the implementation was interrupted by the armed conflict in 2002. The program was suspended in 2004 due to unpaid arrears. After Côte d'Ivoire cleared its arrears, the World Bank adopted the Interim Strategy Note (ISN) for 2008–2009. ISN focused on three strategic objectives: achieving political stability and resolving the conflict, providing humanitarian assistance to war victims, and implementing economic reform and recovery measures. By March 1, 2010, IDA had committed $637 million, of which around half had been disbursed. The CPS (2010–2013) rested on the ISN to support implementation of the PRSP. It sought to "help improve quality of life, boost economic activity and support stabilization in the short term; while continuing to help Côte d'Ivoire lay the groundwork for long term reforms to help achieve sustainable peace and growth and make progress toward the MDGs."[165] CPS focused on four strategic objectives: strengthening governance and institutions, increasing agriculture, revitalizing the private sector, and rebuilding infrastructure and basic services. At the center of these were job creation and gender mainstreaming.

CONCLUSION

At its core, international intervention is an effort to root the UN and other key actors in the international community into the statebuilding process, especially in countries devastated by civil war. Over the past several decades, in an attempt to build stable and well-functioning states after conflict, the international community has encouraged African countries to experiment with a number of neo-liberal policies. This has been done in an effort to enhance peace, democracy, market reforms, and human development. However, such neoliberal policies have not necessarily worked to further successful post–civil war statebuilding in Africa and elsewhere.

In the late 1990s, the discussions about revamping human security fused neoliberalism with the human development approach. This fusion led to what has been referred to as *people-centered liberalism*. People-centered liberalism, which is rooted in democracy, good governance, and human development, clearly has the potential to be a major improvement in the international development and peacebuilding regime. The question we pose here is whether people-centered liberalism can lead to stable, democratic, and economically successful post–civil war states in Africa. Such an approach has the potential to shift new humanitarianism from peacebuilding to positive peace. However, this approach is extremely costly and heavily depends on substantial outside support and large-scale funding from the international community.[166] It is important to ask how long we can expect the international community to maintain their commitments to helping those in need in places such as Sierra Leone, Liberia, and Côte d'Ivoire. Beyond this, questions about ongoing and future challenges, such as corruption, current international political and economic turmoil, Ebola, the COVID-19 pandemic, and nativism, remain. While the results of a people-centered liberal approach have been encouraging, only time will provide us with the necessary empirical evidence of whether it can lead to states that are peaceful, democratic, well-governed, and economically successful.

FIVE

POSTWAR INSTITUTIONAL REFORMS

Human Security and Good Governance

INTRODUCTION

International statebuilding, which has become deeply rooted in new humanitarianism and people-centered liberalism, has three interconnected components: ending widespread violence and human rights violations through peacekeeping operations, mediation aimed at reaching a durable peace agreement and successful transitional democratic elections, and postwar reconstruction to consolidate peace, strengthen democracy, inculcate good governance, and promote sustainable human development.[1] In chapter 3, we discussed the peacekeeping and mediation dimensions of international statebuilding. Chapter 4 analyzed the dominant international development principles and policy framework for good governance and postwar reconstruction. In this chapter, we examine core postwar institutional reform programs geared toward enhancing human security and good governance.

The experiences of Sierra Leone, Liberia, and Côte d'Ivoire show that postwar reconstruction is a process of setting a vision of democracy and material prosperity for the state, defining the political, economic, and social parameters of the state, and undertaking concrete programs to improve the well-being of the people through the consolidation of democracy, good governance, and investment in human development. People-centered liberalism assumes that democracy imbued with good governance has the best chance of creating economic and social conditions for poverty reduction, enhancing the overall well-being of the citizenry, and ensuring human security. In this sense, postwar reconstruction is a visionary process of institutionalizing democracy and good governance and materializing human well-being. Postwar reconstruction agendas are often wrapped in lofty policies of good leadership, prosperity, and equalitarianism that require major institutional reforms to eliminate the corrupt and authoritarian practices that led to civil war. A key part of the postwar reconstruction processes in Sierra Leone, Liberia, and Côte d'Ivoire is the institutional reforms that were undertaken to consolidate peace and democracy. Such reforms typically include major security-sector overhaul to ensure professionalism and civilian control over the military, human rights and judicial reforms, civil society enhancements, and public finance management revisions

Postwar institutional reforms typically begin toward the end of war and accelerate after a successful transitional democratic election. This was the case in both Sierra Leone and Liberia. In Côte d'Ivoire, however, fundamental institutional reforms were hampered by the problematic nature of the transitional 2010 presidential election, which ended in renewed fighting and a military conquest over Laurent Gbagbo. Given the military end to the 2010 presidential election, Côte d'Ivoire did not achieve a truly successful transitional democratic election. It was expected that the subsequent elections with the two-term limit for the presidency would rectify the stalemate. As the Group of Experts on Côte d'Ivoire stated in its April 2014 report, "The Presidential elections in 2015 and the acceptance of its results have to be considered as a benchmark for the political transition and peace process in Côte d'Ivoire."[2] The 2015 presidential election went relatively smoothly, but that gain was shattered in 2020, when Alassane Ouattara violated the presidential limit via a dubious referendum forcing the opposition to boycott the election. As such, fundamental postwar institutional reforms have largely been complicated and half-hearted.[3] Most reform efforts in Côte d'Ivoire have been weak, contested, and slow.

The ideals of democracy and good governance were at the core of the reforms in Sierra Leone, Liberia, and Côte d'Ivoire. Consolidating democracy and enhancing good governance were seen as key to maintaining long-term peace and addressing the underlying roots of poverty. In addition to financial and logistical support for multiparty elections, the international statebuilding effort included numerous postwar programs to support security-sector reforms, the rule of law, civil society, and proper public finance management.[4] The contributions of such programs to international statebuilding rest not only in their individual impacts but in their collective impacts on the governance and political environment of the state.

SECURITY-SECTOR REFORMS: HUMAN SECURITY AND CIVILIAN CONTROL

Security-sector reform, which typically centers on restructuring and retraining the military and police forces, is central to international statebuilding in war-torn countries. Sierra Leone, Liberia, and Côte d'Ivoire each had some form of postwar security-sector reforms, albeit to varying degrees. Such reform can be viewed from two interconnected angles of maintaining state security and ensuring effective law enforcement within the confines of human rights. The state security dimension rests on restructuring and rebuilding the military force, which is often in a state of collapse by the end of civil wars; the new military should not only be capable of defending the country against external threats but must also be trained to be a professional force that respects the principle of civilian control and operates in a manner devoid of sectarianism and human rights violations.[5] State security assumes the existence of a democratic political system that is continuously working toward good governance and the enhancement of human development. The law enforcement dimension rests on rebuilding the police force and related civilian law enforcement apparatus, such as customs and prisons. However, the primary focus is on the national police. Rebuilding the police force largely centers on proper recruitment practices, appropriate training (including in human rights), gender inclusion, the adoption of community policing practices, and the provision of resources for the police. While military reforms are geared toward state security, police reforms are aimed at effective crime management and the delivery of justice within a system that is transparent and effective and ensures human rights. The new military and police forces were expected to gradually replace the United Nations (UN) military and police forces, which were responsible for overall national security and policing functions in the war-torn countries under their peacekeeping mandates.

Military Reforms

One of the most profound postwar security-sector reforms in West Africa took place in Sierra Leone under the International Military Assistance Training Team (IMATT) program initiated by the United Kingdom in 1999.[6] IMATT, the state security component of the postwar security-sector reform in Sierra Leone, aimed to build the military into an effective force under democratic civilian control that will meet the security needs of Sierra Leone.[7] The program was largely funded by Britain and implemented by the British military in partnership with Sierra Leone's Ministry of Defense. In 2007, for example, Britain allocated twelve million pounds sterling to IMATT.[8] IMATT was to build on the Military Reintegration Plan (MRP) envisioned under the Lomé Peace Agreement to integrate former Revolutionary United Front and Civil Defense Forces (RUF) and CDF combatants into a new and restructured army. The new force was to reach 9,500 troops by 2007 and eventually reach a full strength of 12,500 troops.[9] The IMATT program assisted the Armed Forces Training Centre in Benguema with the training of the soldiers recruited under MRP.[10] IMATT's two key components were combat training and professional development. The program trained around 12,500 soldiers (including the air and maritime wings) in basic military skills and provided specialized training for a small group of elite soldiers in logistics, communications, command and control, and other techniques. In addition, IMATT aimed to inculcate professionalism within the new Republic of Sierra Leone Armed Forces (RSLAF). IMATT was to foster policies and practices aimed at eliminating corruption and enhancing military career paths, salaries, and benefits for soldiers. An essential element of the task was ending the corrupt practice of "ghost soldiers" on the payroll. In addition, IMATT was to promote institutional reforms to instill a culture of human rights, loyalty, service, and civilian oversight in the new RSLAF.[11]

During the IMATT program period, British military officers assumed executive roles in Sierra Leone's military affairs.[12] IMATT formally ended on March 31, 2013. It was succeeded by the British-sponsored International Security Advisory Team (ISAT) program, which formally began its mission on April 1, 2013.[13] Overall, IMATT successfully restructured RSLAF, which contributed a battalion to the peacekeeping operations in Somalia. ISAT was scaled back to a general advisory role in the security of Sierra Leone and the surrounding region. Like IMATT, ISAT advised and supported the RSLAF, especially in the area of professional development. However, ISAT's role included providing advice and support to other security agencies, most notably the Sierra Leone Police, the Office of National Security, the National Fire Force, the Prisons Department, the Immigration Office, and the Joint Maritime Committee. It also provided support to the justice sector within the framework of extant Department for International Development (DFID) and United Nations Development Programme (UNDP) programs.

In Liberia, too, security-sector reform entailed rebuilding the military. Like Sierra Leone, Liberia had no functioning national military force by the end of the war. Under the terms of the peace agreement, UNMIL was to disarm all combatants, ensure security for the country, and help with security-sector improvements. UNMIL successfully accomplished its mission of implementing the relevant terms of the Comprehensive Peace Agreement (CPA), which culminated with the installment of an elected government in November 2005. In particular, it disarmed the combatants and ensured the proper conduct of elections. The first phase of the disarmament program, which mostly focused on Monrovia, began in December 2003. The program was extended to the areas close to Monrovia in April 2004. The final phase of disarmament began in July 2004 and targeted the remote areas of the country. By February 2005, 101,495 combatants had been disarmed and demobilized, including 8,523 boys and 2,440 girls. UNMIL collected over 61,000 weapons and nearly 6.5 million rounds of small arms ammunitions.[14] After the disarmament phase, the next critical part was rebuilding the military that would gradually replace UNMIL.

The restructuring of the Liberian military was primarily financed and conducted by the United States. Though the Liberian government officially took responsibility for the Armed Forces of Liberia (AFL) in 2010, international support for the rebuilding of the AFL continued. The new AFL was to be trained according to US military doctrine and reach its full operational strength of two thousand soldiers (146 officers and 1,854 enlisted soldiers) by 2012.[15] The National Defense Strategy of 2014 aimed to increase the force to 2,500 soldiers by 2015.[16] AFL was charged with protecting Liberian territorial integrity and helping in national emergences, including disaster response. The US pledged $210 million to support the rebuilding of the AFL. Other countries also made relatively smaller contributions to the rebuilding of the AFL. Nigeria, Britain, and China trained small groups of Liberian soldiers. China also agreed to construct a base at Tabmanbu to accommodate 780 soldiers.[17] UNMIL trained the AFL on issues of human rights and military-civilian cooperation and on basic skills to operate radios and clear hidden unexploded ordnances from the war.[18]

The military component of security-sector reform in Liberia largely rested on the work of the two private security firms, DynCorp International and Pacific Architects and Engineers (PAE), contracted by the United States to rebuild the AFL. DynCorp was responsible for recruitment and basic training. PAE was in charge of advanced training, structuring the component units of the AFL, and infrastructure projects, such as the construction of barracks and military headquarters.[19] A key part of the rebuilding of the AFL was the establishment of three military bases: Barclay Training Camp, Sandee S. Ware Military Barracks, and Edward B. Kessely Military Barracks.

The rebuilding of the AFL began with the demobilization of around 13,700 soldiers from the old AFL and the termination of a significant number of employees at the Ministry of National Defense.[20] The reformed Ministry of National Defense was staffed by approximately ninety trained civilians.[21] The demobilization allowed for the recruitment of new soldiers vetted on the basis of age and medical fitness, literacy, human rights record, and regional diversity. In particular, the new members of the AFL were expected to have attained at least a twelfth-grade education, be free of drugs, HIV, and tuberculosis, and be between the ages of eighteen and forty-five. A key recruitment target was to get 20 percent of the new AFL to be women.[22] Recruitment took place in all fifteen countries, especially Monrovia.

The training of the Liberian national army progressed, albeit slowly. Only 634 noncommissioned officers and 11 officers completed advanced training by

October 2007.[23] Up to August 2007, women accounted for only 5 percent of the force.[24] By December 2009, two AFL battalions completed the US Army Training and Evaluation program, which brought the force to the level of around two thousand troops and marked the completion of the first phase of training for the new AFL.[25] However, the Liberian government was frequently unable to pay salaries on time, and the Ministry of Defense continuously suffered from poor management.[26] The AFL reached 2,040 soldiers after 134 recruits completed basic training in April 2014.[27]

An essential part of the rebuilding of the AFL was providing advanced training and equipment. In January 2010, sixty-one US military personnel arrived in Liberia to conduct advanced training, which included instruction in the areas of infantry tactics, operational planning, logistics, engineering, communication, medicine, military justice, and administration.[28] By 2014, a total of thirty-two AFL engineers had received intermediate-level training in explosive ordnance disposal from the UN Mine Action Service. Two defender boats were also commissioned in February 2014. A Liberian platoon served at the UN Multidimensional Integrated Stabilization Mission in Mali.[29] In line with the pace of security-sector reform and political developments in Liberia, UNMIL was gradually reduced to 4,619 military personnel in 2014 from its peak of 15,250 troops in 2003.[30] Overall, the rebuilding of the AFL was completed, which paved the way for the termination of UNMIL. As the UN stated, "On 30 June, 2016, UNMIL completed the transfer of security responsibilities to Liberian authorities, in accordance with resolution 2239, adopted on 17 September 2015. UNMIL successfully completed its mandate on 30 March 2018."[31]

The restructuring of the Ivoirian military was far more problematic than that of the military in Sierra Leone and Liberia. The main challenge for Côte d'Ivoire was the fragility of the peace. Because former President Gbagbo and current President Ouattara never peacefully resolved their differences, their supporters were often ready to fight. In 2011, Ouattara issued a decree unifying the National Armed Forces of Côte d'Ivoire and the Forces Nouvelles. However, the Front Populaire Ivoirien (FPI) called for the annulment of the decree and viewed the process as a mere takeover of the Ivoirian military by the former rebel Forces Républicaines de Côte d'Ivoire (FRCI)–cum–Forces Nouvelles de Côte d'Ivoire. This was compounded by the continued existence of former combatants, including the *dozos*, and new armed and militia groups operating in the southwest. On January 22, 2014, Ouattara promoted more than five hundred members of the "unified" FRCI, including several commanders of the Forces Nouvelles (FN).[32]

Côte d'Ivoire struggled with Disarmament, Demobilization and Reintegration (DDR), which was a major step toward any postwar military restructuring. The DDR programmatic framework was only finalized in January 2014. The

African Development Bank promised $30 million, while the EU committed to provide €14 million.[33] The DDR process moved very slowly. By the end of April 2014, only 22,590 former combatants (including 1,596 women) had been disarmed and demobilized. During that period, 6,939 weapons, 531,583 rounds of small arms ammunition, and 8,512 items of explosive ordnance were collected. About seventy operations to disarm and demobilize combatants were conducted at the DDR camp near Abidjan, mostly involving FRCI and FN members. Very few disbandment and demobilization operations took place in the center and southwest of the country. The participation of groups that supported Gbagbo was very low.[34] With respect to the reinsertion of former combatants, UNOCI launched eight community projects in February 2014. The Ivoirian Authority for Disarmament, Demobilization and Reintegration also conducted a resocialization program in March 2014. Around 30,455 people received some form of reinsertion support by the end of April 2014.[35]

In addition to the slow progress on DDR, there were major violations of the arms embargo on Côte d'Ivoire, especially by the Ouattara government. The Ivoirian government imported weapons without reporting them to UNOCI as required under paragraph 5 of UN Security Council Resolution 2101 (2013). This raised serious concerns, including from the Group of Experts on Côte d'Ivoire, that the Ivoirian government was importing weapons in preparation for eventual violence during the presidential elections.[36] The Group of Experts pointed to numerous instances of incompliance with the embargo through the failure to fully disclose the types and quantity of arms imports or the falsification of end-user certificates. Some of the instances included the November 2013 importation of 659 bulletproof jackets, only 200 of which were reported. Also, end-user certificates were not properly submitted for night-vision and observation equipment and fifteen hundred Jericho pistols (9mm). The Group of Experts also observed that vehicles imported by the government (Toyota Land Cruisers) were reconfigured into combat vehicles. These included vehicles produced by military vehicle manufacturer Ateliers de Construction Mécanique de L'Atlantique that had been fitted with heavy machine guns.[37] The group stated, "The reconfiguration of equipment for military purposes after notification to the Committee is a contravention of the sanctions regime, as any conversion to military use requires an exemption by the Committee. The Group would like to reiterate its concern about such cases, particularly those involving transport equipment. Vehicles may be converted for military purposes in order to circumvent the exemption procedures dictated by relevant Security Council resolutions."[38]

Gbagbo supporters also prepared for conflict. The Group of Experts identified a network of Gbagbo supporters who operated in Ghana and South Africa to finance armed groups loyal to Gbagbo through the sale of diamonds and gold, in contravention of the UN sanctions on Côte d'Ivoire. Some of the individuals named in the Group of Experts' report included Abie Zogoé Hervé-Brice, who was a former Ivoirian ambassador to South Africa, and Stephane Kipré, Gbagbo's son-in-law. The group stated: "The illicit diamond network had two main purposes. From one side, it was meant to finance the operations of individuals close to the former administration of Laurent Gbagbo to destabilize Côte d'Ivoire.... The other purpose of the network was to grant personal financial gains to its creators and middlemen through a series of lump sums or facilitation commissions on the value of the sales."[39]

On June 30, 2017, UNOCI's mandate ended. At that time, the Ouattara government had won the fight against Gbagbo and his FPI supporters. Overall, violence had ended and the state was functional, but the reforms did not consolidate peace; rather, the victory of Ouattara only meant that Côte d'Ivoire was sliding back into the state of no war, no peace, and this situation has been further worsened by the prolongation of Ouattara's rule into a third presidential term after the 2020 election, which the opposition boycotted.

Police Reforms

While most of the initial security-sector reforms focused on restructuring the military, police reform remained a critical step. All three countries had some form of police reform, albeit of varying levels of intensity. Sierra Leone and Liberia clearly needed more profound police reform because the states had collapsed, while in Côte d'Ivoire, such reforms were moderate.

Police reform in Sierra Leone began during the civil war period but did not progress until the war ended in 2001. The effort started with the introduction of the Sierra Leone Policing Charter in August 1998 by President Ahmad Tejan Kabbah; the charter established a commitment to upholding community policing practices, protecting human rights, maintaining a sense of professionalism, and ensuring equal opportunity in the police service. It stated: "Our aim is to see a reborn Sierra Leone Police, which will be a 'Force for Good' in our nation."[40] In essence, police reform in Sierra Leone centered on enhancing the management of the police force, providing the necessary equipment to enable the police to do its work, and inculcating community policing practices.

One of the more notable police reform efforts in Sierra Leone was the British-sponsored Commonwealth Community Safety and Security Project (CCSSP), which aimed to make the Sierra Leone Police visible and capable of providing internal security. CCSSP was initiated in 1999, when the Sierra Leone Police had been rendered almost obsolete by the rebel RUF and the renegade military that overthrew the elected government. Police officers were killed, forcing many to abandon their posts and withdraw to the safest areas of Freetown. By the time the war ended, an estimated nine hundred police officers had been killed by the rebels, and the size of the police force fell from 9,317 to 6,600.[41] The management component of the reform was led by Keith Biddle, a retired assistant chief constable from Manchester, UK, who was appointed inspector general of the Sierra Leone Police. Biddle led the police from 1999 to 2003. A key part of the reform was transforming the senior management team of the police and using merit, instead of seniority, as the basis for promotion. Biddle removed some of the old guards through forced retirement. This led to the recruitment and promotion of younger university graduates, who were later trained in Britain and given major leadership roles in the police force. The new management style deviated from orthodox bureaucratic practices and gravitated more toward corporate-style management. An executive management board was established, and emphasis was placed on institutional research and strategic planning.

In terms of reequipping and training the police, officers were furnished with new uniforms, vehicles, and communication equipment. Despite some of the management changes, reforms were hampered by the war. Though recruitment, training, and the construction of barracks went on, efforts to increase the police force to 9,500 and equip it were very slow. Until 2002, the police were barely present outside of Freetown. In 2004, the Sierra Leone force included six thousand officers and seven hundred vehicles. The police reached the target strength of 9,500 in 2005. The inculcation of community policing continued throughout the reform period. Training was based on the principle of Local Needs Policing. At the core of Local Needs Policing were the Local Policing Partnership Boards established to facilitate collaboration and engagement between the police and the communities they served. Each board was coordinated by the police local unit commander and comprised of reputable community members, such as paramount chiefs and religious and women's group leaders. One of the best examples of the application of Local Needs Policing was the development of the Family Support Unit (FSU).

The police reform started under CCSSP was expanded to include more units in the security and justice sectors. In 2005, the Justice Sector Development Program (JSDP) replaced CCSSP. JSDP, which ended in 2011, received around £27.7 million from Britain.[42] The overall goal of JSDP was "to support the development of an effective and accountable justice sector that is capable of meeting the needs and interests of poor, marginalised and vulnerable people." [43] A main objective of JSDP was to improve the quality of the police through effective community policing and enhancing relations between the officers and communities. JSDP was an integrated program that combined police reforms with efforts to better the judicial system, prisons, and civil society organizations. Some of the notable elements of the policing component of JSDP included the training of over 80 percent of senior and middle-ranking police offices in community policing practices, the development of FSUs, and the training of about three hundred community volunteers in community mediation practices.[44] In 2012, JSDP was replaced with the Access to Security and Justice Programme (ASJP), which was to end in 2015. While previous efforts to enhance policing largely centered on Freetown, the main focus of ASJP was to expand the new policing and management practices to the interior of the country. ASJP was launched in several places outside of the capital city, including Waterloo, Kenema, and Moyamba.[45]

FSU was one of the most notable community policing elements of reform in Sierra Leone. It was set up to deal with issues of sexual and gender-based crimes and child abuse through community education and regular police investigation and prosecution practices. This aspect of community policing began in 1999 with the establishment of the Domestic Violence Unit (DVU) at the Kissy Police Station. In 2001, DVU was transformed into FSU and placed within the Criminal Investigation Department of the police. In 2004, the Ministry of Social Welfare, Gender and Children Affairs joined the FSU to provide social work expertise to victims of gender-based crimes. FSU was made an independent unit of the police in 2007, and its work expanded to include crimes committed by or against children. FSU's work was enhanced by the passage of the Anti-Human Trafficking Act (2005), Domestic Violence Act (2007), Child Rights Act (2007), Devolution of Estates Act (2007), and Registration of Customary Marriages and Divorces Act (2009). Over forty-three FSU stations were established throughout the country.[46]

Like military reform, police reform had positive effects on human security in Sierra Leone. The police became visible and operational throughout the country. Though Sierra Leone did not maintain the proper crime statistics to measure the effectiveness of police reforms, there were visible signs of progress in everyday security and human rights. A crime report issued by the police in 2012 indicated that the overall rate of crime decreased from 0.96 percent in 2011 to 0.82 percent in 2012.[47] Despite the reform, the Sierra Leone Police were still plagued by insufficient resources and abuses of power, most notably in the form of corruption. While the lack of resources and petty bribery involving traffic officers were not major threats to national security or the overall state of human rights, police reforms needed to continue to enhance professionalism through proper equipment and practices. Despite the remarkable improvement in security, incidents of armed robbery occurred more frequently. While armed robbery is a common phenomenon in major African cities, postwar countries are particularly challenged when the frequency of such incidents increases. In Freetown, the reality of armed robbery led to a huge private-security industry.[48] While the police force reached the target of 9,500 members, there were concerns that the force was still too small to effectively maintain law and order. There were growing calls to increase the size of the force to twelve thousand. Studies commissioned by the police correctly pointed to some public recognition of improvement in policing practices in Sierra Leone, but the perception that there was corruption continued to be troubling. The problem of petty bribery dovetailed with the poor salaries and inadequate resources for the police, especially in rural areas.[49]

Sierra Leone witnessed a remarkable state of peace after the end of the civil war. Except for some isolated incidents of violence during the 2012 and 2017 elections and periodic cases of armed robbery in Freetown, Sierra Leone did not witness any significant threat to national security until the outbreak of the Ebola epidemic in late 2014 and the controversial sacking of the vice president by President Ernest Bai Koroma on March 18, 2015. However, the events leading to the 2023 elections and the elections themselves have tremendously undermined peace.[50] One of most significant examples of political violence was an attack on the 2012 opposition Sierra Leone People's Party (SLPP) presidential candidate, Julius Maada Bio. The attack took place in Bo in July 2011 during an election campaign event. The fighting left one person dead and twenty injured, and several buildings were burned down, including the local APC party office. Additionally, the minister of Internal Affairs, Musa Tarawali, was attacked in Kono by youths throwing stones. The attack, which allegedly led Tarawali to order his bodyguards to disperse the crowd with gunfire, was said to have been initiated by APC supporters who perceived him to be a potential presidential challenger to the sitting vice president, who is from Kono.[51] More recently, the opposition APC has also been harassed by the current SLPP government led by Bio. Opposition figures have been arbitrarily jailed, and APC offices have also been attacked in what has now become a gradual escalation of conflict and violence between the opposition APC and ruling SLPP.[52]

Though there was not major social unrest outside of the election periods during the immediate postwar period, the 2014 Ebola outbreak sparked tensions, as citizens resisted quarantine regulations or demanded more government action to provide appropriate services to Ebola-affected people. On October 21, 2014, for example, the government imposed a curfew in Koidu Town in Kono after clashes erupted between police and youths who were resisting the effort by police and medical officers to take a ninety-year-old grandmother for an Ebola test. Two people were reported to have been killed during the clash.[53] More recently, COVID-19 restrictions and skyrocketing food prices associated with the Ukraine have triggered violent social unrest.

Liberia's police reform had similar goals of building a professional force capable of maintaining law and order and respecting human rights. By the end of the war, Liberia's police force had been decimated.[54] Most of the efforts to rebuild the Liberian National Police (LNP) were supported by the United States and UN as stipulated in UN Security Council Resolution 1509 of September 19, 2003. In 2009, the United States promised to provide $19.75 million to help rebuild the LNP.[55] However, actual funding was limited, and expectations were that the Liberian government would take responsibility for rebuilding the force. While Liberia was rebuilding its police, United Nations Polic (UNPOL) performed a major policing role in Liberia. By June 2014, Liberian security agencies had assumed responsibility for "81 per cent of static guard duties and all road-bound cash escort functions."[56] Moreover, they were serving as first-line responders. However, UNMIL provided backup to the Liberian security agencies and secured the international airports, two prisons, and the premises of the president of the country. As the UN secretary general noted, "the national security presence remains thin across the country" largely due to the financial and material constraints faced by the Liberian government.[57] According to UNMIL estimates, Liberia would need a police force of eight thousand officers by the time UN peacekeepers fully withdrew. By 2013, however, the LNP had only 4,417 officers. UNPOL was still deployed in thirty-two areas, including twenty-nine zones in Monrovia, providing support to LNP. UNPOL's operational supports to LNP included joint patrols, advising, communication assistance, and crime analysis.[58] Leadership was a major challenge for LNP.

The first effort to rebuild the LNP started in 2004 with the registration of the remnant officers of the defunct LNP and the creation of the Operations Section of UNPOL. UNPOL began rebuilding the LPN by registering about five thousand people believed to be members of the defunct LNP. Most did not have uniforms or receive pay from the Liberian government at the time of their registration. Members of the defunct LPN were engaged in unlawful policing practices such as extorting bribes and operating without a clear command structure. UNPOL vetted and recruited about four hundred of those registered to help maintain law and order. The recruits were fitted with black T-shirts with a police label and given basic office supplies, which allowed them to operate as an ad hoc LNP. UNPOL both provided legitimacy and engaged in public education campaigns about the LNP and its role in the peacebuilding process. UNPOL's Operations Section was tasked with supporting the ad hoc LNP as a way to maintain order and provide basic policing services at the end of the war.[59]

A key step in the efforts to build a real postwar LNP was the establishment of the National Transitional Government of Liberia (NTGL)-UNMIL Rule of Law Implementation Committee, which was tasked with developing policy guidelines for the recruitment and selection of a new LNP. At the start of the recruitment phase, the United States provided $500,000 to support the effort to rebuild the LNP. Other donors, such as Norway, the Netherlands, and Belgium, also provided some support. The initial goal was to train 3,500 officers for the new

LNP.[60] Recruiting was conducted by UNPOL based on criteria established by the NTGL-UNMIL Rule of Law Implementation Committee. The members of the new LNP had to be between the ages of eighteen and thirty-five and attain a twelfth-grade education. In addition, they could not hold a position in a political organization, have a criminal record, or have committed human rights violations.[61] The other dimension of the police reform was the formal deactivation of members of the former LNP who failed to meet the eligibility criteria or simply had not applied to join the new LNP. In 2007, 2,351 members of the former LNP and 870 members of the former Special Security Service were deactivated with a one-time severance pay of around $1,200 per person.[62]

Most of the training of the LNP took place in Liberia with a small group of officers trained in advanced firearms use and leadership outside of Liberia's borders (in Nigeria and Ghana). In addition to meeting the numerical targets, reform measures aimed to enhance police performance, especially in community policing and human rights compliance. In 2004, UNPOL established the National Police Training Academy (NPTA). The NPTA was initially set to train 3,500 recruits in basic police training. A key part of the curriculum was human rights and democratic policing. By June 2007, 3,522 officers (including 203 females) had graduated from the NPTA. The academy was handed over to the LNP in 2007, after the completion of the initial training program. However, UNPOL continued to provide trainers and general support to NPTA. In terms of middle- and senior-level management, seventy-eight officers were trained at the Ghana Institute of Management and Public Administration by 2014. Another set of officers received management training in Liberia at the LNP training center in Harper.[63] Much of the effort to increase the size and quality of the LNP rested on improving the infrastructure by constructing dormitories for police recruits, barracks, stations, and regional headquarters.[64]

The new LNP increased its performance but often received operational support from UNPOL. One of the notable operational achievements was the establishment of the emergency response system (a 355 phone number), which allowed LNP and UNPOL joint patrol officers to respond to law enforcement emergencies. However, the system was often under-resourced, which inhibited proper response. LNP also developed specialized elite police units to deal with major incidents of violence. In particular, the Police Support Unit (PSU) was formed to respond to riots and violent crimes. In 2013, the PSU had around 681 officers.[65] The Emergency Response Unit (ERU) was created to counter organized armed threats and major internal security breaches; it was to include five hundred officers trained in advanced weapons use by American contractor DynCorp. By 2003, ERU had around 321 active officers. The United States provided an initial $5 million in support to ERU, while the UN helped rebuild police stations.[66] Another important part of the reform was enhancing professionalism and addressing abuse of power and corruption. In 2006, the Police Board of Inquiry was replaced with the Professional Standards Division, which was established to enhance accountability within the LNP; it investigated internal and public complaints about police abuse of power and conducted internal audits.[67]

While the rebuilding of the LNP progressed, there were major challenges in terms of size and operational capacity. For example, the LNP was very visible in Monrovia, but there were few officers deployed outside of Monrovia. In 2013, major counties such as Bong, Lofa, and Grand Gedeh had only between 90 and 120 officers each, and some small communities still had no police officers.[68] Not only was the overall size of the force small, but the recruitment and training processes were slow. The other major challenge was a lack of resources and professional capacity. Police officers often complained of low salaries. In 2013, the average salary of a patrol officer was only $135 per month.[69] The LNP did not have sufficient vehicles or essential supplies (e.g., fuel) to properly patrol and respond to crime situations. In many cases, victims of crimes were asked to cover the transportation cost of responding officers. Many police officers engaged in extortion and bribe taking, especially from motorists, petty traders, victims of crimes, and offenders.[70] Public trust in the ability of the police to deal with crimes was low, which further propelled vigilantism and mob justice. Even more troubling was the fact that the ERU and PSU were accused of misusing weapons and robbing citizens at night.[71]

Apart from the abuse of power by individual officers, the police were also involved in the improper use of force and human rights violations. In particular, officers were accused of beating and wounding students during the March 22, 2011, student protest. On November 11, 2011, the police also clashed with supporters of the opposition Congress for Democratic Change, leaving at least one person dead. Both incidents were investigated and led to the dismissal of Police Inspector General Marc Amblard.[72]

Liberia's security-sector reform lagged behind the country's security needs. Though the civil war had ended and overall peace had been restored, there were still significant threats to security beyond regular policing challenges. In fact, the UN kept approximately 3,750 UNMIL troops in Liberia until mid-2015, as approved under UN Security Council resolutions 2066 (2012) and 2116 (2013). It was not until June 2016 that UNMIL completed the transfer of security responsibilities to Liberian authorities, in accordance with Resolution 2239, adopted on September 17, 2015. UNMIL stayed in Liberia until March 30, 2018.

Perhaps the biggest challenge to Liberia's security was the inculcation of good governance to build some trust between the government and citizenry. In June

2014, President Ellen Johnson Sirleaf was openly accused of nepotism and corruption by Christopher Neyor, president of the National Oil Company of Liberia and a candidate for the Montserrado Senate against Sirleaf's son, Robert Sirleaf.[73] Sirleaf was also criticized for appointing her children to top government positions. Apart from political mistrust, there were periodic demonstrations based on economic and political grievances. In July 2014, for example, around five hundred people held a protest against ArcelorMittal Iron Ore Company in Nimba County for noncompliance with social commitments, which resulted in a violent clash with the police. There were also protests against other corporations, such as Golden Veroleum in Grand Kru County and BHP Billiton in Nimba County. The police clashed with supporters of the opposition Congress for Democratic Change. Even more disturbing were reports of plans to overthrow the government. In July 2007, George Koukou (former speaker of the National Transitional Legislative Assembly), Major Charles Julu (former army chief of staff), and Colonel Andrew Dorbor were arrested for an alleged coup plot.[74] Liberia's borders with Côte d'Ivoire and Guinea also continued to be volatile, as refugees, pro-Gbagbo militants, and Liberian mercenaries in Côte d'Ivoire continuously crossed into Liberia. In 2011, over two hundred thousand Ivoirian and Guinean refugees entered the country.[75]

In Côte d'Ivoire, there was minimal progress with police reform. Though the Ivoirian police and gendarmerie were in much better shape than the police in Sierra Leone and Liberia before and during the war, they, too, were in need of major reform. Even before the war, the Ivoirian police and gendarmes were notorious for impunity and plagued by a lack of proper training and equipment.[76] These forces virtually collapsed during the worst points of the Ivoirian war, but by July 2012, 85 percent of police officers and gendarmes had resumed duty. However, reform efforts were minimal and stalled by uncertainty over the peace. Most of the effort to rebuild the police and gendarmes forces centered on acquiring equipment and rebuilding stations. One of the first steps on this front was the effort to distribute weapons recovered by the UN to police officers and gendarmes. UNOCI assisted in the rehabilitation of police stations, gendarmeries, and municipal offices and the training of police officers and gendarmes for the December 2011 legislative elections. In November 2011, France delivered computers and thirty police vehicles following the resumption of security cooperation with Côte d'Ivoire.[77] Though the police and gendarmes forces were operational, Côte d'Ivoire needed fundamental reforms to rebuild trust between them and the citizenry, which would be essential for the inculcation of democracy and long-term peace. Such changes would require real reconciliation between the northern and southern political forces. However, reform of the police and gendarme forces practically stalled.

HUMAN RIGHTS AND JUSTICE

A major aspect of postwar institutional reform is addressing human rights violations committed during war and restoring the rule of law. In Sierra Leone, Liberia, and Côte d'Ivoire, this effort centered on the truth and reconciliation process, prosecutions of persons responsible for war crimes, rebuilding the justice sector, and promoting good governance. All three countries established truth and reconciliation commissions, though of varying quality. Sierra Leone completed its war crimes trials and undertook justice and good-governance reforms. Liberia did not pursue significant war crimes trials, but it engaged in justice and governance reforms. In Côte d'Ivoire, the ICC opened investigations and prosecuted some people. As with the security sector, justice and governance reforms in Côte d'Ivoire were minimal.

Truth and Reconciliation

Overall, the Truth and Reconciliation Commission (TRC) of Sierra Leone was successful in documenting the general nature of the crimes committed during the war, providing a forum for public discourses about the conditions that led to the civil war and the challenges of healing and articulating a vision for national rehabilitation based on social justice and good governance. As envisioned in Article VI(2) of the Lomé Peace Agreement, the TRC of Sierra Leone was established with the passage of the Truth and Reconciliation Act on February 22, 2000. The commission, chaired by Bishop Joseph Humper, was comprised of four Sierra Leoneans, one Canadian, a Gambian, and a South African. The seven commissioners were sworn in on July 5, 2002; at the ceremony, the president of Sierra Leone summed up the mandate of the commission:

> The Commission will investigate and report on the causes, nature and extent of the violations and abuses of human rights and international humanitarian law during the conflict. Of course it will create an impartial historical record of the atrocities perpetrated against innocent civilians during a ten-year period of the war. However, it is absolutely necessary that we look beyond those functions, and see the work of the TRC as a therapeutic process. It was a brutal war. It caused grievous physical and emotional damage for thousands of our compatriots. It also created divisions between families, and among neighbours and friends. To a large extent the conflict also fractured the body politic of the nation. Well, the guns may be silent, but the trauma of the war lingers on. We have a great deal of healing to do. This is why the TRC is, and should also be seen, as an instrument of national reconciliation, and another means of strengthening the peace.[78]

The commission took statements and held public hearings in all the districts of the country. It concluded the public hearings on Aguste 5, 2003, and issued a final report in 2004.

There were contentious debates about the Sierra Leone TRC process, both before the commission was established and after the report was released. Though a TRC process was called for in the Lomé Peace Agreement, many people saw it as a potentially problematic process that could impede reconciliation. Some argued that the TRC would just open up more wounds. Instead of the TRC process favored by NGOs and human rights activists, there was a strong popular desire for a "forgive-and-forget" approach.[79] At a pragmatic level, people were skeptical of the TRC for fear of it undermining the nascent peace, the potential for self-incrimination leading to prosecution by the Special Court for Sierra Leone, and retaliation, especially from ex-combatants and politically vested people. Beyond the practical consideration, forgive-and-forget has been a deeply rooted conflict resolution mechanism in many communities. As Rosalind Shaw observed, "The imperative to remember violence during the TRC was at odds with widespread local techniques of healing and reintegration, which are based on the *social forgetting* of violence."[80] Social forgetting dovetails with the pragmatic considerations of the forgive-and-forget approach. Shaw rightly noted, "Social forgetting is a different process from individual forgetting, in that people still have personal memories of the violence. But speaking of the violence—especially in public—was (and is) viewed as encouraging its return, calling it forth when it is still very close and might at any moment erupt again."[81] Despite the fears, the TRC process passed without undermining the peace or leading to widespread retaliations or prosecutions. As others have contended regarding the experience in Sierra Leone, the "TRC was essentially for the healing of the nation."[82]

The more challenging debates are about the achievements of the TRC process and its impacts on the character of the postwar state. Though the TRC's mandate was largely to impartially investigate and document what happened to persons and their communities during the war, in reality, the TRC was seen as a forum for "truth finding" and identifying durable solutions to the problems that led to the civil war. The expectation that it would not only record what happened to people but also diagnose the causes of the war and recommend solutions led to varying criticisms of the TRC. The TRC itself reified those expectations in its report, which provided both general and specific causes of the civil war and recommendations for building a country that would not be plagued by the corruption, oppression, and abuse of power that had led to the war: "How did a peace-loving nation become engulfed, seemingly overnight, in horror? What events occurred in the history of Sierra Leone to make this conflict possible? Explanations put forward have varied from 'bad governance' and 'the history of the post-colonial period' to 'the urge to acquire the country's diamond wealth' and the roles of Libya or the Liberian faction leader Charles Taylor."[83] Similarly, the report included sweeping recommendations for overhauling the state. These recommendations were grouped into the categories of human rights protection, establishing the rule of law, security services, good governance, fighting corruption, youth and women empowerment, protection and welfare of children, mineral resource management, and reparation.[84] As the commission argued, its recommendations were "designed to facilitate the building of a new Sierra Leone based on the values of human dignity, tolerance and respect for the rights of all persons. In particular, the recommendations are intended to help create an open and vibrant democracy in which all are treated as equal before the law."[85] The commission believed that "the adoption of its recommendations would assist the people of Sierra Leone to rise above the bitter conflicts of the past, which caused unspeakable violations of human rights and left a legacy of dehumanisation, hatred and fear."[86]

Tim Kelsall cast doubts on the validity of the report by questioning the truthfulness of the testimonies presented to the TRC. In the case of the hearings in the Tonkolili district, for example, Kelsall wrote, "the truth—a truth, that is, that was satisfactory to the participants—was not forthcoming. This was so obvious that on the penultimate day of the Commission's hearings, members of the audience were incensed and the hearings appeared to be on the brink of failure, with the community possibly on the verge of renewed violence."[87] Instead of being a truth-telling process, according to Kelsall, the TRC process was a healing ritual. As he further observed in Tonkolili:

> But on the final day of the hearings the atmosphere changed. This was not because the perpetrators eventually told the truth; in fact the truth status of testimony only marginally improved. Rather, the change was due to the addition of a carefully staged reconciliation ceremony to the proceedings, a ritual that created an emotionally charged atmosphere that succeeded in moving many of the participants and spectators, not least the present author, and which arguably opened an avenue for reconciliation and lasting peace. Insofar as this was the case, it suggests that ritual may be more important to reconciliation than truth.[88]

Testimonies at the TRC were often viewed as exaggerated, based on bad memory, or simply deceitful.[89] However, the fact that so many amputations had occurred during the civil war lent physical proof to some of the testimonies. Some of the people who testified were victims of amputation whose scars were visible. While the scars did not tell who committed the violations, where they occurred, or how they occurred, they told a general truth about the war, which was as important as the specific details of the violations. One such victim was

Fatmata Kamara, who told the TRC: "The rebels beheaded my sister and took us to Seven Up garage. They killed two of my friends. At that time I was a virgin, I have done nothing wrong, they killed my sister, my mother and father. . . . After amputating my friend's hand he called one of his boys and he raped me, they said they were still not satisfied, they tied us and chopped off our feet."[90] Though the deficit of truth undermined the TRC's mandate to document, the Sierra Leone TRC process was not too different from others in which the deliberative process and rituals of healing stood in contrast to the deficit of truth as it occurred in both South Africa and Rwanda.[91] This healing and deliberative process was continued by various NGOs that undertook programs to educate the public about the TRC report and furthered the healing process through culturally grounded practices and symbols. One such effort was the work of Fambul Talk.[92]

The recommendations of the TRC in Sierra Leone were widely praised by civil society and activists because of their sweeping calls for human rights, human development, and social justice. Most of the concerns about the report actually centered on the government's implementation effort and the international donor support. As in South Africa, reparation was understood largely in terms of promoting human development, notwithstanding the thirty thousand rands recommended by the TRC for eligible victims.[93] Sierra Leone's entire postwar reconstitution program was congruent with the social justice and human development recommendations of the TRC. While the government of Sierra Leone lacked a clearly defined and comprehensive framework for implementing the recommendations, most of the suggestions dovetailed with the PRSP and the overall postwar statebuilding effort. In particular, the good-governance and human development components of the recommendations were clearly evident in the PRSPs.[94] Two aspects of the TRC report stood out for special implementation outside of the overall national development plan embodied in the PRSR: reparation and human rights.

Reparation centered on both investment in communities devastated by the war and specific payments to people who suffered major abuses, especially amputations and rape. Investments in communities became part of the broader postwar poverty-reduction effort undertaken primarily by the National Commission for Social Action (NaCSA), which implemented small-scale community development projects. Payments to victims of abuse were small and slow, in part due to lack of sufficient donor support. However, some payments were made through the Victims' Trust Fund that was launched in 2009. In 2009, for example, micro grants of around 300,000 leones were awarded to amputees and victims of sexual violence and funded through the $3 million earmarked for reparations under the UN Peacebuilding Grant to Sierra Leone.[95] By March 17, 2011, an estimated 20,107 victims were believed to have each received micro grants of around USD 100.[96]

In 2013, NaCSA provided rehabilitation micro grants to 1,300 victims under the UN Multi-Partner Trust Fund (MPTF).[97]

Based on the Lomé Peace Agreement and the TRC report, the Human Rights Commission of Sierra Leone (HRCSL) was established under Act 19 of 2004 and became operational in 2007. The mission of HRCSL was "to take the lead role in building a culture of human rights (including respect for individual responsibilities) which maintains human dignity for all in Sierra Leone in full compliance with the constitution, laws, international and regional instruments, through effective partnership and collaboration."[98] The Human Rights Commission of Sierra Leone Act of 2004 empowered HRCSL to investigate and report allegations of violations, promote a culture of human rights, review existing laws, draft legislation, advise the government on compliance with domestic and international human rights laws, and publish an annual report on the state of human rights. The commission was given the powers and status of the High Court in matters relating to investigations of human rights issues. It could issue orders to enforce its decision and refer any person unduly refusing to comply to the High Court for contempt of court.[99] HRCSL issued annual human rights reports. It also engaged in public education campaigns. Most of HRCSL's work dovetailed with the justice-sector reform aimed at enhancing the capacity of courts and the prison system to quickly adjudicate cases and treat inmates properly.

In Liberia, the TRC of Liberia, comprised of nine Liberians, was established under the 2005 Truth and Reconciliation Act in line with the 2003 CPA and launched on February 20, 2006. However, the TRC was marred by controversies surrounding the testimonies and its recommendations. Actual hearings began in January 2008, and the final report was released in 2009. The core of the mandate of the TRC was "investigating gross human rights violations and violations of international humanitarian law as well as abuses that occurred, including massacres, sexual violations, murder, extra-judicial killings and economic crimes, such as the exploitation of natural or public resources to perpetuate armed conflicts, during the period January 1979 to October 14, 2003; determining whether these were isolated incidents or part of a systematic pattern; establishing the antecedents, circumstances factors and context of such violations and abuses; and determining those responsible for the commission of the violations and abuses and their motives as well as their impact on victims."[100] However, the law allowed the TRC to address issues prior to 1979. According to the TRC, its report was based on "deliberate planning and engagement with all segments of our society centering on all 15 counties of Liberia and the Diaspora."[101] It collected over 22,000 written statements, conducted several dozen personal interviews, and held over five hundred live public testimonies. It also held consultations with national and local stakeholders and a national conference on reconciliation.[102]

The TRC of Liberia attributed the Liberian civil war to a variety of factors related to poor governance, historic ethnic and social injustices, and ignorance.[103] It also issued recommendations to address poor governance, promote human development, and foster a national memory that provides community reconciliation and memorializes the victims. In particular, it called for a reparation program of approximately USD 500 million over a thirty-year implementation period.[104] It also recommended the formation of a National Palava Hut Forum to promote traditional dispute-resolution mechanisms, the erection of monuments, the issuance of death certificates to relatives of the victims of the war, and the establishment of a National Unification and Memorial Day and a national memorial ceremony for former President William R. Tolbert Jr., who was buried in a mass grave. In addition, it called on the government of Liberia to issue a public apology for the war.[105]

Unlike Sierra Leone, however, the Liberian TRC made very specific recommendations to hold people (including specific individuals) accountable for war crimes. In particular, it called for the establishment of an Extraordinary Criminal Tribunal for Liberia "to try all persons recommended by the TRC for the commission of gross human rights violations including violations of international humanitarian law, international human rights law, war crimes and economic crimes including but not limited to, killing, gang rape, multiple rape, forced recruitment, sexual slavery, forced labor, exposure to deprivation, [the] missing, etc."[106] It listed specific persons and entities to be tried or investigated for such crimes. In addition, it listed forty-nine prominent people, including sitting President Sirleaf, that were to be "barred from holding public office, elected or appointed, for a period of thirty (30) years as of July 1, 2009."[107] According to the commission, those forty-nine people were "by their conduct, leadership, finances, and support, actions or inactions . . . responsible for the commission of gross human rights violations, international humanitarian law violations, international human rights law, war crimes, and egregious domestic law violations."[108]

Liberia's TRC was far more controversial, in terms of both proceedings and recommendations. As with the hearings in Sierra Leone, the truthfulness of the testimonies given to the Liberian TRC were questionable. What was even more problematic with the Liberian TRC hearings was the lack of cooperation and the antagonism from key protagonists in the war. Major players such as Prince Yormie Johnson were reluctant to testify, and when they did, their testimonies and attitude toward the process seemed like a mere joke and an ethnic witch hunt. As Lansana Gberie observed, "I was to see this same attitude on display when I attended the hearings at the Centennial Pavilion. . . . None of the alleged perpetrators who appeared asked for amnesty before they gave their testimonies, and all of them behaved as though what they did—gang-raping women, disemboweling people, participating in mass killings, or leading gangs of fighters (on the orders of Taylor, many said) to invade neighbouring countries where they exported their brand of cruelty—was unusual but not particularly despicable."[109] Given this lack of cooperation, the truthfulness of the TRC report had to be discerned more through the general story of the war than the specific atrocities.

The punitive recommendations of the Liberian TRC were even more controversial, in part due to the call for sweeping punishment directed at many people. One of the biggest blows was that the Liberian Supreme Court ruled in January 2011 that the ban on individuals from holding public office was unconstitutional.[110] Moreover, there were not any meaningful prosecutions as recommended by the TRC. None of the leaders of the warring factions in the civil war were really tried. Taylor was tried and convicted, but only for crimes related to the Sierra Leone civil war. Unlike Sierra Leone's TRC, the Liberian TRC became deeply politicized. Because Liberia did not have a war crimes tribunal, the TRC effectively assumed multiple contradictory roles as a forum for truth seeking, healing, and retribution. In contrast, Sierra Leone's TRC was insulated from being a forum for retribution by the establishment of the Special Court for Sierra Leone, which was given the mandate "to prosecute persons who bear the greatest responsibility for serious violations of international humanitarian law and Sierra Leonean law committed in the territory of Sierra Leone since 30 November 1996."[111] The Liberian government did not even embrace the report. In August 2008, the Liberian parliament stated that it would engage in a yearlong consultation with constituents before it could decide whether to implement the recommendations of the TRC, which became a cover for doing nothing. Similarly, the report's call for reparation was essentially dismissed by the government. In a September 2010 report to parliament, President Sirleaf argued that all Liberian were victims of the war in one way or another, making it impractical to single out specific individuals for a defined payment.[112] Sirleaf took a broadly defined idea of reparation that was imbued in poverty reduction and the development agenda of the country. While such an approach could be appropriate, the government's rejection of defined reparation repayments was also tied to its overall effort to discredit the TRC report.

The Côte d'Ivoire truth and reconciliation process began with the creation of the Commission Dialogue Vérité et Réconciliation (CDVR) by President Ouattara on July 13, 2011.[113] CDVR was headed by Charles Konan Banny, commission president. Banny served as minister under Gbagbo from 2005 to 2007, after the Pretoria Peace Agreement, and as an adviser to Ouattara during the 2010 presidential elections. However, Banny was widely viewed as supportive of Ouattara's presidential ambitions. CDVR also included three vice presidents and seven regular members, the latter of whom represented the Northern region, Southern region, Eastern region, Central region, Western region, Ivoirians in the diaspora, and the foreign residents in Côte d'Ivoire.[114] The eleven commission members were installed on September 28, 2011.[115] CDVR's mandate was "to work independently toward reconciliation and the strengthening of social cohesion among all communities living in Côte d'Ivoire."[116] In particular, CDVR was charged with documenting violations, seeking the truth, identifying those responsible for the crimes associated with the war, and hearing testimonies from victims and perpetrators. The commission was asked to recommend ways to help victims, promote social cohesion and national unity, and combat social injustices such as tribalism and nepotism. In addition, CDVR was to educate the public on the virtues of dialogue and peaceful coexistence and promote diversity and democracy. CDVR was given two years to accomplish its broad mandate and issue a report. It issued a preliminary report in November 2013 and delivered the final report to President Ouattara on December 15, 2014. The report was based on expert testimonies and statements from 72,483 victims (including 28,064 women and 757 children) covering the entire period of the political crisis and war (1990 to 2011).[117]

In contrast to Liberia's government, the government of Côte d'Ivoire embraced the CDVR report. However, this was partly due to the fact that the process was essentially controlled by the government. Under the ordinance creating the CDVR, the president of the republic (Ouattara) appointed the president of the CDVR. He also appointed the members of the commission upon the recommendation of the commission president. The report was essentially friendly to groups that supported Ouattara during the conflict. In his statement at the official release of the CDVR report, Ouattara announced the establishment of a victims compensation fund in 2015 with an initial contribution of ten billion CFA francs from the government of Côte d'Ivoire and requested international partners to contribute to the fund.[118] In May 2015, the government announced that it would start making payments to the roughly 74,000 registered victims.[119] In addition, Ouattara promised that twenty billion CFA francs would be dedicated toward justice-sector reform through funding from international partners. While the government's acceptance of the CDRV report and the compensation payments to victims seemed to be appropriate, both further alienated Gbagbo supporters, who saw the report as biased in favor of Ouattara and his supporters and felt the compensation scheme was skewed in favor of northerners or would be used to influence the 2015 presidential election in favor of Ouattara, the incumbent. Côte d'Ivoire's truth and reconciliation process was complicated by the no war, no peace state of the country. The failure to end the civil war through a peaceful political settlement created an imbalance in the TRC process and prosecution efforts, both of which were largely seen by Gbagbo supporters as a charade to reinforce Ouattara's 2010 victory and pave the way for an unfair advantage in the 2015 presidential election.

War Crimes Trials

The war crimes trials were another component of the postwar effort to promote the rule of law. Like the TRC, these trials were contentious. Prosecutions for war crimes were very limited in Sierra Leone, Liberia, and Côte d'Ivoire. In fact, only Sierra Leone established a war crimes tribunal. Liberia did not conduct war crimes trials; Taylor, however, was tried at the Special Court for Sierra Leone for his role in the Sierra Leone civil war. In Côte d'Ivoire, the ICC prosecuted Gbagbo and some of his supporters, but none of the Ouattara supporters who fought against Gbagbo were arrested or charged.

Liberia did not pursue a war crimes trial largely because major players in the Liberian civil war were in positions of political power, including President Sirleaf and former warlords Prince Johnson and Alhaji Kromah. The debate about war crimes in Liberia stalled between calls for amnesty as suggested in the CPA and demands for trials as recommended by the TRC. Article XXXIV of the CPA stated, "The NTGL shall give consideration to a recommendation for general amnesty to all persons and parties engaged or involved in military activities during the Liberian civil conflict that is the subject of this Agreement."[120] However, no comprehensive amnesty law was passed. Instead, there were contradictory statements of amnesty and references to extant laws that proponents of war crimes saw as efforts to declare self-amnesty. The Liberian government expressed no interest in pursuing war crimes trials and failed to accept the recommendation of the TRC for war crimes prosecution. The fact that Taylor, the central figure in the Liberian civil war, was sentenced to fifty years in prison for war crimes in Sierra Leone and that the key players in the Liberian civil war were entrenched within the government and political opposition made it practically impossible to establish a war crimes tribunal. Though Liberia ratified the Rome Statute on September 22, 2004, it was not very likely that the ICC would prosecute cases related to the country's civil war, in part because the Rome Statute came into force on July 1, 2002, which was toward the end of the war. Article 11 of the Rome Statute states: "The Court has jurisdiction only with respect to crimes committed after the entry into force of this Statute. If a State becomes a Party to this Statute after its entry into force, the Court may exercise its jurisdiction only with respect to crimes committed after the entry into force of this Statute for that State, unless that State has made a declaration under article 12, paragraph 3."[121] By the time Liberia ratified the Rome Statute in 2004, the war had already ended. Liberia did not make a declaration "accepting the exercise of the jurisdiction of the Court pursuant to Article 12, paragraph 3 of the Rome Statute." As such, there is no clear legal basis for ICC prosecution of war crimes committed during the Liberian civil war.

In Côte d'Ivoire, too, the issue of war crimes was complicated. Unlike in Liberia, however, war crimes trials in Côte d'Ivoire were complicated by the no war, no peace situation of the country and the application of a victor's justice by the government. Côte d'Ivoire's CDVR did recommended war crimes trials. There were domestic and international prosecutions for crimes committed during the Ivoirian conflict. While some of these crimes were covered by amnesty, there was room for prosecution. The 2007 Ouagadougou Accord states: "In order to promote forgiveness and national reconciliation and to restore social cohesion and solidarity among Ivoirians, the two Parties to the direct dialogue agree to extend the scope of the amnesty law passed in 2003. To this end, they have decided to adopt, by ordinance, a new amnesty law covering crimes and offences related to national security and arising from the conflict that shook Côte d'Ivoire and which were committed between 17 September 2000 and the date of entry into force of the present Agreement, with the exception of economic crimes, war crimes and crimes against humanity."[122] The amnesty agreed to under the Ouagadougou Accord did not include economic crimes, war crimes, or crimes against humanity and would cover only crimes committed between September 17, 2000, and March 4, 2007, when the accord was signed. Because the Ivoirian civil war erupted again after the 2010 presidential election, resulting in the death of over three thousand people, there were many war crimes that could be prosecuted under Ivoirian and international law. Côte d'Ivoire signed the Rome Statute on November 30, 1998, and ratified it in February 2013. In addition, Côte d'Ivoire accepted Article 12, paragraph 3 of the Rome Statute, which gave the ICC jurisdiction to prosecute crimes dating back to July 1, 2002.[123] Since Ouattara came to power in 2011, Gbagbo and many of his supporters have been arrested, prosecuted, or transferred to the ICC for crimes related to the civil war. Gbagbo and Charles Blé Goudé were acquitted by the ICC in 2019.

The problem with Côte d'Ivoire's effort to deliver justice for crimes related to the civil war was not the absence of arrests or prosecutions but the selective application of justice against Gbagbo supporters. As Doudou Diène stated in his January 2014 expert report to the UN:

> The Independent Expert remains concerned about the calendar for trials
> currently under way. Seeking truth and combating impunity must be the core
> priorities for the courts. Ensuring equitable justice means that the justice
> system must be able to complete the judicial procedures now under way and
> to initiate cases against both sides, as recommended by the International
> Conference on Impunity and Equitable Justice in Côte d'Ivoire, held in
> Yamoussoukro in February 2013. On 10 July 2013 the indictment division
> issued a decision concerning 84 defendants associated with the former

President, Laurent Gbagbo, but no one close to the current Government has been prosecuted for acts committed during the post-election crisis, although according to the report of the National Commission of Inquiry, such persons were allegedly responsible for the deaths of over 500 people. The authorities present only the arrest of Amadé Ouérémi, for the events at Mount Péko, in Duékoué as a sign of balance in the current list of prosecutions. The investigating judge responsible for that case has been transferred to a position as a temporary prosecutor in Bouaké.[124]

Both Gbagbo and his ally Goude, the minister of youth and employment and leader of the Young Patriots, were tried at the ICC after being handed over by the Ivoirian government. In 2019, both men were acquitted. The ICC also issued a warrant of arrest for former first lady Simone Gbagbo, who was held under house arrest by the government of Côte d'Ivoire. In addition, the Ivoirian government detained over a hundred Gbagbo allies in Côte d'Ivoire. By July 2011, the government had charged fifteen pro-Gbagbo associates for crimes related to the civil war and issued international arrest warrants for several others. Another fifteen senior staff members from the Gbagbo government were held under house arrest without charges.[125] However, the arrests fell short of delivering justice. Instead of arresting people suspected of crimes on both sides of the conflict and giving them a free and fair trial, the Ivoirian government pursued a strategy of pacification against the pro-Gbagbo opposition FPI. In particular, the government used prisoners as an instrument of negotiation with the pro-Gbagbo FPI opposition party. One such case was that of Simone Gbagbo, whom the government refused to transfer to the ICC, despite its pledge to cooperate. Simone Gbagbo, who was arrested in April 2011, was sentenced to twenty years for undermining state security by an Ivoirian court on March 10, 2015.[126] In 2018, Ouattara released her as an amnesty. This move was widely seen as part of the political manipulation leading to the 2020 election in which Ouattara violated the two-term limit. In other cases, the government released prisoners as a concession to the opposition FPI, which refused to participate in any dialogue with the Ouattara administration. In August 2013, fourteen pro-Gbagbo top officials, including Michel Gbagbo, were released on bail.[127] Another set of fifty Gbagbo supporters were released in June 2014 with a promise to release 150 more people when the FPI resumed dialogue with the government.[128] Given the precarious nature of the Ivoirian peace, prosecutions for the civil war only fuel the conflict.

The issue of justice in the Ivoirian civil war can only be settled after peace is consolidated. Côte d'Ivoire essentially followed the path of Liberia, where there was no meaningful justice. Unlike in Liberia, the ICC in Côte d'Ivoire can potentially play a major role in delivering justice because it can prosecute any person for war-related crimes that date as far back as July 2002. However, the ICC faces two key challenges. First, it is perceived to be biased because it has only indicted Gbagbo and his supporters. There are no indications that further indictments would include Ouattara or his allies. The other problem is that the ICC is increasingly losing credibility in Africa because it has become a court that is trying only Africans. In fact, the AU has urged member countries not to cooperate with the ICC in prosecuting sitting African presidents.[129] In Kenya, for example, the ICC struggled to try President Uhuru Kenyatta, whom it indicted in 2012. In 2014, the ICC was compelled to drop all charges against him because it was not able to collect enough evidence.[130] Given the growing African resistance to the ICC and the unsettled nature of the Ivoirian conflict, it is highly unlikely that the ICC would prosecute more people for crimes related to the civil war.

Sierra Leone stands out as one of the few African countries that have prosecuted war crimes, even though the Abidjan Peace Accord and the Lomé Peace Agreement provided amnesty. In particular, the Lomé Peace Agreement gave blanket amnesty to Foday Sankoh and members of the RUF, Armed Forces Revolutionary Council (AFRC), ex-Sierra Leone Army (SLA), and CDF for crimes committed from March 1991 to the signing of the Lomé agreement on July 7, 1999. Article IX of the agreement stated:

> 1. . . . the Government of Sierra Leone shall take appropriate legal steps to grant Corporal Foday Sankoh absolute and free pardon.
>
> 2. After the signing of the present Agreement, the Government of Sierra Leone shall also grant absolute and free pardon and reprieve to all combatants and collaborators in respect of anything done by them in pursuit of their objectives, up to the time of the signing of the present Agreement.
>
> 3. . . . the Government of Sierra Leone shall ensure that no official or judicial action is taken against any member of the RUF/SL, ex-AFRC, ex-SLA or CDF in respect of anything done by them in pursuit of their objectives as members of those organisations, since March 1991, up to the time of the signing of the present Agreement. In addition, legislative and other measures necessary to guarantee immunity to former combatants, exiles and other persons, currently outside the country for reasons related to the armed conflict shall be adopted ensuring the full exercise of their civil and political rights, with a view to their reintegration within a framework of full legality.[131]

However, this blanket amnesty was undermined by two factors that allowed for war crimes prosecutions. The first setback was the fact that the UN delegate at the Lomé peace talks opted out of the amnesty clause in the agreement. As the UN secretary general stated, "I instructed my Special Representative to sign the agreement with the explicit proviso that the United Nations holds the understanding that the amnesty and pardon in article IX of the agreement shall not apply to international crimes of genocide, crimes against humanity, war crimes and other serious violations of international humanitarian law."[132] The second setback was that the war continued after the signing of the Lomé Peace Agreement, which meant that war crimes committed after July 7, 1999, were not covered under the amnesty. These two factors allowed for the prosecution of war crimes in Sierra Leone. In fact, the Special Court for Sierra Leone was given the mandate to prosecute crimes dating as far back as November 30, 1996. The only recognized amnesty was the one stipulated under Article 14 of the 1996 Abidjan Peace Accord:

> To consolidate the peace and promote the cause of national reconciliation, the Government of Sierra Leone shall ensure that no official or judicial action is taken against any member of the RUF/SL in respect of anything done by them in pursuit of their objectives as members of that organization up to the time of the signing of this Agreement. In addition, legislative and other measures necessary to guarantee former RUF/SL combatants, exiles and other persons, currently outside the country for reasons related to the armed conflict shall be adopted ensuring the full exercise of their civil and political rights, with a view to their reintegration within a framework of full legality.[133]

The Special Court for Sierra Leone (SCSL) was established in January 2002 under an agreement between the UN and the government of Sierra Leone. The court, which sat in Sierra Leone and operated under international and Sierra Leonean laws, was given a mandate "to prosecute persons who bear the greatest responsibility for serious violations of international humanitarian law and Sierra Leonean law committed in the territory of Sierra Leone since 30 November 1996."[134] The court indicted thirteen people; nine were tried and convicted, and four died before the process was completed. Sankoh, RUF leader, died in custody before his trial began, while Samuel Hinga Norman, CDF leader, died in February 2007 during the course of his trial. RUF Battlefield Commander Sam Bockarie died before he could be arrested, while AFRC Chairman Johnny Paul Koroma fled Sierra Leone shortly before he was indicted. Koroma is officially considered to be at large, though unconfirmed reports indicate that he is dead.

The Sierra Leone trials process began in March 2003 with the indictment of several RUF, AFRC, and DCF members for war crimes and crimes against humanity by the SCSL. The indicted RUF members were Sankoh, Bockarie, Issa Hassan Sesay, Morris Kallon, and Augustine Gbao.[135] Three CDF members (Sam Hinga Norman, Moinina Fofana, and Allieu Kondewa) were also indicted. On the AFRC side, those indicted were Koroma, Alex Tamba Brima, Santigie Borbor Kanu, and Brima Bazzy Kamara. In 2003, the court also indicted Taylor, the former president of Liberia. All nine people tried by the court were found guilty on several or all of the charges and sentenced to prison terms ranging from fifteen to fifty-two years.[136] Taylor was taken to the United Kingdom in October 2013 to serve his prison time, while the other eight people were sent to Mpanga Prison in Rwanda in October 2009.

With the conclusions of the trials and appeals, the SCSL was terminated in 2013. Under a 2010 agreement between the government of Sierra Leone and the UN, the Residual Special Court for Sierra Leone was established to carry out remaining functions relating to the legal and practical obligations of the SCSL. These included ongoing and ad hoc functions such as prisoner supervision, witness protection, preservation and management of the records, the trial of Koroma in the unlikely event that he was arrested, the review of convictions and acquittals, and the prevention of double jeopardy.[137]

In some ways, the SCSL was considered to be a success. First, the trials and convictions affirmed the rule of law. The conviction and imprisonment of Taylor in particular served as a vivid reminder to warlords about the real potential of prosecution and imprisonment. Others have also noted the educational and outreach role of the court in promoting the rule of law and the peace-consolidation process. As Rachel Kerr and Jessica Lincoln noted, "The Special Court's Outreach program is far more extensive and ambitious than anything that has previously been undertaken, and marks a significant departure from the ad hoc tribunals, which were criticized for having made inadequate efforts to reach their target populations."[138] However, others point to the shortcomings of the court. There was a general belief that the court prosecuted too few people, and some were angered by the prosecution of Norman, whom they considered a hero and defender of civilians against the brutality of the RUF at a time when government and international forces were not able to properly protect civilians. Charles Jalloh provides a rich analysis of the SCSL that captures both the merits and shortcomings of the war crimes trials in Sierra Leone. As he argued, "The Court has ensured that punishment is meted out to *some* of those deemed to bear the greatest responsibility for the serious atrocities committed in Sierra Leone."[139] However, Jalloh points to a wide range of concerns that undermine the achievement of the court. These include concerns about the extremely small number of trials due to a narrow interpretation of the court's mandate that left important Sierra Leoneans and non–Sierra Leonean actors free from prosecution and about the prosecution of Norman, "who sacrificed so much to stop rebel atrocities," and Sesay, "who helped to usher peace."[140] The total cost of the court was around $300 million,[141] which many people saw as disproportionately too much spent on the court at the expense of the TRC, strengthening the legal system, and promoting development in general. Friederike Mieth captured a common sentiment about the disconnection between the work of the court and the experience of the vast majority of people in Sierra Leone: "In contrast to the claims by Court officials, many Sierra Leoneans I spoke to describe the work of the Court as irrelevant for them and stated that it has not brought justice to them. Their reasons can be loosely grouped into two categories: that their concept of justice differed from that of the Court, and that their everyday circumstances made the work of the Court less relevant for them."[142]

The shortcomings of the Sierra Leone war crimes process were not unique. Similar problems about prosecutorial decisions and the disproportionate expenditure on war crimes courts as compared to on reparations and human development have been noted in other postwar countries. Rwanda, for example, faced the issue of limited prosecutions and debates about who was most responsible. In the end, a very small proportion of perpetrators were tried. Rwanda sought to make up for this deficit by instituting the Gacaca courts.[143] In South Africa, too, the truth and justice process was criticized. Though South Africa rejected a blanket amnesty and opted for individual amnesty, very few people were prosecuted. The Promotion of National Unity and Reconciliation Act (no. 34 of 1995, July 26, 1995) empowered the TRC to grant "amnesty to persons who make full disclosure of all the relevant facts relating to acts associated with a political objective committed in the course of the conflicts of the past."[144] The TRC granted 849 amnesties and rejected 5,392 applications for amnesty.[145] However, very few cases have been prosecuted. Moreover, the ANC government granted pardons, further reducing the likelihood of prosecution.[146] In the end, South Africa's truth and justice processes have been strongly criticized for failing to deliver justice. As Mahmood Mamdani argued, "To the extent that the TRC did not acknowledge the full truth, the amnesty intended to be *individual* turned into a *group* amnesty. For any perpetrator who was not so identified was a perpetrator who enjoyed impunity."[147] In terms of the cost of war crimes and reparations, Sierra Leone's experience is not too different from that of Rwanda and South Africa. Despite the huge postwar development aid to Rwanda, meaningful reparations did not reach too many of the victims, in large part due to organizational and policy priorities problems.[148] In South Africa, the TRC recommended a one-time payment of thirty thousand rands to eligible victims, which was criticized as inadequate.[149] Sierra Leone's war crimes trial was an important, albeit inadequate, part of the postwar reconstruction program. Yet, the value of the court has to be viewed from the perspective of both what it delivered and what facts and accountability could have been missed out in the absence of war crimes trials that occurred through the SCSL. While a lot more was spent on the court than on other elements of the postwar reconstructions, the court did not necessarily take away money from other programs, as those funds may not have even been available in the absence of a trial. In the end, SCSL has to be accepted for what it achieved and used as a lesson for Sierra Leone.

GOOD GOVERNANCE: CIVIL SOCIETY AND PUBLIC FINANCE MANAGEMENT

The final component of the postwar institutional reform centers on enhancing good-governance practices. While a multiparty election is an indispensable element for good governance, democratic elections alone are not sufficient. The peace agreements and the TRC report as well as studies of the Sierra Leone civil war recognized and identified bad governance, especially corruption, as the key cause of the civil war. Given that fact, enhancing good governance was a critical challenge for postwar reconstruction and the consolidation of peace, and achieving this rested not only on holding regular free and fair multiparty elections but also on strengthening civil society and establishing proper public finance management processes.

Strengthening Civil Society

Civil society has been a key element in the struggles for democracy in Africa that began in the 1990s. In Sierra Leone, civil society organizations, such as Campaign for Good Governance and Fifty-Fifty, were at the forefront to end military rule during the 1996 multiparty election.[150] Organizations like Mano River Women's Peace Network (MAWOPNET) and the Inter-Religious Council continued to campaign against the war and became key actors in the peace process leading to the Lomé Peace Agreement and the eventual end of the civil war.[151] In Liberia, civil society was central to the campaign to end the civil war. Women's organizations and interfaith religious bodies were critical in the peace process.[152] In Côte d'Ivoire, civil society was at the forefront in the democratization process, which forced long-term ruler Felix Houphouët-Boigny to open the country to multiparty elections.[153] While civil society was instrumental in the effort to end one-party rule and oust the military from power, its role in the civil war also became divisive as the conflict increasingly took a regional and ethnic character. Because the Ivoirian conflict was not peacefully ended, the role of civil society continued to be muddled, as different organizations harbored strong pro-government or pro-Gbagbo positions. Due to their critical role, civil society organizations received support in the form of contracts and grants from both the national and foreign governments and international organizations. As such, these organizations have become important actors in the delivery of programs aimed at promoting civic awareness on national issues, including human rights, governance, natural resources, and human development, and empowering citizens to hold government accountable.[154]

Civil society organizations handled a plethora of programs, and some were aimed directly at helping key players, such as the media, improve their capacity to promote good governance. In 2004, for example, the Partnership for Media and Conflict Prevention in West Africa (which included the UN and UNESCO) and the Press Union of Liberia started the Liberia Media Center (LCM) to enhance civil society and the role of media in Liberia. LCM, which received around $85,100 in startup costs, focused on providing media workers with professional skills on how to investigate and report on crime, corruption, human rights violations, and HIV/AIDS.[155] It also provided resources (e.g., IT services, office space, information sources) for journalists and monitored the state of freedom of expression in the major cities of Liberia.

In Sierra Leone, the US Agency for International Development (USAID) provided around $4.5 million in 2005 and nearly $4 million in 2006 for the Strengthening Democracy program,[156] which aimed to broaden community-based political participation and combat corruption. At the grassroots level, it supported community radio programs promoting public discourse on good governance. In terms of leadership development, it organized training and mentoring programs for parliamentarians and local leaders to promote informed dialogues, transparency, and strong community participation in governance.

As often happens during conflict, politicians and other elites in Côte d'Ivoire used the media as a tool to mobilize and consolidate support, in turn aggravating intergroup divisions and contributing to the violence. In the aftermath of the civil war and the divisive and destructive 2010 presidential elections, donor partners of Côte d'Ivoire provided resources in an attempt to use the media to reduce the potential of violent conflict and promote a responsive state and an inclusive civil society. In one clear example, USAID's Office of Transition Initiatives (OTI) funded a series of activities known as the Côte d'Ivoire Transition Initiative program (CITI).[157] OTI launched CITI in September 2011, four months after the end of the postelection violence in the country. The short-term transition CITI program ended five years later, in March 2016, after having sponsored 345 separate activities valued at 10.8 billion CFA francs ($18 million), reaching over five hundred thousand beneficiaries.[158] According to the US Embassy in Abidjan, the 2016 closing of the CITI office demonstrated "the confidence of the United States Government that Côte d'Ivoire has definitively turned the page after a long period of conflict."[159]

CITI was designed to help push forward reconciliation and the peacebuilding process in Côte d'Ivoire and to discourage a repeat of violence in the lead-up to the 2015 presidential elections, which had the potential to exacerbate enduring tensions around the issues of nationality and identity.[160] The various CITI activities focused on building state capacity and encouraged community engagement.

OTI worked with the Ivoirian government and local groups to identify and respond to community-prioritized needs and encourage a peaceful transition. Radio and television were considered critical tools for facilitating postconflict peace and reconciliation, with a television series promoting women's participation in the 2015 elections being seen as a particular success.[161] CITI programs "mobilized actors as diverse as women, transporters, youth, traditional leaders, religious leaders, victims and those affected by the war, radio station owners and radio animators, community and civic organizations, and many others."[162] Overall, OTI's CITI program tried to help increase cohesion among local communities affected by the decade-long conflict in Côte d'Ivoire and support a peaceful, inclusive, transparent, and credible 2015 presidential election.

Public Finance Management Reform

At the heart of good governance is proper public finance management. In Liberia and Sierra Leone, where corruption was a major factor leading to the civil war, major programs have been launched to ensure proper management of revenues from minerals and overall public finances. In 2005, the UNDP established the Diamonds for Development program in Liberia "to facilitate the establishment of a transparent and accountable revenue management system based on a fair and equitable distribution of revenues."[163] The program was in line with the terms of UN Security Council Resolution 1343 of 2001, which established an embargo on Liberian rough diamonds and required compliance with the Kimberley Process Certification Scheme. The program, which cost around $6,898,200 (2005 to 2010), centered on making changes in the mining laws to enhance revenue management and local control over mineral resources (especially diamonds, gold, iron ore, bauxite, timber, and rubber). The new laws that were passed aimed to decrease bureaucratic inefficiencies and decentralize national resource management while increasing independent oversight so as to enhance transparency and accountability in the way revenues from mineral resources were generated.[164] With respect to local development, the program sought to ensure that up to 25 percent of profits, taxes, or incomes from minerals was directed to the local governments where the natural resources were extracted. In addition, the program called for the formation of local development funds and microfinanced mining cooperatives to benefit local communities.

In Sierra Leone, the World Bank provided $4 million for the Mining Technical Assistance Project (MTAP) in 2010. MTAP was renamed the Extractive Industries Technical Assistance Project (EITAP) in 2011.[165] MTAP was initiated against the backdrop of the resumption of large-scale mining in Sierra Leone after its collapse during the civil war. After the UN embargo on rough diamonds from

Sierra Leone was lifted in June 2003, diamond exports increased to $126.65 million in 2004, a 67 percent increase from 2003. Additionally, Sierra Rutile Limited resumed its operations in 2006 with a twenty-five-million-euro credit from the EU. Also, Sierra Mineral Limited opened its bauxite operation. MTAP sought to promote overarching legal and regulatory reform of the mining sector to ensure sustainable development.[166] In particular, it called for mechanisms to monitor the environmental and social impacts of mines and adoption of the Environment and Social Management Framework (ESMF). ESMF outlined procedures for environmental and social screenings and assessments to measure and mitigate the potential negative impacts of mining. MTAP called for the establishment of a resettlement policy, regulations for underground mining, and trading and licensing rules in line with the Kimberley Process. MTAP also provided material and technical assistance to the National Minerals Agency in areas such as geodata management and geochemical surveys and support for pilot studies on land rehabilitation and the identification of alternative livelihoods for people affected by mining. While MTAP focused more on environmental issues, EITAP's core objective was to "build the capacity of the Government to manage and regulate the extractive industries sector."[167] One key indicator of progress toward proper management was admission to and compliance with the Extractive Industries Transparency Initiative (EITI), for which Sierra Leone became a candidate country in 2007. Unfortunately, Sierra Leone was suspended from EITI in 2013 and asked to undertake remedial steps for it to be reinstated.[168] The country was readmitted into EITTI in 2014.

Much of the effort to promote good governance was focused on broader public finance management reforms beyond the mining sector. In Sierra Leone, this began in 2006 with the Institutional Support Project to Strengthen the Public Financial Management and the Energy Sectors (ISPSPFMES), which received UAC 2,790,000 (note: UA 1 = SDR 1; UA 1 = 3,954.06 leones; UA 1 = USD 1.45183) from the African Development Bank (AfDB) to help the government implement its National Strategy for Good Governance (NSGG). The government of Sierra Leone contributed UAC 150,000, which brought the project total to UAC 2,940,000.[169] The cornerstone of NSGG was public finance management reform. ISPSPFMES aimed to assist in building the required capacity to strengthen Public Financial Management at the Ministry of Finance, especially in the Debt Management Unit, the Office of the Auditor Genera, the Office of Accountant General, and the National Revenue Authority[170]

In 2009, Sierra Leone received $15 million from AfDB under the Economic Governance Reform Program (EGRP).[171] EGRP II, which was launched in 2011, received UA 58.2 million in grants and USD 6.2 million in credit for 2011–2012.[172] The funding was to be provided by AfDB's Fragile States Facility, World Bank,

European Commission (EC), and DFID.[173] EGRP was aimed at enhancing public finance management reforms. In particular, it focused on strengthening public expenditure management and improving revenue governance in the mining and energy sectors. In terms of public expenditure management, the program called for effective payroll control through the use of biometric verification of public employee payrolls to eliminate the fraud and inaccurate record costs associated with ghost employees. EGRP I introduced biometric verification to the payroll of civil servants and health-sector employees. The biometric system reduced the civil service payroll from 16,000 to 12,000, and associated salary savings of SLE500 million per month were realized. EGRP II extended the biometric to teachers, who constituted about 50 percent of public employees. It was to establish a physical verification of all teachers and ensure accurate employment records were maintained by the Human Resources Management Office and with the Integrated Financial Management and Information System (IFMIS). The program also called for the establishment of a Teachers Commission to maintain teacher records and ensure effective management of the workforce and payroll control. The other component of public expenditure management was proper auditing and oversight, especially by Audit Service Sierra Leone, the Accountant General Department, and Parliament.

With respect to revenue governance in the mining and energy sectors, EGRP II focused on enhancing transparency and accountability. It built on the 2009 Mines and Mineral Act and the efforts to review mining contracts, restructure the Ministry of Mines and Mineral Resources, and comply with the EITI to ensure that the mining sector contributed to socioeconomic development. EGRP focused on ensuring implementation of the 2010 EITI reconciliation and validation reports on Sierra Leone, implementing reforms at the Ministry of Mines and Mineral Resources, and ensuring proper disclosure of mining revenues by the Minister of Finance and Economic Development. In the energy sector, EGRP II concentrated on restructuring the National Power Authority (NPA) and other utility companies through parliamentary and other regulatory mechanisms, undertaking an electricity tariff study, implementing a new electricity tariff system, formalizing power sales from the Bumbuna hydro dam to NPA through a legally binding power purchase agreement, and expanding the use of prepaid electricity meters to enhance revenue-collection transparency.

Similarly, the World Bank provided Sierra Leone a grant of SDR 2.7 million in 2009 to implement the Sierra Leone Integrated Public Financial Management Reform Project (PFMRP).[174] Sierra Leone was to also contribute $2 million, which it received from AfDB, toward PFMRP. PFMRP was aimed at helping Sierra Leone sustainably improve the credibility, control, and transparency of its fiscal management.[175] In particular, it sought to reduce variance in expenditures, reduce payment arrears, increase the share of actual-to-budgeted spending on pro-poor expenditure priorities, and increase compliance with procurement regulations. PFMRP had four main components: strengthening macrofiscal coordination and budget management, reinforcing the control system for improved service delivery, strengthening central finance functions, and assisting nonstate actors (NSAs) with oversight over public finances.

The first component, macrofiscal coordination and budget management, focused on budget formulation and execution and debt management practices. It called for developing a macroeconomic and fiscal framework incorporating realistic aggregate fiscal estimates, improving procedures for revenue forecasting, establishing expenditure ceilings through the medium-term expenditure framework, strengthening the strategic planning capacity, aid policy, and management processes, and streamlining and implementing control procedures for all central government expenditures. With respect to debt management, PFMRP called for the development of a policy on the criteria and limits of public debts and guarantees, the adoption and implementation of a plan to reduce domestic debts and expenditure arrears, the strengthening of the debt database, and the regular analysis of the fiscal position of state-owned enterprises.[176]

The second component of PFMRP, reinforcing control systems, centered on legal reforms and improving procurement, accounting, payroll, and auditing practices. PFMRP called for revision of the Government Budgeting and Accountability Act of 2005 and the Financial Management Regulations of 2007 statutory instruments, completion of the necessary local government financial administration regulations, and the strengthening of parliamentary oversight. It also called for the introduction of processes that were in line with the IFMIS and the improvement of standards for financial reporting by various public agencies.

The third component of PFMRP focused on technology and capacity building to enhance public finance management. PFMRP called for the creation of a disaster recovery plan for the IFMIS, the implementation of the budgeting, asset, and stock management modules of the system, the provision of accounting software to local government authorities, and the establishment of ICT support structures within the Ministry of Finance and Economic Development (MOFED) and other ministries, departments, and agencies (MDAs) and an up-to-date website for MOFED. PFMRP also sought to build the human resources capacity of MOFED and the National Public Procurement Authority through personnel training and improved salaries.

The final component of PFMRP was to increase citizens' oversight over the budget and develop a procitizen public finance management system. PFMRP specifically called for effective information sharing with NSAs (including the media), the dissemination of public finance management information at the national and local levels, and enhancement of the public finance management capacity of NSAs. In addition, NSAs were to be provided grants to help them monitor national and local government budgets and engage in public finance advocacy. The NSAs Secretariat was established within the Ministry of Finance to increase civil society oversight over public finances as called for in PFMRP. NSAs Secretariat undertook public information workshops and issued reports on the annual budgets, primarily focusing on the notion of citizens budgets, which rested on the principles of public participation in defining spending priorities and transparency in the ways revenues were spent.[177]

Another important project in Sierra Leone was Public Financial Management Improvement and Consolidation (PFMIC), which was approved on November 27, 2013, for a four-year period (March 31, 2014, to March 31, 2018). The total cost of PFMIC was $28.5 million credit, funded by the World Bank and other international agencies. The World Bank itself provided $12 million toward the project, and the other contributors were the UK Department of International Development ($11.19 million), AfDB ($3.5 million), and EU ($1.81 million). PFMIC, which was aligned with pillar seven of Sierra Leone's PRSP III (Agenda for Prosperity, 2013–2018), expanded on the previous public finance reform programs. PFMIC had five components: enhancing budget planning and credibility; financial control, accountability, and oversight; supporting the strengthening of revenue mobilization and administration systems; strengthening the local governance, financial management, and accountability systems component; and public financial management reform coordination and project management. The project's activities were mostly centered on providing equipment to the Ministry of Finance and related agencies in Sierra Leone, training for staff (budget experts, auditors, legislator, civil society actors, etc.), and developing manuals and protocols for the proper management of public finance. PFMIC allocated $1.52 million toward enhancing budget planning and credibility. The activities under this component included improving the forecasting of mineral resources revenues, fiscal-risk stocktaking, establishing a database of identified risks, designing reporting formats for risks, and helping the Budget Bureau adopt a Government Finance Statistics 2001 compliant budget classification.[178]

The financial control, accountability, and oversight component was allocated $15.28 million. Its activities extended the IFMIS to forty-three government ministries, departments, and agencies (MDAs). IFMIS was also extended to on-budget donor-funded projects. IFMIS interfaced with the Bank of Sierra Leone debt management system and the customs and tax system. Other key systems created included a treasury single account, a document management system, and an electronic fund transfer system. The financial control, accountability, and oversight component also included the development of internal audit mechanisms to MDAs. Various manuals were to be developed and staff trained to ensure the proper management of debts and funds and enhanced auditing practices. In addition, the operational capacity of civil society/nonstate actors and legislative oversight bodies (the Public Accounts Committee, the Public Finance Committee, and the Transparency and Accountability Committee) were to be improved.

Another $4.56 million was allocated for supporting the strengthening of revenue mobilization and administration systems component.[179] This included providing expert technical assistance to the Reform and Tax Policy Unit and the acquisition and implementation of a robust off-the-shelf tax administration system that would address the limitations of the Domestic Tax Information System and facilitate the transition to ASYCUDA World (Customs Automated System). Other activities included providing technical assistance to facilitate IPSAS compliance of local councils' financial reports, establishing mechanisms to enhance revenue mobilization, auditing local governments, providing energy-supply equipment to facilitate the work of local councils, and holding training workshops for stakeholders at the local council level.

In Liberia, too, public finance management reform was a key part of the postwar reconstruction. In 2008, the World Bank started the Economic Governance and Institutional Reform Project (EGIR) in Liberia, which sought to "improve the efficiency and transparency in managing public financial and human resources, focusing on revenue administration, public procurement, budget execution and payroll management."[180] EGIR was funded through an $11 million loan ($8.5 million for public financial management and $2.5 million for civil service reform) and implemented by the Public Financial Management Unit of the Liberian Ministry of Finance in partnership with the World Bank.[181] EGIR had two components: public financial management reform and civil service reform. The public financial management reform focused on assisting Liberia's Ministry of Finance by providing technical expertise and IT resources and updating public financial management laws and auditing and reporting practices. EGIR brought in expatriates and provided funding to the University of Liberia's public financial management training school to increase local expertise. With respect to IT resources, EGIR introduced Magnetic Ink Character Recognition technology and upgraded computer networks and accounting software to help the Ministry of Finance streamline banking and accounting procedures and reduce the gap between balances and outstanding payments. Additionally, EGIR sought to promote comprehensive tax reforms, increase taxpayer compliance, and enlarge the tax base. Special attention was directed at helping Liberian agencies establish transparent systems for collecting and reporting mining revenues and payments. EGIR also directed resources to help the General Auditing Commission improve its efficiency by providing additional training to its auditors and recruiting more auditors. EGIR included similar initiatives with respect to civil service reform. It installed a computerized human resource management information system to ameliorate fraud in payroll and pension systems and provided funding to the Liberian Institute of Public Administration to train future Liberian civil servants.[182]

Liberia's EGIR was complemented with other public finance reform projects, most notably the IFMIS, which became the Integrated Public Financial Management Reform (IPFMR) project in December 2011. In 2008, Liberia was granted $3.7 million from the World Bank for IFMIS. The project was to last from 2009 to February 2012. IFMIS aimed to "to improve the efficiency of the Government's accounting system through the provision and installation of a computerized financial management information system in the Ministry of Finance and through strengthening manual accounting systems in line ministries and counties."[183] Most of the funds were for the procurement of basic equipment, software programs, and office materials for rebuilding the capacity of the ministry to perform its core functions.

IPFMR was approved on December 15, 2011; it continued and expanded IFMIS. IPFMR, which Liberia received a $28.55 million loan for, was very similar to Sierra Leone's PFMIC. The Swedish International Development Cooperation provided $15.10 million. The other contributors were the World Bank ($5 million), AfDB ($4.6 million), and USAID ($3.85 million). The overall objective of IPFMR was to improve "budget coverage, fiscal policy management, financial control, and oversight of government finances of Liberia."[184] Anchored in Liberia's "Agenda for Transformation, Liberia Rising 2030" vision, IPFMR was based on the idea that "through strengthened institutional capacity for the delivery of effective PFM and oversight, the government will be able to expand and deepen the scope of reforms in support of reduced corruption and improved service delivery, particularly to vulnerable groups, thereby reducing poverty."[185] The five components of IPFMR were the improvement of budget-planning systems, coverage, and credibility; the strengthening of PFM legal framework, budget execution, accounting, and reporting; revenue mobilization and administration; the enhancement of transparency and accountability; and program governance and project management. IPFMR was to provide a wide range of training and technical assistance to finance experts, auditors, legislators, and civil society organizations. It was also intended to develop systems to enhance revenue collection and management at the national and local levels, and it helped to procure appropriate materials (computers, software, vehicles, etc.), refurbish offices, and boost the overall capacity of critical agencies.

Another important effort in Liberia was the Public Sector Modernization Project (PSMP), approved on February 10, 2014, for a five-year period (2014 to

2019) at a total cost of $10.71 million in credit provided by USAID ($5.04 million), Swedish International Development Cooperation ($3.67 million), and the World Bank ($2 million).[186] PSMP, which aligned with Liberia's PRSP, sought "to improve pay and performance management in participating ministries, and strengthen payroll management in the civil service in Liberia."[187] PSMS focused on key ministries (Education, Finance, Health and Social Welfare, Internal Affairs, Justice, Information and Tourism, and Foreign Affairs), which had around 26,000 civil servants, accounting for nearly 75 percent of the entire Liberian civil service. PSMP was designed to complement other reforms in Liberia, most notably pay-scale improvements, payroll cleaning to eliminate ineligible names, and revisions to the mandates and functions of ministries and agencies, and decentralization. PSMP was expected to boost transparency and predictability in hiring, salaries, and promotion, which would benefit civil servants and Liberia as a whole. Moreover, it would provide a well-structured compensation regime and improve the management of the government wage bill. PSMP had four components: improved pay management ($3.18 million), strengthened payroll management ($3.05 million), improved performance ($3.38 million), and project and program management ($1.1 million). As with the other projects, PSMP largely centered on providing training, research, recruitment, and technical assistance, and help with the procurement of essential materials and facilities for effective payroll management.

The first component (improved pay management) centered on two key problems: how to attract and retain competent managerial and professional staff and how to handle low motivation and engagement among civil servants. To address these problems, PSMP would map out civil servants into grades, conduct remuneration surveys, revise HR policy manuals, develop a pay strategy, and train civil servants for key HR functions. A main goal was getting civil service agencies to submit a pay strategy to the Liberian government for cabinet approval. The second component (strengthened payroll management) was a response to the lack of effective payroll discipline and the weak institutional control, which facilitated corruption in the government payroll. To address these problems, PSMP would prepare and disseminate HR planning procedures, identify staffing requirements, strengthen personnel records, decentralize the Human Resource Information Management System to civil service outreach centers, help the General Auditing Commission conduct independent payroll and HR systems audits, train staff in payroll management, and update personnel files. A major goal was reducing the discrepancy between salaries paid and the personnel roster to no more than 5 percent. The improved performance component sought to increase civil servant accountability and ensure that they delivered on their duties. These problems were addressed by mapping and redesigning existing organizational structures, reviewing the mandates and functions of ministries, preparing draft legislation to amend the structures and functions of ministries, implementing performance management in the civil service, and developing policy frameworks for the establishment of a civil service commission and the appointment of principal administrative officers. The key target for this component was to ensure that each ministry would complete three annual cycles of performance appraisal for grade P and grade E grade civil servants.

In Côte d'Ivoire, promoting good governance was also a crucial part of the rebuilding process, but a lot of the programs lagged due to the intermittent relapses into violence. In 2001, the AfDB initiated the National Good Governance and Capacity Building Programme (PNBGRC) in Côte d'Ivoire to strengthen the rule of law, promote sound public resources management, and reduce poverty.[188] PNBGRC had four components. The first was to support the legal system by boosting the capacity of the office of Inspection Générale des Services Juridictionnels et Pénitentiaires and other judicial bodies through training and IT resources. The second was to provide technical assistance and IT to improve the human resources capacities for decentralization. The third was to enhance public resource management by providing direct capacity-building support to core financial management agencies, namely the General Directorate of the Treasury, the Directorate of Public Debt, the Judicial Agency of the Treasury, the General Directorate of the Economy, the Directorate of Economic Analysis and Projection, the General Inspectorate of Finance, and the Chamber of Accounts of the Supreme Court. The final component was to support the National Capacity Building Secretariat (SNRC), which would coordinate the other three components. Training for SNRC included civil society and private sector involvement. The overriding goal of the PNBGRC was to restore the confidence of the citizenry in state institutions. AfDB provided UA 3.79 million through its Technical Assistance Fund, which covered 95 percent of the program cost.

An important public finance management program in Côte d'Ivoire was the World Bank–supported Economic Governance and Recovery Grant (EGRG), which was approved on April 1, 2008. EGRG I was largely a grant package to help Côte d'Ivoire clear its arrears to the World Bank dating back to 2004 and thereby restore normal relations with lenders. Under EGRG I, Côte d'Ivoire received $308 million to help repay its loans and $35 million in budget support from the World Bank.[189] EGRG I also concentrated on "supporting government-owned reforms to improve governance, transparency and efficiency in public expenditure management as well as advance structural reforms aimed at strengthening governance and transparency in the key sectors of the economy (energy, cocoa and financial sector)."[190] EGRG I focused on policy reforms aimed at enhancing fiscal sustainability, private-sector confidence, and transparency of state institutions.

EGRG II, which was approved on March 31, 2009, coincided with significant progress in Côte d'Ivoire toward the adoption of its first PRSP and qualification for debt relief under Heavily Indebted Poor Countries (HIPC). EGRG II was a $150 million grant from the World Bank to expand on the public finance reforms that were started under EGRG I. Though the public finance management and good-governance challenges of Côte d'Ivoire had long been identified and were starting to be addressed, the reality was that the country's failure to fully resolve the conflict hampered progress. In fact, the World Bank recognized this problem and classified Côte d'Ivoire as a high-risk country for lending. The main source of risk was the nation's failure to peacefully resolve the conflict. As the World Bank stated, "The proposed operation is of high risk. The principal risks are: (i) political risk stemming from the fragility of the peace process, the upcoming presidential elections, delays in disarmament, demobilization and reintegration, and possible changes of reform-minded ministers after the presidential elections; (ii) macroeconomic risk . . . and (iii) governance and fiduciary risk, arising from vested interests and political intervention, notably in the cocoa, energy and finance sectors, which remain strong and could stall reforms."[191]

Ensuring proper public finance management was critical to meeting the development goals set in Côte d'Ivoire's PRSP. As the World Bank noted, achieving the strategic goals of the PRSP would require "improving governance, transparency and economic efficiency and strengthening the basic functions of government, based on accountability and the rule of law. This will involve: (i) continued and deeper reforms to strengthen public financial management to improve efficiency and effectiveness in public resources and hold the Government accountable for the appropriate use of public funds; and (ii) enhancing transparency, accountability and efficiency of state institutions and processes in the cocoa, energy and financial sectors, which are the two key generators of exports and public revenues."[192] In addition to the political crisis it faced, Côte d'Ivoire continued to deal with public finance management challenges, most notably in the critical sectors of energy, cocoa, and banking. Some of the challenges included distorted budget cycles, a lack of transparency, expenditure execution problems, inadequate budget nomenclature and classification, a lack of clear rules for budget transfers to local governments, and inadequate controls to prevent corruption. EGRG II specifically sought to address such problems. As the World Bank stated, "The key objective of the proposed EGRG II is to support government-owned reforms to improve governance, transparency and efficiency in public expenditure management as well as advance structural reforms aimed at strengthening governance and transparency in key sectors of the economy. Specifically, it would focus on supporting the Government's efforts to restore the normal budget cycle and strengthen budget preparation, execution, controls and accountability. In addition, it would contribute to enhancing private sector confidence, investment and growth recovery through improved governance and transparency in the energy, cocoa, and financial sectors."[193] EGRG II focused on a range of public finance management problems in four specific areas: public expenditure management, the energy sector, the cocoa sector, and the financial sector.

According to the World Bank, "Public expenditure management has suffered from a distorted budget cycle, worsening transparency, and expenditure execution problems."[194] EGRG therefore supported reforms and the development of new mechanisms that would improve governance, transparency, and efficiency. The key targets were getting approval of the 2008 budget by presidential ordinance and a cabinet decision on the budget published in the official gazette and major newspapers; ensuring that the Ministry of Economy and Finance submitted draft budget execution bills for fiscal years 2005 and 2006 to the Chamber of Accounts; ensuring that less than 15 percent of cumulative expenses (excluding wages and salaries, debt servicing, and expenditures) in 2008 were executed through treasury advances, instead of the revolving-fund cash account mechanism or external resources mechanism; and ensuring adoption by the Ministry of Economy and Finance of a time-bound road map to separate policy functions from execution and control functions in public procurement.[195]

In the energy sector, one key problem was the huge financial deficit, which drained 60 billion CFA francs from the government budget in 2008. The poor financial state of the energy sector was largely due to rising fuel costs, a greater reliance on thermal power, low power tariffs, and a low rate of bill collection, especially from government customers and northern clients. As such, EGRG supported the completion of a full audit of the electricity sector. The audit was to produce recommendations for improving efficiency and financial viability. EGRG also expected improvements to be made regarding the natural resources aspect of the energy sector, such as oil and gas production. The full adoption of EITI regulations was essential. As such, EGRG supported the effort to make the National Committee for EITI operational. In particular, EGRG required the Ministry of Economy and Finance to adopt a work program and budget for the committee for 2008–2009.[196]

The World Bank noted that the cocoa sector "has long been saddled with excessive taxation and significant governance problems and has been in need of a thorough reform and improvement in governance and transparency."[197] Because cocoa generated around 17 percent of public revenues in Côte d'Ivoire, addressing the problems was critical to the country's ability to achieve the development goals outlined in its PRSP. As the world's largest cocoa producer, accounting for about 40 percent of total world production, Côte d'Ivoire had huge potentials that were impeded by poor governance and inefficiencies in the cocoa sector.

EGRG II focused on three key actions. The first was to reduce levies on cocoa in 2008/2009 by 15 CFA francs per kilogram from the 2007/2008 rates. The other two actions centered on accountability and transparency reforms. In particular, the government was required to submit to the World Bank quarterly reports on investment projects and the implementation status for 2008 projects approved under the Fonds d'Investissement en Milieu Rural (Rural Investment Funds), Fonds de Développement et de Promotion des Activités des Producteurs du Café et du Cacao (Development Fund for the Promotion of Coffee and Cocoa Producers' Activities, FDPCC), and Fonds de Régulation et de Contrôle du Café et du Cacao (Fund for the Regulation and Control of Coffee and Cocoa, FRC). EGRG II also required steps to be taken toward the proper auditing and restructuring of the cocoa sector. In particular, internal audit reports were required for Autorité de Régulation du Café et du Cacao (Coffee and Cocoa Regulatory Agency), Bourse du Cacao et du Café (Cocoa and Coffee Exchange), FRC, and FDPCC. A committee was to be established to manage the restructuring, and the government was required to adopt a cocoa-sector policy that was satisfactory to the World Bank.[198]

The objective of the Third Economic Governance and Recovery Grant Program (EGRG III) for Côte d'Ivoire was to support government-owned reforms to improve governance, transparency, and efficiency in public expenditure management and to deepen structural reforms aimed at strengthening governance and transparency in key sectors. The focus was on supporting the government's efforts to improve budget preparation, execution, controls, and accountability and enhancing governance, transparency, and efficiency in the energy, cocoa, and financial sectors. The operation provided financial support to the government in light of the unfavorable global economic environment and the fact that Côte d'Ivoire's annual debt service to the World Bank would remain considerable until attainment of the HIPC completion point. A rapid improvement in public financial management and governance and transparency in the energy, cocoa, and financial sectors was critical to sustain the peace process and financially recover. Specifically, the government needed to ensure that scarce public resources were utilized efficiently and transparently to provide essential public services, that resources raised in the cocoa sector were effectively used to rebuild the sector, and that the overall tax burden was reduced to ensure that the farmers obtained a higher share of the world price.

CONCLUSION: INSTITUTIONAL REFORMS, GOOD GOVERNANCE, AND DEMOCRATIC CONSOLIDATION

This chapter examined a number of postwar institutional reform programs aimed at enhancing human security and promoting good governance across the three cases. Central to the post–civil war reconstruction processes in Sierra Leone, Liberia, and Côte d'Ivoire were a number of institutional reform programs undertaken in order to consolidate peace and democracy. These international efforts are deeply rooted in new humanitarianism and people-centered liberalism. The concept of people-centered liberalism holds that democracy needs to be built solidly on good governance. This, in turn, provides the best opportunity for creating the necessary economic and social conditions to reduce poverty, enhance the overall well-being of the population, and ensure human security. Accordingly, the foundation of post–civil war rebuilding lies on institutionalizing democracy around the practices of good governance while enhancing human well-being at the same time. Three interconnected components are at the core of these ideas and their manifestations in postconflict realities.[199] The first is ending the war-related violence and protecting at-risk populations with the deployment of international peacekeepers. Next is mediating the achievement of a durable peace agreement and the proper timing of transitional democratic elections. The third is gaining the support of the international donor community for postwar reconstruction to consolidate peace, strengthen democracy, instill good governance, and promote sustainable human development.

The experiences of Sierra Leone, Liberia, and Côte d'Ivoire show that postwar reconstruction based on the ideals of new humanitarianism and people-centered liberalism—including peacebuilding and statebuilding efforts—is a long, complicated process. Rebuilding after war involves, among other things, setting forth a vision for democratic governance and defining the parameters of state reach into the political, economic, and social spheres, not to mention putting into action programs aimed at ameliorating the overall well-being of the citizenry. In general, postwar institutional reconstruction frequently includes a number of activities, including security-sector reforms of the military and police, the amelioration of human rights and justice through TRCs and war crimes trials, and the strengthening of good governance by supporting civil society and improving public finance management. All of these were examined in detail in this chapter.

Postwar reconstruction agendas are often couched in language referring to the lofty principles of good leadership, shared prosperity, equalitarianism, and so on. These highly theoretical concepts, when correctly applied, can help create deep institutional reforms and changes in overall political behavior that are designed to root out the corrupt and authoritarian practices that led to war in the first place. That said, the promotion of democracy and good governance was central to the reforms in Sierra Leone, Liberia, and Côte d'Ivoire. Their consolidation was seen as the critical element to achieving long-term peace and addressing the underlying roots of poverty. As explored in this chapter, the international peacebuilding and statebuilding efforts included a number of postwar programs aimed at supporting security-sector reforms, human rights, justice, good governance, civil society, and proper public finance management. It is true that in these three cases, the contributions of such programs to peacebuilding and statebuilding processes and outcomes did vary. Nonetheless, these reforms frequently went far, not only in their individual impact but also in their ability to create substantial change in the respective states and the given societies as a whole.

SIX

—ᴍ—

CONCLUSION

State Decay, International Statebuilding, and Institutional Design

INTRODUCTION

The international community played an important part in ending the civil wars in Sierra Leone, Liberia, and Côte d'Ivoire. While the configuration of external actors—whether from the subregion, the continent, the United Nations (UN), or former colonial powers—differed in each context, they all moved in to end the conflicts and protect at-risk populations. However, bringing an end to the fighting is easier than consolidating peace by building inclusive and democratic states on a path to sustainable peace and development.

In the case of Sierra Leone, the civil war played out in a single phase that lasted almost eleven years, from March 1991 to January 2002. It ended after the British armed forces, acting with UN troops under a renewed UN mandate, took control of Freetown, defeating the Revolutionary United Front (RUF) insurgency. The civil war in Sierra Leone led to a significant loss of life and destroyed much of the country's infrastructure. After the war, the country, with significant help from the international community, made slow but steady progress in terms of democratic governance and economic development. Yet, it remains extremely poor in terms of the Human Development Index (HDI), and its democracy is becoming increasingly tenuous; corruption and the ethnic and regional political divide are growing, as evidenced by the controversial 2023 elections.

In Liberia, the civil war happened in two phases, with actors from Economic Community of West African States (ECOWAS) (primarily Nigeria) and the UN playing important roles in ending the war. The first period of the civil war began with the invasion by Charles Taylor's forces in December 1989 and lasted through his eventual election as president in August of 1997. The second phase of the

209

conflict lasted from April 1999 to August 2003, when Taylor was removed from power. Since the end of the war, Liberia has maintained democracy, albeit with significant struggles. Overall, Liberia has maintained low economic growth and has not properly recovered from its brutal civil war. It remains one of the poorest countries in the world based on HDI rankings, and its democracy is marred by deep suspicion, animosity, and corruption among the political elite.

Côte d'Ivoire enjoyed decades of relative peace and prosperity, but then came its civil war, which also played out in two phases. During the first conflict, which began in September 2002 and ended in March 2007, the country experienced intermittent but brutal fighting. The subsequent peace process failed to result in permanent institutional accommodations between the warring factions, leading to significant postelection violence in phase two of the conflict, which lasted from November 2010 to April 2011. The international community, led by France, played a significant role in ending the violence during both phases. Yet, the international community remained sidelined for much of the peace process. Today, the situation has stabilized largely due to the military defeat of the southern supporters of Laurent Gbagbo. However, the Ivoirian peace process has stalled.

These three West African civil wars provide us with excellent opportunities to explore our central themes in this book, and taken together with the pursuant peacebuilding and postwar reconstruction efforts undertaken by the international community, they raise important questions about the challenges of building states after war in Africa and beyond. Our overall goal in this research is to spark a discussion on future policymaking concerning the nexus between international peacebuilding and statebuilding. Additionally, we hope to stimulate and focus the debate around the interconnections between the causes of civil wars and postwar institutional design as a way to gauge the prospect of consolidating peace and building an inclusive and democratic multiethnic postcolonial state. We are guided by the desire to shed light on the idea that civil wars can potentially bring positive opportunities, even given the horrors that such conflicts undoubtedly produce. However, the critical question is whether postwar reconstruction entails creative and robust institutional design efforts to address the root causes of the civil wars. The interconnections between state decay, international humanitarian intervention, and statebuilding in war-torn postcolonial multiethnic states are the crux of this book.

As a starting point, it is important to point out that over the past three decades, intrastate conflicts have emerged as the most prominent form of warfare on the planet. Put more specifically, empirical evidence shows that there has been a sharp rise in the number of civil wars since the end of the Cold War. Such civil wars across Africa, as well as those outside the continent, are terribly devastating. They destroy infrastructure and cause human suffering on an almost unimaginable scale. The wars in Côte d'Ivoire, Liberia, and Sierra Leone cost countless human lives and created legacies of violence that outlive the fighting. These types of horrendous events are incredibly difficult to overcome and more often than not require major peacekeeping, peace-mediation, and peacebuilding efforts on the part of the international community. Robust international humanitarian interventions to help end war and undertake significant postwar reconstruction designed to keep such civil wars from reoccurring are clearly necessary, given the realities and research on the topic. As we see in these three West African cases, not to mention others, the international community can play a pivotal role in ending the fighting, forging a political solution to the fighting, and providing critical assistance to help build peace.

In this study, we attempt to shed light on the relationship between the practices of peacebuilding and statebuilding in the contexts of state decay and collapse across several African civil war situations. We seek to advance existing debates on the delicate interplay between these processes by closely examining the postwar reconstruction and political developments across our cases. The cases examined in this book provide clear empirical evidence about how states in Africa can be remade after civil war while getting at the nexus of the interaction between peace building and statebuilding. We pursue a clear and coherent theoretical argument in this book, stating that the processes of peacebuilding and statebuilding are linked together, with the international community playing a significant role, if it is willing to do so. That said, we also posit that postwar realities, as tough as they may be, can be viewed not just as setbacks but as opportunities for building more inclusive states. Internal violent conflicts such as the three discussed here can be seen as opportunities to construct a better future by restructuring the state and redesigning political institutions in order to better manage conflict and deal with political divisions and societal grievances. Creative institutional design practices are especially important.

There is an overarching research question in this study: How can a war-torn postcolonial multiethnic country be transformed into a peaceful and democratic state? This question provokes other related questions about the case countries: What are the causes of state collapse and the civil wars? How did the international community respond to state collapse and the civil wars? How were the causes of the civil wars addressed? What kinds of institutional arrangements have been established to ensure durable peace and inclusive democracy? These lines of inquiry provide the core focus of our book. Accordingly, our book makes three central arguments that contribute to the existing body of scholarly and policy literature: there is a clear nexus between the concepts and practices of peace building and statebuilding; peacebuilding and statebuilding are not simply domestic matters alone but are also matters of international intervention, notably under the principles of new humanitarianism and people-centered liberalism; and civil wars can be viewed as opportunities for statebuilding through creative postwar institutional design efforts. These three lines of argument are often fragmented and isolated in the extant literatures on peace and conflict, democracy, and international development.

We ask if the postwar state can become a vehicle capable of promoting peaceful and democratic governance while improving the well-being of its citizens. To answer this critical question, we need to push forward the often fragmented and isolated ideas in the existing literatures on the topic.[1] The wide variety of problems of a number of postwar African states have featured prominently in the peace and conflict, democracy, and development literature.[2] Yet, considerable deficits exist in each body of scholarship. Our examination of three West Africa case studies tries to address these gaps and further our understanding of the challenges and opportunities of internationally supported peacebuilding and statebuilding in the context of civil war. We aimed to reorient this discussion. This book does this by bridging the isolated discourses on peace/conflict, democracy, and development, and our work also focuses on providing new theoretical and policy insights to arrive at a better understanding of the links between the three.

The causes of civil wars and their tremendous humanitarian and security implications have been well examined in the peace and conflict literature.[3] However, this body of scholarship often fails to examine the link between civil wars and the transformation of the postwar state in order to avoid future relapse into violence. That is to say, apart from the deplorable humanitarian tragedy that civil wars produce, such conflicts can potentially act as catalysts for ending state decay, reworking failed states, and facilitating difficult intergroup dialogue and bargaining needed to promote democracy. Peacebuilding cannot just be about ending war; it must be about creating sustainable and positive peace, and therefore creating situations and institutional frameworks that can help negotiate conflict, avoid a relapse into violence, and consolidate democracy. Accordingly, we argue that civil wars can be opportunities for statebuilding, mainly through creative postwar institutional design.

Some of the critical questions in the democracy literature, as it applies to peace building and statebuilding, relate to the manner in which civil wars are resolved, the kinds of political and institutional arrangements that are put in place to address the underlying cause of conflict, and the extent of postwar reform that is aided by key external actors.[4] Designing democratic institutional arrangements that can facilitate peaceful intergroup bargaining constitutes a pillar of peacebuilding activities focused on resolving armed conflicts, and democratization and the establishment of the rule of law are important elements. The UN and most international donors clearly view democratic reform as a critical part of peacebuilding and postwar statebuilding. However, there is debate as to what extent democratization can be aided from the outside by the international development community, especially when it is overly based on orthodox liberal notions of electoral democracy.

Finally, much of the development literature is concerned with the role of external actors in restoring and rebuilding the state in postwar situations. Rebuilding after war is clearly an expensive endeavor that frequently outstrips the available resources of the afflicted country. Nevertheless, given this reality, what role should the international development community play in peacebuilding and statebuilding after conflict beyond simply financing reform? While the international community has been involved in these activities on behalf of a number of postwar states in Africa and beyond, some authors argue that donors should be aware of the limits of externally driven postwar development.[5] This point of debate in the literature is clear. However, we conclude that outside actors from the international community can clearly play an important role in facilitating change after a civil war, and we agree with the widely shared analysis that, in many cases, the root causes of conflicts involve the fragility of governance, which necessitates extensive economic development assistance and significant contributions from international actors. Together, local domestic actors and their international partners can create opportunities to build a new regime based on inclusive democratic governance while addressing the underlying problems of corruption and the fundamental injustices plaguing the particular society, not to mention promoting economic and social development at the same time.

THE PEACEBUILDING/STATEBUILDING NEXUS

With this book, we aim to further the discussion about how the three West African countries examined here exemplify how the wider issues of poor governance and corrosive ethnicity-driven democracy can exacerbate underlying state decay and lead to state collapse under the weight of civil war. Such civil wars are ultimately the manifestation of fundamental problems underlying the state, especially in Africa but not exclusively so. These conflicts arise from deep questions about statehood, colonial/foreign institutional origins, and the underlying lack of political freedoms, social justice, economic opportunity, and so on. Civil wars most frequently emerge in places suffering from significant levels of state decay. Weak authority and unresponsive states (including strong states) can further increase the likelihood of civil war. At the same time, violent internal conflict can exacerbate the characteristics of a decaying state and state collapse. State decay may cause civil war, and inversely, civil war may exacerbate state decay and lead to collapse; clearly, there is a complex relationship between the two. Civil wars not only expose the instability of some states but also bring forth the issues that impede the development of reasonably stable, democratic, and prosperous states, particularly in Africa. The interrelated concepts and practices of peacebuilding and statebuilding represent efforts to overcome the problems of state decay, civil war, and state collapse.

As a starting point, peacebuilding is primarily about creating situations of nonviolent coexistence despite prevailing incompatibilities. It is a response to and a consequence of civil war. According to a definition provided by the UN, peacebuilding involves a range of measures to reduce the risk of the outbreak or relapse of conflict, to strengthen national capabilities at all levels for conflict management, and to provide a foundation for sustainable peace and lasting development.[6] Furthermore, the most successful peacebuilding strategies should be coherent and tailored to meet the specific needs of the country concerned, be based on the idea of national ownership of the process, and be comprised of a carefully prioritized, sequenced, and therefore relatively targeted set of activities aimed at securing sustainable peace.[7] In the cases we examined, peacebuilding was driven by new humanitarianism and involved robust peacekeeping missions, mediation geared toward holding multiparty elections, and postwar reconstruction.

In a related manner, the contemporary state can be conceptualized as primarily being designed to deliver benefits, such as key goods and services, for the people within its borders. The state's ability to manage expectations and conflicts as well as statebuilding processes is strongly influenced by the degree of legitimacy it has in the eyes of its population. That is to say, statebuilding is at its simplest the development of state capacity constructed on top of legitimacy. Accordingly, it is a process designed to enhance capacity, institutions, and the overall legitimacy of the state. The term *statebuilding* here refers to the various types of political, economic, and social institutional arrangements that can be used to ensure a durable peace and inclusive democratic governance. Statebuilding practices in part involve reciprocal relations between a state that delivers services for its people and social and political groups who constructively engage with their state. The overall goal is to create inclusive political-institutional arrangements and processes that can build bargaining relationships able to negotiate potentially difficult interactions between the state and society. In the three case countries, ethnic inclusion in the political system and institutions of the state is critical, because ethnic marginalization has been a key factor in state decay. The overarching question here is how a postcolonial multiethnic country wracked by civil war can be transformed into a peaceful and democratic state. This is the crux of statebuilding. The three cases examined here allow us to explore these processes.

The practices of statebuilding are closely linked with political interactions and power relations between the elite holding the reins of power in a given country and the organized groups that oppose them. The way that they negotiate and manage any conflicts has a huge impact on the nature of the state. Throughout history, this process has often been extremely violent; nonetheless, it has still provided the fundamental basis for developing the scope of capacity and even the overall legitimacy of the state. Yet, at times, the various groups involved in these processes can identify, or even be encouraged or helped to identify, a critical number of interrelated common interests and negotiate ways to pursue them in a mutually beneficial manner. This not only reinforces statebuilding; it can provide the core of it. Even more, such practices and institutions of accommodation and consociation can be critical ingredients of postwar institutional design arrangements.

As we argue here, statebuilding has been fragmented and undermined by a wide variety of contradicting agendas and interests. The key elements of statehood, such as defined territorial boundaries, central government, and security apparatuses, were established during colonial rule. It goes without saying that the imposition of a state and its institutions with foreign origins has had a significant impact on many of the countries on the African continent, not to mention colonial entities everywhere. Despite their distinctly different colonial experiences, Liberia, Sierra Leone, and Côte d'Ivoire faced very similar predicaments. In all three cases, the state was an alien political and economic structure brought in from the outside. As independent countries, they adopted models of Western state institutions but mostly failed to foster the common national identity needed to transform the multiethnic state into a cohesive nation. All three countries eventually strayed from more democratic norms of political behavior toward an ethnicity-driven dictatorship. This undermined the legitimacy of the state and intensified interethnic and regional animosities. These states were simply not conceived as cohesive cultural units that could be transformed into nations. Instead of promoting nationhood, the colonial agenda undermined it. This made arriving at a national consensus on how to build a state, what the state should be, and how state power and resources would be distributed extremely difficult. This book examines how such a consensus can be helped via comprehensive peacebuilding and statebuilding efforts geared toward a creative institutional design aimed at fostering an inclusive democracy, especially after devastating and divisive civil wars. Our work shows the limit of winner-takes-all multiparty elections in the multiethnic postcolonial state. This should be an impetus for more inclusive models of democracy that are consociational in nature. Even more, such inclusivity needs to go beyond mere power-sharing governments and conventional electoral models of proportionality in representation. Inclusivity has to encompass the totality of the state institutions and be designed in a deliberate manner to fit the historical and cultural contexts of the country and the contemporary social and economic development needs of the citizenry.

The concepts of peacebuilding and statebuilding have evolved considerably in international policymaking and scholarly communities recently. There are clear conceptual convergences and linkages between these two practices. Both represent the development of institutional capacity and the growth of domestic legitimacy in order to further effective governance and sustainable development. Peacebuilding is also closely associated with the process of statebuilding through the mutual development of institutional conflict-management mechanisms. One of the objectives of both practices is to facilitate bargaining and build situations within which this type of interaction can lay the basis for future institutional arrangements that inculcate an inclusive and democratic multiethnic state.

Here, we argue that there is a clear relationship between peacebuilding and statebuilding. Furthermore, the two not only go together in tandem but are in all actuality mutually reinforcing processes. Building peace means increasing state responsiveness and its ability to manage conflict. This is necessary not only during wartime but even more so after a brutal civil war. Put another way, along with addressing the root causes of social and political conflict, these practices strengthen governmental structures as well as build more peaceful intergroup relations through creative institutional design arrangements.

The objective of contemporary statebuilding is to reconstruct the state and its institutions so that it can be more responsive and facilitate intergroup bargaining, thereby avoiding future violent conflict. Peacebuilding aims to transform the interrelations between the state and the various societal groups that might be at odds with each other. Both practices attempt to ameliorate the bond between state and society. They also try to build inclusive political systems that can unite a fractured society after war. In reality, both interact in an extremely complex but interrelated manner and have a clear impact on state-society relations. The three cases discussed here present illuminating opportunities for understanding the nexus between civil war and international statebuilding across Africa and beyond.

Since the end of the Cold War, now some three decades ago, statebuilding has been an integral part of the peacebuilding process and has seen a growing collaboration between domestic actors and the international community. The UN and various regional and subregional organizations and other major international actors all play critical roles in the effort to help reestablish peace and rebuild the state in war-torn countries. They do so by introducing comprehensive peacebuilding and statebuilding strategies. In our three case studies, as with other similar cases across the planet, we clearly see a delicate interplay between peacebuilding and statebuilding, both on a domestic and international level.

NEW HUMANITARIANISM AND PEOPLE-CENTERED LIBERALISM: THE INTERNATIONAL PRAXIS OF PEACEBUILDING AND STATEBUILDING

Peacebuilding is commonly perceived as being an internal matter designed to build up the state, improve state-society relations, and provide conflict-management mechanisms to ease intergroup relations. Similarly, statebuilding is frequently viewed as being exclusively a domestic affair. The efforts to redesign the state internally can be the result of a new homegrown political and civic awareness that emerged out of the horrors of war. However, we argue that peacebuilding and statebuilding are not just matters confined to the domestic arena but are intrinsic elements of international military and humanitarian interventions, especially under the banner of new humanitarianism. Alone, states emerging from civil war are severely limited in their ability to build peace and come back from violent conflict. Furthermore, outside players, acting both in a multilateral or unilateral manner, frequently have a higher level of capacity, increased resources, and at times the will to intervene and stop widespread human rights violations from happening. Given the destructive nature of such conflicts, the affected states often lack the capacity to get themselves back on track. In this light, peacebuilding and statebuilding can be seen as exercises of administrative assistance provided by the international community to facilitate peaceful intergroup relations, build good governance, and develop institutional capacity in countries impacted by civil war.[8] Intervening in such civil wars where institutions of authority have been destroyed or significantly disrupted can be exceptionally challenging for outsiders. However, in the cases of Côte d'Ivoire, Liberia, and Sierra Leone, the international community felt that human security and local, regional, and international order were being frayed so much that it was necessary to intervene. As a part of the concept of new humanitarianism, the international community has a collective responsibility to confront such problems of human security and order. The fear that the state decay-conflict spiral could further undermine human security and therefore pose a substantial threat to international order led regional and global players to eventually intervene in all three conflicts discussed here. Those interventions epitomize what we have termed *new humanitarianism* and *people-centered liberalism* in international peacebuilding and statebuilding.

As we argue, the international community can definitely play a critical role in countries on the verge of state collapse. For decades, the international community has been deeply involved in postwar reconstruction aimed at protecting at-risk populations, restoring state capacity, and providing the foundation for democracy and economic development. Foreign aid agencies in many instances have gone on to provide a wide number of critical services on the part of the state.

The actions of the international community may be mixed, however. They are frequently motivated by a combination of both liberal morality and their own realist security interests. These humanitarian interventions propelled by new humanitarianism and people-centered liberalism have accordingly been viewed by many with some skepticism. Furthermore, the results of many of these actions on the part of the international community have been questionable at best. The international community has frequently been accused of failing to build peace by not properly targeting the underlying causes of conflict and of not being able to push forward peace processes toward a negotiated settlement that adequately addresses the fundamental causes of conflict and eventually leads to sustainable peace. The overarching interests of the international actors involved are seen by some as coming before those from the affected country. Nonetheless, it is important to remember that the various players that make up the international community are critical in contemporary peacebuilding and statebuilding for the previously mentioned reasons.

We are particularly interested in civil wars during which there has been significant international intervention under the banners of new humanitarianism and people-centered liberalism. In each of the three West African cases examined here, the international community, along with key regional actors, played critical roles in the future development of the postwar states. The peacebuilding and statebuilding practices in these three countries differ from those in cases such as Nigeria; following the Biafran Civil War (1967–1970), the Nigerian state was radically reconstructed primarily by domestic actors.[9] On the contrary, the termination of the wars and the development of the state in each of the three cases examined in this book had major international and regional input. Actors such as ECOWAS, the UN, the World Bank, the African Development Bank, the United Kingdom, and France, among others, played important roles in achieving an end to these and to the future development of the postwar state. Interestingly, while the military force provided by the international community served to bring an end to each of the civil wars, the role of outside actors to secure a sustainable peace has been equally far-reaching.

Humanitarian intervention has been frequently equated with the use of armed force by a member or members of the international community; consider the controversial actions by the United States in places like Somalia, Bosnia-Herzegovina, and Kosovo. Humanitarian intervention by the international community has historically been defined as "the threat or use of force across state borders by a state (or group of states) aimed at preventing or ending widespread and grave violations of the fundamental human rights."[10] Yet, as we argue, the international community also has an important role in developing the concepts of humanitarianism, peace, and the promotion of democratic governance within war-torn countries. This goes beyond the use of military force. New humanitarianism is the global embodiment of the idea of human compassion. The notion of extending and providing care to those in need and restoring state capacity is at the heart of international humanitarian intervention in situations such as the three West African civil wars examined in this book. This is epitomized in the doctrines of new humanitarianism and people-centered liberalism that have been applied to Sierra Leone, Liberia, and Côte d'Ivoire.

These three massive international humanitarian interventions have been largely viewed as necessary in order to restore security within these states, as well as in the West African subregion as a whole, and perhaps more importantly to fulfill the moral obligations of the international community to protect at-risk populations. However, it is critical to note that the attention from international actors was not the same in all three cases. Interestingly, in Liberia and Sierra Leone, there were rather robust regional and international humanitarian-military interventions as well as significant postwar reconstruction efforts buttressed by extensive development aid packages from donors. Since intervening in these two cases, the international community has subsequently turned to far-reaching statebuilding efforts. In contrast, Côte d'Ivoire points not only to the possibilities for international statebuilding but also to its limitations. The international community played a critical supportive role in ending the fighting in Côte d'Ivoire and trying to forge a political solution to the conflict, albeit with limited success. The external intervention was mostly limited to securing a buffer zone, mediating a political solution to the conflict, and supporting the implementation of the various peace agreements. In this case, interestingly, the Ivoirians actually went on to sidestep the international community and eventually negotiate a fairly successful peace agreement on their own, with some help from subregional actors. However, in the end, international forces briefly intervened to oust Gbagbo after he lost the 2010 presidential election. These processes, which have led to the end of three brutal civil wars, can provide opportunities for a better, more peaceful future if the postwar reconstruction efforts can address the root causes of state decay and civil war.

INSTITUTIONAL DESIGN: CIVIL WARS AND THE OPPORTUNITIES FOR STATEBUILDING

Today, as in the past, war and its consequences have played a large role in determining the structures of states. There is a clear relationship between war and statebuilding; wars have spurred and created opportunities for statebuilding throughout history. As Anthony Giddens observes, states have transformed themselves in order to conduct war and, perhaps more importantly here, as a result of war.[11] In Africa and beyond, state decay and collapse connected to civil wars must be treated not only as crises to be quelled but as potential opportunities to rethink the state and build better political, economic, and social institutions that are sustainable. Advancing this discussion is at the core of our efforts in this book. Our task is not to provide a blueprint for institutional design. Rather, our work raises this issue and shows a variety of reforms efforts that have been undertaken with the hope of accentuating the importance of creative institutional design aligned to the root causes of war. Based on the current postwar state of peace and democracy in Sierra Leone, Liberia, and Côte d'Ivoire, the need for more creative institutional design is even greater.

It goes without saying that civil war leaves a tremendous imprint on any society. Clearly, such conflicts are first and foremost humanitarian disasters that rip societies to tatters. The legacy of such wars, in Africa and elsewhere, has mostly been tremendous human suffering that can have a major impact for decades, long after the fighting has ended. The underlying dysfunctional conditions of many states across Africa, including political instabilities, poor economic and social conditions, and divisive ethnic politics—all exacerbated by poor governance and leadership—combine to make statebuilding an extremely difficult process. These challenges are even more acute in brittle, decaying, and war-torn countries.

Nonetheless, civil wars can provide a unique opportunity for statebuilding. There can be a positive angle to the end of civil war despite the horror it entails. Such conflicts can be an opportunity to build a better state by addressing fundamental problems. In our cases, notwithstanding all the devastation of the civil wars in Liberia, Sierra Leone and Côte d'Ivoire, scholars and policymakers should be seeking to understand the opportunities for transforming the state from an oppressive political and economic apparatus into a political system that fosters freedom, social justice, and economic development. These opportunities could take the form of a fundamental break with the prewar political system aimed at fostering significant postwar changes in the political culture and state institutions; this could make such civil wars catalysts for inclusive democracy and economic development. As with the three cases examined in this study, such changes could be the result of the deployment of international forces and humanitarian agencies to provoke a transformation in the domestic political culture and state institutions. Clearly, statebuilding should not be limited to restoring old institutions and setting up new social programs. It should also address existential questions of statehood (citizenship, ethnic representation, justice, rights, power, and development) by being more deliberate and creative with institutional design. It should generate a sense of local consciousness and grassroots participation in national issues, hopefully leading to a wide-ranging social transformation. These changes are frequently born out of a combination of homegrown political and civic awareness brought on by the civil war and the efforts of international actors and humanitarian agencies to foster and support such reforms.

Important opportunities for institutional design existed in all three of the cases discussed. However, successful postwar institutional reform is contingent on improving good-governance practices and the efficient use of economic resources. Enhancing good governance was a critical challenge for postwar reconstruction and the consolidation of peace. The proper management of public finance and natural endowments lies at the heart of good-governance reforms. In Liberia and Sierra Leone, where corruption was a critical factor leading to the civil war, major programs were launched to ensure proper management of revenues from minerals and overall public finances. As for Côte d'Ivoire, where cocoa revenues represent a critical source of government income, the international community helped push forward transparency in that sector.

In Sierra Leone, reconstruction and good-governance reform emphasized significant changes in the mining sector. The international community, led by the World Bank, initiated several projects in line with the Kimberley Process and with the Extractive Industries Transparency Initiative (EITI) that were aimed at helping Sierra Leone resume large-scale mining in an equitable and sustainable manner after the end of the civil war.[12] They focused on enhancing transparency and accountability in the mining industries with the hope of enabling the country to better use its natural resources for more sustainable development. These efforts built on the 2009 Mines and Mineral Act and led to the review of mining contracts, the restructuring of the Ministry of Mines and Mineral Resources, and pressure to comply with the EITI in order to ensure that the sector contributed to socioeconomic development.

In Liberia, improvements in public finance management were a key part of postwar reconstruction. International actors such as the United Nations Development Programme (UNDP) and the World Bank helped the country make important reforms relating to good governance and economic resource management. Two programs had a particularly significant impact—the Diamonds for Development program and the Economic Governance and Institutional Reform Project (EGIR). In 2005, the UNDP established the Diamonds for Development program in Liberia "to facilitate the establishment of a transparent and accountable revenue management system based on a fair and equitable distribution of revenues."[13] The program called for the formation of a local development fund and microfinanced mining cooperatives to benefit communities throughout the country. Furthermore, in 2008, the World Bank started the EGIR in Liberia. This project sought to "improve the efficiency and transparency in managing public financial and human resources, focusing on revenue administration, public procurement, budget execution and payroll management."[14] Special attention was directed at assisting Liberian agencies establish transparent systems for the collection and reporting of mining revenues and payments.

In Côte d'Ivoire, too, promoting good governance was a critical part of the postwar rebuilding process. The cocoa sector was of particular importance. As the largest cocoa producer, accounting for approximately 40 percent of the total world production (not to mention that the commodity represents the primary source of the country's public revenues), Côte d'Ivoire had huge potentials that were impeded by poor governance and inefficiencies in the cocoa sector. Accordingly, the World Bank, through the Economic Governance and Recovery Grant (both EGRG I and EGRG II), sought to improve accountability and transparency.

All three countries—with help from key external actors from the international community—were able to undertake significant institutional reforms that led to important changes in economic resource management. These transformations allowed for the development of better good-governance practices that have had a clear impact. Despite these various postwar reconstruction programs, there have been significant missed opportunities for creative institutional design. Notably, none of the countries introduced consociational arrangements to ensure that the various ethnic groups and regions were properly represented in the government and state institutions more broadly. Instead, they have all continued regular winner-takes-all multiparty democracy, which is already creating problems as they slide back into pseudodemocracy and authoritarianism. The failure to design new institutional mechanisms to enhance inclusive politics is leading to significant problems that can negate the gains made as ethnically driven politics undermine the rules of law and increase nepotism and corruption. All three countries missed the opportunity to institute major constitutional reforms that would address the nature of the state and the way the different ethnic groups and regions can be meaningfully represented, despite the fact that the peace agreements and the reports of the truth and reconciliation commissions clearly noted the problems of ethnic and regional marginalization.

CONCLUSION

This book goes beyond merely connecting the literature on peace and conflict, democracy, and international development. Significantly, it offers detailed comparative case studies and developed novel concepts. While these countries have been separately discussed in the peace and conflict, democracy, and international development literatures, we provide a holist and comparative study that furthers our understanding of the case countries and a comprehensive analysis of the security and international interventions in the West African region at large. In the process, we developed novel concepts and applications in the scholarly and policy debates about civil wars, international interventions, and development. We go beyond the familiar concepts of failed states, Responsibility to Protect (R2P), peacekeeping, peace mediation, democracy, and human development. Notably, we introduce and enhance the concepts of state decay, new humanitarianism, people-centered liberalism, and institutional design. These concepts emerge out of the analysis of the historical and international contexts of the civil wars and the efforts to end the wars. They add richness to the scholarly works on peace and conflict, democracy, and development and to the international policy debates on governance, human security, and human development. In sum, the book adds to our understanding of the roots of civil wars, the complexities of peacebuilding, the possibilities for statebuilding, and the interconnections between human security, state security, and regional-cum-international security. While the book is not a blueprint for statebuilding, it provides critical lessons that local and international actors can draw from as they try to figure out practical solutions to the political, economic, and social problems that impede the development of peaceful and democratic multiethnic postcolonial states in Africa.

Moreover, the book provides a close analysis of the realities of the civil war and the international intervention in West Africa, offering important lessons for that region and beyond. The three countries examined here present illuminating cases for understanding the relationship between civil war, peacebuilding, and statebuilding in West Africa and the possibilities they bring for change. The international community has played a critical and supportive role in ending the fighting and forging a long-term political solution to the civil wars in Sierra Leone, Liberia, and Côte d'Ivoire. Yet, these peacebuilding efforts raise important questions about the challenges of building states in Africa after civil war. As we have argued in this work, civil wars must be treated not only as crises to be quelled but as opportunities to rethink the state and build better institutions. Indeed, we cannot ignore the fact that the horrors of war may create the potential for sustainable peace, democracy, and positive change. These countries need to continue their peacebuilding and postwar reconstruction efforts by drawing lessons from their past and exploring new institutional arrangements. Sierra Leone has been debating the need for a national conference and potential changes to the constitution in line with the Lomé Peace Agreement. However, that discussion has stalled. Côte d'Ivoire made constitutional changes in 2000 and 2016, but the changes were geared toward exclusion rather than inclusion. Both changes undermined democracy. Southerners used the 2000 constitutional change to narrow citizenship, while Alassane Ouattara used the 2016 change to violate the term limit for the presidency. Indeed, constitutional amendments can be opportunities to redesign the state, but there is the danger of changing constitutions in ways that undermine democracy; this is not what we mean by institutional design. Institutional design should lead to more ethnic and regional inclusion among other principles of democracy. In Côte d'Ivoire, the constitutional changes failed to incorporate the lessons learned about north-south power sharing under the Ouagadougou Peace Accord and the dangers of ethnic and regional marginalization. The critical point is that constitutional changes need to be deliberative processes geared toward making the state more inclusive and representative of its various ethnic groups and regions. This remains a huge deficit in the postwar reconstruction efforts in Sierra Leone, Liberia, and Côte d'Ivoire.

NOTES

1. INTRODUCTION

1. Abu Bakarr Bah, "State Decay: A Conceptual Frame of Failing and Failed States in West Africa," *International Journal of Politics, Culture, and Society* 25, no. 1 (2012): 71–89; S. N. Sangmpam, "Neither Soft nor Dead: The African State Is Alive and Well," *African Studies Review* 36, no. 2 (1993): 73–94.

2. Interview, assistant professor at the University of Liberia, Monrovia, 2008.

3. Bah, *Breakdown and Reconstitution: Democracy, the Nation-State, and Ethnicity in Nigeria* (Lanham, MD: Lexington, 2005); Bah, "Approaches to Nation Building in Post-Colonial Nigeria," *Journal of Political and Military Sociology* (renamed *Political and Military Sociology: An Annual Review*) 32, no. 1 (Summer 2004): 45–60; Rotimi Suberu, *Federalism and Ethnic Conflict in Nigeria* (Washington, DC: United States Institute of Peace, 2001); Larry Diamond, *Class, Ethnicity and Democracy in Nigeria: The Failure of the First Republic* (Syracuse, NY: Syracuse University Press, 1988); Matthijs Bogaards, "Ethnic Party Bans and Institutional Engineering in Nigeria," *Democratization* 17, no. 4 (2010): 730–749.

4. Adekeye Adebajo, *Building Peace in West Africa: Liberia, Sierra Leone, and Guinea-Bissau* (Boulder, CO: Lynne Rienner, 2002); Adebajo and Ismail Rashid, eds., *West Africa's Security Challenges: Building Peace in a Troubled Region* (Boulder, CO: Lynne Rienner, 2004); John Kabia, *Humanitarian Intervention and Conflict Resolution in West Africa: From ECOMOG to ECOMIL* (Burlington, VT: Ashgate, 2009); Amadu Sesay, Charles Ukeje, Osman Gbla, and Olawale Ismail, *Post War Regimes and State Reconstruction in Liberia and Sierra Leone* (Dakar, SN: Codresia, 2009).

5. Bah, "Democracy and Civil War: Citizenship and Peacemaking in Côte d'Ivoire," *African Affairs* 109, no. 437 (2010): 597–615.

6. Bah, *Post-Conflict Institutional Design: Peacebuilding and Democracy in Africa* (London: Zed, 2020).

7. Charles Tilly, "War Making and State Making as Organized Crime," in *Bringing the State Back In*, ed. Peter Evans, Dietrich Rueschemeyer, and Theda Skocpol (Cambridge, UK: Cambridge University Press, 1985).

8. Reyko Huang, *The Wartime Origins of Democratization: Civil War, Rebel Governance, and Political Regime* (Cambridge, UK: Cambridge University Press, 2016).

9. Robert Blair, *Peacekeeping, Policing, and the Rule of Law after Civil War* (Cambridge, UK: Cambridge University Press, 2020).

10. Roland Paris, *At War's End: Building Peace after Civil Conflict* (Cambridge, UK: Cambridge University Press, 2004).

11. William Reno, *Corruption and State Politics in Sierra Leone* (New York: Cambridge University Press, 2008).

12. Bah and Ibrahim Bangura, "Landholding and the Creation of Lumpen Tenants in Freetown: Youth Economic Survival and Patrimonialism in Postwar Sierra Leone," *Critical Sociology* (2023).

13. Robert H. Bates, *When Things Fell Apart: State Failure in Late-Century Africa* (New York: Cambridge University Press, 2008).

14. Bah, "State Decay: A Conceptual Frame," 71–89; Bah, "State Decay and Civil War: A Discourse on Power in Sierra Leone," *Critical Sociology* 37, no. 2 (2011): 199–216; Paul Collier and Anke Hoeffler, "Greed and Grievance in Civil War," *Oxford Economic Papers* 56, no. 4 (2004): 563–595; Reno, *Corruption and State Politics in Sierra Leone*; Robert H. Jackson and Carl G. Rosberg, *Personal Rule in Black Africa: Prince, Autocrat, Prophet, Tyrant* (Berkeley: University of California Press, 1982); Jean-Francois Bayart, *The Illusion of Cultural Identity* (London: Hurst, 2005); Michael Bratton and Nicolas Van de Walle, *Democratic Experiments in Africa: Regime Transitions in Comparative Perspective* (New York: Cambridge University Press, 1997); Patrick Chabal and Jean-Pascal Daloz, *Africa Works: Disorder as Political Instrument* (Bloomington: Indiana University Press, 1999).

15. Bratton and Van de Walle, *Democratic Experiments in Africa*; Van de Walle, "Africa's Range of Regimes," *Journal of Democracy* 13, no. 2 (2002): 66–80; Vicky Randall and Lars Svåsand, "Political Parties and Democratic Consolidation in Africa," *Democratization* 9, no. 3 (2002): 30–52; Danielle Resnick and Van de Walle, eds., *Democratic Trajectories in Africa: Unravelling the Impact of Foreign Aid* (Oxford: Oxford University Press, 2013).

16. Ashraf Ghani and Clare Lockhart, *Fixing Failed States: A Framework for Rebuilding a Fractured World* (Oxford: Oxford University Press, 2008).

17. Tanja Schümer, *New Humanitarianism: Britain and Sierra Leone, 1997–2003* (New York: Palgrave Macmillan, 2008).

18. Peace A. Medie, *Global Norms and Local Action: The Campaigns to End Violence against Women in Africa* (New York: Oxford University Press, 2020).

19. Suzannah Linton, "Cambodia, East Timor and Sierra Leone: Experiments in International Justice," *Criminal Law Forum* 12 (2001): 185–246; Richard Wilson, *The Politics of Truth and Reconciliation in South Africa: Legitimizing the Post-apartheid State* (Cambridge, UK: Cambridge University Press, 2001); Elizabeth M. Evenson, "Truth and Justice in Sierra Leone: Coordination between Commission and Court," *Columbia Law Review* (2004): 730–767; Allison Corey and Sandra F. Joireman, "Retributive Justice: The Gacaca Courts in Rwanda," *African Affairs* 103, no. 410 (2004): 73–89; Rosalind Shaw, "Memory Frictions: Localizing the Truth and Reconciliation Commission in Sierra Leone," *International Journal of Transitional Justice* 1, no. 2 (2007): 183–207; Charles Chernor Jalloh, "Special Court for Sierra Leone: Achieving Justice?," *Michigan Journal of International Law* 32, no. 3 (2011): 395–460.

20. Osman Gbla, "Security Sector Reform under International Tutelage in Sierra Leone," *International Peacekeeping* 13, no. 1 (2006): 78–93; Adedeji Ebo, "The Challenges and Lessons of Security Sector Reform in Post-conflict Sierra Leone: Analysis," *Conflict, Security & Development* 6, no. 4 (2006): 481–501; Edward Sawyer, "Remove or Reform? A Case for (Restructuring) Chiefdom Governance in Post-conflict Sierra Leone," *African Affairs* 107, no. 428 (2008): 387–403; Bah, "The Contours of New Humanitarianism: War and Peacebuilding in Sierra Leone," *Africa Today* 60, no. 1 (2013): 3–26.

21. David M. Anderson and Jacob McKnight, "Kenya at War: Al-Shabaab and Its Enemies in Eastern Africa," *African Affairs* 114, no. 454 (2015): 1–27; Caroline Thomas, "Global Governance, Development and Human Security: Exploring the Links," *Third World Quarterly* 22, no. 2 (2001): 159–175; Mark Duffield, *Global Governance and the New Wars: The Merging of Development and Security* (London: Zed, 2001); Schümer, *New Humanitarianism*; Lisa Denney, "Reducing Poverty with Teargas and Batons: The Security–Development Nexus in Sierra Leone," *African Affairs* 110, no. 439 (2011): 275–294; Bah, "The Contours of New Humanitarianism," 3–26.

22. Neta Crawford, *Argument and Change in World Politics: Ethics, Decolonization, and Humanitarian Intervention* (Cambridge, UK: University Press Cambridge, 2002).

23. Séverine Autesserre, *The Trouble with the Congo: Local Violence and the Failure of International Peacebuilding* (Cambridge, UK: Cambridge University Press, 2010).

24. Autesserre, *Peaceland: Conflict Resolution and the Everyday Politics of International Intervention* (Cambridge, UK: Cambridge University Press, 2014).

25. Scott Straus, *The Order of Genocide: Race, Power, and War in Rwanda* (Ithaca, NY: Cornell University Press, 2013); Autesserre, *The Trouble with the Congo*; Bah, "State Decay and Civil War: A Discourse on Power in Sierra Leone"; Bah, "The Contours of New Humanitarianism," 3–26; Krijn Peters, *War and the Crisis of Youth in Sierra Leone* (Cambridge, UK: Cambridge University Press, 2011); Danny

Hoffman, "The Civilian Target in Sierra Leone and Liberia: Political Power, Military Strategy, and Humanitarian Intervention," *African Affairs* 103, no. 411 (2004): 211–226; Adebajo, *Building Peace in West Africa*; Stephen Ellis, *The Mask of Anarchy: The Destruction of Liberia and the Religious Dimension of an African Civil War* (New York: New York University Press, 1999).

26. Adebajo, *Building Peace in West Africa*.

27. Alfred B. Zack-Williams, "Sierra Leone: The Political Economy of Civil War, 1991–98," *Third World Quarterly* 20 (1999): 143–162; Michael Ross, "How Do Natural Resources Influence Civil War? Evidence from Thirteen Cases," *International Organization* 58, no. 1 (2004): 35–68; Michael L. Ross, "What Do We Know about Natural Resources and Civil War?," *Journal of Peace Research* 41 (2004): 337–356.

28. Alan Bryman, *Social Research Methods* (Oxford: Oxford University Press, 2016); Charles C. Ragin and Lisa M. Amoroso, *Constructing Social Research: The Unity and Diversity of Method* (Thousand Oaks, CA: Pine Forge, 2011); Antony Bryant, "The Grounded Theory Method," in *Reviewing Qualitative Research in the Social Sciences*, ed. Audrey Trainor and Elizabeth Graue, 120–136 (New York: Routledge, 2013); Barney G. Glaser and Anselm L. Strauss, *The Discovery of Grounded Theory: Strategies for Qualitative Research* (New Brunswick, NJ: AldineTransaction, 1967).

29. Auguste Comte, *Auguste Comte and Positivism: The Essential Writings* (Piscataway, NJ: Transaction, 1975); Robert C. Tucker, ed., *The Marx-Engels Reader* (New York, W. W. Norton, 1978); Max Weber, *Max Weber: Essays in Sociology* (New York: Routledge, 2009); Emile Durkheim, *Emile Durkheim: Selected Writings* (Cambridge, UK: Cambridge University Press, 1972); Bronislaw Malinowski, *A Scientific Theory of Culture and Other Essays* (UNC Press, 2015).

30. Theda Skocpol and Margaret Somers, "The Uses of Comparative History in Macrosocial Inquiry," *Comparative Studies in Society and History* 22, no. 2 (1980): 174.

31. James Mahoney, "Comparative-Historical Methodology," *Annual Review of Sociology* 30 (2004): 81–101.

32. Barrington Moore, *Social Origins of Dictatorship and Democracy: Lord and Peasant in the Making of the Modern World* (Boston, MA: Beacon, 1966); Skocpol, *States and Social Revolutions: A Comparative Analysis of France, Russia, and China* (Cambridge, UK: Cambridge University Press, 1979); Tilly, *Big Structures, Large Processes, Huge Comparisons* (New York: Russell Sage Foundation, 2006); Immanuel Wallerstein, *The Capitalist World-Economy* (Cambridge, UK: Cambridge University Press, 1979).

33. Mahoney, *Colonialism and Postcolonial Development: Spanish America in Comparative Perspective* (Cambridge, UK: Cambridge University Press, 2010); Andrew Arato, *Constitution Making Under Occupation: The Politics of Imposes Revolution in Iraq* (New York: Columbia University Press, 2009); Nic Cheeseman,

Democracy in Africa: Successes, Failures, and the Struggle for Political Reform (Cambridge, UK: Cambridge University Press, 2015); Bratton and Van de Walle, *Democratic Experiments in Africa*.

34. Crawford, *Argument and Change in World Politics*; Paris, *At War's End: Building Peace after Civil Conflict*; Mohammed Ayoob, *The Third World Security Predicament: State Making, Regional Conflict, and the International System* (Boulder, CO: Lynne Rienner, 1995).

35. Ali A. Mazrui, *The African Condition: A Political Diagnosis* (Cambridge, UK: Cambridge University Press, 1980); Mahmood Mamdani, *Citizen and Subject: Contemporary Africa and the Legacy of Late Colonialism* (Princeton, NJ: Princeton University Press, 2018); Gilbert M. Khadiagala, *Meddlers or Mediators? African Interveners in Civil Conflicts in Eastern Africa* (Leiden, NL: Martinus Nijhoff, 2007).

36. Mahoney, "Comparative-Historical Methodology," 93.

37. Weber, *Max Weber*; Durkheim, *Emile Durkheim*.

38. Ragin and Amoroso, *Constructing Social Research*, 49.

39. Ragin and Amoroso, *Constructing Social Research*, 61.

40. Ragin and Amoroso, *Constructing Social Research*, 71.

41. Mahoney, "Comparative-Historical Methodology," 93.

42. Skocpol and Somers, "The Uses of Comparative History in Macrosocial Inquiry," 176

43. Skocpol and Somers, "The Uses of Comparative History in Macrosocial Inquiry," 178.

44. Skocpol and Somers, "The Uses of Comparative History in Macrosocial Inquiry," 192.

45. Skocpol and Somers, "The Uses of Comparative History in Macrosocial Inquiry," 181.

46. Skocpol and Somers, "The Uses of Comparative History in Macrosocial Inquiry," 187.

47. The field data collection in New York and West Africa were conducted by first author Bah with the support of Northern Illinois University, the West African Research Association, and the Council of American Overseas Research Centers (CAORC).

48. Andreas Rauber, Andreas Aschenbrenner, and Oliver Witvoet, "Austrian Online Archive Processing: Analyzing Archives of the World Wide Web," *International Conference on Theory and Practice of Digital Libraries* (Berlin: Springer, 2002); Scott L. Miller, "History on the Cheap: Using the Online Archive to Make Historicists out of Undergrads," *Pedagogy* 5, no. 1 (2005): 97–101; Christopher Power et al., "Improving Archaeologists' Online Archive Experiences through User-Centred Design," *Journal on Computing and Cultural Heritage* 10, no. 1 (2017): 1–20.

49. Bill Tally and Lauren B. Goldenberg, "Fostering Historical Thinking with Digitized Primary Sources," *Journal of Research on Technology in Education* 38, no. 1 (2005): 3.

50. Chaim Noy, "Sampling Knowledge: The Hermeneutics of Snowball Sampling in Qualitative Research," *International Journal of Social Research Methodology* 11, no. 4 (2008): 327–344.

51. The field data collection in New York and West Africa were conducted by first author Bah with the support of Northern Illinois University, the West African Research Association, and CAORC. There was one research assistant in each of the countries. The paid research assistants were recent graduates from local universities working with grassroots organizations dealing with issues of development and security. The research assistants were recommended by colleagues in the case countries. Stipends were directly negotiated with the research assistants. In addition to the stipend, research assistants were reimbursed for research-related expenses, such as transportation, phone calls, and making photocopies. These research assistants did not conduct the interviews or gain access to the interview recordings or transcripts. While the research assistants know the respondents, the interviews did not take place in their direct presence. Their roles were limited to helping with logistical issues in the data-collection process.

52. The original taped interviews were later downloaded from the recording device and saved on university computers that are password protected.

53. Bryman and Bob Burgess, eds., *Analyzing Qualitative Data* (London, UK: Routledge, 2002); Matthew B. Miles and A. Michael Huberman, *Qualitative Data Analysis: An Expanded Sourcebook* (Thousand Oaks, CA: Sage, 1994); Bryman, *Social Research Methods*.

54. Ragin and Amoroso, *Constructing Social Research*; Bryant, "The Grounded Theory Method"; Glaser and Strauss, *The Discovery of Grounded Theory*.

55. Johnny Saldaña, "Coding and Analysis Strategies," *The Oxford Handbook of Qualitative Research* (Oxford, UK: Oxford University Press, 2014).

56. Bah, "Ethnic Conflicts and Management Strategies in Bulgaria, Sierra Leone and Nigeria," *Programme on Ethnic and Federal Studies Monograph New Series* 3 (Ibadan, NG: John Archers, 2003); Bah, *Breakdown and Reconstitution*.

57. Daryll Forde and Phyllis Mary Kaberry, *West African Kingdoms in the Nineteenth Century* (New York: Oxford University Press, 1967); John D. Hargreaves, *Prelude to the Partition of West Africa* (New York: Macmillan, 1963); Katherine E. Reece, *West African Kingdoms: Empires of Gold and Trade* (Vero Beach, FL: Rourke, 2005); Falola Toyin, *The Power of African Cultures* (Rochester, NY: University of Rochester Press, 2008); Toyin, ed., *Africa: African History Before 1885* (Durham, NC: Academic Press, 2000); J. F. Ade Ajayi, ed., *Africa in the Nineteenth Century until the 1880s* (Paris: UNESCO and Heinemann International, 1998).

58. Jack Goody, "Feudalism in Africa?," *Journal of African History* 4, no. 1 (1963): 1–18; Michael Crowder, *West Africa Under Colonial Rule* (Evanston, IL: Northwestern University Press, 1968); Ade Ajayi and Crowder, *History of West Africa* (New York: Columbia University Press, 1976); Crowder and Obara Ikime,

West African Chiefs: Their Changing Status Under Colonial Rule and Independence (New York: Africana Publishing, 1970); Mamdani, *Citizen and Subject*; Ismael Montana, *The Abolition of Slavery in Ottoman Tunisia* (Tampa: University Press of Florida, 2013).

59. Sheldon Gellar, *Statebuilding and Nation-Building in West Africa* (Bloomington: International Development Research Center, Indiana University, 1972); Mamdani, *Citizen and Subject*; James S. Coleman, *Nigeria: Background to Nationalism* (Berkeley, University of California Press, 1958); Lewis H. Gann and Peter Duignan, eds., *Colonialism in Africa, 1870–1960* (London: Cambridge University Press, 1975); Achille Mbembe, *On the Postcolony* (Berkeley: University of California Press, 2001).

60. J. Ayodele Langley, *Pan-Africanism and Nationalism in West Africa, 1900–1945: A Study in Ideology and Social Classes* (Gloucestershire, UK: Clarendon, 1973); Coleman, "Nationalism in Tropical Africa," *American Political Science Review* 48, no. 2 (1954): 404–426; Bah, *Post-Conflict Institutional Design*.

61. Isaac Land and Andrew Schocket, "New Approaches to the Founding of the Sierra Leone Colony, 1786–1808," *Journal of Colonialism and Colonial History* 9, no. 3 (2008); Hilary Blood, "History of Sierra Leone," *African Affairs* 62, no. 246 (1963): 76; A. B. C. Sibthorpe, *The History of Sierra Leone* (London: Frank Cass, 1970).

62. Jimmy D. Kandeh, "Politicization of Ethnic Identities in Sierra Leone," *African Studies Review* 35, no. 1 (1992): 81–99; Joseph Bangura, "Understanding Sierra Leone in Colonial West Africa: A Synoptic Socio-Political History," *History Compass* 7, no. 3 (2009): 583–603.

63. Leo Spitzer, *The Creoles of Sierra Leone: Responses to Colonialism, 1870–1945* (Madison: University of Wisconsin Press, 1974); Coleman, "Nationalism in Tropical Africa," 404–426; Anthony D. Smith, ed., *Nationalist Movements* (London: Macmillan, 1976).

64. Interview, Solomon Berewa, former vice president of Sierra Leone, Freetown, 2008.

65. G. I. C. Eluwa, "Background to the Emergence of the National Congress of British West Africa," African Studies Review 14, no. 2 (1971): 205–218.

66. A. Adu Boahen, *Africa Under Colonial Domination: 1880–1935* (Paris: UNESCO and Heinemann Educational Books, 1985).

67. Kandeh, "Politicization of Ethnic Identities," 81–99.

68. Santosh C. Saha, ed., *The Politics of Ethnicity and National Identity* (New York: Peter Lang, 2007); Bah, "State Decay and Civil War," 199–216; Kandeh, "Politicization of Ethnic Identities," 81–99; David Keen, *Conflict and Collusion in Sierra Leone* (Oxford: James Currey, 2005).

69. Tony Chafer, *The End of Empire in French West Africa: France's Successful Decolonization?* (Gordonsville, VA: Berg, 2002); Timothy C. Weiskel, *French Colonial Rule and the Baule Peoples: Resistance and Collaboration, 1889–1911* (Gloucestershire: Clarendon, 1980); Djibril Tamsir Niane and Joseph Ki-Zerbo,

Africa from the Twelfth to the Sixteenth Century (Oxford: James Currey, 1998); Paul M. Lubeck, *The African Bourgeoisie: Capitalist Development in Nigeria, Kenya, and the Côte d'Ivoire* (Boulder, CO: Lynne Rienner, 1987); Hargreaves, *West Africa: The Former French States* (Englewood Cliffs, NJ: Prentice-Hall, 1967); Thomas Hodgkin and Ruth Schachter, *French-Speaking West Africa in Transition* (Washington, DC: Carnegie Endowment for International Peace, 1961); Crowder, "Indirect Rule: French and British Style," *Journal of the International Africa Institute* 34, no. 3 (1964): 197–205; Martin A. Klein, *Slavery and Colonial Rule in French West Africa* (New York: Cambridge University Press, 1998); Virginia McLean Thompson and Richard Adloff, *French West Africa* (Stanford, CA: Stanford University Press, 1957); A. S. Kanya-Forstner, *The Conquest of Western Sudan: A Study in French Military Imperialism* (New York: Cambridge, 1969).

70. Crowder, "Indirect Rule," 197–205; Mamdani, *Citizen and Subject*; Conklin, *A Mission to Civilize*; Crowder, *West Africa Under Colonial Rule*.

71. Mamdani, *Citizen and Subject*; Kathryn Firmin-Sellers, "Institutions, Context, and Outcomes: Explaining French and British Rule in West Africa," *Comparative Politics* (2000): 253–272.

72. Coleman, "Nationalism in Tropical Africa," 404–426; Chafer, *The End of Empire in French West Africa*.

73. Jean-François Havard, "Tuer les 'Pères des Indépendances?' Comparaison de Deux Générations Politiques Post-Indépendances au Sénégal et en Côte d'Ivoire," *Revue Internationale de Politique Comparée* 16, no. 2 (2009): 315–331.

74. Aristide R. Zolberg, *One-Party Government in the Côte d'Ivoire* (Princeton, NJ: Princeton University Press, 1964); Pierre Nandjui, *Houphouët-Boigny: l'homme de la France en Afrique* (Paris: L'Harmattan, 1995); Charles F. Andrain, "The Pan-African Movement: The Search for Organization and Community," *Phylon* 23, no. 1 (1962): 5–17; James S. Magee, "What Role for ECA? Or Pan-Africanism Revisited," *Journal of Modern African Studies* 9, no.1 (2008): 73–89; Jean-Pierre Dozon, "La Côte d'Ivoire entre démocratie, nationalisme et ethnonationalisme," *Politique Africaine* 78, no. 2 (2000): 45–62; Kevin Shillington, ed., *Encyclopedia of African History Volume 1: A-G* (New York: Taylor and Francis, 2005).

75. Nandjui, *Houphouët-Boigny*; interview, a professor of anthropology, University of Cocody, Abidjan, 2008.

76. Ruth Marshall-Fratani, "The War of 'Who is Who': Autochthony, Nationalism, and Citizenship in the Ivoirian Crisis," *African Studies Review* 49, no. 2 (2006): 9–44; Dozon, "La Côte d'Ivoire," 45–62; Dwayne Woods, "The Tragedy of the Cocoa Pod: Rent-Seeking, Land and Ethnic Conflict in Côte d'Ivoire," *Journal of Modern African Studies* 41, no. 4 (2003): 641–655; Bah, "Democracy and Civil War," 597–615.

77. Thomas J. Bassett, *The Peasant Cotton Revolution in West Africa: Coté d'Ivoire 1880-1995* (New York: Cambridge University Press, 2001); Lubeck, *The African Bourgeoisie*; I. William Zartman and Christopher L. Delgado, eds., *The*

Political Economy of Côte d'Ivoire (New York: Praeger, 1984); Richard C. Crook, "Patrimonialism, Administrative Effectiveness and Economic Development in Côte d'Ivoire," *African Affairs* 88, no. 351 (1989): 205–228; John Rapley, *Ivoirien Capitalism: African Entrepreneurs in Côte d'Ivoire* (Boulder, CO: Lynne Reiner, 1993); Antony G. Hopkins, *An Economic History of West Africa* (New York: Longman, 1973); Crowder, *West Africa Under Colonial Rule.*

78. Zelijko Bogetic, John Noer, and Carlos Espina, "Côte d'Ivoire: From Success to Failure: A Story of Growth, Specialization, and the Terms of Trade," World Bank Policy Research Working Paper 4414, 2007; Robert M. Hecht, "The Ivory Coast Economic 'Miracle': What Benefits for Peasant Farmers?," *Journal of Modern African Studies* 21, no.1 (2008): 25–53; Bastiaan A. Den Tuinder, *Côte d'Ivoire, the Challenge of Success: Report of a Mission Sent to the Ivory Coast by the World Bank* (Baltimore, MD: Johns Hopkins University Press, 1978); Richard Sandbrook, "The State and Economic Stagnation in Tropical Africa," *World Development* 14, no. 3 (1986): 319–332.

79. Interview, an adviser to the president, Office of the President, Abidjan, 2008.

80. Bah, "Democracy and Civil War," 597–615; Marshall-Fratani, "The War of 'Who is Who,'" 9–44.

81. Interview, a professor of anthropology, University of Cocody, Abidjan, 2008.

82. George Klay Kieh, *The First Liberian Civil War: the Crises of Underdevelopment* (New York: Peter Lang, 2008).

83. "Maps of Liberia, 1830–1870," Library of Congress, accessed October 28, 2023, https://www.loc.gov/collections/maps-of-liberia-1830-to-1870/about-this -collection/; "U.S. Relations with Liberia," US Department of State, August 2, 2019, https://www.state.gov/u-s-relations-with-liberia/; Harry Johnston, *Liberia Vol. 1* (London: Hutchinson, 1906); Edwin Wiley, Albert Bushnell Hart, and Irving Everett Rines, eds., *Lectures on the Growth and Development of the United State, Vol. 6* (Washington, DC: American Educational Alliance, 1915); John Hanson Thomas McPherson, *History of Liberia* (Whitefish, MT: Kessinger, 2004); Abayomi Wilfrid Karnga, *History of Liberia* (Liverpool: D. H. Tyte, 1926).

84. Svend E. Holsoe, "A Study of the Relations Between Settlers and Indigenous Peoples in Western Liberia, 1821–1847," *African Historical Studies* 4, no. 2 (1971): 331–362; George William Brown, *The Economic History of Liberia* (Gainesville, FL: Associated Publishers, 1941); David Brown, "On the Category 'Civilised' in Liberia and Elsewhere," *Journal of Modern African Studies* 20, no. 2 (1982): 287–303; Amos Sawyer, "Proprietary Authority and Local Administration in Liberia," in *The Failure of the Centralized State: Institiutions and Self-Governance in Africa*, ed. James Wunsch and Dele Oluwu (Boulder, CO: Westview, 1990); Mamdani, *Citizen and Subject.*

85. D. Elwood Dunn, *Liberia and the United States During the Cold War: Limits of Reciprocity* (New York: Palgrave-Macmillan, 2009); Robert A. Smith, *The American Foreign Policy in Liberia: 1822–1971* (Granite Bay, CA: Providence, 1972); Wayne

Chatfield Taylor, *Firestone Operations in Liberia* (Washington, DC: National Planning Association, 1956); Alusine Jalloh and Toyin Falola, *The United States and West Africa: Interactions and Relations* (Rochester, NY: University of Rochester Press, 2008); Dew Tuan-Wleh Mayson and Sawyer, "Labour in Liberia," *Review of African Political Economy* 14 (1979): 3–15.

86. Interview, member of TRC of Liberia and the Inter Religious Council, Monrovia, June 2008.

87. Merran Fraenkel, *Tribe and Class in Monrovia* (London: Oxford University Press, 1964); David Levinson, *Ethnic Groups Worldwide: A Ready Reference Handbook* (Phoenix: Oryx, 1998).

88. Interview, official at the Liberian Mission to the UN, New York, 2005.

89. Bates, *When Things Fell Apart*.

90. Interview, civil society activist and member of the Network of Education and Peace Caretakers, Abidjan, 2008.

91. Interview, lecturer, Abidjan, 2008.

92. Interview, assistant professor at the University of Liberia, Monrovia, 2008.

93. Interview, senior official at the Sierra Leonean Ministry of Foreign Affairs, Freetown, 2008.

94. Adebajo, *Building Peace in West Africa*; Adebajo and Rashid, *West Africa's Security Challenges*; Ademola Adeleke, "The Politics and Diplomacy of Peacekeeping in West Africa: The ECOWAS Operation in Liberia," *Journal of Modern African Studies* 33, no. 4 (1995): 569–593; Kabia, *Humanitarian Intervention*.

95. Sesay et al., *Post-War Regimes and State Reconstruction*.

96. Bah, "Democracy and Civil War," 597–615.

97. Gianfranco Poggi, *The State: Its Nature, Development, and Prospects* (Palo Alto, CA: Stanford University Press, 1990); Tilly, "Reflections on the History of European State-Making," in *The Formation of National States in Western Europe*, ed. Gabriel Ardant and Tilly (Princeton, NJ: Princeton University Press, 1975); Weber, *Max Weber*; Rogers Brubaker, *Citizenship and Nationhood in France and Germany* (Cambridge, MA: Harvard University Press, 1992); Wallerstein, *Modern World System: Capitalist Agriculture and the Origins of the European World Economy in the Sixteenth Century* (New York: Academic Press, 1974); Michael I. Handel, *Weak States in the International System* (London: Frank Cass, 1990); Robert Owen Keohane, *International Institutions and State Power: Essays in International Relations Theory* (Boulder, CO: Westview, 1989); Christopher S. Clapham, *Africa and the International System: The Politics of State Survival* (New York: Cambridge University Press, 2002); John W. Meyer, John Boli, George M. Thomas, and Francisco O. Ramirez, "World Society and the Nation-State," *American Journal of Sociology* 103, no. 1 (1997): 144–181; Joseph R. Strayer, *On the Medieval Origins of the Modern State* (Princeton, NJ: Princeton University Press, 1970); Ghani and Lockhart, *Fixing Failed States*; Evans, Rueschemeyer, and Skocpol, eds., *Bringing the State Back In*.

98. Strayer, *Medieval Origins of the Modern State*; Eiko Ikegami, *The Taming of the Samurai: Honorific Individualism and the Making of Modern Japan* (Cambridge, MA: Harvard College, 1995); Moore, Social Origins of Dictatorship and Democracy; Hendrik Spruyt, "The End of the Empire and the Extension of the Westphalian System: The Normative Basis of the Modern State Order," *International Studies Review* 2, no. 2 (2000): 65–92; Crawford Young, "The End of the Post-Colonial State in Africa? Reflections on Changing African Political Dynamics," *African Affairs* 103, no. 410 (2004): 23–49; Robin M. Grier, "Colonial Legacies and Economic Growth," *Public Choice* 98 (1999): 317–335; Kwame Nkrumah, *Neo-Colonialism: The Last Stage of Imperialism* (London: Thomas Nelson, 1965); Young, *The African Colonial State in Comparative Perspective* (New Haven, CT: Yale University, 1995).

99. Skocpol, *States and Social Revolutions*; Ikegami, *The Taming of the Samurai*; Tilly and Ardant, *The Formation of National States in Western Europe* (Princeton, NJ: Princeton University Press, 1975).

100. Even Ethiopia and Liberia were affected by colonialism. Their boundaries were practically drawn by Western colonial powers.

101. Weber, *Max Weber*.

102. Juan J. Linz and Alfred Stepan, *Problems of Democratic Transition and Consolidation: Southern Europe, South America, and Post-Communist Europe* (Baltimore, MD: Johns Hopkins University Press, 1996); Bah, "Changing World Order and the Future of Democracy in Sub-Saharan Africa," *Proteus, A Journal of Ideas* 21, no. 1 (2004): 3–12; Huang, *The Wartime Origins of Democratization*; Blair, *Peacekeeping, Policing, and the Rule of Law after Civil War*.

103. Samuel E. Finer, "The One-Party Regimes in Africa: Reconsiderations," *Government and Opposition* 2, no. 4 (1967): 491–509; Zolberg, "The Structure of Political Conflict in the New States of Tropical Africa," *American Political Science Review* 62, no.1 (1968): 70–87; Zolberg, "The Military Decade in Africa," *World Politics* 25, no. 2 (1973): 309–321; Jackson and Rosberg, *Personal Rule in Black Africa*; Bah, *Post-Conflict Institutional Design*.

104. Bratton and Van de Walle, "Neopatrimonial Regimes and Political Transitions in Africa," *World Politics* 46, no. 4 (1994): 453–489; Bratton and Robert B. Mattes, "Support for Democracy in Africa: Intrinsic or Instrumental?," *British Journal of Political Science* 31, no. 3 (2001): 447–474; Bratton and Van de Walle, *Democratic Experiments in Africa*; Samuel Decalo, "The Process, Prospects, and Constraints of Democratization in Africa," *African Affairs* 91, no. 362 (1992): 7–35.

105. Thomas Humphrey Marshall, *Class, Citizenship, and Social Development* (New York: Greenwood, 1964).

106. Brubaker, *Citizenship and Nationhood*; Benedict Anderson, *Imagined Communities: Reflections on the Origin and Spread of Nationalism* (New York: Verso, 1991).

107. Smith, *Nationalism and Modernism: A Critical Survey of Recent Theories of Nations and Nationalism* (London: Routledge, 1998); Eric Hobsbawm, *On History*

(London: Weidenfeld and Nicolson, 1997); Johann G. Herder, *Reflections on the Philosophy of the History of Man* (Chicago: University of Chicago Press, 1968); Florian Znaniecki, *Modern Nationalities: A Sociological Study* (Urbana: University of Illinois Press, 1952); Bayart, *The Illusion of Cultural Identity*.

108. Charles Taylor, *Multiculturalism: Examining the Politics of Recognition* (Princeton, NJ: Princeton University Press, 1994); Mamdani, *Citizen and Subject*; Peter Geschiere, *The Perils of Belonging: Autochthony, Citizenship, and Exclusion in Africa and Europe* (Chicago: University of Chicago Press, 2009); Wale Adebanwi, "Contesting Exclusion: The Dilemmas of Citizenship in Nigeria," *African Anthropologist* 12, no. 1 (2005): 11–45.

109. Marshall-Fratani, "The War of 'Who is Who,'" 9–44; Bah, "Democracy and Civil War," 597–615.

110. Juan J. Linz, "Statebuilding and Nation Building," *European Review* 1, no. 4 (1993): 355–369; Jean-Marie Guéhenno, *The End of the Nation-State*, trans. Victoria Elliott (Minneapolis: University of Minnesota Press, 1995).

111. Paris Yeros, ed., *Ethnicity and Nationalism in Africa: Constructivist Reflections and Contemporary Politics* (New York: Macmillan, 1999).

112. Bah, *Post-Conflict Institutional Design*.

113. Ellis, *The Mask of Anarchy*; Bah, "State Decay and Civil War," 199–216.

114. Marshall-Fratani, "The War of 'Who is Who,'" 9–44; Dozon, "La Côte d'Ivoire," 45–62.

115. Barry Buzan, "From International System to International Society: Structural Realism and Regime Theory Meet the English School," *International Organization* 47, no. 3 (1993): 327–352; Ayoob, *The Third World Security Predicament*; Thomas M. Franck, "Legitimacy in the International System," *American Journal of International Law* 82, no. 4 (1988): 705–759; Hedley Bull, *The Anarchical Society: A Study of Order in World Politics* (New York: Columbia University Press, 1977); Alan James, *Sovereign Statehood: The Basis of International Society* (East Melbourne, AU: Allen and Unwin, 1986); John Gerard Ruggie, "Territoriality and Beyond: Problematizing Modernity in International Relations," *International Organization* 47, no. 1 (1993): 139–174; Kenneth N. Waltz, "The Emerging Structure of International Politics," *International Security* 18, no. 2 (1993): 44–79.

116. Handel, *Weak States in the International System*; Wallerstein, *World Systems Analysis: An Introduction* (Durham, NC: Duke University Press, 2004); Bull, *The Anarchical Society*; Martha Finnemore, *National Interests in International Society* (Ithaca, NY: Cornell University Press, 1996); Waltz, "The Emerging Structure of International Politics," 44–79; Duffield, *Global Governance and the New Wars*; Bah, "People-Centered Liberalism: An Alternative Approach to International Statebuilding in Sierra Leone and Liberia," *Critical Sociology* 43, no. 7–8 (2017): 989–1007.

117. Ronnie D. Lipschutz, "Reconstructing World Politics: The Emergence of Global Civil Society," *Millenium: Journal of International Studies* 21 (1992): 389–420;

Ulrich Beck, *What Is Globalization?*, trans. P. Camiller (Malden: Polity, 2000); Hugh Seton-Watson, *Nations and States: An Enquiry into the Origins of Nations and the Politics of Nationalism* (New York: Routledge, 2019).

118. Wallerstein, *World Systems Analysis.*

119. Wallerstein, "The Rise and Future Demise of the World Capitalist System: Concepts for Comparative Analysis," *Comparative Studies in Society and History* 16, no. 4 (1974): 387–415; Wallerstein, *Historical Capitalism: with Capitalist Civilization* (London: Verso Trade, 2011).

120. Clapham, *Africa and the International System*; Andrew Fenton Cooper and Agata Antkiewicz, eds., *Emerging Powers in Global Governance: Lessons From the Heiligendamm Process* (Waterloo, Ontario: Wilfrid Laurier University Press, 2008).

121. Interview, senior diplomat, Sierra Leone Mission to the UN, New York, 2005.

122. Robert Owen Keohane, ed., *Power and Governance in a Partially Globalized World* (London: Routledge, 2002); Bah, ed., *International Security and Peacebuilding: Africa, the Middle East, and Europe* (Bloomington: Indiana University Press, 2017).

123. Roberta Cohen and Francis Mading Deng, *Masses in Flight: The Global Crisis of Internal Displacement* (Washington, DC: Brookings Institution, 1998); Paul F. Diehl, Daniel Druckman, and James Wall, "International Peacekeeping and Conflict Resolution: A Taxonomic Analysis with Implications," *Journal of Conflict Resolution* 42, no. 1 (1998): 33–55.

124. Kofi A. Annan, "Two Concepts of Sovereignty," *The Economist* 18, no. 9 (1999); Commission on Human Security, *Human Security Now* (New York: United Nations Publications, 2003); S. Neil MacFarlane and Yuen Foong-Khong, *Human Security and the UN: A Critical History* (Bloomington: Indiana University Press, 2006).

125. Clifford Geertz, *Old Societies and New States: The Quest for Modernity in Asia and Africa* (NewYork: Free Press of Glencoe, 1963); Joane Nagel and Susan Olzak, "Ethnic Mobilization in New and Old States: An Extension of the Competition Model," *Social Problems* 30, no. 2 (1982): 127–143.

126. Thomas Blom Hansen and Finn Stepputat, eds., *States of Imagination: Ethnographic Explorations of the Postcolonial State* (Durham, NC: Duke University Press, 2001); John S. Saul, "The State in Post-Colonial Societies: Tanzania," *Socialist Register* 11 (1974): 349–371; Mamdani, *Citizen and Subject*; J. F. Médard, "Patrimonialism, Neo-Patrimonialism, and the Study of the Postcoloniaal State in Sub-Saharan Africa," in *Political Corruption: Concepts and Contexts*, ed. Arnold J. Heidenheimer and Michael Johnston (New Brunswick, NJ: Transaction, 2009); Collin Leys, "The 'Overdeveloped' Post Colonial State: A Re-evaluation," *Review of African Political Economy* 3, no. 5 (1976): 39–48; Karen Dawisha and Bruce Parrott, *Russia and the New States of Eurasia: The Politics of Upheaval* (New York: University of Cambridge, 1994); Ian Bremmer and Ray Taras, *Nation and Politics in the Soviet Successor States* (New York: Cambridge University Press, 1993).

127. Dirk Hoerder, Christiane Harzig, and Adrian Shubert, *The Historical Practice of Diversity: Transcultural Interactions from the Early Modern Mediterranean to the Postcolonial World* (New York: Berghahn, 2003); Ewin N. Wilmsen and Patrick McAllister, *The Politics of Difference: Ethnic Premises in a World of Power* (Chicago: University of Chicago Press, 1996); Arjun Appadurai, *Modernity at Large: Cultural Dimensions of Globalization* (Minneapolis: University of Minnesota Press, 1996); Jan Nederveen Pieterse, "Deconstructing/Reconstructing Ethnicity," *Nations and Nationalism* 3, no. 3 (1997): 365–395; Gerard Delanty and Krishan Kumar, *The SAGE Handbook of Nations and Nationalism* (Thousand Oaks, CA: Sage, 2006); Michael A. Burayidi, *Multiculturalism in a Cross-National Perspective* (Lanham, MD: University of America Press, 1997); Rainer Forst, "The Basic Right to Justification: Towards a Constructivist Concept of Human Rights," *Constellations: An International Journal of Critical and Democratic Theory* 6, no. 1 (1999): 35–60.

128. Don Cupitt, *After God: The Future of Religion* (New York: Basic Books, 1997); David Bennett, *Multicultural States: Rethinking Difference and Identity* (New York: Routledge, 1998); Donald L. Horowitz, *Ethnic Groups in Conflict* (Berkeley: University of California Press, 1985); Anderson, *Imagined Communities*; Tilly, "Reflections on the History of European State-Making"; Ian S. Lustick, Dan Miodownik, and Roy J. Eidelson, "Secessionism in Multicultural States: Does Sharing Power Prevent or Encourage It?," *American Political Science Review* 98, no. 2 (2004): 209–229; Taylor, *Multiculturalism*.

129. Zachary Elkins and John Sides, "Can Institutions Build Unity in Multiethnic States?," *American Political Science Review* 101, no. 4 (2007): 693–708; Feliks Gross, *Citizenship and Ethnicity: The Growth and Development of a Democratic Multiethnic Institution* (Oxford: Greenwood, 1999); Uri Ra'anan, "The Nation-State Fallacy," in *Conflict and Peacemaking in Multiethnic Societies*, ed. Joseph V. Montville (Lexington, MA: Lexington Books, 1990).

130. "World Economic and Social Survey 2010: Retooling Global Development 2010," United Nations, Department of Economic and Social Affairs, 2010.

131. "World Bank Country and Lending Groups: Country Classification," World Bank, accessed October 30, 2023, http://data.worldbank.org/about /country-classifications?print&book_recurse.

132. Jeni Klugman, *Human Development Report 2009: Overcoming Barriers— Human Mobility and Development*, United Nations Development Programme, 2009.

133. Seymour Martin Lipset, "Some Social Requisites of Democracy: Economic Development and Political Legitimacy," *American Political Science Review* 53, no. 1 (1959): 69–105; Linz and Stepan, *Problems of Democratic Transition and Consolidation*.

134. Collier and Hoeffler, "Greed and Grievance in Civil War," 563–595; Robert I. Rotberg, "The Failure and Collapse of Nation-States: Breakdown, Prevention, and Repair," in *When States Fail: Causes and Consequences*, ed. Rotberg (Princeton,

NJ: Princeton University Press, 2004); I. William Zartman, ed., *Collapsed States: The Disintegration and Restoration of Legitimate Authority* (Boulder, CO: Lynne Rienner, 1995); Jean-Germain Gros, "Towards a Taxonomy of Failed States in the New World Order: Decaying Somalia, Liberia, Rwanda and Haiti," *Third World Quarterly* 17, no. 3 (1996): 455–471; Bah, "State Decay: A Conceptual Frame," 71–89.

135. Weak states can be found in both democratic and nondemocratic countries. In democratic nations, weak states can result from excessive institutionalized restraints that hamper the ability of the government to achieve policy goals or from conditions of oppressive rule that lack legitimacy. See Michael M. Atkinson and William D. Coleman, "Strong States and Weak States: Sectoral Policy Networks in Advanced Capitalist Economies," *British Journal of Political Science* 19, no. 1 (1989): 47–67; Joel S. Migdal, *Strong Societies and Weak States: State-Society Relations and State Capabilities in the Third World* (Princeton, NJ: Princeton University Press, 1988). However, weak democratic states are fundamentally different from weak nondemocratic states, which are the subject of this study.

136. Rotberg, "Failed States, Collapsed States, Weak States: Causes and Indicators," in *State Failure and State Weakness in a Time of Terror*, ed. Rotberg (Washington, DC: Brookings Institution, 2003), 4.

137. Gros, "Towards a Taxonomy of Failed States," 455–471.

138. Zartman, *Collapsed States*.

139. Rotberg, *State Failure and State Weakness*, 9.

140. Stephen Holmes, "Constitutionalism, Democracy, and State Decay," in *Deliberative Democracy and Human Rights*, ed. Harold Hongju Koh and Ronald C. Slye (New Haven, CT: Yale University Press, 1999); Bah, "State Decay and Civil War"; Bah, "State Decay: A Conceptual Frame," 71–89.

141. Jackson and Rosberg, "Why Africa's Weak States Persist: The Empirical and the Juridical in Statehood," *World Politics* 35, no.1 (1982): 1–24; Zartman, *Collapsed States*; Rotberg, "Failed States, Collapsed States, Weak States."

142. The five categories are *critical, in danger, borderline, stable,* and *most stable.*

143. Erwin van Veen. "Global Developments in State Failure. A Brief Analysis of the Failed States 2005 – 2010." The Hague, Holland: Netherlands Institute of International Relation, March 2011. https://www.clingendael.org/sites/default/files/2016-02/20110304_cru_publicatie_evanveen.pdf (accessed 12/29/2023).

144. Rotberg, *State Failure and State Weakness*, 10–13.

145. Rotberg, *State Failure and State Weakness*, 16–17.

146. Stephen Skowronek, *Building a New American State: The Expansion of National Administrative Capacities, 1877–1920* (New York: Cambridge University Press, 1982).

147. Francis Fukuyama, "The Imperative of Statebuilding," *Journal of Democracy* 15, no. 2 (2004): 17–31.

148. Arnold Rivkin, *Nation-Building in Africa: Problems and Prospects* (Piscataway, NJ: Rutgers University Press, 1969).

149. Ghani and Lockhart, *Fixing Failed States*.

150. Interview, policy specialist, UNDP, Monrovia, June 3, 2008.

151. Marshall, *Citizenship and Social Class and Other Essays* (Cambridge, UK: Cambridge University Press, 1950); Lipset, "Some Social Requisites of Democracy," 69–105.

152. The goals are to eradicate extreme poverty and hunger; achieve universal primary education; promote gender equality and empower women; reduce child mortality; improve maternal health combat HIV/AIDS, malaria, and other diseases; ensure environmental sustainability; and develop a global partnership for development. See *The Millennium Development Goals Report, 2010*, United Nations, 2010.

153. Connor Walker, "National-Building or Nation-Destroying?," *World Politics* 24, no. 3 (1972): 319–355; Rivkin, *Nation-Building in Africa*; Ade Ajayi, "The Place of African History and Culture in the Process of Nation-Building in Africa South of the Sahara," *Journal of Negro Education* 30, no. 3 (1961): 206–213; Dominic Richard David Thomas, *Nation-Building, Propaganda, and Literature in Francophone Africa* (Bloomington: Indiana University Press, 2002); Gellar, *Statebuilding and Nation-Building*; Christophe Bonneuil, "Development as Experiment: Science and Statebuilding in Late Colonial and Postcolonial Africa, 1930–1970," *Osiris* 15, no. 1 (2000): 258–281.

154. See Samuel Obeng, *Selected Speeches of Kwame Nkrumah* (Ghana: Afram, 1997); Nelson Obeng, *Long Walk to Freedom: The Autobiography of Nelson Mandela* (Boston: Little Brown, 1994); Julius Nyerere, *Ujamaa: Essays on Socialism* (New York: Oxford University Press, 1968).

155. Schachter, "Single-Party Systems in West Africa," *American Political Science Review* 55, no. 2 (1961): 294–307; Kofi Abrefa Busia, *Africa in Search of Democracy* (Santa Barbara, CA: Praeger, 1967); Zolberg, *One-Party Government in the Ivory Coast*; Zolberg, "The Structure of Political Conflict," 70–87; Anton Bebler, ed., *Military Rule in Africa: Dahomey, Ghana, Sierra Leone, and Mali* (Santa Barbara, CA: Praeger, 1973); Bah, *Post-Conflict Institutional Design*.

156. Bratton and Van de Walle, Democratic Experiments in Africa; John A. Wiseman, *The New Struggle for Democracy in Africa* (Aldershot: Avebury, 1996); Bah, "Changing the World Order," 3–12.

157. Bratton and Mattes, "Support for Democracy in Africa," 447–474.

158. Bah, "Democracy and Civil War," 597–615; Collier and Hoeffler, "Greed and Grievance in Civil War," 563–595; Håvard Hegre, "Toward a Democratic Civil Peace? Democracy, Political Change, and Civil War, 1816–1992," *American Political Science Review* 95, no.1 (2002): 33–48; Bratton and Van de Walle, *Democratic Experiments in Africa*; Mary H. Moran, *Liberia: The Violence of Democracy* (Philadelphia: University of Pennsylvania Press, 2006).

159. Richard Caplan contrasts third-party state building from indigenous state building; see Caplan, "International Authority and Statebuilding: The

Case of Bosnia and Herzegovina," *Global Governance* 10 (2004): 53–65. See also
Andy Aitchison, *Making the Transition: International Intervention, Statebuilding
and Criminal Justice Reform in Bosnia and Herzegovina*, Series on Traditional
Justice (Cambridge, UK: Intersentia, 2011); Marina Ottaway, "Rebuilding State
Institutions in Collapsed States," *Development and Change* 33, no. 5 (2002):
1001–1023; Simon Chesterman, *You, the People: The United Nations, Transitional
Administration, and Statebuilding* (New York: Oxford University Press, 2005);
Joanna Macrae, ed., "The New Humanitarianisms: A Review of Trends in Global
Humanitarian Action," *Humanitarian Policy Group, Overseas Development Institute*
11 (2002); "The Responsibility to Protect: Report of the International Commission
on Intervention and State Sovereignty," International Development Research
Centre, 2001.

160. Adam Roberts, "The Road to Hell: a Critique of Humanitarian
Intervention," *Harvard International Review* 16, no.1 (1993): 10–14; Stanley
Hoffmann, Robert C. Johansen, James T. Sterba, and Raimo Vayrynen, *The Ethics
and Politics of Humanitarian Intervention* (Notre Dame, IN: University of Notre
Dame Press, 1996); "The Responsibility to Protect"; Terry Nardin, "The Moral
Basis of Humanitarian Intervention," *Ethics and International Affairs* 16, no. 1
(2002): 57–70; Thomas George Weiss, *Humanitarian Intervention: Ideas in Action*
(Cambridge, UK: Polity, 2007); Bah, *International Security and Peacebuilding*; Bah,
"The Contours of New Humanitarianism," 3–26; Bah, "Civil Non-State Actors in
Peacekeeping and Peacebuilding in West Africa," 313–336.

161. Jan Nederveen Pieterse, "Sociology of Humanitarian Intervention: Bosnia,
Rwanda and Somalia Compared," *International Political Science Review* 18, no. 1
(1997): 71–93; "The Responsibility to Protect"; Weiss, *Humanitarian Intervention*;
Cohen and Deng, *Masses in Flight*.

162. Pratap Bhanu Mehta, "From State Sovereignty to Human Security (via
Institutions?)," *Humanitarian Intervention* 47 (2006): 257–285; Hoffmann et
al., *The Ethics and Politics of Humanitarian Intervention*; Ayoob, "Humanitarian
Intervention and International Society," *Global Governance* 7, no. 3 (2001): 225–230;
Ayoob, "Third World Perspective on Humanitarian Intervention and International
Administration," *Global Governance* 10 (2004): 99–118; Roberts, "The Road to
Hell," 10–14; "Declaration of the Group of 77 South Summit held in Havana from
10 to 14 April 2000," Non-Aligned Movement, 2000, https://www.g77.org
/summit/Declaration_G77Summit.htm; ; Bah, *International Security and
Peacebuilding*.

163. Annan, "Two Concepts of Sovereignty"; Commission on Human Security,
Human Security Now; MacFarlane and Foong-Khong, *Human Security and the UN*;
Boutros Boutros-Ghali, "An Agenda for Peace Preventive Diplomacy, Peacemaking
and Peace-Keeping," *International Relations* 11, no. 3 (1992).

164. Macrae, "The New Humanitarianisms"; Michael Barnett, *Eyewitness to a
Genocide: The United Nations and Rwanda* (Ithaca, NY: Cornell University Press,

2002); Tim Allen and David Styan, "A Right to Interfere? Bernard Kouchner and the New Humanitarianism," *Journal for International Development* 12, no. 6 (2000): 825–842.

165. Bah, "The Contours of New Humanitarianism," 3–26.

166. "The Responsibility to Protect," 39.

167. Macrae, "The New Humanitarianisms."

168. Caplan, "International Authority and State Building," 53–65.

169. Jens Meierhenrich, "Forming States After Failure," in *When States Fail: Causes and Consequences*, ed. Rotberg (Princeton, NJ: Princeton University Press, 2004); Ottaway, "Rebuilding State Institutions in Collapsed States," 1001–1023; Jennifer Milliken, *State Failure, Collapse and Reconstruction* (Malden, MA: Blackwell, 2003); Shahar Hameiri, "Capacity and its Fallacies: International Statebuilding as State Transformation," *Millenium: Journal of International Studies* 38, no. 1 (2009): 55–81; Kumar, ed., *Rebuilding Societies After Civil War: Critical Roles for International Assistance* (Boulder, CO: Lynne Rienner, 1997).

170. Fukuyama, *Statebuilding: Governance and World Order in the 21st Century* (Ithaca, NY: Cornell University Press, 2004); Fukuyama, "The Imperative of Statebuilding"; Ghani and Lockhart, *Fixing Failed States*.

171. Ray Salvatore Jennings, "The Road Ahead: Lessons in Nation Building from Japan, Germany, and Afghanistan for Postwar Iraq," *Peaceworks* 49, United States Institute of Peace (April 2003); James F. Dobbins et al., *America's Role in Nation-Building: From Germany to Iraq* (Santa Monica, CA: RAND, 2003); Bah, "The Contours of New Humanitarianism," 3–26.

172. Sesay et al., *Post-War Regimes and State Reconstruction*; Norrie MacQueen, *United Nations Peacekeeping in Africa Since 1960* (London: Longman, 2002); Kabia, *Humanitarian Intervention*; Pieterse, "Sociology of Humanitarian Intervention," 71–93; Barnett, *Eyewitness to a Genocide*; Adebajo, *Building Peace in West Africa*; Adebajo and Rashid, *West Africa's Security Challenges*; Adeleke, "The Politics and Diplomacy of Peacekeeping," 569–593; Funmi Olonisakin, *Peacekeeping in Sierra Leone: The Story of UNAMSIL* (Boulder, CO: Lynne Rienner, 2008).

173. Interview, a senior diplomat, Sierra Leone Mission to the UN, 2005; interview, diplomat, UK Mission to the UN, 2005.

174. Bah, "Democracy and Civil War," 597–615; Center on International Cooperation, *Annual Review of Global Peace Operations 2010* (Boulder, CO: Lynne Rienner, 2010).

175. Interview, diplomat, EU Commission Delegation to Côte d'Ivoire, 2008.

176. Bah, *Breakdown and Reconstitution*; Bah, "Democracy and Civil War," 597–615.

177. Meierhenrich, "Forming States After Failure."

178. Bratton, "Second Elections in Africa," *Journal of Democracy* 9, no. 3 (1998): 51–66; Wiseman, *The New Struggle for Democracy in Africa*; Collier and Hoeffler, "Greed and Grievance in Civil War," 563–595; Clapham, ed., *African Guerrillas*

(Bloomington: Indiana University Press, 1998); Bates, *Markets and States in Tropical Africa: the Political Basis of Agricultural Policies* (Berkeley: University of California Press, 2005); Bassett, *The Peasant Cotton Revolution.*

179. Bah, *Breakdown and Reconstitution*; Clapham, *Private Patronage and Public Power: Political Clientelism in the Modern State* (London: Pinter, 1982); Leonardo R. Arriola, "Patronage and Political Stability in Africa," *Comparative Political Studies* 42, no. 10 (2009): 1339–1362; Reno, "African Weak States and Commercial Alliances," *African Affairs* 96, no. 383 (1997): 165–185; Reno, *Corruption and State Politics in Sierra Leone*; Ebenezer Obadare and Wale Adebanwi, eds., *Governance and The Crisis of Rule in Africa: Leadership in Transformation* (New York: Palgrave-Macmillan, 2016); Sangmpam, "Neither Soft nor Dead," 73–94.

180. Mamdani, *Citizen and Subject*; Diamond, "Class Formation in the Swollen African State," *Journal of Modern African Studies* 25, no. 4 (1987): 567–596; Richard A. Joseph, "Class, State, and Prebendal Politics in Nigeria," *Commonwealth & Comparative Politics* 21, no. 3 (1983): 21–38.

181. Kurt Mills and Richard Norton, "Refugees and Security in the Great Lakes Region of Africa," *Civil Wars* 5, no. 1 (2002): 1–26; Patricia Daley, "Population Displacement and the Humanitarian Aid Regime: The Experience of Refugees in East Africa," in *Mobile Africa: Changing Patterns of Movement in Africa and Beyond,* ed. Mirjam de Bruijn, Rijk Adrianus van Dijk, and Dick Foeken (Leiden, NL: Brill, 2001); Jean-Paul Azam and Hoeffler, "Violence against Civilians in Civil Wars: Looting or Terror?," *Journal of Peace Research* 39, no. 4 (2002): 461–485; Taisier M. Ali and Robert O. Matthews, *Civil Wars in Africa: Roots and Resolution* (Québec: McGill-Queen's University Press, 1999); Kumar, *Rebuilding Societies After Civil War*; Assefaw Bariagaber, *Conflict and the Refugee Experience: Flight, Exile, and Repatriation in the Horn of Africa* (Burlington, VT: Ashgate, 2006); E. Elbadawi and N. Sambanis, "Why Are There So Many Civil Wars in Africa? Understanding and Preventing Violent Conflict," *Journal of African Economies* 9, no. 3 (2000): 244–269.

182. Kumar, *Rebuilding Societies After Civil War*; Marrack Goulding, "The United Nations and Conflict in Africa Since the Cold War," *African Affairs* 98, no. 391 (1999): 155–166; Andreas Mehler, "Peace and Power Sharing in Africa: A Not so Obvious Relationship," *African Affairs* 108, no. 432 (2009): 453–473.

183. Macharia Munene, J. D. Olewe Nyunya, and Korwa Gombe Adar, *The United States and Africa: From Independence to the End of the Cold War* (Nairobi: East African Educational Publishers, 1995); John Willis Harbeson and Donald S. Rothchild, eds., *Africa in World Politics: Post-Cold War Challenges* (Boulder, CO: Westview, 1995); Domingos Jardo Muekalia, "Africa and China's Strategic Partnership", *African Security Review* 3, no. 1 (2004): 5–11; Elizabeth Asiedu, "Foreign Direct Investment in Africa: The Role of Natural Resources, Market Size, Government Policy, Institutions and Political Instability," *World Economy* 29, no. 1 (2006): 63–77; Nancy Birdsall, Stijn Claessens, and Ishac Diwan, "Policy Selectivity Forgone: Debt and Donor Behavior in Africa," *World Bank Economic*

Review 17, no. 3 (2003): 409–435; Bade Onimode, ed., *The IMF, the World Bank and the African Debt: The Social and Political Perspectives* (London: Zed, 1989).

184. Adebayo Oyebade and Abiodun Alao, *Africa after the Cold War: The Changing Perspectives on Security* (Trenton, NJ: African World Press, 1998); William Hale and Eberard Kienle, eds., *After the Cold War: Security and Democracy in Africa and Asia* (London: I. B. Tauris, 1998).

185. Fantu Cheru, *The Silent Revolution in Africa: Debt, Development and Democracy* (London: Zed, 1989).

186. Bah and Nikolas Emmanuel, "Migration Cooperation between Africa and Europe: Understanding the Role of International Incentives," *Oxford Research Encyclopedia of International Studies*, September 15, 2022, https://doi.org/10.1093/acrefore/9780190846626.013.735.

2. STATE DECAY AND CIVIL WAR

1. TRC of Sierra Leone, *Witness to Truth: Report of the Sierra Leone Truth & Reconciliation Commission*, vol. 1 (2004), 2, accessed November 3, 2023, https://www.sierraleonetrc.org/index.php/view-the-final-report.

2. For report by the TRC of Liberia, see https://www.trcofliberia.org/reports/final-report.html.

3. TRC, *Witness to Truth*, 2, app. 1; Abu Bakarr Bah, "Democracy and Civil War: Citizenship and Peacemaking in Côte d'Ivoire," *African Affairs* 109, no. 437 (2010): 597–615; Bah, "State Decay and Civil War: A Discourse on Power in Sierra Leone," *Critical Sociology* 37, no. 2 (2011): 199–216; Adekeye Adebajo, *Building Peace in West Africa: Liberia, Sierra Leone, and Guinea-Bissau* (Boulder, CO: Lynne Rienner, 2002); John Hirsch, *Sierra Leone: Diamonds and the Struggle for Democracy* (Boulder, CO: Lynne Rienner, 2001); Paul Richards, "To Fight or to Farm? Agrarian Dimensions of the Mano River Conflicts (Liberia and Sierra Leone)," *African Affairs* 104, no. 417 (2005): 571–590.

4. Bah, "State Decay and Civil War," 199–216; Bah, "State Decay: A Conceptual Frame of Failing and Failed States in West Africa," *International Journal of Politics, Culture, and Society* 25, no. 1 (2012): 71–89.

5. Richard Sandbrook, "The State and Economic Stagnation in Tropical Africa," *World Development* 14, no. 3 (1986): 319–332; Donal B. Cruise O'Brien, "A Lost Generation? Youth Identity and State Decay in West Africa," in *Postcolonial Identities in Africa*, ed. Richard Werbner and Terence Ranger (London: Zed, 1996); William Reno, "Reinvention of an African Patrimonial State: Charles Taylor's Liberia," *Third World Quarterly* 16, no. 1 (1995): 109–120; Reno, *Corruption and State Politics in Sierra Leone* (New York: Cambridge University Press, 2008).

6. Christopher Clapham, "The Global-Local Politics of State Decay," in *When States Fail: Causes and Consequences*, ed. Robert Rotberg (Princeton, NJ: Princeton University Press, 2004).

7. Stephen Holmes, "Constitutionalism, Democracy, and State Decay," in *Deliberative Democracy and Human Rights*, ed. Harold Hongju Koh and Ronald C. Slye (New Haven, CT: Yale University Press, 1999).

8. Abdel-Fatau Musah, "A Country Under Siege: State Decay and Corporate Military Intervention in Sierra Leone," in *Mercenaries: An African Security Dilemma*, ed. Abdel-Fatau Musah and J. Kayode-Fayemi (Sterling, VA: Pluto, 2000).

9. Georges Nzongola-Ntalaja, *The Congo from Leopold to Kabila: A People's History* (UK: Zed, 2002).

10. Gary King, Robert O. Keohane, and Sidney Verba, *Designing Social Inquiry: Scientific Inference in Qualitative Research* (Princeton, NJ: Princeton University Press, 1994).

11. Bah, "State Decay: A Conceptual Frame," 71–89.

12. Interview, defense counsel, Special Court for Sierra Leone, Freetown, 2008.

13. Liberia, the Declaration of Independence, https://afrikadu.cois.it/?p=1417&lang=en. #.

14. Arthur J. Klinghoffer, *Soviet Perspectives on African Socialism* (Rutherford, NJ: Dickinson University Press, 1969); Oye Ogunbadejo, "Soviet Policies in Africa," *African Affairs* 17, no. 316 (New York: 1980): 239–244; Elliott P. Skinner, *Beyond Constructive Engagement: United States Foreign Policy Toward Africa* (Saint Paul: Paragon House, 1986).

15. This movement continued as part of the struggle against white settler rule in Southern Africa.

16. Frantz Fanon, *Toward the African Revolution: Political Essays* (New York: New Grove, 1988).

17. Boubacar N'Diaye, "The Military in the Politics of West Africa," *Journal of Political and Military Sociology* 28 (Winter 2000), 187–190; Pierre Nandjui, *Houphouët-Boigny: l'homme de la France en Afrique* (Paris: L'Harmattan, 1995); Jennifer A. Widner, "Two Leadership Styles and Patterns of Political Liberalization," *African Studies Review* 37, no. 1 (1994): 151–174.

18. Interview, diplomat, Liberian Mission to the UN, New York, 2005.

19. Alusine Jalloh and Toyin Falola, *The United States and West Africa: Interactions and Relations* (Rochester, NY: University of Rochester Press, 2008).

20. See Article 1, section two; Article II, and Article III, https://www.refworld.org/docid/3ae6b6030.html.

21. "Sovereignty belongs to the people. No section of the people nor any individual can take the exercise of it."

22. Bankole Thompson, *The Constitutional History and Law of Sierra Leone (1961–1995)* (Lanham, MD: University Press of America, 1997).

23. Wayne Chatfield Taylor, *Firestone Operations in Liberia* (Washington, DC: National Planning Association, 1956); Stephen Ellis, "Liberia 1989–1994: A Study of Ethnic and Spiritual Violence," *African Affairs* 94, no. 375 (1995): 165–197; Ellis, *The*

Mask of Anarchy: The Destruction of Liberia and the Religious Dimension of an African Civil War (New York: New York University Press, 1999); Earl Conteh-Morgan and Shireen Kadivar, "Ethnopolitical Violence in the Liberian Civil War," *Journal of Conflict Studies* 15, no 1 (1995): 30–44.

24. Bah, "State Decay and Civil War," 199–216; Humphrey J. Fisher, "Elections and Coups in Sierra Leone, 1967," *Journal of Modern African Studies* 7, no. 4 (1969): 611–636.

25. Aristide R. Zolberg, *One-Party Government in the Ivory Coast* (Princeton, NJ: Princeton University Press, 1964); Widner, "Single Party States and Agricultural Policies: The Cases of Ivory Coast and Kenya," *Comparative Politics* 26, no. 2 (1994): 127–147; N'Diaye, *The Challenge of Institutionalizing Civilian Control: Botswana, Côte d'Ivoire* (Lanham, MD: Lexington, 2001); N'Diaye, "The Military in the Politics of West Africa," 187–190.

26. Alex de Waal, "Mission without End? Peacekeeping in the African Political Market Place," *International Affairs* 85, no. 1 (2009): 99–113; Sandbrook, *The Politics of African Economic Stagnation* (New York: Cambridge University Press, 1986); Bah and Ibrahim Bangura, "Landholding and the Creation of Lumpen Tenants in Freetown: Youth Economic Survival and Patrimonialism in Postwar Sierra Leone," *Critical Sociology* (2023); Bah and Margaret Nasambu Barasa, "Indigenous Knowledge and the Social Construction of Patriarchy: The Case of the Bukusu of Kenya," *Critical Sociology* 49, no. 2 (2023): 217–232.

27. Bah, "State Decay: A Conceptual Frame," 71–89.

28. Peter Harrold, Malathi Jayawickrama, and Deepak Bhattasali, *Practical Lessons for Africa from East Asia in Industrial and Trade Policies* (Washington, DC: World Bank, 1996).

29. Harrold, Jayawickrama, and Bhattasali, *Practical Lessons for Africa*.

30. *World Development Report, 1989*, World Bank, accessed October 12, 2023, https://openknowledge.worldbank.org/handle/10986/2124.

31. *World Development Report, 1989*, 194.

32. Bah, "State Decay: A Conceptual Frame," 71–89.

33. Somalia had the lowest GDP per capita of $93.30 in 1991. See "Per Capita GDP at Current Prices—US Dollars," UN Data: A World of Information, accessed October 12, 2023, http://data.un.org/Data.aspx?q=GDP+per+capita&d=SNAAM A&f=grID%3a101%3bcurrID%3aUSD%3bpcFlag%3a1.

34. "Per Capita GDP at Current Prices."

35. Bah, "State Decay: A Conceptual Frame," 71–89.

36. Some of the years used in the tables slightly deviate from the ideal periods due to a lack of data. The available data for the closest years are used in the tables.

37. Bah, "State Decay: A Conceptual Frame," 71–89.

38. US dollar figures (not listed on table 2.1) are based on an exchange rate of USD 1: SLL 0.71 (1964), USD 1: SLL 0.86 (1974), USD 1: SLL 1.24 (1982), USD 1: SLL1.89

(1983), USD 1: SLL 2.51 (1984), and USD 1: SLL 295.34 (1991). All figures, including those not listed on the table, are from the sources noted in table 2.1.

39. Bah, "State Decay: A Conceptual Frame," 71–89.

40. US dollar figures (not listed on table 3.2) are based on an exchange rate of USD 1: 1 LRD. The official 1:1 exchange rate of the Liberian dollar to the US dollar was abandoned at the end of August 1998. See Katherine Murison, Africa South of the Sahara (London: Europa Publications, 2004), 617. All figures, including those not listed on the table, are from the sources noted in table 3.2.

41. Bah, "State Decay: A Conceptual Frame," 71–89.

42. Francs refer to CFA francs. US dollar figures (not listed on table 2.3) are based on an exchange rates of USD 1: 245.0 CFA francs (1964), USD 1: 212.72 CFA francs (1979), USD 1: 211.2 CFA francs (1980), USD 1: 381.06 CFA francs (1983), USD 1: 297.85 CFA francs (1988), USD 1: 283.1 CFA francs (1993), USD 1: 555.20 CFA francs (1994), USD 1: 499.15 CFA francs (1995), USD 1: 696.9 CFA francs (2002). All figures are from the sources noted in table 2.3.

43. Bah, "State Decay: A Conceptual Frame," 71–89.

44. Loucoumane Coulibaly and Ange Aboa, "Ivory Coast Opposition Says Third Term for Ouattara Would Destabilise Country," Reuters, August 7, 2020, https://www.reuters.com/article/us-ivorycoast-politics/ivory-coast-opposition-says-third-term-for-ouattara-would-destabilise-country-idUSKCN2531QD.

45. Some of the years used in the tables slightly deviate from the ideal periods due to the lack of data. The available data for the closest years are used in the tables.

46. Bah, "State Decay: A Conceptual Frame," 71–89.

47. Bah, "State Decay: A Conceptual Frame," 71–89.

48. Bah, "State Decay: A Conceptual Frame," 71–89.

49. Zolberg, "The Structure of Political Conflict in the New States of Tropical Africa," *American Political Science Review* 62, no.1 (1968): 70.

50. Michael Bratton and Nicolas Van de Walle, "Neopatrimonial Regimes and Political Transitions in Africa," *World Politics* 46, no. 4 (1994): 453–489; Bratton and Van de Walle, *Democratic Experiments in Africa: Regime Transitions in Comparative Perspective* (New York: Cambridge University Press, 1997); Nathan Jensen and Leonard Wantchekon, "Resource, Wealth, and Political Regimes in Africa," *Comparative Political Studies* 37, no. 7 (2004): 816–841; Paul Collier and Anke Hoeffler, "Resource Rents, Governance, and Conflict," *Journal of Conflict Resolution* 49, no. 4 (2005): 625–633; Ian Bannon and Collier, eds., *Natural Resources and Violent Conflict: Options and Actions* (Washington, DC: World Bank, 2003); Robert H. Bates, *Markets and States in Tropical Africa: The Political Basis of Agricultural Policies* (Berkeley: University of California Press, 2005); David K. Leonard and Scott Straus, *Africa's Stalled Development: International Causes and Cures* (Boulder, CO: Lynne Rienner, 2003); Jeffrey D. Sachs and Andrew M. Warner, "Sources of Slow Growth in African Economies," *Journal of African Economies* 6, no. 3 (1997): 335–376; Van de Walle, *African Economies and the Politics*

of Permanent Crisis, 1979–1999 (Cambridge, MA: Cambridge University Press, 2001).

51. Ebenezer Obadare and Wale Adebanwi, eds., *Governance and the Crisis of Rule in Contemporary Africa: Leadership in Transformation* (New York: Palgrave-Macmillan, 2016).

52. Bah, *Post-Conflict Institutional Design: Peacebuilding and Democracy in Africa* (London: Zed, 2020).

53. Bah, "State Decay: A Conceptual Frame," 71–89.

54. Ian Spears, *Believers, Skeptics and Failure in Conflict Resolution* (Cham: Palgrave, 2019).

55. Seymour Martin Lipset, "Some Social Requisites of Democracy: Economic Development and Political Legitimacy," *American Political Science Review* 53, no. 1 (1959): 69–105; Juan J. Linz and Alfred Stepan, *Problems of Democratic Transition and Consolidation: Southern Europe, South America, and Post-Communist Europe* (Baltimore, MD: Johns Hopkins University Press, 1996).

56. Peter Anyang' Nyong'o, "Africa: The Failure of One-Party Rule," *Journal of Democracy* 3, no. 1 (1992): 90–96; Bratton and Van de Walle, *Democratic Experiments in Africa*; John Wiseman, *Democracy and Political Change in Sub-Saharan Africa* (London: Routledge, 1995); Stephen P. Riley, "The Democratic Transition in Africa: An End to the One-Party State?," *Conflict Studies* 245 (1991): 1–37; Morris Szeftel, "Clientelism, Corruption & Catastrophe," *Review of African Political Economy* 27, no. 85 (2000): 427–441; Bratton and Van de Walle, "Neopatrimonial Regimes and Political Transitions in Africa," 453–489; Robert H. Jackson and Carl G. Rosberg, *Personal Rule in Black Africa: Prince, Autocrat, Prophet, Tyrant* (Berkeley: University of California Press, 1982).

57. Morten Bøås, "Liberia and Sierra Leone—Dead Ringers? The Logic of Neopatrimonial Rule," *Third World Quarterly* 22, no. 5 (2001): 697–723; Widner, "Single Party States," 127–147; Zolberg, *One-Party Government*; Martin L. Kilson, "Authoritarian and Single-Party Tendencies in African Politics," *World Politics* 15, no. 2 (1963): 262–294; Fisher, "Elections and Coups," 611–636; Reno, *Corruption and State Politics in Sierra Leone*.

58. Jackson and Rosberg, *Personal Rule in Black Africa*.

59. Patrick Chabal and Jean-Pascal Daloz, *Africa Works: Disorder as Political Instrument* (Bloomington: Indiana University Press, 1999).

60. Jimmy D. Kandeh, "What Does the 'Militariat' Do When It Rules? Military Regimes: The Gambia, Liberia and Sierra Leone," *Review of African Political Economy* 23, no. 69 (1996): 387–404; Julius O. Ihonvbere, "Are Things Falling Apart? The Military and the Crisis of Democratization in Nigeria," *Journal of Modern African Studies* 34, no. 2 (1996): 193–225.

61. Chabal and Daloz, *Africa Works*; Kempe R. Hope and Bornwell C. Chikulo, eds., *Corruption and Development in Africa: Lessons From Country Case-Studies* (New York: Palgrave, 2000); John M. Mbaku, *Corruption in Africa: Causes,*

Consequences, and Cleanups (Lanham, MD: Lexington, 2007); Ernest Harsch, "Accumulators and Democrats: Challenging State Corruption in Africa," *Journal of Modern African Studies* 31, no. 1 (1993): 31–48; Jean-Pierre Olivier de Sardan, "A Moral Economy of Corruption in Africa?," *Journal of Modern African Studies* 37, no. 1 (1999): 25–52; Sandbrook, "The State and Economic Stagnation," 319–332.

62. Reno, *Corruption and State Politics in Sierra Leone*; Bah, "State Decay and Civil War," 199–216; Ishmail Rashid, "Subaltern Reactions, Lumpen, Students and the Left," *Africa Development* 22, no. 3–4 (1997): 19–43; Ibrahim Abdullah, "Bush Path to Destruction: The Origin and Character of the Revolutionary United Front," *Journal of Modern African Studies* 36, no. 2 (1998): 203–235; Kayode-Fayemi, "Governing Insecurity in Post-Conflict States: The Case of Sierra Leone and Liberia," in *Reform and Reconstruction of the Security Sector*, ed. Alan Bryden and Heiner Hänggi (New Brunswick, NJ: Transaction, 2004); Kandeh, "Politicization of Ethnic Identities in Sierra Leone," *African Studies Review* 35, no. 1 (1992): 81–99.

63. David F. Luke and Riley, "The Politics of Economic Decline in Sierra Leone," *Journal of Modern African Studies* 27, no. 1 (1989): 133–141; Steve Riley and Max Sesay, "Sierra Leone: the Coming Anarchy?," *Review of African Political Economy* 22, no. 63 (1995): 121–126; Gerald H. Smith, "The Dichotomy of Politics and Corruption in a Neopatrimonial State: Evidence from Sierra Leone, 1968–1993," *A Journal of Opinion* 25, no. 1 (1997): 58–62; Sahr J. Kpundeh, "The Fight Against Corruption in Sierra Leone," in *Curbing Corruption: Toward a Model for Building National Integrity*, ed. Rick Stapenhurst and Kpundeh (Washington, DC: World Bank, 1999); Thompson and Gary Potter, "Governmental Corruption in Africa: Sierra Leone as a Case Study," *Crime, Law, and Social Change* 28, no. 2 (1997): 137–154.

64. Kayode-Fayemi, "Governing Insecurity in Post-Conflict States."

65. Tuan Wreh, *The Love of Liberty: The Rule of President William V. S. Tubman in Liberia, 1944–1971* (New York: Universe Books, 1976); Reno, "Anti-corruption Efforts in Liberia: Are They Aimed at the Right Targets?," *International Peacekeeping* 15, no. 3 (2008): 387–404; Jackson and Rosberg, *Personal Rule in Black Africa*.

66. Ellis, "Liberia 1989–1994," 165–197; David Harris, "From Warlord to Democratic President: How Charles Taylor Won the 1997 Liberian Elections," *Journal of Modern African Studies* 37, no. 3 (1999): 431–455; Sesay, "Security and State-Society Crises in Sierra Leone and Liberia," in *Globalization, Human Security, and the African Experience*, ed. Caroline Thomas and Peter Wilkin (Boulder, CO: Lynne Rienner, 1999); Michael Clough, *Free at Last? U.S. Policy Toward Africa and the End of the Cold War* (New York: Council on Foreign Relations Press, 1992).

67. Ellis, *The Mask of Anarchy*; Kandeh, "What Does the 'Militariat' Do," 387–404; Henry Bienen, "Populist Military Regimes in West Africa," *Armed Forces & Society* 11, no. 3 (1985): 357–377.

68. Jacques Baulin, *La Politique Intérieure d'Houphouët-Boigny* (Paris: Eurafor, 1982); Baulin, *La Politique Africaine d'Houphouët-Boigny* (Paris: Eurafor, 1980); Widner, "Two Leadership Styles," 151–174.

69. Baulin and Gilbert Comte, *La Succession d'Houphouët-Boigny: Les Débuts de Konan Bédié* (Paris: Karthala, 2000); Thomas J. Bassett, *The Peasant Cotton Revolution in West Africa: Cotê d'Ivoire 1880–1995* (New York: Cambridge University Press, 2001); Bastiaan A. Den Tuinder, *Côte d'Ivoire, the Challenge of Success: Report of a Mission Sent to the Ivory Coast by the World Bank* (Baltimore, MD: Johns Hopkins University Press, 1978); Robert M. Hecht, "The Ivory Coast Economic 'Miracle': What Benefits for Peasant Farmers?," *Journal of Modern African Studies* 21, no.1 (2008): 25–53; John Rapley, *Ivoirian Capitalism: African Entrepreneurs in Côte d'Ivoire* (Boulder, CO: Lynne Reiner, 1993); Jeanne Maddox Toungara, "The Apotheosis of Côte d'lvoire's Nana Houphouët-Boigny," *Journal of Modern African Studies* 28, no. 1 (1990): 23–54; Richard C. Crook, "Patrimonialism, Administrative Effectiveness and Economic Development," *African Affairs* 88, no. 351 (1989): 205–228.

70. Amadou K. Koné, *Houphouët-Boigny et la Crise Ivoirienne* (Paris: Karthala, 2003); Dwayne Woods, "The Tragedy of the Cocoa Pod: Rent-Seeking, Land and Ethnic Conflict in Côte d'Ivoire," *Journal of Modern African Studies* 41, no. 4 (2003): 641–655; Ruth Marshall-Fratani, "The War of 'Who is Who': Autochthony, Nationalism, and Citizenship in the Ivoirian Crisis," *African Studies Review* 49, no. 2 (2006): 9–44; Nandjui, *Houphouët-Boigny*; Woods, "Elites, Ethnicity, and 'Home Town' Associations in the Côte d'Ivoire: An Historical Analysis of State Society Links," *Africa* 64, no.4 (1994): 465–483; Crook, "Politics, the Cocoa Crisis, and Administration in Côte d'Ivoire," *Journal of Modern African Studies* 28, no. 4 (1990): 649–669; Crook, "Patrimonialism, Administrative Effectiveness and Economic Development," 205–228.

71. Jean-Pierre Dozon, "La Côte d'Ivoire entre démocratie, nationalisme et ethnonationalisme," *Politique Africaine* 78, no. 2 (2000): 45–62; Richard Banégas and Bruno Losch, "La Côte d'Ivoire au Bord de l'implosion," *Politique Africaine* 87 (2002): 139–161; Bah, "Democracy and Civil War," 597–615.

72. Walter Rodney, "How Europe Underdeveloped Africa," in *Beyond Borders: Thinking Critically About Global Issues*, ed. Paula S. Rothenberg (New York: Worth, 2006); Leonard and Straus, *Africa's Stalled Development*; Thad Dunning, "Conditioning the Effects of Aid: Cold War Politics, Donor Credibility, and Democracy in Africa," *International Organization* 58, no. 2 (2004): 409–423; Clough, *Free at Last?*; Frederick Cooper, "Africa and the World Economy," *African Studies Review* 24, no. 2–3 (1981): 1–86; Bates, *Markets and States in Tropical Africa*; Jacques Delacroix and Charles C. Ragin, "Structural Blockage: A Cross-National Study of Economic Dependency, State Efficacy, and Underdevelopment," *American Journal of Sociology* 86, no. 6 (1981): 1311–1347; James D. Fearon, "International Financial Institutions and Economic Policy Reform in Sub-Saharan Africa," *Journal of Modern African Studies* 26, no. 1 (1988): 113–137; Samir Amin, "Underdevelopment and Dependence in Black Africa: Historical Origin," *Journal of Peace Research* 9, no. 2 (1972): 105–119; Amin, *Neo-Colonialism in West Africa* (New York: Penguin, 1973);

Amin, "Accumulation and Development: A Theoretical Model," *Review of African Political Economy* 1, no. 1 (1974): 9–26; Patrick J. McGowan, "Economic Dependence and Economic Performance in Black Africa," *Journal of Modern African Studies* 14, no. 1 (1976): 25–40; James Ferguson, *Global Shadows: Africa in the Neoliberal World Order* (Durham, NC: Duke University Press, 2006); Robert Calderisi, *The Trouble with Africa: Why Foreign Aid Isn't Working* (New York: Palgrave-MacMillan, 2006); Stephen N. Ndegwa, *The Two Faces of Civil Society: NGOs and Politics in Africa* (West Hartford, CT: Kumarian, 1996).

73. Catherine Gegout, *Why Europe Intervenes in Africa: Security, Prestige, and the Legacy of Colonialism* (London: Hurst, 2017).

74. Sheldon Gellar, *State-Building and Nation-Building in West Africa* (Bloomington: International Development Research Center, Indiana University, 1972); Mahmood Mamdani, *Citizen and Subject: Contemporary African and the Legacy of Late Colonialism* (Princeton, NJ: Princeton University Press, 1996); Basil Davidson, *The Black Man's Burden: Africa and the Curse of the Nation-State* (New York: Times Press, 1993).

75. Clapham, *Africa and the International System: The Politics of State Survival* (New York: Cambridge University Press, 2002); Fred Marte, *Political Cycles in International Relations: The Cold War and Africa, 1945–1990* (Amsterdam: Paul Publishing Consortium, 1994); Peter Schwab, "Cold War on the Horn of Africa," *African Affairs* 77, no. 306 (1978): 6–20; Olewe Nyunya Munene and Korwa Gombe, *The United States and Africa: From Independence to the End of the Cold War* (Nairobi: East African Educational Publishers, 1995); Jackson and Rosberg, *Personal Rule in Black Africa*.

76. Bah, *Post-Conflict Institutional Design*.

77. Gegout, *Why Europe Intervenes in Africa*.

78. Adebayo Oyebade and Abiodun Alao, *Africa After the Cold War: The Changing Perspectives on Security* (Trenton, NJ: African World Press, 1998); Bratton and Van de Walle, *Democratic Experiments in Africa*; Graham Harrison, *The World Bank and Africa: The Construction of Governance States* (New York: Routledge, 2004); Deborah A. Bräutigam and Stephen Knack, "Foreign Aid, Institutions, and Governance in Sub-Saharan Africa," *Economic Development and Cultural Change* 52, no. 2 (2004): 255–285.

79. Li Anshan, "China and Africa: Policy and Challenges," *China Security* 3, no. 3 (2007): 69–93; Domingos Jardo Muekalia, "Africa and China's Strategic Partnership," *African Security Review* 3, no. 1 (2004): 5–11; Andrea Goldstein, Nicolas Pinaud, Helmut Reisen, and Xiaobao Chen, "China and India: What's in it for Africa?," Organization for Economic Cooperation and Development Centre (2006).

80. Interview, senior official, Coalition for Justice and Accountability, Freetown.

81. Interview, senior official, Network of Education and Peace Caretakers, Abidjan, 2008.

82. Interview, senior official, West African Network for Peacebuilding, Monrovia, 2008.

83. Adebajo, *Building Peace in West Africa*; Bøås, "Liberia and Sierra Leone," 697–723; Ellis, *The Mask of Anarchy*.

84. Interview, member of parliament, Monrovia, 2008.

85. United Liberation Movement for Democracy, which was later renamed United Liberation Movement of Liberia for Democracy.

86. Interview, member of parliament, Monrovia, 2008.

87. Adebajo, *Building Peace in West Africa*; Hirsch, *Sierra Leone*; Richards, "To Fight or to Farm?," 571–590; Ellis, *The Mask of Anarchy*.

88. "United Nations Mission in Liberia," UN Peacekeeping, accessed October 12, 2023, https://unmil.unmissions.org/.

89. Interview, secretary general for the Inter-Religious Council of Liberia, Monrovia, 2008.

90. *United Nations Development Assistance Framework (UNDAF) Liberia 2008–2012*, UN in Liberia, Monrovia, LR, 200.

91. *United Nations Development*, 1.

92. *Statistical Yearbook 2003: Trends in Displacement, Protection and Solutions*, UNHCR, Geneva, 2005, annex A.6.

93. *Statistical Yearbook 2003*.

94. Angela Thompsell, "A Brief History of The African Country of Liberia," ThoughtCo., September 9, 2020, https://www.thoughtco.com/brief-history-of-liberia-4019127#.

95. There is much speculation that the war in Sierra Leone was instigated by Taylor as retaliation against the government of Momoh for allowing ECOMOG to use Sierra Leone as a base to launch its operations in Liberia. However, the TRC has clearly noted that "it was years of bad governance, endemic corruption and the denial of basic human rights that created the deplorable conditions that made conflict inevitable." While external forces facilitated the war, the war was purely a RUF-led rebellion by the people of Sierra Leone. See TRC, *Witness to Truth*, vol. 1, 10.

96. Foday Saybana Sankoh, "Footpaths to Democracy: Toward a New Sierra Leone," Revolutionary United Front Manifesto, 1995.

97. "World: Africa Sierra Leone Rebels Reject Peace Offer," *BBC News*, June 23, 1999, http://news.bbc.co.uk/2/hi/africa/376323.stm; UN Development Fund for Women, *Women, Peace and Security: UNIFEM Supporting Implementation of Security Council Resolution 1325*, New York, 2004, 28.

98. *Statistical Yearbook 2003*.

99. *Statistical Yearbook 2003*, table A.6.

100. *United Nations Development Assistance Framework (UNDAF) Sierra Leone 2004–2007*, UN Country Team, Freetown, SL, 2003.

101. TRC, *Witness to Truth*.

102. Abdullah, "Bush Path to Destruction"; Lansana Gberie, *A Dirty War in West Africa: The RUF and the Destruction of Sierra Leone* (Bloomington: University of Indiana Press, 2005).

103. Bah, "The Contours of New Humanitarianism: War and Peacebuilding in Sierra Leone," *Africa Today* 60, no. 1 (2013): 3–26.

104. TRC, *Witness to Truth*; Hirsch, *Sierra Leone*.

105. Zubairu Wai, "Rethinking War and Violence in Sierra Leone: The RUF and the Nature and Condition of Insurgency Violence," *African Conflict & Peacebuilding Review* 13, no. 1 (2023): 44–76.

106. Interview, member, RUF and Promoters of Justice and Peace, Freetown, 2008.

107. Interview, Solomon Berewa, vice president of Sierra Leone, Freetown, 2008; David J. Francis, "Torturous Path to Peace: The Lomé Accord and Postwar Peacebuilding," *Sierra Leone Security Dialogue* 31, no. 3 (2000): 357–373; Hirsch, *Sierra Leone*; Adebajo, *Building Peace in West Africa*; Yusuf Bangura, "Strategic Policy Failure and Governance in Sierra Leone," *Journal of Modern African Studies* 38, no. 4 (2000): 551–577; Larry J. Woods and Timothy R. Reese, *Military Interventions in Sierra Leone: Lessons from a Failed State* (Seattle, WA: CreateSpace, 2008); Julius Mutwol, *Peace Agreements and Civil Wars in Africa: Insurgent Motivations, State Responses and Third Party Peacemaking in Liberia, Rwanda, and Sierra Leone* (Amherst, NY: Cambria, 2009).

108. Interview, senior official, UNDP, Freetown, 2008.

109. Olusegun Obasanjo, "Nigeria, Africa and the World in the Next Millennium: Statement by President Olusegun Obasanjo," General Debate of the 54th Session of the United Nations General Assembly, 1999.

110. Adebajo, *Building Peace in West Africa*, 91.

111. Resolution 1181, UN Security Council, July 13, 1998.

112. Resolution 1289, UN Security Council, February 7, 2000.

113. Resolution 1346, UN Security Council, March 30, 2001.

114. *Ninth Report of the Secretary-General on the United Nations Mission in Sierra Leone*, UN Security Council, March 14, 2001.

115. *Fourth Report of the Secretary-General on the United Nations Mission in Sierra Leone*, UN Security Council, May 19, 2000.

116. "Security Council Establishes UN Integrated Office in Sierra Leone to Further Address Root Causes of Conflict," UN Security Council, August 31, 2005.

117. Bah, "Democracy and Civil War," 597–615.

118. Bah, "Democracy and Civil War," 597–615; Marshall-Fratani, "The War of 'Who is Who,'" 9–44; Toungara, "Francophone Africa in Flux: Ethnicity and Political Crisis in Côte d'Ivoire," *Journal of Democracy* 12, no. 3 (2001): 63–72.

119. Interview, Ivoirian diplomat, New York, 2005; Interview, lecturer, University of Cocody, Abidjan, June 6, 2008; Dozon, "La Côte d'Ivoire entre démocratie," 45–62; Marshall-Fratani, "The War of 'Who is Who,'" 9–44.

120. Bah, "Democracy and Civil War," 597–615.

121. Marshall-Fratani, "The War of 'Who is Who,'" 9–44; Toungara, "Francophone Africa in Flux," 63–72; Peter Geschiere, *The Perils of Belonging: Autochthony, Citizenship, and Exclusion in Africa and Europe* (Chicago: University of Chicago Press, 2009); Banégas, "Côte d'Ivoire: Patriotism, Ethno-nationalism, and Other African Modes of Self-Writing," *African Affairs* 105, no. 421 (2006): 535–552.

122. Article 35 of the 2000 Constitution.

123. Ouattara lived out of the country and is believed to have held a Burkina Faso passport. See Toungara, "Francophone Africa in Flux," 63–72.

124. Marshall-Fratani, "The War of 'Who is Who,'" 9–44; Toungara, "Francophone Africa in Flux," 63–72; Bah, "Democracy and Civil War," 597–615.

125. Banégas, "Côte d'Ivoire," 542.

126. Daniel Chirot, "The Debacle in Côte d'Ivoire," *Journal of Democracy* 17, no. 2 (2006): 63–77; Marshall-Fratani, "The War of 'Who is Who,'" 9–44; Interview, northern businessman and community leader, Abidjan, June 7, 2008.

127. Interview, lawyer and community leader, Abidjan, 2008.

128. Arnim Langer, "Horizontal Inequalities and Violent Group Mobilization in Côte d'Ivoire," *Oxford Development Series* 33, no. 1 (2005): 25–45.

129. Banégas and Losch, "La Côte d'Ivoire au Bord de l'Implosion," 139–161.

130. "Clashes at Côte d'Ivoire Army Camp," *BBC News*, October 25, 2000, http://news.bbc.co.uk/2/hi/africa/988935.stm; "Côte d'Ivoire Bars Opposition Leader," *BBC News*, October 6, 2000, http://news.bbc.co.uk/2/hi/africa/960415.stm; "Côte d'Ivoire Reins In Soldiers," *BBC News*, October 30, 2000, http://news.bbc.co.uk/2/hi/africa/998144.stm; John Akokpari, "'You Don't Belong Here' Citizenship, the State & Africa's Conflicts: Reflections on Côte d'Ivoire," in *The Roots of African Conflicts: The Causes and Costs*, ed. Alfred G. Nhema and Paul Zeleza Tiyambe (Athens: Ohio University Press, 2008).

131. Woods, "The Tragedy of the Cocoa Pod," 641–655; Marshall-Fratani, "The War of 'Who is Who,'" 9–44.

132. Akokpari, "'You Don't Belong Here'"; Banégas, "Côte d'Ivoire," 535–552.

133. "Heavy Gunfire in Ivoirian City," *BBC News*, September 19, 2002, http://news.bbc.co.uk/2/hi/africa/2267971.stm.

134. Paul Welsh, "Côte d'Ivoire: Who Are the Rebels?," *BBC News*, 2003, http://news.bbc.co.uk/2/hi/africa/2662655.stm.

135. The FN also includes *dozos* (traditional hunters) and dissident soldiers supporting General Guéï.

136. Ivoirité is "no more or no less than a xenophobic concept. The word Ivoirité in its true sense means nothing other than: 'Côte d'Ivoire to Ivoirians,' that is to say in plain language, to those who are from the South, the Northerners are considered foreigners in their own country." See Guillaume Soro and Serge Daniel, *Pourquoi je Suis Devenu un Rebelle: La Côte d'Ivoire au Bord du Gouffre; Entretiens avec Serge Daniel* (Paris: Hachette Littératures, 2005), 20.

137. *First Report of the Secretary-General on the United Nations Operation in Côte d'Ivoire (S/2004/443)*, UN Security Council, June 2, 2004.

138. *First Report of the Secretary-General.*

139. *First Report of the Secretary-General.*

140. *First Report of the Secretary-General.*

141. Bah, "Democracy and Civil War," 597–615.

142. Collier and Hoeffler, "Greed and Grievance in Civil War," *Oxford Economic Papers* 56, no. 4 (2004): 563–595; Gberie, *A Dirty War in West Africa*; Mary Kaldor, *New and Old Wars: Organized Violence in a Global Era* (Stanford, CA: Stanford University Press, 2007); Thomas George Weiss, *Humanitarian Intervention: Ideas in Action* (Cambridge, UK: Polity, 2007).

143. Bassett, "Dangerous Pursuits: Hunter Associations (*Donzo Ton*) and National Politics in Côte d'Ivoire," *Africa* 73, no 1 (2003): 1–30; Bassett, "Containing the Donzow: The Politics of Scale in Côte d'Ivoire," *Africa Today* 50, no. 4 (2004): 31–49.

3. HUMANITARIAN INTERVENTION AND PEACE BUILDING

1. Abu Bakarr Bah, *Breakdown and Reconstitution: Democracy, the Nation-State, and Ethnicity in Nigeria* (Lanham, MD: Lexington, 2005); Adekeye Adebajo and Ismail Rashid, eds., *West Africa's Security Challenges: Building Peace in a Troubled Region* (Boulder, CO: Lynne Rienner, 2004); Kenneth Omeje, "The State, Conflict & Evolving Politics in the Niger Delta, Nigeria," *Review of African Political Economy* 31, no. 101 (2004): 425–440; Amos Sawyer, "Violent Conflicts and Governance Challenges in West Africa: The Case of the Mano River Basin Area," *Journal of Modern African Studies* 42, no. 3 (2004): 437–363; Adebajo, *Building Peace in West Africa: Liberia, Sierra Leone, and Guinea-Bissau* (Boulder, CO: Lynne Rienner, 2002); Bah, "Changing World Order and the Future of Democracy in Sub-Saharan Africa," *Proteus, A Journal of Ideas* 21, no. 1 (2004): 3–12; Kathryn Nwajiaku, "The National Conferences in Benin and Togo Revisited," *Journal of Modern African Studies* 32, no. 3 (1994): 429–447; Boubacar N'Diaye, Abdoulaye Saine, and Matturin Houngnikpo, *Not Yet Democracy: West Africa's Slow Farewell to Authoritarianism* (Durham, NC: Carolina Academic Press, 2005).

2. Augustine Ikelegbe, "Civil Society, Oil and Conflict in the Niger Delta Region of Nigeria: Ramifications of Civil Society for a Regional Resource Struggle," *Journal of Modern African Studies* 39, no. 3 (2001): 437–469; Dimieari Von Kemedi, "The Changing Predatory Styles of International Oil Companies in Nigeria," *Review of African Political Economy* 30, no. 95 (2003): 134–139; J. Shola Omotola, "From Political Mercenarism to Militias: The Political Origin of Niger Delta Militias," *Journal of Alternative Perspective in the Social Sciences* (2009): 91–124; Michael Nwankpa, "Understanding the Local-Global Dichotomy and Drivers of the Boko Haram Insurgency," *African Conflict and Peacebuilding Review* 10, no. 2 (2020): 43–64.

3. Gérard Prunier, *The Rwanda Crisis: History of a Genocide* (New York: Columbia University Press, 1997); Michael Barnett, *Eyewitness to a Genocide: The United Nations and Rwanda* (Ithaca, NY: Cornell University Press, 2002); Bruce D. Jones, *Peacemaking in Rwanda: The Dynamics of Failure* (Boulder, CO: Lynn Rienner, 2001); Samuel Totten and Eric Markusen, *Genocide in Darfur: Investigating the Atrocities in the Sudan* (New York: Routledge, 2006); Judy Mayotte, "Civil War in Sudan: The Paradox of Human Rights and National Sovereignty," *Journal of International Affairs* 47, no. 2 (1994): 497–524; David Laitin, "Somalia: Civil War and International Intervention," in *Civil Wars, Insecurity, and Intervention*, ed. Barbara F. Walter and Jack Snyder (New York: Columbia University Press, 1999); Morten Bøås and Kevin C. Dunn, eds., *African Guerillas: Raging Against the Machine* (Boulder, CO: Lynn Rienner, 2007); Mohamoud A. Abdullah, *State Collapse and Post-Conflict Development in Africa: The Case of Somalia (1960–2001)* (West Lafayette, IN: Purdue University Press, 2006); Jan Nederveen Pieterse, "Sociology of Humanitarian Intervention: Bosnia, Rwanda and Somalia Compared," *International Political Science Review* 18, no. 1 (1997): 71–93; Séverine Autesserre, *The Trouble with the Congo: Local Violence and the Failure of International Peacebuilding* (Cambridge, UK: Cambridge University Press, 2010); Autesserre, *Peaceland: Conflict Resolution and the Everyday Politics of International Intervention* (Cambridge, UK: Cambridge University Press, 2014).

4. Judy Atkins, "A New Approach to Humanitarian Intervention? Tony Blair's Doctrine of the International Community," *British Politics* 1 (2006): 274–283; Georges Abi-Saab, "Whither the International Community?," *European Journal of International Law* 9, no. 2 (1998): 248–265; Dianne Otto, "Subalternity and International Law: The Problems of Global Community and the Incommensurability of Difference," *Social & Legal Studies* 5, no. 3 (1996): 337–364; Bardo Fassbender, *The United Nations Charter as the Constitution of the International Community* (Leiden, NL: Matinus Nijhoff, 2009); Howard M. Hensel, *Sovereignty and the Global Community: The Quest for Order in the International System* (Aldershot, UK: Ashgate, 2004); Bah, Abu Bakarr. (ed.) 2024. *African Security Local Issues and Global Connections*. Athens: Ohio University Press.

5. Arun Agrawal and Clark C. Gibson. "Enchantment and Disenchantment: The Role of Community in Natural Resource Conservation," *World Development* 27, no. 4 (1999): 629–649; Elizabeth Frazer, *The Problems of Communitarian Politics Unity and Conflict* (Oxford: University Press, 2000); Anthony P. Cohen, *The Symbolic Construction of Community* (London: Tavistock, 1985); Tim Jordan, "Community, Everyday and Space," in *Understanding Everyday Life*, ed. Tony Bennett and Diane Watsons (Oxford: Wiley-Blackwell, 2002); Michael Young and Peter Willmott, *Family and Kinship in East London* (Harmondsworth, UK: Penguin, 1957); Alison Gilchrist, *A Well-Connected Community: A Net Working Approach to Community Development* (Bristol, UK: Policy, 2004).

6. Adam Roberts, "The Road to Hell: A Critique of Humanitarian Intervention," *Harvard International Review* 16, no.1 (1993): 10–13; Stanley Hoffmann, Robert C. Johansen, James T. Sterba, and Raimo Vayrynen, *The Ethics and Politics of Humanitarian Intervention* (Notre Dame, IN: University of Notre Dame Press, 1996); ICISS, "The Responsibility to Protect: Report of the International Commission on Intervention and State Sovereignty," International Development Research Centre, 2001; Terry Nardin, "The Moral Basis of Humanitarian Intervention," *Ethics and International Affairs* 16, no. 1 (2002): 57–70; Thomas George Weiss, *Humanitarian Intervention: Ideas in Action* (Cambridge, UK: Polity, 2007).

7. Bah, "The Contours of New Humanitarianism: War and Peacebuilding in Sierra Leone," *Africa Today* 60, no. 1 (2013): 3–26.

8. Pieterse, "Sociology of Humanitarian Intervention," 71–93; ICISS, "The Responsibility to Protect"; Weiss, *Humanitarian Intervention*.

9. Johansen, "Limits and Opportunities in Humanitarian Intervention," in *The Ethics and Politics of Humanitarian Intervention*, ed. Hoffman, Johansen, Sterba, and Väyrynen (Notre Dame, IN: University of Notre Dame Press, 1996).

10. ICISS, "The Responsibility to Protect," 11.

11. Bah, ed., *International Security and Peacebuilding: Africa, the Middle East, and Europe* (Bloomington: Indiana University Press, 2017).

12. Nardin, "The Moral Basis of Humanitarian Intervention," 57–70.

13. ICISS, "The Responsibility to Protect."

14. Hoffmann et al., *The Ethics and Politics of Humanitarian Intervention*; Mohammed Ayoob, "Third World Perspective on Humanitarian Intervention and International Administration," *Global Governance* 10 (2004): 99–118; Bah, *International Security and Peacebuilding*.

15. *Declaration of the South Summit*, Group of 77 South Summit, Havana, CU, April 10–14, 2000, para. 54.

16. Neta Crawford, *Argument and Change in World Politics: Ethics, Decolonization, and Humanitarian Intervention* (Cambridge, UK: University Press Cambridge, 2002).

17. Roberts, "The Road to Hell," 10–13; Pieterse, "Sociology of Humanitarian Intervention," 71–93.

18. Bah, *International Security and Peacebuilding*.

19. Hoffmann et al., *The Ethics and Politics of Humanitarian Intervention*; Nardin, "The Moral Basis of Humanitarian Intervention," 57–70; Weiss, *Humanitarian Intervention*.

20. Kofi A. Annan, "Two Concepts of Sovereignty," *The Economist* 18, no. 9 (1999): 49–50; Commission on Human Security, *Human Security Now* (New York: United Nations Publications, 2003); S. Neil MacFarlane and Yuen Foong-Khong, *Human Security and the UN: A Critical History* (Bloomington: Indiana University Press, 2006).

21. Commission on Human Security, *Human Security Now*, iv.

22. Roberta Cohen and Francis Mading Deng, *Masses in Flight: The Global Crisis of Internal Displacement* (Washington, DC: Brookings Institution, 1998); Annan, "Two Concepts of Sovereignty," 49–50; ICISS, "The Responsibility to Protect."

23. Bah, "The Contours of New Humanitarianism: War and Peacebuilding in Sierra Leone," *Africa Today* 60, no. 1 (2013): 3–26.

24. Paul Collier and Anke Hoeffler, "Greed and Grievance in Civil War," *Oxford Economic Papers* 56, no. 4 (2004): 563–595; Lansana Gberie, *A Dirty War in West Africa: The RUF and the Destruction of Sierra Leone* (Bloomington: University of Indiana Press, 2005); Mary Kaldor, *New and Old Wars: Organized Violence in a Global Era* (Stanford, CA: Stanford University Press, 2007); Bah, "Civil Non-State Actors in Peacekeeping and Peacebuilding in West Africa," *Journal of International Peacekeeping* 17, no. 3–4 (2013): 313–336.

25. Weiss, *Humanitarian Intervention*, 73.

26. Barnett, "Humanitarianism Transformed," *Perspectives on Politics*, 3, no. 4 (2005): 723–740; Joanna Macrae, ed., "The New Humanitarianisms: A Review of Trends in Global Humanitarian Action," *Humanitarian Policy Group, Overseas Development Institute* 11 (2002).

27. Bah, "The Contours of New Humanitarianism," 3–26.

28. Note that in both Liberia and Sierra Leone, the transition to new humanitarianism occurred after the international community was able to delineate between good guys and bad guys—in Sierra Leone after the coup, in Liberia after Taylor's implication in the Sierra Leone war, and in Côte d'Ivoire perhaps after the 2010 presidential elections.

29. "Ivory Coast Policemen Die in Clashes in Abidjan," *BBC News*, January 12, 2011, http://www.bbc.co.uk/news/world-africa-12170838; Mark Doyle, "No Rush to Military Intervention in Côte d'Ivoire," *BBC News*, December 31, 2010, http://www.bbc.co.uk/news/world-africa-12096437; Thomas Fessy, "Côte d'Ivoire: Life Inside Ouattara's Hotel," *BBC News*, December 23, 2010, http://www.bbc .co.uk/news/world-africa-12068131; "Ghana President Questions Côte d'Ivoire Military Option," *BBC News*, January 7, 2011, http://www.bbc.co.uk/news/world -africa-12136353; "Ivory Coast Unity Cabinet Possible, Says UN Ambassador," *BBC News*, January 11, 2011, http://www.bbc.co.uk/news/world-africa-12157810; "Côte d'Ivoire: Gbagbo 'Expels UK and Canada Envoys,'" *BBC News*, January 7, 2011, http://www.bbc.co.uk/news/world-africa-12132835.

30. The RUF fought the APC government of Joseph Momoh (1985–1992), NPRC military regime of Valentine Strasser (1992–1996), and SLPP government of Kabbah (1996–2007).

31. Hirsch, *Sierra Leone*; Truth and Reconciliation Commission of Sierra Leone, *Witness to Truth: Report of the Sierra Leone Truth & Reconciliation Commission*, vol. 1, 2, 3A, and 3B (2004), accessed November 3, 2023, https://www.sierraleonetrc .org/index.php/view-the-final-report; Funmi Olonisakin, "Nigeria, ECOMOG,

and the Sierra Leone Crisis," in *Between Democracy and Terror: The Sierra Leone Civil War*, ed. Ibrahim Abdullah (Dakar, SN: Codresia, 2004).

32. ECOWAS, "Final Communiqué," Ministers of Foreign Affairs meeting, Conakry, GN, June 26, 1997.

33. Resolution 1132, UN Security Council, October 8, 1997; Commonwealth Heads of Government, "The Edinburgh Communiqué," Commonwealth Secretariat, London, 1998; Council of Ministers, Decisions Adopted by the Sixty-Sixth Ordinary Session of the Council of Ministers, Organization of African Unity, Harare, ZW, May 28–31, 1997.

34. For some details on ECOMOG, see Europa Publications, *The Europa World Year Book 2004*, vol. 1 (London: Routledge, 2004), 198; Europa Publications, *Africa South of the Sahara* (London: Psychology Press, 2004), 829.

35. Resolution 1181, UN Security Council, July 13, 1998.

36. Interview, official, UN Department of Political Affairs, New York, 2005; Interview, senior official, Office of National Security, State House, Freetown, 2008.

37. Resolution 1289, UN Security Council, February 7, 2000.

38. Resolution 1346, UN Security Council, March 30, 2001.

39. *Ninth Report of the Secretary-General on the United Nations Mission in Sierra Leone*, UN Security Council, March 14, 2001, 9.

40. Interview, official, Nigerian Mission to the UN, New York, 2005; Interview, official, UN Peace and Security Department, New York, 2005.

41. Interview, Solomon Berewa, vice president of Sierra Leone, Freetown, 2008.

42. Paul Richards, "The Political Economy of Internal Conflict in Sierra Leone," Netherlands Institute of International Relations, Clingendael Conflict Research Unit, 2003.

43. Tanja Schümer, *New Humanitarianism: Britain and Sierra Leone, 1997–2003* (New York: Palgrave Macmillan, 2008).

44. UNAMSIL, "UNAMSIL: A Success Story in Peacekeeping," United Nations Department of Public Information: Peace and Security Section, December 2005, accessed November 3, 2023, https://peacekeeping.un.org/mission/past/unamsil /Overview.pdf.

45. Interview, diplomat, UK Mission to the UN, New York, 2005; Interview, official, Nigerian Mission to the UN, New York, 2005; Interview, official, Mission of Guinea to the UN, New York, 2005.

46. Interview, official, Bureau for Crisis Prevention and Management, UNDP, New York, 2005.

47. "Sierra Leone," Amnesty International, https://www.amnesty.org/en /location/africa/west-and-central-africa/sierra-leone/; John Kabia, *Humanitarian Intervention and Conflict Resolution in West Africa: From ECOMOG to ECOMIL* (Burlington, VT: Ashgate, 2009).

48. Adebajo, *Building Peace in West Africa*.

49. Council of Ministers, Decisions Adopted by the Sixty-Sixth Ordinary Session; Commonwealth Heads of State, "The Edinburgh Communiqué."

50. Resolution 1132, UN Security Council.

51. *Fourth Report of the Secretary-General on the United Nations Mission in Sierra Leone*, UN Security Council, May 19, 2000.

52. Andrew Dorman, *Blair's Successful War: British Military Intervention in Sierra Leone* (Burlington, VT: Ashgate, 2009).

53. Christopher Tuck, "Every Car or Moving Object Gone: The ECOMOG Intervention in Liberia," *African Studies Quarterly* 4, no. 1 (2000): 1–16.

54. Comfort Ero, "ECOWAS and the Subregional Peacekeeping in Liberia," *Journal of Humanitarian Assistance* (1995).

55. Adebajo, *Building Peace in West Africa*; Sawyer, "Violent Conflicts and Governance Challenges in West Africa," 437–463; Max Sesay, "'Bringing Peace to Liberia,'" in *The Liberian Peace Process 1990–1996*, ed. J. Armon and A. Carl (London: Conciliation Resources, 1996), 9–26, 75–79.

56. Ikechi Mgbeoji, *Collective Insecurity: The Liberian Crisis, Unilateralism, and Global Order* (Vancouver: University of British Columbia Press, 2003).

57. Liberia. *Cotonou Agreement*, July 25,1993, https://www.refworld.org /docid/3ae6b5796.html.

58. "Past Peace Operations," UN Peacekeeping, accessed October 14, 2023, https://peacekeeping.un.org/en/past-peacekeeping-operations.

59. Resolution 866, UN Security Council, September 22, 1993.

60. Resolution 866 UN Security Council.

61. Resolution 1020, UN Security Council, November 10, 1995.

62. Liberia. *Cotonou Agreement*, July 25,1993, accessed January 10, 2024. https://www.refworld.org/docid/3ae6b5796.html.

63. Liberia. *Cotonou Agreement*, July 25,1993, accessed January 10, 2024. https://www.refworld.org/docid/3ae6b5796.html.

64. "Past Peace Operations."

65. "Past Peace Operations."

66. "Past Peace Operations."

67. "Past Peace Operations."

68. "Past Peace Operations."

69. "Past Peace Operations."

70. Interview, official, Liberian Women Initiative, Monrovia, 2008; Interview, official, Center for Media Studies and Peacebuilding, Monrovia, 2008; Interview, member of Parliament, Monrovia, 2008.

71. Interview, official, South African Mission to the UN, New York, 2005; Interview, official, Nigerian Mission to the UN, New York, 2005.

72. Interview, official, UN Department of Peacekeeping Operations, New York, 2005.

73. "Thousands Cheer U.S. Troops in Liberia," *CNN World*, August 14, 2003, http://edition.cnn.com/2003/WORLD/africa/08/14/us.liberia/index.html; "US

Pulls Out of Liberia," *BBC News*, September 30, 2003, http://news.bbc.co.uk/2/hi/africa/3150650.stm.

74. "UNMIL: Background," UN Peacekeeping, accessed October 14, 2023, https://unmil.unmissions.org/background.

75. Resolution 1509, UN Security Council, September 19, 2003.

76. Resolution 1638, UN Security Council, November 11, 2005, 1.

77. Resolution 1509, UN Security Council.

78. "UNMIL: Background"; "UNMIL: Fact Sheet," United Nations, accessed October 14, 2023, https://peacekeeping.un.org/en/mission/unmil; "UNMIL: DDR," UN Peacekeeping, accessed October 14, 2023, https://unmil.unmissions.org/disarmament-demobilization-and-reintegration-ddr.

79. "UNMIL: Background"; "UNMIL: Fact Sheet"; "UNMIL: DDR."

80. "UNMIL: Background"; "UNMIL: Fact Sheet"; "UNMIL: DDR."

81. "UNMIL: Background"; "UNMIL: Fact Sheet"; "UNMIL: DDR."

82. "UNMIL Fact Sheet."

83. Interview, official, Embassy of Germany, Abidjan, 2008; Interview, official, EU Commission Delegation to Côte d'Ivoire, Abidjan, 2008; Interview, official, Embassy of Senegal, Abidjan, 2008; Interview, senior adviser, Office of the President, Abidjan, 2008.

84. "MINUCI: Background," UN Peacekeeping, accessed October 14, 2023, https://peacekeeping.un.org/en/mission/past/minuci/background.html.

85. Novosseloff, Alexandra. "The Many Lives of a Peacekeeping Mission: The Un Operation In Côte D'ivoire." New York: International Peace Institute, June 2018. https://www.ipinst.org/wp-content/uploads/2018/06/1806_Many-Lives-of-a-Peacekeeping-Mission.pdf.

86. *Report of the Secretary-General on Côte d'Ivoire*, UN Security Council, March 26, 2003; "Côte d'Ivoire: ECOWAS Approves Beefed-Up ECOMICI Contingent," *New Humanitarian*, April 8, 2003, https://www.thenewhumanitarian.org/news/2003/04/08/ecowas-approves-beefed-ecomici-contingent.

87. Donald C. F. Daniel, Patricia Taft, and Sharon Wiharta. *Peace Operations: Trends, Progress, and Prospects* (Washington, DC: Georgetown University Press, 2007).

88. Resolution 1479, UN Security Council, May 13, 2003.

89. Resolution 1528, UN Security Council, February 27, 2004.

90. Resolution 1528, UN Security Council; Resolution 1609, UN Security Council, June 24, 2005; Resolution 1739, UN Security Council, January 10, 2007; Resolution 1765, UN Security Council, July 16, 2007.

91. Resolution 1572, UN Security Council, November 15, 2004, para. 7.

92. Resolution 1967, UN Security Council, January 19, 2011.

93. Bah, "Democracy and Civil War: Citizenship and Peacemaking in Côte d'Ivoire," *African Affairs* 109, no. 437 (2010): 597–615.

94. Cabinet du Premier Ministre, République de Côte d'Ivoire, "Communique du Porte-Parole du Premier Ministre (01/050308)," March 6, 2008; UN Security

Council, *Nineteenth Progress Report of the Secretary-General on the United Nations Operation in Côte d'Ivoire*, January 8, 2009; Gouvernement de Côte d'Ivoire, "Conseil des Ministres: L'election presidentielle fixee au 29 novembre 2009," May 14, 2009, https://news.abidjan.net/articles/331069/conseil-des-ministres-hier -lelection-presidentielle-fixee-au-29-novembre-2009. .

95. Interview, official, UNDP, Freetown, 2008.

96. Interview, professor, University of Liberia, Monrovia, 2008.

97. Bah and Nikolas Emmanuel, "Positive Peace and the Methodology of Costing Peacebuilding Needs," *Administrative Theory & Praxis* 43, no. 3 (2020): 299–318.

98. Bah, *Post-Conflict Institutional Design: Peacebuilding and Democracy in Africa* (London: Zed, 2020).

99. Julius Mutwol, *Peace Agreements and Civil Wars in Africa: Insurgent Motivations, State Responses and Third Party Peacemaking in Liberia, Rwanda, and Sierra Leone* (Amherst, NY: Cambria, 2009), 233; Gberie, "First Stages on the Road to Peace: The Abidjan Process (1995–96)," *Accord: An International Review of Peace Initiatives* 9 (2000): 18–25.

100. Mutwol, *Peace Agreements and Civil Wars in Africa*, 232–237.

101. Interview, Solomon Berewa, vice president of Sierra Leone, Freetown, 2008.

102. Bah, "The Contours of New Humanitarianism," 3–26.

103. Republic of Sierra Leone, "Abidjan Peace Accord," Sierra Leone Web, November 30, 1996, http://www.sierra-leone.org/abidjanaccord.html.

104. Republic of Sierra Leone, "Abidjan Peace Accord," article 26.

105. Hirsch, *Sierra Leone*, 55.

106. Republic of Sierra Leone, "Lomé Peace Agreement," Sierra Leone Web, June 3, 1999, http://www.sierra-leone.org/lomeaccord.html, article XVI.

107. Republic of Sierra Leone, "Lomé Peace Agreement."

108. Patricia O'Brien, "Statement by Ms. Patricia O'Brien Under-Secretary-General for Legal Affairs, The Legal Counsel. Office of Legal Affairs," United Nations, New York, September 23, 2009, 7.

109. Interview, civil society activist, Network of Education & Peace Caretakers, Abidjan, 2008.

110. Interview, member of the Inter-religious Council and the Human Right Commission, Freetown, 2008.

111. *Fourth Report of the Secretary-General*, UN Security Council, 5.

112. Bah, "The Contours of New Humanitarianism," 3–26.

113. "World Briefing: Africa—Sierra Leone: U.N. Prosecutor Demands Body," *New York Times*, May 14, 2003, http://www.nytimes.com/2003/05/14/world /world-briefing-africa-sierra-leone-un-prosecutor-demands-body.html?src=pm.

114. Bah, "The Contours of New Humanitarianism," 3–26.

115. Republic of Sierra Leone, "Abuja Ceasefire Agreement," Sierra Leone Web, November 10, 2000, http://www.sierra-leone.org/ceasefire1100.html.

116. Mark Malan, Phenyo Rakate, and Angela McIntyre, *Monograph 68: Peacekeeping in Sierra Leone: UNAMSIL Hits the Home Straight* (Pretoria, ZA: Institute for Security Studies, 2002).

117. UNAMSIL, "UNAMSIL: A Success Story in Peacekeeping," 1.

118. Guinea was in favor of the intervention.

119. Mitikishe M. Khobe, "The Evolution and Conduct of ECOMOG Operations in West Africa," in *Monograph 44: Boundaries of Peace Support Operations* (Pretoria, ZA: Institute for Security Studies, 2000).

120. The agreements signed during the civil war include: Bamako Ceasefire Agreement (November 1990), Banjul Agreement (December 1990), Lomé Agreement (February 1991), three agreements in Yamoussoukro (April to September 1991), Yamoussoukro IV Agreement (October 1991), Geneva Ceasefire Agreement (July 1993), Cotonou Agreement (July 1993), Akosombo Agreement (September 1994), Agreement on the Clarification of the Akosombo Agreement (December 1994), Acceptance and Accession Agreement (December 1994), Abuja Accord (August 1995), Supplement to the Abuja Accord (August 1996), Agreement on Ceasefire and Cessation of Hostilities Between the Government of the Republic of Liberia and Liberians United for Reconciliation and Democracy and the Movement for Democracy in Liberia (Accra June 2003), and Comprehensive Peace Agreement (August 2003); Conciliation Resources, "The Liberian Peace Process 1990–1996," *Accord: An International Review of Peace Initiatives* 1 (1996).

121. These positions include members of the Council of State, Supreme Court Justices, members of the Elections Commission, cabinet ministers, members of the Transitional Legislative Assembly, managing directors or heads of public corporations and autonomous agencies.

122. For example, the AFL supported Liberian Peace Council (September 1993), the NPFL supported Lofa Defense Force (December 1993), and the split of ULIMO into ULIMO-K and ULIMO-J (May 1994).

123. The LNC held several national conferences, including the 1994 conference in Monrovia.

124. Interview, official, Mano River Women's Peace Network, Monrovia, 2008.

125. The ICGL (established in 2002) includes Ghana, Nigeria, Morocco, France, the United Kingdom, the United States, the AU, ECOWAS Secretariat, the European Union, and the UN.

126. Interview, senior official, West African Network for Peacebuilding, Monrovia, 2008.

127. Bah, "Civil Non-State Actors," 313–336.

128. Republic of Liberia, "Agreement on Ceasefire and Cessation of Hostilities between the Government of the Republic of Liberia and Liberians United for Reconciliation and Democracy and the Movement for Democracy in Liberia," United States Institute of Peace, June 17, 2003, https://www.usip.org/sites/default

/files/file/resources/collections/peace_agreements/liberia_ceasefire_06172003
.pdf.

129. By the time the agreement was signed, Taylor had resigned and been sent into exile. The GOL was headed by Taylor's deputies in the NPFL and NPP, most notably Moses Blah, who was the vice president, and Daniel L. Chea Sr., who was the minister of National Defence. Blah became president after Taylor's resignation.

130. Some of the notable civic organizations include the Inter-religious Council for Liberia (IRCL) and the Manor River Women Peace Network (MARWOPNET).

131. Liberia. Comprehensive Peace Agreement Between the Government of Liberia and the Liberians United for Reconciliation and Democracy (LURD) and the Movement for Democracy in Liberia (MODEL) and Political Parties Accra, August 18, 2003. Article 11 https://www.usip.org/publications/2003/08/peace-agreements-liberia.

132. Interview, member of parliament, Monrovia, 2008.

133. Liberia. Comprehensive Peace Agreement Between the Government of Liberia and the Liberians United for Reconciliation and Democracy (LURD) and the Movement for Democracy in Liberia (MODEL) and Political Parties Accra, August 18, 2003. (Article XXIX) https://www.usip.org/publications/2003/08/peace-agreements-liberia.

134. Liberia. Comprehensive Peace Agreement Between the Government of Liberia and the Liberians United for Reconciliation and Democracy (LURD) and the Movement for Democracy in Liberia (MODEL) and Political Parties Accra, August 18, 2003. (Article XXIII) https://www.usip.org/publications/2003/08/peace-agreements-liberia.

135. Liberia. Comprehensive Peace Agreement Between the Government of Liberia and the Liberians United for Reconciliation and Democracy (LURD) and the Movement for Democracy in Liberia (MODEL) and Political Parties Accra, August 18, 2003. (Article III) https://www.usip.org/publications/2003/08/peace-agreements-liberia; ECOMIL and US forces were deployed in August 2003. See: "Annualized implementation data on comprehensive intrastate peace accords, 1989–2012." Madhav Joshi, Jason Michael Quinn, and Patrick M. Regan. Journal of Peace Research 52 (2015): 551-562.

136. Liberia. Comprehensive Peace Agreement Between the Government of Liberia and the Liberians United for Reconciliation and Democracy (LURD) and the Movement for Democracy in Liberia (MODEL) and Political Parties Accra, August 18, 2003. (Article XXIX) https://www.usip.org/publications/2003/08/peace-agreements-liberia.

137. Liberia. Comprehensive Peace Agreement Between the Government of Liberia and the Liberians United for Reconciliation and Democracy (LURD) and the Movement for Democracy in Liberia (MODEL) and Political Parties Accra, August 18, 2003 (Article VII) https://www.usip.org/publications/2003/08/peace-agreements-liberia.

138. The agreement temporarily superseded the constitutional statutes and other laws that were incompatible with the agreement, such as the composition and powers of the three organs of the government.

139. In some cases, the agreement referred to the three branches of the government as the NTGL. However, in most parts of the agreement, the executive branch was referred to as NTGL, while the legislature was referred to as the NTLA and the judiciary as the Supreme Court.

140. Liberia. Comprehensive Peace Agreement Between the Government of Liberia and the Liberians United for Reconciliation and Democracy (LURD) and the Movement for Democracy in Liberia (MODEL) and Political Parties Accra, August 18, 2003. (Article IX) https://www.usip.org/publications/2003/08/peace-agreements-liberia.

141. The agreements are Linas-Marcousis (2003), Accra II (2003), Accra III (2004), and Pretoria (2005).

142. Bah, "Democracy and Civil War," 597–615.

143. Interview, UN official, New York, 2005; Interview, European diplomat, Abidjan, 2008; Marrack Goulding, "The United Nations and Conflict in Africa since the Cold War," *African Affairs* 98, no. 391 (1999): 155–166.

144. Bah, "Democracy and Civil War," 597–615.

145. Bah, "Democracy and Civil War," 597–615.

146. The parties to the agreement are the major political parties (PDCI, RDR, FPI), rebel groups (MPCI, MJP, MPIGO), and smaller political parties (Mouvement des Forces de l'Avenir, Parti Ivoirien des Travailleurs, Union Democratique et Citoyenne, and Union pour la Democratie et la Paix en Côte d' Ivoire).

147. Interview, Ivoirian diplomat, New York, 2005; Interview, African diplomat, Abidjan, June 7, 2008; "Ivoirian Rebels Stick to Peace Deal," *BBC News*, February 4, 2003, http://news.bbc.co.uk/2/hi/africa/2724805.stm; "Ivoirian Peace Deal Provokes Fury," *BBC News*, February 1, 2003, http://news.bbc.co.uk/2/hi/africa/2715779.stm; "Côte d'Ivoire: All Sides Pledge Commitment to Peace Process Again, but Will Anything Change?," *New Humanitarian*, December 7, 2004, https://www.thenewhumanitarian.org/news/2004/12/07/all-sides-pledge-commitment-peace-process-again-will-anything-change.

148. UN Security Council, Linas-Marcoussis Agreement, New York, January 27, 2003.

149. Bah, "Democracy and Civil War," 597–615.

150. Office for the Coordination of Humanitarian Affairs (OCHA), Reliefweb, "Linas-Marcoussis Agreement: Cote d'Ivoire," January 23, 2003. https://reliefweb.int/report/c%C3%B4te-divoire/linas-marcoussis-agreement-cote-divoire.

151. Présidence de la République de Côte d'Ivoire. Constitution De 2000. La Deuxieme Constitution. Loi N°2000-513 DU 1 er AOÛT 2000 Portant Constitution De La Côte D'ivoire. August 1, 2000. https://www.presidence.ci/constitution-de-2000; /; Republic of Côte d'Ivoire, Constitution of 2000 accessed January 10, 2024. https://www.constituteproject.org/constitution/Cote_DIvoire_2000.

152. Bah, "Democracy and Civil War," 597–615.

153. Interview, northern businessman and community leader, Abidjan, June 7, 2008.

154. Ruth Marshall-Fratani, "The War of 'Who is Who': Autochthony, Nationalism, and Citizenship in the Ivoirian Crisis," *African Studies Review* 49, no. 2 (2006): 9–44; Peter Geschiere, *The Perils of Belonging: Autochthony, Citizenship, and Exclusion in Africa and Europe* (Chicago: University of Chicago Press, 2009); Richard Banégas, "Côte d'Ivoire: Patriotism, Ethno-nationalism, and Other African Modes of Self-Writing," *African Affairs* 105, no. 421 (2006): 535–552; John Akokpari, "'You Don't Belong Here' Citizenship, the State & Africa's Conflicts: Reflections on Côte d'Ivoire," in *The Roots of African Conflicts: The Causes and Costs*, ed. Alfred G. Nhema and Paul Zeleza Tiyambe (Athens: Ohio University Press, 2008); Bah, "Democracy and Civil War," 597–615.

155. Bah, "Democracy and Civil War," 597–615.

156. "Ivoirian Rebels Stick to Peace Deal."

157. République de Côte d'Ivoire, "Accord Accra II (Ghana) sur la Crise en Côte d'Ivoire," Accra, GH, March 7, 2003.

158. Bah, "Democracy and Civil War," 597–615.

159. "Accra III Agreement on Côte d'Ivoire," UN Security Council, July 30, 2004.

160. "Pretoria Agreement on the Peace Process in the Côte d'Ivoire," Republic of Côte d'Ivoire, Pretoria, ZA, 2005.

161. Bah, "Democracy and Civil War," 597–615

162. "Côte d'Ivoire: Les demi-mesures ne suffiront pas," *International Crisis Group Africa* 33 (2005); "PM Signals New Ivoirian Stand-Off," *BBC News*, November 8, 2006, http://news.bbc.co.uk/2/hi/africa/6130248.stm.

163. Bah, "Democracy and Civil War," 597–615

164. Interview, adviser to the president, Abidjan, 2008; Interview, African diplomat, Abidjan, June 7, 2008.

165. *Twelfth Progress Report of the Secretary-General on the United Nations Operation in Côte d'Ivoire*, UN Security Council, March 8, 2007; Nico Colombant and Guillaume Michel, "Gbagbo Speech Divides Ivoirians," *Voice of America*, October 31, 2009, https://www.voanews.com/a/a-13-2006-12-20-voa26/319336 .html.

166. Resolution 1721 UN Security Council, November 1, 2006.

167. Interview, adviser to the president, Abidjan, 2008.

168. "Direct Dialogue: Ouagadougou Political Agreement," UN Security Council, (S/2007/144) March 4, 2007. https://peaceaccords.nd.edu/wp-content /accords/Ouagadougou_Political_Agreement_OPA.pdf

169. Bah, "Democracy and Civil War," 597–615.

170. United Nations Security Council. "Direct Dialogue: Ouagadougou Political Agreement." March 4, 2007 (Article 1). https://peaceaccords.nd.edu/wp-content /accords/Ouagadougou_Political_Agreement_OPA.pdf.

171. Bah, "Democracy and Civil War," 597–615.

172. United Nations Security Council. "Direct Dialogue: Ouagadougou Political Agreement." March 4, 2007 (Article 1.1.2)

173. United Nations Security Council. "Direct Dialogue: Ouagadougou Political Agreement." March 4, 2007 (Article 1.3).

174. Société d'Application Générales Electriques et Mécaniques was the technical agency.

175. Bah, "Democracy and Civil War," 597–615.

176. République de Côte d'Ivoire, Loi n° 61–416 du 14 Décembre 1961 Portant Code de la Nationalité Ivoirienne, modifiée par la loi n° 72–852 du 21 décembre 1972. For a full discussion of the citizenship law from 1961 to 2010, see Magali L. B. Chelpi, *Militarized Youths in Western Côte d'Ivoire: Local Processes of Mobilization, Demobilization, and Related Humanitarian Interventions (2002–2007)* (Leiden, NL: African Studies Centre, 2011).

177. Présidence de la République de Côte d'Ivoire. Constitution De 2000. La Deuxieme Constitution. Loi N°2000-513 DU 1 er AOÛT 2000 Portant Constitution De La Côte D'ivoire. August 1, 2000. https://www.presidence.ci /constitution-de-2000; Republic of Côte d'Ivoire, Constitution of 2000. https:// www.constituteproject.org/constitution/Cote_DIvoire_2000.

178. In addition to the challenges of Ouattara's citizenship, he was also disqualified from the elections on the ground that he does not meet the residency criteria for the presidency. In subsequent elections, he was able to meet the residency criteria because he was permanently based in Côte d'Ivoire.

179. Bah, "Democracy and Civil War," 597–615.

180. Republic of Côte d'Ivoire, "Foire aux Questions," *Audience Foraines*, November 2007, http://www.audiencesforaines.gouv.ci/foire.php.

181. Présidence de la République de Côte d'Ivoire. Constitution De 2000. La Deuxieme Constitution. Loi N°2000-513 DU 1 er AOÛT 2000 Portant Constitution De La Côte D'ivoire. August 1, 2000. https://www.presidence.ci /constitution-de-2000/; Republic of Côte d'Ivoire, *Constitution of 2000*, https:// www.constituteproject.org/constitution/Cote_DIvoire_2000.

182. Ouattara betrayed Soro in the run-up to the 2020 election by altering the constitution to allow him to run for a third term.

183. "Côte d'Ivoire: The War Is Not Yet Over," *International Crisis Group Africa* 72 (2003).

184. SAPA-AFP, "Ouattara Camp Urges Ivoirians to Help Take Government Sites," *Times Live, Africa,* December 14, 2010, https://www.timeslive.co.za/news /africa/2010-12-14-ouattara-camp-urges-ivorians-to-help-take-government-sites/; "Thabo Mbeki Begins Côte d'Ivoire Mediation Mission," *BBC News*, December 5, 2010, http://www.bbc.co.uk/news/world-africa-11920739; "Ivoirian Rival Ouattara Tells Gbagbo to Leave," *BBC News*, December 12, 2010, http://www.bbc.co.uk /news/world-africa-11977920.

185. *Nineteenth Progress Report*, UN Security Council.

186. Cabinet du Premier Ministre, République de Côte d'Ivoire, "Communique du Porte-Parole."

187. *Nineteenth Progress Report*, UN Security Council.

188. "Conseil des Ministres," Gouvernement de Côte d'Ivoire.

189. "Côte d'Ivoire Presidential Elections October 31, 2010," UNOCI, November 25, 2010, https://peacekeeping.un.org/sites/default/files/past/unoci/documents/cote_d'ivoire_elections_round2_%20factsheet24112010.pdf.

190. *Nineteenth Progress Report*, UN Security Council.

191. Bah, "Democracy and Civil War," 597–615.

192. *Nineteenth Progress Report*, UN Security Council.

193. "Concerned at Delay Plans in Côte d'Ivoire Elections, Security Council, in Presidential Statement, Urges Parties to Work for Poll by Spring 2009," UN Security Council, November 7, 2008.

194. "Statement attributable to the Spokesperson for the Secretary-General on the Presidential Election in Côte d'Ivoire," UN Secretary-General, December 3, 2010, https://www.un.org/sg/en/content/sg/statement/2010-12-03/statement-attributable-spokesperson-secretary-general-presidential.

195. "Côte d'Ivoire: Amnesty Warns Over Rights Abuses," *BBC News*, February 22, 2011, http://www.bbc.co.uk/news/world-africa-12540968; "Côte d'Ivoire Government Takes Control of Foreign Banks," *BBC News*, February 17, 2011, http://www.bbc.co.uk/news/business-12500544; "Côte d'Ivoire Cocoa Farmers Protest at EU Sanctions," *BBC News*, February 17, 2011, http://www.bbc.co.uk/news/business-12497524.

196. "Côte d'Ivoire: Army and Ex-Rebels 'Breach Ceasefire,'" *BBC News*, February 24, 2011, http://www.bbc.co.uk/news/world-africa-12569372; "Côte d'Ivoire: Rebels Take Western Town Zouan-Hounien," *BBC News*, February 25, 2011, http://www.bbc.co.uk/news/world-africa-12582014; Imogen Foulkes, "Côte d'Ivoire: UN Warns of Forgotten Humanitarian Crisis," *BBC News*, March 22, 2011, http://www.bbc.co.uk/news/world-africa-12827243; "Ouattara's Men Waiting to March on Abidjan, Côte d'Ivoire," *BBC News*, March 21, 2011, http://www.bbc.co.uk/news/world-africa-12804613; "Côte d'Ivoire: Besieged Gbagbo 'in Basement' of Residence," *BBC News*, April 5, 2011, http://www.bbc.co.uk/news/world-africa-12967610.

197. See the Annex of the agreement.

198. Ian Spears, "Africa: The Limits of Power-Sharing," *Journal of Democracy* 13, no. 3 (July 2002): 123–136.

199. "MINUCI: Background," UN Peacekeeping; Geohive, "Côte d'Ivoire," accessed January 10, 2024. https://peacekeeping.un.org/es/mission/past/minuci/background.html.

200. Côte d'Ivoire is administratively divided into nineteen regions. Each region is divided into administrative units referred to as departments. The administrative

regions are divided according to the north-south regional divide, which is largely based on social, cultural, and economic distinction between the northern half and the southern half of the country.

201. There are a significant number of northern immigrant workers living among the Baoule plantation owners. See Thomas J. Bassett, *The Peasant Cotton Revolution in West Africa: Cotê d'Ivoire 1880–1995* (New York: Cambridge University Press, 2001); Dwayne Woods, "The Tragedy of the Cocoa Pod: Rent-Seeking, Land and Ethnic Conflict in Côte d'Ivoire," *Journal of Modern African Studies* 41, no. 4 (2003): 641–655.

202. "Category Archives: Côte d'Ivoire—African Review 2011," World Elections, accessed October 14, 2023, http://welections.wordpress.com/category/cote -divoire/; "CEI," Commission Electorale Indépendante de Côte d'Ivoire, accessed October 14, 2023, http://www.ceici.org/elections/ci/index.php.

203. "Category Archives," World Elections; "CEI," Commission Electorale Indépendante de Côte d'Ivoire.

204. John James, "Cocoa Farmers: A Mirror to Côte d'Ivoire's Divisions," *BBC News*, November 25, 2010, http://www.bbc.co.uk/news/mobile/world -africa-11832982; "Ivory Coast Set for Presidential Election Run-Off," *BBC News*, November 4, 2010, http://www.bbc.co.uk/news/world-africa-11681134.

205. Bah, *Breakdown and Reconstitution*.

206. "Côte d'Ivoire: Odinga Makes Fresh AU Mediation Attempt," *BBC News*, January 17, 2011, http://www.bbc.co.uk/news/world-africa-12204139.

207. Bah, "TV Interview, Côte d'Ivoire Civil War, Prof. Abu Bakarr Bah," Al Jazeera TV, August 12, 2022, YouTube video, 7:32, https://www.youtube.com /watch?v=VQAMUE2hmqQ.

208. "Côte d'Ivoire: AU Panel of Leaders to Seek Way Forward," *BBC News*, January 29, 2011, http://www.bbc.co.uk/news/world-africa-12314022.

209. Compaoré was unable to join the other four presidents in Côte d'Ivoire due to security threats against him.

4. PEOPLE-CENTERED LIBERALISM AND INTERNATIONAL STATEBUILDING

1. Interview, policy specialist, UNDP, Monrovia, 2008.

2. Abu Bakarr Bah, "People-Centered Liberalism: An Alternative Approach to International Statebuilding in Sierra Leone and Liberia," *Critical Sociology* 43, no. 7–8 (2017): 989–1007.

3. Bah, "People-Centered Liberalism," 989–1007.

4. David K. Leonard and Scott Straus, *Africa's Stalled Development: International Causes and Cures* (Boulder, CO: Lynne Rienner, 2003); Aristide R. Zolberg, *One-Party Government in the Ivory Coast* (Princeton, NJ: Princeton University Press, 1964); Robert H. Bates, *Markets and States in Tropical*

Africa: The Political Basis of Agricultural Policies (Berkeley: University of California Press, 2005); Robert H. Jackson and Carl G. Rosberg, *Personal Rule in Black Africa: Prince, Autocrat, Prophet, Tyrant* (Berkeley: University of California Press, 1982).

5. *Economic Development Report 2011: Fostering Industrial Development in Africa in the New Global Environment*, UN Industrial Development Organization (UNIDO) and UN Conference on Trade and Development (UNCTAD), New York, 2011; Patrick Conway, "IMF Lending Programs: Participation and Impact," *Journal of Development Economics* 45, no. 2 (1994): 365–391; William Easterly, "What Did Structural Adjustment Adjust?: The Association of Policies and Growth with Repeated IMF and World Bank Adjustment Loans," *Journal of Development Economics* 76, no. 1 (2005): 1–22; Fantu Cheru, *The Silent Revolution in Africa: Debt, Development and Democracy* (London: Zed, 1989); J. Barry Riddell, "Things Fall Apart Again: Structural Adjustment Programmes in Sub-Saharan Africa," *Journal of Modern African Studies* 30, no. 1 (1992): 53–68.

6. John A. Wiseman, *The New Struggle for Democracy in Africa* (Aldershot, UK: Avebury, 1996); Michael Bratton and Nicolas Van de Walle, *Democratic Experiments in Africa: Regime Transitions in Comparative Perspective* (New York: Cambridge University Press, 1997).

7. Bah, "People-Centered Liberalism," 989–1007; Roland Paris, *At War's End: Building Peace after Civil Conflict* (Cambridge, UK: Cambridge University Press, 2004).

8. David Williams and Tom Young, "Governance, the World Bank and Liberal Theory," *Political Studies* 42, no. 1 (1994): 84–100; Carlos Santiso, "Good Governance and Aid Effectiveness: The World Bank and Conditionality," *Georgetown Public Policy Review* 7, no. 1 (2001): 1–22; Graham Harrison, *The World Bank and Africa: The Construction of Governance States* (New York: Routledge, 2004); Ray Kiely, "Neoliberalism Revised? A Critical Account of the World Bank Concepts of Good Governance and Market Friendly Intervention," *Capital & Class* 22, no. 1 (1998): 63–88.

9. Resolution 46/137, UN General Assembly, December 17, 1991; Resolution 44/146, UN General Assembly, December 15, 1989; Resolution 45/150, UN General Assembly, December 18, 1990; Resolution 1989/51, UN Commission on Human Rights, March 7, 1989.

10. International Covenant on Civil and Political Rights (Resolution 2200A [XXI]), UN General Assembly, December 16, 1996; Universal Declaration of Human Rights (Resolution 3/217A), UN General Assembly, December 10, 1948.

11. United Nations General Assembly. Resolution 46/137. December 17, 1991.

12. UN General Assembly. Enhancing the Effectiveness of the Principle of Periodic and Genuine Elections UNGA 197; A/RES/46/137 (December 17, 1991). http://www.worldlii.org/int/other/UNGA/1991/197.pdf.

13. In 1994, UNEAU was renamed Electoral Assistance Division (EAD) and made a part of the UN Department of Political Affairs.

14. me*UNDP and Electoral Assistance: Ten Years of Experience*, UN Development
Programme (UNDP), New York, November 15, 2015, https://www.undp.org/content
/undp/en/home/librarypage/democratic-governance/electoral_systemsandprocesses
/undp-and-electoral-assistance-10-years-of-experience.html, 1.

15. United Nations Millennium Declaration (Resolution 55/2), UN General
Assembly, September 8, 2000.

16. "We Can End Poverty: Millennium Development Goals and Beyond 2015,"
UN, accessed October 17, 2023, https://www.un.org/millenniumgoals/.

17. UN, "Official List of MDG Indicators," Statistics Division, January 15, 2008,
https://www.developmentgoals.org/About_the_goals.html.

18. "Positive Peace Report 2019: Analysing the Factors that Sustain Peace,"
Institute for Economics and Peace, October 2019, https://www.economicsandpeace
.org/wp-content/uploads/2020/08/PPR-2019-web.pdf; Bah and Nikolas
Emmanuel, "Positive Peace and the Methodology of Costing Peacebuilding
Needs," *Administrative Theory & Praxis* 43, no. 3 (2020): 299–318.

19. Bah, "People-Centered Liberalism," 989–1007.

20. "Communiqué of the Interim Committee of the Board of Governors of the
International Monetary Fund," International Monetary Fund, press release no.
96/49, 1996.

21. "Good Governance: The IMF's Role," IMF, Washington, DC, 1997.

22. Arch Puddington, *Freedom in the World 2012: The Arab Uprisings and Their
Global Repercussions* (New York: Freedom Publications, 2012); "The Ibrahim Index,
2011," Mo Ibrahim Foundation, accessed October 17, 2023, https://mo.ibrahim
.foundation/iiag.

23. Sudhir Anand and Amartya Sen, "Human Development and Economic
Sustainability," *World Development* 28, no. 12 (2000): 2029–2049; Kamal
Taori, *Sustainable Human Development: Issues and Challenges* (New Delhi, IN:
Concept, 2000); Bill Hopwood, Mary Mellor, and Geoff O'Brien, "Sustainable
Development: Mapping Different Approaches," *Sustainable Development* 13, no. 1
(2005): 38–52; Bob Giddings, Hopwood, and O'Brien, "Environment, Economy,
and Society: Fitting them Together into Sustainable Development," *Sustainable
Development* 10, no. 4 (2002): 187–196; Jennifer A. Elliott, *An Introduction to
Sustainable Development* (New York: Routledge, 2006); Susan Pick and Jenna T.
Sirkin, *Breaking the Poverty Cycle: The Human Basis for Sustainable Development*
(New York: Oxford University Press, 2010); Anand and Sen, "Sustainable Human
Development: Concepts and Priorities," paper written for the UNDP *Human
Development Report*, March 1994.

24. *Report of the World Commission on Environment and Development: Our
Common Future*, UN, 1987, https://digitallibrary.un.org/record/139811?ln=en.

25. *Report of the World Commission*, UN.

26. UNDP, *Human Development Report 1990* (Oxford: Oxford University Press,
1990), 11.

27. UNDP, *Human Development Report 1996* (Oxford: Oxford University Press, 1996), 10.

28. Anand and Sen, "Human Development and Economic Sustainability," 2029–2049; Taori, *Sustainable Human Development*; Hopwood, Mellor, and O'Brien, "Sustainable Development," 38–52; Giddings, Hopwood, and O'Brien, "Environment, Economy, and Society," 187–196; Elliot, *An Introduction to Sustainable Development*; Pick and Sirkin, *Breaking the Poverty Cycle.*

29. Anand and Sen, *Sustainable Human Development*, 4.

30. UNDP, *Human Development Report 1996.*

31. Anand and Sen, *Sustainable Human Development*, 4.

32. Anand and Sen, *Sustainable Human Development*, 2038.

33. Anand and Sen, *Sustainable Human Development*, 3–4.

34. Bah, "People-Centered Liberalism," 989–1007.

35. Bah, "People-Centered Liberalism," 989–1007.

36. Bah, "People-Centered Liberalism," 989–1007.

37. "Debt Relief Under Heavily Indebted Poor Countries (HIPC) Initiative," International Monetary Fund, 2011, accessed November 2, 2023, http://www.imf .org/external/np/exr/facts/hipc.htm.

38. "The Extended Credit Facility," International Monetary Fund, 2012, accessed November 2, 2023, http://www.imf.org/external/np/exr/facts/ecf.htm.

39. "The Multilateral Debt Relief Initiative," International Monetary Fund, 2012, http://www.imf.org/external/np/exr/facts/mdri.htm.

40. Burkina Faso, Burundi, Central African Republic, Congo (Dem. Rep. of), Ethiopia, The Gambia, Ghana, Guinea-Bissau, Liberia, Madagascar, Malawi, Mali, Mozambique, Niger, Rwanda, São Tomé and Príncipe, Sierra Leone, Tanzania, Togo, Uganda, Benin, Congo Republic, Cameroon, Mauritania, Senegal, Zambia. See IMF, "The Multilateral Debt Relief Initiative."

41. "UNDG Guidance Note to United Nations Country Teams on the PRSP," final version, UNDG, November 8, 2001, http://www.undg.org/index.cfm?P=16, 2.

42. "UNDG Guidance Note," UNDG, 3.

43. "NEPAD: A Programme of the African Union," New Partnership for Africa's Development (NEPAD), accessed December 18, 2023, https://www.nepad.org /news/au-un-and-oecd-unveil-their-first-joint-report-africas-need-diversification.

44. The other key programs are Climate Change and National Resource Management, Regional Integration and Infrastructure, Human Development, and Cross-Cutting Issues, including Gender, Capacity Development, and ICT. See "African Union Development Agency (AUDA-NEPAD)," NEPAD, accessed December 18, 2023, http://www.nepad.org/.

45. "Economic and Corporate Governance: Overview," NEPAD, accessed October 17, 2023, https://www.nepad.org/.

46. "African Peer Review Mechanism (APRM)," NEPAD, accessed December 25, 2024, https://www.undp.org/sites/g/files/zskgke326/files/publications/Users -Guide-Measuring-Corruption-Anticorruption.pdf.

47. Patrick Chabal, "The Quest for Good Government and Development in Africa: Is NEPAD the Answer?," *International Affairs* 78, no. 3 (2002): 447–462; John K. Akokpari, "The AU, NEPAD, and the Promotion of Good Governance in Africa," *Nordic Journal of African Studies* 13, no. 3 (2004): 243–263; 'Kunle Amuwo, "Globalisation, *Nepad* and the Governance Question in Africa," *African Studies Quarterly* 6, no. 3 (2002): 65–82; Charles Ukeje, "Rethinking Africa's Security in the Age of Uncertain Globalisation: NEPAD and Human Security in the 21st Century," Paper submitted to the 11th CODESRIA General Assembly, Maputo, MZ, 2005, 6–10.

48. "Ibrahim Prize for Achievement in African Leadership," Mo Ibrahim Foundation, accessed October 17, 2023, https://mo.ibrahim.foundation/prize.

49. "Ibrahim Prize for Achievement in African Leadership," Mo Ibrahim Foundation.

50. Dambisa Moyo, *Dead Aid: Why Aid Is Not Working and How There Is a Better Way for Africa* (New York: Farrar, Straus and Giroux, 2010), xix.

51. Roger Riddell, *Aid in the 21st Century*, ODS Discussion Paper Series 6, United Nations, New York, 1996; Deborah A. Bräutigam and Stephen Knack, "Foreign Aid, Institutions, and Governance in Sub-Saharan Africa," *Economic Development and Cultural Change* 52, no. 2 (2004): 255–285; Todd Moss, Gunilla Pettersson, and Van de Walle, "An Aid-Institutions Paradox? A Review Essay on Aid Dependency and Statebuilding in Sub-Saharan Africa," Mario Einaudi Center for International Studies, 2005; Howard White, ed., *Aid and Macro-Economic Performance: Theory, Empirical Evidence and Four Country Cases* (Basingstoke, UK: Palgrave Macmillan, 1998); Craig Burnside and David Dollar, "Aid, Policies and Growth," *American Economic Review* 90, no. 4 (2000): 847–868; Peter S. Heller, "Pity the Finance Minister: Issues in Managing a Substantial Scaling Up of Aid Flows," International Monetary Fund (Working Paper 05/180, 2005); Raghuram G. Rajan and Arvind Subramanian, "What Undermines Aid's Impact on Growth?," National Bureau of Economic Research (Working Paper 11657, 2005).

52. Riddell, *Aid in the 21st Century*; Paul Collier, "Aid 'Dependency': A Critique," *Journal of African Economies* 8, no. 4 (1999): 528–545; Jeffrey Sachs and John W. McArthur, "Moyo's Confused Attack on Aid for Africa," *HuffPost*, May 27, 2009, http://www.huffingtonpost.com/jeffrey-sachs/moyos-confused-attack-on -b_208222.html.

53. Sachs and McArthur, "Moyo's Confused Attack on Aid for Africa."

54. Ministerial Declaration (WT/MIN(01)/DEC/1), World Trade Organization (WTO), Doha, QA, November 14, 2001.

55. *Aid for Trade and LDCs: Starting to Show Results*, WTO and Organization for Economic Co-Operation and Development (OECD), 2011, accessed November 4, 2023, https://www.oecd.org/aidfortrade/48294296.pdf.

56. Commission for Africa, "Our Common Interest: Report of the Commission for Africa," Council on Foreign Relations, 2005.

57. Commission for Africa, "Still Our Common Interest: Commission for Africa Report," Council on Foreign Relations, 2010.

58. Africa Growth and Opportunities Act (AGOA), "About AGOA," AGOA. info, accessed October 17, 2023, https://agoa.info/about-agoa.html.

59. "Generalized System of Preference (GSP)," Office of the United States Trade Representative, accessed February 9, 2021, https://ustr.gov/issue-areas /trade-development/preference-programs/generalized-system-preference-gsp.

60. AGOA, "About AGOA."

61. H.R. 434, Trade and Development Act of 2000, US Congress, 106th Congress (2000); see section 104.

62. Collier and Anthony J. Venables, "Rethinking Trade Preferences: How Africa Can Diversify its Exports," *World Economy* 30, no. 8 (2007): 1326–1345; Marcelo Olarreaga and Çaglar Özden, "AGOA and Apparel: Who Capturers the Tariff Rent in the Presence of Preferential Market Access," *World Economy* 28, no. 1 (2005): 63–77; Bedassa Tadesse and Bichaka Fayissa, "The Impact of African Growth and Opportunity Act (AGOA) on U.S. Imports from Sub-Saharan Africa (SSA)," *Journal of International Development* 20, no. 7 (2008): 920–941.

63. H.R. 434, US Congress; see section 102.

64. European Union, Proposal for a Regulation of the European Parliament and of the Council: Applying a Scheme of Generalized Tariff Preferences, United Nations, Brussels, October 5, 2011.

65. "Generalized System of Preferences (GSP)," European Union.

66. "Generalized System of Preferences (GSP)," European Union.

67. European Union, Proposal for a Regulation, 5.

68. William Wallis and Tom Burgis, "Africa-China Trade: Continent Drives a Harder Bargain," *Financial Times*, June 14, 2010, http://www.ft.com/intl/cms /de832bb2-7500-11df-aed7-00144feabdco.pdf, 1.

69. Progress in Intra-African Trade (E/ECA/CTRC/7/5), UN Economic Commission for Africa, Addis Ababa, May 16, 2011, 1.

70. Progress in Intra-African Trade, UN Economic Commission for Africa, 1.

71. *Annual Report and Financial Statements for the Year Ended December 31, 2010,* African Export-Import Bank, Cairo, 2012, 28–29.

72. "Regional Trade for Global Gains: Programme for Building African Capacity for Trade," International Trade Centre (ITC), accessed March 29, 2010, https://www.intracen.org/uploadedFiles/intracenorg/Content/About_ITC /Where_are_we_working/Multi-country_programmes/Pact_II/PACT %20II%20Factsheet_FINAL.pdf; "Programme for Building African Capacity for Trade: PACT II: Programme Logical Framework," ITC, June 2009, https://www .intracen.org/uploadedFiles/intracenorg/Content/About_ITC/Where _are_we_working/Multi-country_programmes/Pact_II/PACT%20II %20Logframe_5June2009.pdf; "Programme for Building African Capacity for Trade: PACT II: Programme Summary," ITC, March 2009, https://www.intracen .org/uploadedFiles/intracenorg/Content/About_ITC/Where_are_we_working /Multi-country_programmes/Pact_II/PACT%20II%20Programme

%20Summary-June09.pdf; "Women Access! Export Success: The Voice For African Businesswomen," ITC, accessed March 29, 2010. https://www.intracen .org/uploadedFiles/intracenorg/Content/About_ITC/Where_are_we_working /Multi-country_programmes/Pact_II/3.%20ACCES-Case-Studies-fin.pdf.

73. "Regional Trade for Global Gains," ITC.

74. Wallis and Burgis, "Africa-China Trade," 1.

75. Alexis Arieff, Martin A. Wiess, and Vivian C. Jones, "The Global Economic Crisis: Impact on Sub-Saharan Africa and Global Policy Responses," Congressional Research Service, April 6, 2010, 10.

76. Nilanjana Bhowmick, "India Pledges $5bn to Help African States Meet the MDGs," *The Guardian*, May 25, 2011, http://www.guardian.co.uk/global -development/poverty-matters/2011/may/25/india-pledges-5bn-to-help -african-states-meet-mdgs.

77. Bhowmick, "India Pledges $5bn."

78. Deborah Brautigam, "Chinese Development Aid in Africa: What, Where, Why, and How Much?," in *Rising China: Global Challenges and Opportunities*, ed. Jane Golley and Ligang Song (Canberra: Australian National University Press, 2011).

79. "China-Africa Development Fund," China-Africa Development Fund, accessed October 17, 2023, http://en.cadfund.com; "China's Policy Bank: China Development Bank—The Muscle behind China's Global Expansion," Thornhill Capital, April 1, 2013, http://thornhillcapital.info/featured-articles/chinas-policy -bank-china-development-bank-the-muscle-behind-chinas-global-expansion.

80. Brautigam, "Chinese Development Aid in Africa," 211.

81. "China Pledges $10bn Africa Loans," *BBC News*, November 8, 2009, http://news.bbc.co.uk/2/hi/africa/8349020.stm.

82. These include: Universal Declaration of Human Rights, UN General Assembly, December 10, 1948; International Covenant on Civil and Political Rights, UN General Assembly, December 16, 1996; Resolution 1989/51, UN Commission on Human Rights, March 7, 1989; Resolution 44/146, UN Commission on Human Rights, December 15, 1989; Resolution 46/137, UN General Assembly, December 17, 1991; For specific UN resolutions on elections, see "Political and Peacebuilding Affairs: Elections," UN, accessed October 17, 2023, https://dppa.un.org/en /elections. See also "Law Reform," United Republic of Tanzania; "Declaration on the Principles of Governing Democratic Elections in Africa AHG/Decl. 1 (XXXVIII)," Organization of African Unity/African Union, Durban, ZA, 2002.

83. Robert Dahl, *Polyarchy: Participation and Opposition* (New Haven, CT: Yale University Press, 1971); Joseph A. Schumpeter, *Capitalism, Socialism, and Democracy* (New York: Harper, 1942); Juan J. Linz and Alfred Stepan, *Problems of Democratic Transition and Consolidation: Southern Europe, South America, and Post-Communist Europe* (Baltimore, MD: Johns Hopkins University Press, 1996); Adam

Przeworski, *Democracy and the Market: Political and Economic Reforms in Eastern Europe and Latin America* (Cambridge, UK: Cambridge University Press, 1991).

84. Declaration on the Principles Governing Democratic Elections in Africa, OAU/AU.

85. Declaration on the Principles Governing Democratic Elections in Africa, OAU/AU, 2.

86. "Lomé Declaration of July 2000 on the Framework for an OAU Response to Unconstitutional Changes of Government (AHG/Decl.5 [XXXVI])," Office of the United Nations High Commissioner for Human Rights, accessed November 3, 2023, https://www2.ohchr.org/english/law/compilation_democracy/lomedec .htm; African Charter on Democracy, Elections, and Government, African Union, Addis Ababa, January 30, 2007.

87. "Security Council Extends Ivory Coast Mission Until 24 June, With Intention to Renew for Further 7 Months," UN Security Council, June 3, 2005; Thomas J. Bassett, "Winning Coalition, Sore Loser: Côte d'Ivoire's 2010 Presidential Elections," *African Affairs* 110, no. 440 (2011): 469–479.

88. Sierra Leone's recently conducted general elections in 2023 were widely considered not to be credible. The opposition has rejected the official results of the presidential election and is refusing to participate in any part of the government. International observers have also expressed doubts about the credibility of the elections. See Abdul R. Thomas, "President Bio Throws Insults at Britain, USA, Germany, Ireland and the EU over Rigged Election Results," *Sierra Leone Telegraph*, July 5, 2023, https://www.thesierraleonetelegraph.com/president-bio -throws-insults-at-britain-usa-germany-ireland-and-the-eu-over-rigged-election -results/.

89. The UN was actually given the role of supervising the 2010 Ivoirian presidential election. "The Priority Is Economic Recovery," *Africa Renewal*, October 3, 2011, https://www.un.org/africarenewal/web-features/%E2%80 %98-priority-economic-recovery%E2%80%99.

90. Interview, assistant professor with the University of Liberia, Monrovia, 2008.

91. *Enhancing the Effectiveness of the Principle of Periodic and Genuine Elections— Report of the Secretary-General* (A/49/675), UN General Assembly, November 17, 1994.

92. *Enhancing the Effectiveness*, UN General Assembly.

93. Y. J. Choi, SRSG, and UNOCI, "Statement of the Certification of the Result of the Second Round of the Presidential Election Held on 28 November 2010," United Nations, December 3, 2010; Resolution 1721, UN Security Council, November 1, 2006 ; Resolution 1765, UN Security Council, July 16, 2007.

94. "Elections Unit," African Union, accessed October 17, 2023, https://au.int /en/elections; Declaration on the Principles Governing Democratic Elections in Africa, OAU/AU.

95. "Elections Unit," African Union.

96. Declaration on the Principles Governing Democratic Elections in Africa, OAU/AU, 5.

97. The definitions of poverty in each of the three countries are consistent with the MDG definition of poverty: consumption of less than USD 1 per day for extreme poverty and consumption of less than USD 2 per day for poverty.

98. PRSP, 4; $1 = 447.81 CFA francs in 2008.

99. Sierra Leone's PRSP I, 56–57.

100. *Liberia: Poverty Reduction Strategy Paper*, IMF, country report no. 08/219, 2008, 25.

101. Sierra Leone's PRSP I, 109.

102. Sierra Leone's PRSP I, 78.

103. Sierra Leone's PRSP I, 108.

104. *Liberia: Poverty Reduction Strategy Paper*, IMF, 41.

105. *Côte d'Ivoire: Poverty Reduction Strategy Paper*, IMF, country report no. 09/156, 2009, 85.

106. Côte d'Ivoire's PRSP, 86.

107. Côte d'Ivoire's PRSP, 86.

108. Côte d'Ivoire's PRSP, 86.

109. *Côte d'Ivoire: Poverty Reduction Strategy Paper*, IMF, 85.

110. Richard Banegas, "Post-election Crisis in Côte d'Ivoire: The *Gbonhi* War," *African Affairs* 110, no. 440 (2011): 457–468; Straus, "'It's Sheer Horror Here': Patterns of Violence during the First Four Months of Côte d'Ivoire's Post-electoral Crisis," *African Affairs* 110, no. 440 (2011): 481–489.

111. Bassett, "Winning Coalition, Sore Loser," 469–470.

112. *Liberia: Poverty Reduction Strategy Paper*, IMF, 53.

113. Miranda Gaanderse and Kristen Valasek, eds., *The Security Sector and Gender in West Africa: A Survey of Police, Defense, Justice and Penal Services in ECOWAS States* (Geneva: DCAF, 2011).

114. International Monetary Fund. Sierra Leone: Poverty Reduction Strategy Paper. June 10, 2005 (stock no. 1SLEEA2005002). https://www.imf.org/en/Publications/CR/Issues/2016/12/31/Sierra-Leone-Poverty-Reduction-Strategy-Paper-18313, 112.

115. *Liberia: Poverty Reduction Strategy Paper*, IMF, 84.

116. International Monetary Fund. Sierra Leone: Poverty Reduction Strategy Paper. June 10, 2005 (stock no. 1SLEEA2005002). https://www.imf.org/en/Publications/CR/Issues/2016/12/31/Sierra-Leone-Poverty-Reduction-Strategy-Paper-18313, 113.

117. Côte d'Ivoire's PRSP, 138.

118. International Monetary Fund. Sierra Leone: Poverty Reduction Strategy Paper. June 10, 2005 (stock no. 1SLEEA2005002). https://www.imf.org/en/Publications/CR/Issues/2016/12/31/Sierra-Leone-Poverty-Reduction-Strategy-Paper-18313, 127.

119. 62 percent toward pillar four in Liberia, 52 percent toward outcome three in Côte d'Ivoire, and 31.7 percent toward pillar three in Sierra Leone.

120. International Monetary Fund. *Côte d'Ivoire: Poverty Reduction Strategy Paper.* Country report no. 09/156, 2009, 122.

121. International Monetary Fund. *Côte d'Ivoire: Poverty Reduction Strategy Paper.* Country report no. 09/156, 2009, vi.

122. International Monetary Fund. *Côte d'Ivoire: Poverty Reduction Strategy Paper.* Country report no. 09/156, 2009, 125–129.

123. International Monetary Fund. *Côte d'Ivoire: Poverty Reduction Strategy Paper.* Country report no. 09/156, 2009, 131.

124. International Monetary Fund. *Côte d'Ivoire: Poverty Reduction Strategy Paper.* Country report no. 09/156, 2009, 134.

125. International Monetary Fund. *Côte d'Ivoire: Poverty Reduction Strategy Paper.* Country report no. 09/156, 2009, 137.

126. International Monetary Fund. *Côte d'Ivoire: Poverty Reduction Strategy Paper.* Country report no. 09/156, 2009, 114.

127. International Monetary Fund. *Côte d'Ivoire: Poverty Reduction Strategy Paper.* Country report no. 09/156, 2009, 114.

128. International Monetary Fund. Sierra Leone: Poverty Reduction Strategy Paper. June 10, 2005 (stock no. 1SLEEA2005002). https://www.imf.org/en /Publications/CR/Issues/2016/12/31/Sierra-Leone-Poverty-Reduction-Strategy -Paper-18313, 94.

129. International Monetary Fund. *Côte d'Ivoire: Poverty Reduction Strategy Paper.* Country report no. 09/156, 2009, 105.

130. International Monetary Fund. *Côte d'Ivoire: Poverty Reduction Strategy Paper.* Country report no. 09/156, 2009, 105.

131. International Monetary Fund. Sierra Leone: Poverty Reduction Strategy Paper. June 10, 2005 (stock no. 1SLEEA2005002), 123–124.

132. International Monetary Fund. *Côte d'Ivoire: Poverty Reduction Strategy Paper.* Country report no. 09/156, 2009, 104.

133. *Liberia: Poverty Reduction Strategy Paper,* IMF, 22.

134. International Monetary Fund. *Côte d'Ivoire: Poverty Reduction Strategy Paper.* Country report no. 09/156, 2009, 33.

135. International Monetary Fund. Sierra Leone: Poverty Reduction Strategy Paper. June 10, 2005 (stock no. 1SLEEA2005002)., 123.

136. International Monetary Fund. *Côte d'Ivoire: Poverty Reduction Strategy Paper.* Country report no. 09/156, 2009, 103.

137. International Monetary Fund. *Côte d'Ivoire: Poverty Reduction Strategy Paper.* Country report no. 09/156, 2009, 103.

138. International Monetary Fund. *Côte d'Ivoire: Poverty Reduction Strategy Paper.* Country report no. 09/156, 2009, 73–76.

139. International Monetary Fund. *Côte d'Ivoire: Poverty Reduction Strategy Paper.* Country report no. 09/156, 2009. Figure aggregated from the figures on the table on page 108.

140. International Monetary Fund. *Côte d'Ivoire: Poverty Reduction Strategy Paper.* Country report no. 09/156, 2009, 109.

141. International Monetary Fund. Sierra Leone: Poverty Reduction Strategy Paper. June 10, 2005 (stock no. 1SLEEA2005002)., 121.

142. Interview, official, Network of Education and Peace Caretakers, Abidjan, 2008.

143. Pillar one, $585.6 million (34.2%); pillar two, $588 million (34.3%); and pillar three, $543.5 million (31.7%)—total: USD 1,786,700,000.

144. International Monetary Fund. Sierra Leone: Poverty Reduction Strategy Paper. June 10, 2005 (stock no. 1SLEEA2005002)., vx; Also see "IMF Approves in Principle US$169 Million Three-Year PRGF Arrangement for Sierra Leone," IMF, press release no. 01/39, 2001; "IMF Executive Board Completes Sixth and Final Review Under Sierra Leone's PRGF Arrangement and Approves US$20.8 Million Disbursement," IMF, press release no. 05/130, 2005.

145. Republic of Sierra Leone. Agenda for Change: Second Poverty Reduction Strategy Paper (PRSP II), 2008-2012, Freetown, June 2008, https://www.undp.org /sites/g/files/zskgke326/files/2022-05/agenda_for_change.pdf, 5.

146. Republic of Sierra Leone. Agenda for Change: Second Poverty Reduction Strategy Paper (PRSP II), 2008-2012, Freetown, June 2008, https://www.undp.org /sites/g/files/zskgke326/files/2022-05/agenda_for_change.pdf, 127.

147. *Liberia: Poverty Reduction Strategy Paper*, IMF, 136.

148. 472.19 CFA francs = USD 1 in 2009. See *International Financial Statistics Yearbook, 2011*, IMF, International Financial Statistics, July 19, 2011, 255. (17,645.05 billion CFA francs is the same as 17.645 trillion CFA francs; 2,518.55 billion CFA francs is the same as 2.518 trillion CFA francs.).

149. International Monetary Fund. *Côte d'Ivoire: Poverty Reduction Strategy Paper.* Country report no. 09/156, 2009, 145–149.

150. "472.19 CFA francs = USD 1 in 2009." See *International Financial Statistics Yearbook, 2011*, IMF, 255.

151. "IMF and World Bank Support Sierra Leone's Completion Point under the Enhanced HIPC Initiative and Approve Debt Relief under the Multilateral Debt Relief Initiative," IMF, press release no. 06/286, 2006.

152. "Liberia Qualifies for Complete Debt Relief under HIPC Initiative," World Bank, June 29, 2010, https://www.worldbank.org/en/news/feature/2010/06/29 /liberia-qualifies-for-complete-debt-relief-under-hipc-initiative.

153. "Liberia Hails $1.2bn Debt Pardon by Paris Club," *BBC News*, September 17, 2010, http://www.bbc.co.uk/news/business-11341667.

154. "US Cancels Liberia's $391m Debt," *BBC News*, February 13, 2007, http:// news.bbc.co.uk/2/hi/business/6358665.stm; "Liberia's US$194.1 Million Debt

Cancelled by Japan," *Shout-Africa,* March 11, 2011, http://www.shout-africa.com /news/liberia%E2%80%99s-us194-1-millin-debt-cancelled-by-japan/; Devex, "Germany Cancels Liberia's Debts," *Newswire Newsletter,* February 15, 2007, https://www.devex.com/news/germany-cancels-liberia-s-debts-50223.

155. "IMF and World Bank Announce More Than US$4 Billion in Debt Relief for Côte d'Ivoire," World Bank, June 26, 2012, https://www.worldbank.org/en/news /press-release/2012/06/26/imf-world-bank-announce-more-than-4-billion-debt -relief-cote-divoire; "Côte d'Ivoire Reaches Decision Point Under the Enhanced HIPC Debt Relief Initiative," IMF, press release no. 09/104, 2009; "Debt Relief Under Heavily Indebted Poor Countries (HIPC) Initiative," IMF.

156. *Sierra Leone—Country Assistance Strategy for the Period FY2006-2009 (Report no. 31793-SL),* World Bank, May 5, 2005; *Sierra Leone—Joint Country Assistance Strategy for the Period FY10-FY13 (Report no. 52297-SL),* World Bank, March 4, 2010.

157. *Sierra Leone—Country Assistance,* World Bank, 9.

158. *Sierra Leone—Country Assistance,* World Bank, 9.

159. *Sierra Leone—Country Assistance,* World Bank, 14.

160. *Sierra Leone—Joint Country Assistance,* World Bank, 4.

161. *Liberia—Joint Country Assistance Strategy for the Period FY09-FY11 (Report no. 47928-LR),* World Bank, March 31, 2009.

162. *Liberia—Joint Country Assistance,* World Bank, 23.

163. *Liberia—Joint Country Assistance,* World Bank, 36.

164. *Côte d'Ivoire—Country Partnership Strategy for the Period FY10-FY13 (Report no. 53666-CI),* World Bank, April 1, 2010.

165. *Côte d'Ivoire—Country Partnership Strategy,* World Bank, 19–20.

166. Bah and Emmanuel, "Positive Peace and the Methodology of Costing Peacebuilding Needs," 299–318.

5. POSTWAR INSTITUTIONAL REFORMS

1. Abu Bakarr Bah, "The Contours of New Humanitarianism: War and Peacebuilding in Sierra Leone," *Africa Today* 60, no. 1 (2013): 3–26; Bah and Nikolas Emmanuel, "Positive Peace and the Methodology of Costing Peacebuilding Needs," *Administrative Theory & Praxis* 43, no. 3 (2020): 299–318.

2. *Final Report of the Group of Experts on Côte d'Ivoire Pursuant to Paragraph 19 of Security Council Resolution 2101 (2013),* United Nations Security Council, April 14, 2014, para. 9.

3. John M Mbaku, "African Elections in 2015: A Snapshot for Côte d'Ivoire, Tanzania, Burkina Faso and Sudan," in *Foresight Africa: Top Priorities for the Continent in 2015,* ed. Africa Growth Initiative (Washington, DC: Brookings Institution, 2015).

4. Lisa Denney, *Justice and Security Reform: Development Agencies and Informal Institutions in Sierra Leone* (New York: Routledge, 2014).

5. Kenneth W. Kemp and Charles Hudlin, "Civil Supremacy over the Military: Its Nature and Limits," *Armed Forces and Society* 19, no. 1 (1992): 7–26.

6. Osman Gbla, "Security Sector Reform Under International Tutelage in Sierra Leone," *International Peacekeeping* 13, no. 1 (2006): 78–93; Gbla, "Security Sector Reform in Sierra Leone," in *Monograph 135: Challenges to Security Sector Reform in the Horn of Africa*, ed. Yemane Kidane and Len le Roux (Pretoria, ZA: Institute for Security Studies, 2007); Denney, *Justice and Security Reform*.

7. "The Military Mission in Sierra Leone," Reuters, May 30, 2007, http://uk.reuters.com/article/idUKL3070034720070530; Mark Malan, "Security and Military Reform," *Monograph 80: Sierra Leone: Building the Road to Recovery* (Pretoria, ZA: Institute for Security Studies, 2010); Malan, Phenyo Rekate, and Angela McIntyre, *Peacekeeping in Sierra Leone: UNAMSIL Hits the Home Straight*, Institute for Security Studies (January 1, 2002); Al-Hassan K. Kondeh, "Formulating Sierre Leone's Defence White Paper," in *Security System Transformation in Sierra Leone, 1997–2007*, ed. Paul Jackson and Peter Albrecht (London: International Alert, 2008); "Overseas Deployment: Africa," British Army, 2010, https://www.medal-medaille.com/sold/product_info.php?products_id=8542.

8. "The Military Mission in Sierra Leone."

9. International Monetary Fund. *Republic of Sierra Leone. Interim Poverty Reduction Strategy Paper*. Freetown, June 2001, https://www.imf.org/external/np/prsp/2001/sle/01/063101.pdf.

10. Malan, Rekate, and McIntyre, *Peacekeeping in Sierra Leone*.

11. Malan, Rekate, and McIntyre, *Peacekeeping in Sierra Leone*.

12. Kondeh, "Formulating Sierra Leone's Defence."

13. Rick Shearn, "In Sierra Leone—IMATT to ISAT," *Sierra Express Media*, March 29, 2013, https://sierraexpressmedia.com/?p=54524; "Report of the Visit of the Peacebuilding Commission to Sierra Leone," UN, February 15–20, 2013, https://www.un.org/peacebuilding/content/report-visit-peacebuilding-commission-sierra-leone; Brian Jones, "Graduation—The End and Beginning of a Journey," Foreign and Commonwealth Office, October 8, 2013, http://blogs.fco.gov.uk/ukinsierraleone/2013/10/08/graduation-the-end-and-beginning-of-a-journey.

14. "Mission in Liberia," UN, accessed December 20, 2023 https://unmil.unmissions.org/.

15. Center on International Cooperation, *Annual Review of Global Peace Operations 2012* (Boulder, CO: Lynne Rienner, 2012). Note the prewar troop level of AFL was six thousand soldiers. Malan, *Security Sector Reform in Liberia: Mixed Results from Humble Beginnings* (Carlisle, PA: US Army Strategic Studies Institute, 2008).

16. *Twenty-Eighth Progress Report of the Secretary-General on the United Nations Operation in Liberia*, August 15, 2014, UN Security Council.

17. Malan, *Security Sector Reform in Liberia*.

18. Center on International Cooperation, *Annual Review of Global Peace Operations 2012*.

19. Center on International Cooperation, *Annual Review of Global Peace Operations 2012*; Malan, *Security Sector Reform in Liberia*.

20. Malan, *Security Sector Reform in Liberia*.

21. International Monetary Fund, *Liberia: Poverty Reduction Strategy Paper*, (Washington, DC: IMF, 2008).

22. Malan, *Security Sector Reform in Liberia*.

23. Center on International Cooperation, *Annual Review of Global Peace Operations 2012*.

24. Malan, *Security Sector Reform in Liberia*.

25. *Twentieth Progress Report of the Secretary-General on the United Nations Operation in Liberia*, UN Security Council, February 17, 2010.

26. Malan, *Security Sector Reform in Liberia*.

27. *Twenty-Eighth Progress Report*, UN Security Council.

28. *Twenty-First Progress Report of the Secretary-General on the United Nations Operation in Liberia*, UN Security Council, August 11, 2010.

29. *Twenty-Eighth Progress Report*, UN Security Council.

30. *Twenty-Eighth Progress Report*, UN Security Council.

31. "UNMIL Fact Sheet," United Nations, accessed October 14, 2023, https://peacekeeping.un.org/en/mission/unmil.

32. *Thirty-Fourth Report of the Secretary-General on the United Nations Operation in Côte d'Ivoire*, UN Security Council, May 15, 2014.

33. *Thirty-Fourth Report*, UN Security Council.

34. *Thirty-Fourth Report*, UN Security Council.

35. *Thirty-Fourth Report*, UN Security Council.

36. *Final Report of the Group of Experts*, UN Security Council, para. 9.

37. *Final Report of the Group of* Experts, UN Security Council, para. 9.

38. *Final Report of the Group of Experts*, UN Security Council, para. 43.

39. *Final Report of the Group of Experts*, UN Security Council, para. 279–280.

40. Joseph P. C. Charley and Freida I. M'Cormack, *Becoming and Remaining a 'Force for Good'—Reforming the Police in Post-conflict Sierra Leone* (Brighton, UK: Institute of Development Studies, 2011).

41. Bruce Baker, "Sierra Leone Police Reform: The Role of the UK Government," Grips Policy Research Center, 2010.

42. "Justice Sector Development Programme (GB-1-104594)," Department for International Development, accessed January 9, 2024, https://devtracker.fcdo.gov.uk/projects/GB-1-104594/summary#.

43. "Justice Sector Development Programme," Department for International Development.

44. "Justice Sector Development Programme," British Council, accessed November 2, 2023, http://www.britishcouncil.org/partner/track-record/justice-sector-development-programme.

45. Peter Albrecht, Olushegu Garber, Ade Gibson, and Sophy Thomas, *Community Policing in Sierra Leone—Local Policing Partnership Boards* (Copenhagen, DK: Danish Institute for International Studies, 2014).

46. *Guidelines on SGBV Case Management: A Reference Handbook for the FSU*, UN Development Programme, Freetown, SL.

47. *Annual Crime Management Statistical Report for January-December, 2012*, Sierra Leone Police, Freetown, SL, 2012.

48. Rita Abrahamsen and Michael Williams, *The Globalisation of Private Security. Country Report: Sierra Leone* (Aberystwyth: University of Wales, 2005).

49. Baker, "Sierra Leone Police Reform," 7, 12.

50. The 2023 election falls a bit out of the scope of the study, as this work had been completed. However, the violence that emerged during the 2023 election seems to be a continuation of a pattern that started during the 2017 election.

51. "Ahead of Elections, Sierra Leone Focuses on Mitigating Political Violence Election Security, All Electoral Integrity and Transparency," International Foundation for Electoral Systems, January 17, 2012, http://www.ifes.org/Content /Publications/News-in-Brief/2012/Jan/Ahead-of-Elections-Sierra-Leone-Focuses -on-Mitigating-Political-Violence.aspx; Daou, Awa Faye. "Sierra Leone: an election without violence." Institute for Security Studies, ISS Today, February 27, 2013, https://issafrica.org/iss-today/sierra-leone-an-election-without-violence.

52. Abdul R. Thomas, "Dr Sylvia Blyden Arrested as US Government Signs Multi-Million Dollar Grant Aid with President Bio," *Sierra Leone Telegraph*, December 16, 2020, https://www.thesierraleonetelegraph.com/dr-sylvia -blyden-arrested-as-us-government-signs-multi-million-dollar-grant-aid-with -president-bio/; Thomas, "The Palo Conteh Treason Trial—Lesson Learnt," *Sierra Leone Telegraph*, July 5, 2020, https://www.thesierraleonetelegraph.com /the-palo-conteh-treason-trial-lesson-learnt/.

53. "Curfew in Sierra Leone Town after Rioting, Shooting over Ebola Case," Reuters, October 21, 2014, https://www.reuters.com/article/us-health-ebola -leone/curfew-in-sierra-leone-town-after-rioting-shooting-over-ebola-case -idUSKCN0IA2AY20141021.

54. Valerie Brender, *"No Money, No Justice": Police Corruption and Abuse in Liberia* (New York: Human Rights Watch, 2013).

55. Winston P. Parley, "LNP, Much Expected," *New Dawn*[Liberia], June 10, 2011.

56. *Twenty-Eighth Progress Report*, UN Security Council.

57. *Twenty-Eighth Progress Report*, UN Security Council.

58. Malan, *Security Sector Reform in Liberia*.

59. Malan, *Security Sector Reform in Liberia*.

60. Malan, *Security Sector Reform in Liberia*.

61. Malan, *Security Sector Reform in Liberia*.

62. Malan, *Security Sector Reform in Liberia*.

63. *Twenty-Eighth Progress Report*, UN Security Council.

64. Center on International Cooperation, *Annual Review of Global Peace Operations 2012*.

65. Brender, *"No Money, No Justice."*

66. Malan, *Security Sector Reform in Liberia*.

67. Brender, *"No Money, No Justice."*

68. Brender, *"No Money, No Justice."*

69. Brender, *"No Money, No Justice."*

70. Brender, *"No Money, No Justice."*

71. Brender, *"No Money, No Justice."*

72. *New Dawn*, "Liberia: Police Boss Marc Amblard Sacked," allAfrica, November 28, 2011, http://allafrica.com/stories/201111280821.html; Brender, *"No Money, No Justice."*

73. UN Security Council, *Twenty-Eighth Progress Report*.

74. Center on International Cooperation, *Annual Review of Global Peace Operations 2008*, (Boulder, CO: Lynne Rienner, 2008).

75. Center on International Cooperation, *Annual Review of Global Peace Operations 2008*.

76. Center on International Cooperation, *Annual Review of Global Peace Operations 2012*.

77. Center on International Cooperation, *Annual Review of Global Peace Operations 2012*.

78. Truth and Reconciliation Commission (TRC) of Sierra Leone, *Witness to Truth: Report of the Sierra Leone Truth & Reconciliation Commission*, vol. 1 (2004), 27, accessed November 3, 2023, https://www.sierraleonetrc.org/index.php /view-the-final-report.

79. Interview, member of RUF and the Promoters of Peace and Justice, Freetown, 2008.

80. Rosalind Shaw, *Rethinking Truth and Reconciliation Commissions: Lessons from Sierra Leone (Special Report No. 130)* (Washington, DC: United States Institute of Peace, 2005), 3.

81. Shaw, 9.

82. Interview, Bishop Joseph Humper, chair of the Sierra Leonean Truth and Reconciliation Commission, Freetown, 2008.

83. TRC, *Witness to Truth*, vol. 3, 3.

84. TRC, *Witness to Truth*, vol. 2, 124.

85. TRC, *Witness to Truth*, vol. 2, 117.

86. TRC, *Witness to Truth*, vol. 2, 117.

87. Tim Kelsall, "Truth, Lies, Ritual: Preliminary Reflections on the Truth and Reconciliation Commission in Sierra Leone," *Human Rights Quarterly* 27, no. 2 (2005): 361–391, 363.

88. Kelsall, "Truth, Lies, Ritual," 363.

89. Shaw, "Memory Frictions: Localizing the Truth and Reconciliation Commission in Sierra Leone," *International Journal of Transitional Justice* 1, no. 2 (2007): 183–207.

90. TRC, *Witness to Truth*, app. 3, part 1, 95.

91. Christopher J. Colvin, "'Brothers and Sisters, Do Not Be Afraid of Me': Trauma, History and the Therapeutic Imagination in the New South Africa," in *Contested Pasts: The Politics of Memory*, ed. Katharine Hodgkin and Susannah Radstone (New York: Routledge, 2003); Mahmood Mamdani, "Amnesty or Impunity? A Preliminary Critique of the Report of the Truth and Reconciliation Commission of South Africa (TRC)," *Diacritics* 32, no. 3 (2002): 32–59; Jacobus A. Du Pisani and Kwang-Su Kim, "Establishing the Truth about the Apartheid Past: Historians and the South African Truth and Reconciliation Commission," *African Studies Quarterly* 8, no. 1 (2004): 77–95; Allison Corey and Sandra F. Joireman, "Retributive Justice: The Gacaca Courts in Rwanda," *African Affairs* 103, no. 410 (2004): 73–89; Peter Uvin and Charles Mironko, "Western and Local Approaches to Justice in Rwanda," *Global Governance* 9 (2003): 219–231; Jacques Fierens, "*Gacaca* Courts: Between Fantasy and Reality," *Journal of International Criminal Justice* 3, no. 4 (2005): 896–919.

92. "Home Page," Fambul Tok, accessed January 9, 2024, http://www .fambultok.org.

93. Richard Wilson, *The Politics of Truth and Reconciliation in South Africa: Legitimizing the Post-apartheid State* (Cambridge, UK: Cambridge University Press, 2001); Hein Marais, *South Africa: Limits to Change: The Political Economy of Transition* (New York: Zed, 2001).

94. Bah, "People-Centered Liberalism: An Alternative Approach to International Statebuilding in Sierra Leone and Liberia," *Critical Sociology* 43, no. 7–8 (2017): 989–1007.

95. "War-Wounded Get Micro-Grants," *New Humanitarian*, November 12, 2009, http://www.irinnews.org/report/87007/sierra-leone-war-wounded-get -micro-grants.

96. Aruna Turay, "In Sierra Leone, NaCSA Certifies Female War Victims," *Awareness Times*, [Sierra Leone] March 17, 2011.

97. Sanusi Savage and Paul K. Kargbo, "Sierra Leone Conflict Victims Receive Reparations," International Organization for Migration, October 4, 2013, https:// www.iom.int/news/sierra-leone-conflict-victims-receive-reparations.

98. "Vision, Mission and Core Values," Human Rights Commission of Sierra Leone, accessed December 15, 2023, https://www.hrc-sl.org/Mission_Vision.aspx.

99. Human Rights Commission of Sierra Leone Act of 2004, Government of Sierra Leone, August 20, 2004.

100. TRC of Liberia mandate enacted on May 12, 2005, by the National Transitional Legislative Assembly. The TRC mandate is the act that established the TRC of Liberia.

101. TRC, *Final Report*, vol. 2, Consolidated Final Report, xxiv.

102. TRC, *Final Report*, xxiv.

103. TRC, *Final Report*, 16.

104. TRC, *Final Report*, 378.

105. TRC, *Final Report*.

106. TRC, *Final Report*, 349.

107. TRC, *Final Report*, 361.

108. TRC, *Final Report*, 361.

109. Lansana Gberie, "Truth and Justice on Trial in Liberia," *African Affairs* 107, no. 428 (2008): 455–465, 459.

110. Terence Sesay, "Liberia Supreme Court: TRC Ban on Politicians Unconstitutional," *African Press International*, January 27, 2011, https://africanpress .wordpress.com/2011/01/27/liberia-supreme-court-trc-ban-on-politicians -unconstitutional.

111. Agreement Between the United Nations and the Government of Sierra Leone on the Establishment of a Special Court for Sierra Leone, UN, Freetown, SL, April 12, 2002.

112. Tamba, "Liberia Won't Pay Reparations to Civil War Victims," *Africa Review*, September 17, 2010.; *New Dawn*, "Liberia: Disabled Press for Reparation from Government," allAfrica, April 17, 2013, https://allafrica.com/stories/201304170838 .html.

113. Ordonnance N° 2011-167 Du 13 Juillet 2011 Portant Creation, Attributions, Organisation Et Fonctionnement De La Commission Dialogue, Verite Et Reconciliation, Republic of Côte d'Ivoire, Office of the President of the Republic, July 13, 2011.

114. "Côte d'Ivoire: la liste des membres de la Commission vérité et réconciliation est publiée," RFI, June 9, 2011, http://www.rfi.fr/afrique/20110905 -cote-ivoire-liste-membres-commission-verite-reconciliation-est-publiee/.

115. "Remise du rapport de la CDVR: Allocution de SEM Alassane Ouattara," Abidjan.Net, December 16, 2014, http://news.abidjan.net/h/518251.htm.

116. Author translation of "La CDVR a pour mission d'oeuvrer en toute indépendance à la réconciliation et au renforcement de la cohésion sociale entre toutes les communautés vivant en Côte d'Ivoire." Ordonnance N° 2011-167, Republic of Côte d'Ivoire, Office of the President of the Republic Du 13 Juillet 2011 Portant Creation, Attributions, Organisation Et Fonctionnement De La Commission Dialogue, Verite Et Reconciliation; Article 5.

117. Remise du rapport final de la CDVR: Charles Konan Banny Recommande Des Journées Nationales De La Mémoire Et Du Pardon, Republic of Côte d'Ivoire, December 15, 2015, https://www.gouv.ci/_actualite-article.php?d=1&recordID =5153&p=296

118. Abidjan.Net. Remise du rapport de la CDVR: Allocution de SEM Alassane Ouattara, Republic of Côte d'Ivoire, December 16, 2014, https://news.abidjan.net /articles/518251/remise-du-rapport-de-la-cdvr-allocution-de-sem-alassane-ouattara.

119. "Ivory Coast to Compensate Civil Conflict Victims," *BBC News*, May 6, 2015, http://www.bbc.com/news/world-africa-32606494.

120. Liberia. Comprehensive Peace Agreement Between the Government of Liberia and the Liberians United for Reconciliation and Democracy (LURD) and the Movement for Democracy in Liberia (MODEL) and Political Parties Accra, August 18, 2003, https://www.usip.org/sites/default/files/file/resources /collections/peace_agreements/liberia_08182003.pdf.

121. International Criminal Court. "Rome Statute of the International Criminal Court: Article 11," International Criminal Court, 1998, 8.

122. United Nations Security Council. "Direct Dialogue: Ouagadougou Political Agreement." March 4, 2007.

123. "Registry," International Criminal Court, accessed January 9, 2024, https:// www.icc-cpi.int/about/registry/default.

124. Doudou Diène, *Report of the Independent Expert on the Situation of Human Rights in Côte d'Ivoire*, United Nations, Geneva, June 24, 2013.

125. "Paving the Way for Justice in Côte d'Ivoire," *New Humanitarian*, July 22, 2011, http://www.irinnews.org/report/93307/analysis-paving-the-way-for-justice -in-c%C3%B4te-d-ivoire.

126. "Côte d'Ivoire's Former First Lady Simone Gbagbo Jailed," *BBC News*, March 10, 2015, http://www.bbc.com/news/world-africa-31809073.

127. "Côte d'Ivoire's Laurent Gbagbo Son Michel Calls for Peace," *BBC News*, August 8, 2013, https://www.bbc.com/news/world-africa-23612701.

128. Babatunde Akinsola, "UN Expert Welcomes Release Of 50 Gbagbo Loyalists by Côte d'Ivoire's Govt," *Naija247News*, June 9, 2014, https://www.naija247news .com/2014/06/09/un-expert-welcomes-release-of-50-gbagbo-loyalists-by-cote -divoires-govt/#.YDc4-OhKjIU.

129. Matthew Pomy, "African Union Urges Members to Stand Against ICC Trials of Presidents," *The Jurist*, February 1, 2014, https://www.jurist.org/news/2014/02 /african-union-urges-members-to-stand-against-icc-trials-of-presidents.

130. "ICC Drops Uhuru Kenyatta Charges for Kenya Ethnic Violence," *BBC News*, December 5, 2014, http://www.bbc.com/news/world-africa-30347019.

131. Republic of Sierra Leone. "Lomé Peace Agreement." Sierra Leone Web, June 3, 1999. http://www.sierra-leone.org/lomeaccord.html.

132. *Seventh Report of the Secretary-General on the United Nations Observer Mission in Sierra Leone*, UN Security Council, July 30, 1999, para. 7.

133. Republic of Sierra Leone. "Abidjan Peace Accord." Sierra Leone Web, November 30, 1996. http://www.sierra-leone.org/abidjanaccord.html.

134. Agreement Between the United Nations and the Government of Sierra Leone, UN; African Union Panel of the Wise, *Peace, Justice, and Reconciliation in Africa: Opportunities and Challenges in the Fight Against Impunity*, African Union Series (New York: International Peace Institute, 2013); Michael P. Scharf, "The Special Court for Sierra Leone," *American Society of International Law: Insights* 5, no. 14 (2000).

135. The indictments against Sankoh and Bockarie were withdrawn after their deaths in 2003.

136. The sentences were Fofana (fifteen years), Kondewa (twenty years), Sesay (fifty-two years), Kallon (forty years), Gbao (twenty-five years), Brima (fifty years), Kanu (fifty years), Kamara (forty-five years), and Taylor (fifty years).

137. "Mandate of the Residual Special Court for Sierra Leone," Residual Court of Sierra Leone, accessed February 25, 2021, https://rscsl.org/the-rscsl/mandate -of-the-residual-special-court-for-sierra-leone/.

138. Rachel Kerr and Jessica Lincoln, *The Special Court for Sierra Leone: Outreach, Legacy and Impact (Final Report)*, War Crimes Research Group, King's College, London, 2008, 11.

139. Charles Chernor Jalloh, "Special Court for Sierra Leone: Achieving Justice?," *Michigan Journal of International Law* 32, no. 3 (2011): 458.

140. Jalloh, "Special Court for Sierra Leone," 418–428.

141. Gberie, "The Special Court for Sierra Leone Rests—for Good," *Africa Renewal*, April 2014, http://www.un.org/africarenewal/magazine/april-2014/special-court -sierra-leone-rests-%E2%80%93-good.

142. Friederike Mieth, "Bringing Justice and Enforcing Peace? An Ethnographic Perspective on the Impact of the Special Court for Sierra Leone," *International Journal of Conflict and Violence* 7, no. 1 (2013): 10–12, 15.

143. Jeremy Sarkin, "The Tension Between Justice and Reconciliation in Rwanda: Politics, Human Rights, Due Process and the Role of the *Gacaca* Courts in Dealing with the Genocide," *Journal of African Law* 45, no. 2 (2001): 143–172; Corey and Joireman, "Retributive Justice," 73–89; Gary J. Bass, *Stay the Hand of Vengeance: The Politics of War Crimes Tribunals* (Princeton, NJ: Princeton University Press, 2014).

144. National Unity and Reconciliation Act (no. 34 of 1995), Republic of South Africa, Office of the President, July 26, 1995, http://www.justice.gov.za/legislation /acts/1995-034.pdf.

145. "Welcome to the Official Truth and Reconciliation Commission Website," Republic of South Africa, TRC, accessed October 20, 2023, https://www.justice .gov.za/trc/.

146. *Truth Commission: South Africa*, US Institute of Peace, December 1, 1995, http://www.usip.org/publications/truth-commission-south-africa.

147. Mamdani, "Amnesty or Impunity?," 32–59.

148. Peter Uvin, "Difficult Choices in the New Post-Conflict Agenda: The International Community in Rwanda after the Genocide," *Third World Quarterly* 22, no. 2 (2001): 177–189; Barbara Oomen, "Donor-Driven Justice and Its Discontents: The Case of Rwanda," *Development and Change* 36, no. 5 (2005): 887–910.

149. "Reparation & Rehabilitation Committee Transcripts, Policies & Articles," TRC of South Africa, accessed October 20, 2023, http://www.justice

.gov.za/trc/reparations/index.htm; Brandon Hamber and Richard A. Wilson, "Symbolic Closure Through Memory, Reparation and Revenge in Post-Conflict Societies," *Journal of Human Rights* 1, no. 1 (2002): 35–53; "Ignoring Cries for Justice, South Africa Fails Victims of Apartheid-era Crimes," International Center for Transitional Justice, January 7, 2013, https://www.ictj.org/news /ignoring-cries-justice-south-africa-fails-victims-apartheid-era-crimes.

150. Robert M. Press, "Sierra Leone's Peaceful Resistance to Authoritarian Rule," *African Conflict and Peacebuilding Review* 2, no. 1 (2012): 31–57.

151. Bah, "Civil Non-State Actors in Peacekeeping and Peacebuilding in West Africa," *Journal of International Peacekeeping* 17, no. 3–4 (2013): 313–336.

152. Bah, "Civil Non-State Actors," 313–336; Peace A. Medie, *Global Norms and Local Action: The Campaigns to End Violence against Women in Africa* (New York: Oxford University Press, 2020).

153. Thomas J. Bassett, *The Peasant Cotton Revolution in West Africa: Côte d'Ivoire, 1880–1995* (New York: Cambridge University Press, 2001).

154. Interview, official, Campaign for Governance, Freetown, 2008.

155. UNESCO, "Professional Development and Access to Technical Resources," Liberia Media Centre (with support from members of Partnership for Media and Conflict Prevention in West Africa), Project PDC/51 LIR/01; "Liberia Media Center is Five," *Analyst Newspaper*, August 27, 2010, http://www.analystliberia.com/index .php?option=com_content&view=article&id=430:liberia-media-center-is-five &catid=41:top-headlines&Itemid=95.

156. Management Systems International, accessed December 31, 2008, http:// www.msiworldwide.com; "Funders and Donors," Search for Common Ground, accessed December 31, 2008, http://www.sfcg.org/sfcg/sfcg_funders.html; "Our Mission and Vision," Search for Common Ground, accessed December 31, 2008, http://www.sfgc.org/sfcg/sfc g_mission.html; "Data Sheet," United States Agency for International Development, accessed December 31, 2008, http://www.usaid .gov/policy/budget/cbj2006/afr/pdf/sl636-002.pdf; "Structure and Funding," World Vision International, accessed December 31, 2008, http://www.wvi.org /wvi/wviweb.nsf/maindocs/39F905AE21E265C1882573750075074B?opendocu ment; "Who We Are," World Vision International, accessed December 31, 2008, http://www.wvi.org/wvi/wviweb.nsf/maindocs/3F50B250D66B7629882573640 0663F21?opendocument.

157. "Office of Transition Initiatives CITI Program in Côte d'Ivoire," United States Agency for International Development, accessed October 1, 2020, https:// www.usaid.gov/stabilization-and-transitions/closed-programs/cote-divoire.

158. "Closing OTI and its Côte d'Ivoire Transition Initiatives (CITI) Program," US Embassy in Côte d'Ivoire, March 29, 2016, https://ci.usembassy.gov/closing-of -the-office-of-transition-initiatives-oti-and-its-cote-divoire-transition-initiatives -citi-program/.

159. "Closing OTI," US Embassy in Côte d'Ivoire.

160. "Côte d'Ivoire Radio Stations Promote Healing and Disclosure," United States Agency for International Development, July 2015, https://2012-2017.usaid .gov/results-data/success-stories/local-radio-stations-du%C3%A9kou %C3%A9-promote-reconciliation.

161. "Office of Transition Initiatives CITI Program in Côte d'Ivoire," USAID.

162. "Closing OTI," US Embassy in Côte d'Ivoire.

163. "Diamonds for Development Programme Framework," UN Development Programme, 2005, 4.

164. Michael D. Beevers, "Natural Resource Reforms in Postwar Liberia and Sierra Leone: Contradictions and Tensions," in *Post-Conflict Institutional Design: Peacebuilding and Democracy in Africa*, ed. Bah (London, UK: Zed, 2020).

165. *Project Paper on a Proposed Additional Grant and Proposed Restructuring of Original Project in the Amount of SDR 2.6 Million (US$4.0 Million Equivalent) to the Republic of Sierra Leone for an Extractive Industries Technical Assistance Project (Report no. 59466-SL)*, World Bank, March 29, 2011.

166. *Mining Technical Assistance Project: Environmental and Social Management Framework (Report no. E2691)*, World Bank, September 24, 2009.

167. *Project Paper on a Proposed Additional Grant*, World Bank.

168. "EITI Implementation," Extractive Industries Transparency Initiative, accessed January 9, 20204, http://eiti.org/SierraLeone/implementation.

169. *Institutional Support Project to Strengthen the Public Financial Management and the Energy Sectors (Appraisal Report)*, African Development Bank Group, September 2004.

170. *Institutional Support Project*, African Development Bank Group.

171. *Programme: Economic Governance Reform Grant I, Country: Sierra Leone (Appraisal Report)*, African Development Bank Group, April 10, 2009; Sahr Morris Jr., "Sierra Leone: U.S. $15 Million Economic Reform Package," allAfrica, May 22, 2009, https://allafrica.com/stories/200905220668.html.

172. *Economic Governance Reform Program II (EGRP II). Country: Sierra Leone (Appraisal Report)*, African Development Bank Group, July 2011.

173. As of May 2011, 1 Unit of Account (UA) = USD 1.57305; *Economic Governance Reform Program II (EGRP II)*, African Development Bank Group.

174. "Financing Agreement (Integrated Public Financial Management Reform Project) between REPUBLIC OF SIERRA LEONE and INTERNATIONAL DEVELOPMENT ASSOCIATION," World Bank, October 19, 2009, accessed January 25, 2011, http://www-wds.worldbank.org/external/default/WDSContentServer /WDSP/AFR/2010/06/09/F02928C642C280C9852576660068E22F/2_0/Rendered /PDF/IPFMRP0FA101Conf.1.pdf.

175. "Financing Agreement (Integrated Public Financial Management Reform Project)," World Bank, 5.

176. "Financing Agreement (Integrated Public Financial Management Reform Project)," World Bank, 5.

177. Interview, senior official, Ministry of Finance, Freetown, 2008.

178. *Project Appraisal Document on a Proposed Credit in the Amount of SDR 7.9 Million (US$12 Million Equivalent) to the Republic of Sierra Leone for the Public Financial Management & Consolidated Project*, World Bank, October 31, 2013.

179. *Project Appraisal Document on a Proposed Credit in the Amount of SDR 7.9 Million (US$12 Million Equivalent) to the Republic of Sierra Leone for the Public Financial Management & Consolidated Project*, World Bank, October 31, 2013.

180. *Emergency Project Paper for an IDA Grant*, World Bank: 2008, 9.

181. *Project Information Document (PID) Concept Stage (Report no. AB3782)*, World Bank, March 28, 2008.

182. *Project Paper on a Proposed Additional Credit in the Amount of SDR 4.5 Million (US$7 Million Equivalent) to the Republic of Liberia for an Economic Governance and Institutional Reform Project (Report no. 58891-LR)*, World Bank, March 14, 2001.

183. *Restructuring Paper on a Proposed Project Restructuring of LR-Public Financial Management—IFMIS—Project Grant: Main Report (Report no. 66453 vol. 1)*, World Bank, January 4, 2012.

184. *International Development Association Project Appraisal Document on a Proposed Credit in the Amount of SDR 3.20 Million (US$5 Million Equivalent) to the Republic of Liberia for an Integrated Public Financial Management Reform Project (Report no. 64363-LR)*, World Bank, November 18, 2011, 7.

185. *International Development Association Project Appraisal Document on a Proposed Credit in the Amount of SDR 3.20 Million*, World Bank, 7–8.

186. *International Development Association Project Appraisal Document on a Proposed Credit in the Amount of SDR 1.4 Million (US$2.0 Million Equivalent) to the Republic of Liberia for a Public Sector Modernization Project (Report no. 83735-LR)*, World Bank, January 15, 2014.

187. *International Development Association Project Appraisal Document (Report no. 83735-LR)*, World Bank, 8.

188. Ahmed Zejly and Gilbert Galibaka, *Appraisal Report: The National Good Governance and Capacity Building Programme (PNBGRC) Republic of Côte d'Ivoire*, African Development Fund, West Region, October 2001.

189. *Financing Agreement (Economic Governance and Recovery Grant) between Republic of Côte d'Ivoire and International Development Association (H3500-CI)*, World Bank, April 1, 2008; "World Bank Approves US$150 Million Grant to Support Côte d'Ivoire's Economic Recovery and Governance Program," World Bank press release no. 2009/269/AFR, March 31, 2009.

190. "World Bank Approves US$150 Million Grant."

191. *International Development Association Program Document for the Second Economic Governance and Recovery Grant in the Amount of SDR 96.4 Million (US$150 Million Equivalent) to the Republic of Côte d'Ivoire (Report no. 46167-CI)*, World Bank, March 4, 2009, vii.

192. *International Development Association Program Document for the Second Economic Governance and Recovery Grant*, World Bank, 10.

193. *International Development Association Program Document for the Second Economic Governance and Recovery Grant*, World Bank, 28.

194. *International Development Association Program Document for the Second Economic Governance and Recovery Grant*, World Bank, 11.

195. *International Development Association Program Document for the Second Economic Governance and Recovery Grant*, World Bank, 30.

196. *International Development Association Program Document for the Second Economic Governance and Recovery Grant*, World Bank, 30.

197. *International Development Association Program Document for the Second Economic Governance and Recovery Grant*, World Bank, 30.

198. *International Development Association Program Document for the Second Economic Governance and Recovery Grant*, World Bank, 30.

199. Bah, "Contours of New Humanitarianism," 3–26; Bah and Emmanuel, "Positive Peace and the Methodology of Costing Peacebuilding Needs," 299–318.

6. CONCLUSION

1. Mahmood Mamdani, *Citizen and Subject: Contemporary African and the Legacy of Late Colonialism* (Princeton, NJ: Princeton University Press, 1996); Larry Diamond, "Class Formation in the Swollen African State," *Journal of Modern African Studies* 25, no. 4 (1987): 567–596; Richard A. Joseph, "Class, State, and Prebendal Politics in Nigeria," *Commonwealth & Comparative Politics* 21, no. 3 (1983): 21–38.

2. Michael Bratton, "Second Elections in Africa," *Journal of Democracy* 9, no. 3 (1998): 51–66; John A. Wiseman, *The New Struggle for Democracy in Africa* (Aldershot, UK: Avebury, 1996); Paul Collier and Anke Hoeffler, "Greed and Grievance in Civil War," *Oxford Economic Papers* 56, no. 4 (2004): 563–595; Christophe S. Clapham, ed., *African Guerrillas* (Bloomington: Indiana University Press, 1998); Robert H. Bates, *Markets and States in Tropical Africa: The Political Basis of Agricultural Policies* (Berkeley: University of California Press, 2005).

3. Kurt Mills and Richard Norton, "Refugees and Security in the Great Lakes Region of Africa," *Civil Wars* 5, no. 1 (2002): 1–26; Patricia Daley, "Population Displacement and the Humanitarian Aid Regime: The Experience of Refugees in East Africa," in *Mobile Africa: Changing Patterns of Movement in Africa and Beyond*, ed. Mirjam de Bruijn, Rijk Adrianus van Dijk, and Dick Foeken (Leiden, NL: Brill, 2001); Jean-Paul Azam and Hoeffler, "Violence against Civilians in Civil Wars: Looting or Terror?," *Journal of Peace Research* 39, no. 4 (2002): 461–485; Taisier M. Ali and Robert O. Matthews, *Civil Wars in Africa: Roots and Resolution* (Québec: McGill-Queen's University Press, 1999); Krishna Kumar, ed., *Rebuilding Societies After Civil War: Critical Roles for International Assistance* (Boulder, CO: Lynne Rienner, 1997); Assefaw Bariagaber, *Conflict and the Refugee Experience: Flight, Exile, and Repatriation in the Horn Africa* (Burlington, VT: Ashgate, 2006);

E. Elbadawi and N. Sambanis, "Why Are There So Many Civil Wars in Africa? Understanding and Preventing Violent Conflict," *Journal of African Economies* 9, no. 3 (2000): 244–269.

4. Kumar, *Rebuilding Societies After Civil War*; Marrack Goulding, "The United Nations and Conflict in Africa since the Cold War," *African Affairs* 98, no. 391 (1999): 155–166; Mehler, "Peace and Power Sharing in Africa: A Not so Obvious Relationship," *African Affairs* 108, no. 432 (2009): 453–473.

5. Thomas Carothers, "The 'Sequencing' Fallacy," *Journal of Democracy* 18 (2007): 12–27.

6. United Nations (UN), "UN Peace-Building: An Orientation," New York, 2010.

7. Abu Bakarr Bah and Nikolas Emmanuel, "Positive Peace and the Methodology of Costing Peacebuilding Needs: The Case of Burundi," *Administrative Theory & Praxis* 43, no. 3 (2020): 299–318.

8. David Chandler, "Peacebuilding as Statebuilding," in *Peacebuilding: The Twenty Years' Crisis, 1997–2017*, ed. David Chandler, 69–94 (London: Palgrave Macmillan, 2017); Bah, ed., *International Security and Peacebuilding: Africa, the Middle East, and Europe* (Bloomington: Indiana University Press, 2017).

9. Bah, *Breakdown and Reconstitution: Democracy, the Nation-State, and Ethnicity in Nigeria* (Lanham, MD: Lexington, 2005).

10. J. L. Holzgrefe and Robert Owen Keohane, *Humanitarian Intervention: Ethical, Legal, and Political Dilemmas* (New York: Cambridge University Press, 2008), 18.

11. Anthony Giddens, *The Nation-State and Violence: Volume Two of a Contemporary Critique of Historical Materialism* (Cambridge: Polity, 1996), 112.

12. *Project Paper on a Proposed Additional Grant and Proposed Restructuring of Original Project in the Amount of SDR 2.6 Million (US$4.0 Million Equivalent) to the Republic of Sierra Leone for an Extractive Industries Technical Assistance Project (Report no. 59466-SL)*, World Bank, March 29, 2011.

13. "Diamonds for Development Programme Framework," UN Development Programme, 2005, 4.

14. *Emergency Project Paper for an IDA Grant in the Amount of SDR6.7 Million (US$11.0 Million Equivalent) to the Republic of Liberia for an Economic Governance and Institutional Reform Project (Report no. 42836-LR)*, World Bank, April 29, 2008, 9.

REFERENCES

Abdullah, Ibrahim. "Bush Path to Destruction: The Origin and Character of the Revolutionary United Front." *Journal of Modern African Studies* 36, no. 2 (1998): 203–235.

Abdullah, Mohamoud A. *State Collapse and Post-Conflict Development in Africa: The Case of Somalia (1960–2001)*. West Lafayette, IN: Purdue University Press, 2006.

Abidjan.Net. Remise du rapport de la CDVR: Allocution de SEM Alassane Ouattara, Republic of Côte d'Ivoire, December 16, 2014. https://news.abidjan.net /articles/518251/remise-du-rapport-de-la-cdvr-allocution-de-sem-alassane-ouattara.

Abiodun Alao, Charles. "Commentary on the Accords." *Accord: An International Review of Peace Initiatives* 1 (1996): 33–36, 70–74.

Abi-Saab, Georges. "Whither the International Community?" *European Journal of International Law* 9, no. 2 (1998): 248–265.

Aboa, Ange, and Loucoumane Coulibaly. "UN rejects Gbagbo Win in Ivoirian Poll." Reuters, December 3, 2010. https://www.reuters.com/article/uk-ivorycoast -election-events-idUKTRE6B25K420101204.

Abrahamsen, Rita, and Michael Williams. *The Globalisation of Private Security: Country Report: Sierra Leone*. Aberystwyth: University of Wales, 2005.

Ade Ajayi, J. F., ed. *Africa in the Nineteenth Century until the 1880s*. Portsmouth, NH: UNESCO and Heinemann International, 1998.

Ade Ajayi, J. F. "The Place of African History and Culture in the Process of Nation-Building in Africa South of the Sahara." *Journal of Negro Education* 30, no. 3 (1961): 206–213.

Ade Ajayi, J. F., and Michael Crowder. *History of West Africa*. New York: Columbia University Press, 1976.

Adebajo, Adekeye. *Building Peace in West Africa: Liberia, Sierra Leone, and Guinea-Bissau*. Boulder, CO: Lynne Rienner, 2002.

Adebajo, Adekeye. *Liberia's Civil War: Nigeria, ECOMOG, and Regional Security in West.* Boulder, CO: Lynn Rienner, 2002.

Adebajo, Adekeye, and Ismail Rashid, eds. *West Africa's Security Challenges: Building Peace in a Troubled Region.* Boulder, CO: Lynne Rienner, 2004.

Adebanwi, Wale. "Contesting Exclusion: The Dilemmas of Citizenship in Nigeria." *African Anthropologist* 12, no. 1 (2005): 11–45.

Adeleke, Ademola. "The Politics and Diplomacy of Peacekeeping in West Africa: The ECOWAS Operation in Liberia." *Journal of Modern African Studies* 33, no. 4 (1995): 569–593.

Adibe, Clement E. "The Liberian Conflict and the ECOWAS-UN Partnership." In *Beyond UN Subcontracting: Task-Sharing with Regional Security Arrangements and Service-Providing NGOs,* edited by Thomas G. Weiss. New York: St. Martin's, 1998.

Africa Growth and Opportunities Act. "About AGOA." AGOA.info. Accessed October 17, 2023. https://agoa.info/about-agoa.html.

African Development Bank Group. *Economic Governance Reform Program II (EGRP II). Country: Sierra Leone (Appraisal Report).* African Development Bank, July 2011.

African Development Bank Group. *Institutional Support Project to Strengthen the Public Financial Management and the Energy Sectors (Appraisal Report).* African Development Bank, September 2004.

African Development Bank Group. *Programme: Economic Governance Reform Grant I, Country: Sierra Leone (Appraisal Report).* African Development Bank, April 10, 2009.

African Export-Import Bank. *Annual Report and Financial Statements for the Year Ended December 31, 2010.* Cairo, 2012.

African Union. African Charter on Democracy, Elections, and Government. Addis Ababa, January 30, 2007.

African Union. "Elections Unit." Accessed October 17, 2023. https://au.int/en/elections.

African Union Panel of the Wise. *Peace, Justice, and Reconciliation in Africa: Opportunities and Challenges in the Fight Against Impunity.* African Union Series. New York: International Peace Institute, 2013.

Africa Renewal. "The Priority Is Economic Recovery," October 3, 2011. https:// www.un.org/africarenewal/web-features/%E2%80%98-priority-economic -recovery%E2%80%99.

Agrawal, Arun, and Clark C. Gibson. "Enchantment and Disenchantment: The Role of Community in Natural Resource Conservation." *World Development* 27, no. 4 (1999): 629–649.

Aitchison, Andy. *Making the Transition: International Intervention, Statebuilding and Criminal Justice Reform in Bosnia and Herzegovina.* Series on Traditional Justice. Cambridge, UK: Intersentia, 2011.

Akinsola, Babatunde. "UN Expert Welcomes Release of 50 Gbagbo Loyalists by Côte d'Ivoire's Govt." *Naija247News,* June 9, 2014. https://www.naija247news .com/2014/06/09/un-expert-welcomes-release-of-50-gbagbo-loyalists-by-cote -divoires-govt/#.YDc4-OhKjIU.

Akokpari, John. "The AU, NEPAD, and the Promotion of Good Governance in Africa." *Nordic Journal of African Studies* 13, no. 3 (2004): 243–263.

Akokpari, John. "'You Don't Belong Here' Citizenship, the State & Africa's Conflicts: Reflections on Côte d'Ivoire." In *The Roots of African Conflicts: The Causes and Costs*, edited by Alfred G. Nhema and Paul Zeleza Tiyambe. Athens: Ohio University Press, 2008.

Albrecht, Peter, Olushegu Garber, Ade Gibson, and Sophy Thomas. *Community Policing in Sierra Leone—Local Policing Partnership Boards*. Copenhagen, DK: Danish Institute for International Studies, 2014.

Alcock, Antony Evelyn. *A History of the Protection of Regional Cultural Minorities in Europe: From the Edict of Nante to the Present Day*. New York: St. Martin's, 2000.

Ali, Taisier M., and Robert O. Matthews. *Civil Wars in Africa: Roots and Resolution*. Québec: McGill-Queen's University Press, 1999.

Allen, Tim, and David Styan. "A Right to Interfere? Bernard Kouchner and the New Humanitarianism." *Journal for International Development* 12, no. 6 (2000): 825–842.

Amin, Samir. "Accumulation and Development: A Theoretical Model." *Review of African Political Economy* 1, no. 1 (1974): 9–26.

Amin, Samir. "Africa: Living on the Fringe." *Monthly Review* 53, no. 10 (2002): 41–50.

Amin, Samir. *Neo-Colonialism in West Africa*. New York: Penguin, 1973.

Amin, Samir. "Underdevelopment and Dependence in Black Africa: Historical Origin." *Journal of Peace Research* 9, no. 2 (1972): 105–119.

Amnesty International. "Sierra Leone." Accessed January 11, 2024. https://www .amnesty.org/en/location/africa/west-and-central-africa/sierra-leone/.

Amuwo, 'Kunle. "Globalisation, *Nepad* and the Governance Question in Africa." *African Studies Quarterly* 6, no. 3 (2002): 65–82.

Analyst Newspaper. "Liberia Media Center is Five." August 27, 2010. http://www .analystliberia.com/index.php?option=com_content&view=article&id=430:liberia -media-center-is-five&catid=41:top-headlines&Itemid=95.

Anand, Sudhir, and Amartya Sen. "Human Development and Economic Sustainability." *World Development* 28, no. 12 (2000): 2029–2049.

Anand, Sudhir, and Amartya Sen. "Sustainable Human Development: Concepts and Priorities." Paper written for the UNDP *Human Development Report*, March 1994.

Anderson, Benedict. *Imagined Communities: Reflections on the Origin and Spread of Nationalism*. New York: Verso, 1991.

Anderson, David M., and Jacob McKnight. "Kenya at War: Al-Shabaab and Its Enemies in Eastern Africa." *African Affairs* 114, no. 454 (2015): 1–27.

Andrain, Charles F. "The Pan-African Movement: The Search for Organization and Community." *Phylon* 23, no. 1 (1962): 5–17.

Annan, Kofi A. "Two Concepts of Sovereignty." *The Economist* 18, no. 9 (1999): 49–50.

Anshan, Li. "China and Africa: Policy and Challenges." *China Security* 3, no. 3 (2007): 69–93.

Appadurai, Arjun. *Modernity at Large: Cultural Dimensions of Globalization.* Minneapolis: University of Minnesota Press, 1996.

Arato, Andrew. *Constitution Making Under Occupation: The Politics of Imposes Revolution in Iraq.* New York: Columbia University Press, 2009.

Arieff, Alexis, Martin A. Wiess, and Vivian C. Jones. "The Global Economic Crisis: Impact on Sub-Saharan Africa and Global Policy Responses." Congressional Research Service, April 6, 2010.

Arriola, Leonardo R. "Patronage and Political Stability in Africa." *Comparative Political Studies* 42, no. 10 (2009): 1339–1362.

Asiedu, Elizabeth. "Foreign Direct Investment in Africa: The Role of Natural Resources, Market Size, Government Policy, Institutions and Political Instability." *World Economy* 29, no. 1 (2006): 63–77.

Atkins, Judy. "A New Approach to Humanitarian Intervention? Tony Blair's Doctrine of the International Community." *British Politics* 1, no. 2 (2006): 274–283.

Atkinson, Michael M., and William D. Coleman. "Strong States and Weak States: Sectoral Policy Networks in Advanced Capitalist Economies." *British Journal of Political Science* 19, no. 1 (1989): 47–67.

Autesserre, Séverine. *Peaceland: Conflict Resolution and the Everyday Politics of International Intervention.* Cambridge, UK: Cambridge University Press, 2014.

Autesserre, Séverine. *The Trouble with the Congo: Local Violence and the Failure of International Peacebuilding.* Cambridge, UK: Cambridge University Press, 2010.

Ayoob, Mohammed. "Humanitarian Intervention and International Society." *Global Governance* 7, no. 3 (2001): 225–230.

Ayoob, Mohammed. "Third World Perspective on Humanitarian Intervention and International Administration." *Global Governance* 10 (2004): 99–118.

Ayoob, Mohammed. *The Third World Security Predicament: State Making, Regional Conflict, and the International System.* Boulder, CO: Lynne Rienner, 1995.

Azam, Jean-Paul, and Anke Hoeffler. "Violence against Civilians in Civil Wars: Looting or Terror?" *Journal of Peace Research* 39, no. 4 (2002): 461–485.

Bah, Abu Bakarr. (ed.) 2024. *African Security Local Issues and Global Connections.* Athens: Ohio University Press.

Bah, Abu Bakarr. "Approaches to Nation Building in Post-Colonial Nigeria." *Journal of Political and Military Sociology* (renamed *Political and Military Sociology: An Annual Review*) 32, no. 1 (Summer 2004): 45–60.

Bah, Abu Bakarr. *Breakdown and Reconstitution: Democracy, the Nation-State, and Ethnicity in Nigeria.* Lanham, MD: Lexington, 2005.

Bah, Abu Bakarr. "Changing World Order and the Future of Democracy in Sub-Saharan Africa." *Proteus, A Journal of Ideas* 21, no. 1 (2004): 3–12.

Bah, Abu Bakarr. "Civil Non-State Actors in Peacekeeping and Peacebuilding in West Africa." *Journal of International Peacekeeping* 17, no. 3–4 (2013): 313–336.

Bah, Abu Bakarr. "The Contours of New Humanitarianism: War and Peacebuilding in Sierra Leone." *Africa Today* 60, no. 1 (2013): 3–26.

Bah, Abu Bakarr. "Democracy and Civil War: Citizenship and Peacemaking in Côte d'Ivoire." *African Affairs* 109, no. 437 (2010): 597–615.

Bah, Abu Bakarr, ed. *International Security and Peacebuilding: Africa, the Middle East, and Europe.* Bloomington: Indiana University Press, 2017.

Bah, Abu Bakarr. "Ethnic Conflicts and Management Strategies in Bulgaria, Sierra Leone and Nigeria." *Programme on Ethnic and Federal Studies Monograph New Series* 3. Ibadan, NG: John Archers, 2003.

Bah, Abu Bakarr. "People-Centered Liberalism: An Alternative Approach to International Statebuilding in Sierra Leone and Liberia." *Critical Sociology* 43, no. 7–8 (2017): 989–1007.

Bah, Abu Bakarr. *Post-Conflict Institutional Design: Peacebuilding and Democracy in Africa.* London: Zed, 2020.

Bah, Abu Bakarr. "State Decay: A Conceptual Frame of Failing and Failed States in West Africa." *International Journal of Politics, Culture, and Society* 25, no. 1 (2012): 71–89.

Bah, Abu Bakarr. "State Decay and Civil War: A Discourse on Power in Sierra Leone." *Critical Sociology* 37, no. 2 (2011): 199–216.

Bah, Abu Bakarr, "TV Interview, Côte d'Ivoire Civil War, Prof. Abu Bakarr Bah," Al Jazeera TV, August 12, 2022, YouTube video, 7:32, https://www.youtube.com/watch?v=VQAMUE2hmqQ.

Bah, Abu Bakarr, and Ibrahim Bangura. "Landholding and the Creation of Lumpen Tenants in Freetown: Youth Economic Survival and Patrimonialism in Postwar Sierra Leone." *Critical Sociology* 49, no. 7-8 (2023): 1289-1305.

Bah, Abu Bakarr, and Margaret Nasambu Barasa. "Indigenous Knowledge and the Social Construction of Patriarchy: The Case of the Bukusu of Kenya." *Critical Sociology* 49, no. 2 (2023): 217–232.

Bah, Abu Bakarr, and Nikolas Emmanuel. "Migration Cooperation between Africa and Europe: Understanding the Role of International Incentives." *Oxford Research Encyclopedia of International Studies,* September 15, 2022. https://doi.org/10.1093/acrefore/9780190846626.013.735.

Bah, Abu Bakarr, and Nikolas Emmanuel. "Positive Peace and the Methodology of Costing Peacebuilding Needs." *Administrative Theory & Praxis* 43, no. 3 (2020): 299–318.

Baker, Bruce. "Sierra Leone Police Reform: The Role of the UK Government." Grips Policy Research Center (2010).

Banégas, Richard. "Côte d'Ivoire: Patriotism, Ethno-nationalism, and Other African Modes of Self-Writing." *African Affairs* 105, no. 421 (2006): 535–552.

Banégas, Richard. "Post-election Crisis in Côte d'Ivoire: The *Gbonhi* War." *African Affairs* 110, no. 440 (2011): 457–468.

Banégas, Richard, and Bruno Losch. "La Côte d'Ivoire au Bord de l'implosion." *Politique Africaine* 3, no. 87 (2002): 139–161.

Bangura, Joseph. "Understanding Sierra Leone in Colonial West Africa: A Synoptic Socio-Political History." *History Compass* 7, no. 3 (2009): 583–603.

Bangura, Yusuf. "Strategic Policy Failure and Governance in Sierra Leone." *Journal of Modern African Studies* 38, no. 4 (2000): 551–577.

Bannon, Ian, and Paul Collier, eds. *Natural Resources and Violent Conflict: Options and Actions*. Washington, DC: World Bank, 2003.

Bariagaber, Assefaw. *Conflict and the Refugee Experience: Flight, Exile, and Repatriation in the Horn Africa*. Burlington, VT: Ashgate, 2006.

Barnett, Michael. *Eyewitness to a Genocide: The United Nations and Rwanda*. Ithaca, NY: Cornell University Press, 2002.

Barnett, Michael. "Humanitarianism Transformed." *Perspectives on Politics*, 3, no. 4 (2005): 723–740.

Bass, Gary J. *Stay the Hand of Vengeance: The Politics of War Crimes Tribunals*. Princeton, NJ: Princeton University Press, 2014.

Bassett, Thomas J. "Containing the Donzow: The Politics of Scale in Côte d'Ivoire." *Africa Today* 50, no. 4 (2004): 31–49.

Bassett, Thomas J. "Dangerous Pursuits: Hunter Associations (*Donzo Ton*) and National Politics in Côte d'Ivoire." *Africa* 73, no 1 (2003): 1–30.

Bassett, Thomas J. *The Peasant Cotton Revolution in West Africa: Cotê d'Ivoire 1880–1995*. New York: Cambridge University Press, 2001.

Bassett, Thomas J. "Winning Coalition, Sore Loser: Côte d'Ivoire's 2010 Presidential Elections." *African Affairs* 110, no. 440 (2011): 469–479.

Bates, Robert H. *Markets and States in Tropical Africa: The Political Basis of Agricultural Policies*. Berkeley: University of California Press, 2005.

Bates, Robert H. *When Things Fell Apart: State Failure in Late-Century Africa*. New York: Cambridge University Press, 2008.

Baulin, Jacques. *La Politique Africaine d'Houphouët-Boigny*. Paris: Eurafor, 1980.

Baulin, Jacques. *La Politique Intérieure d'Houphouët-Boigny*. Paris: Eurafor, 1982.

Baulin, Jacques, and Gilbert Comte. *La Succession d'Houphouët-Boigny: Les Débuts de Konan Bédié*. Paris: Karthala, 2000.

Bayart, Jean-Francois. *The Illusion of Cultural Identity*. London: Hurst, 2005.

BBC News. "China Pledges $10bn Africa Loans." November 8, 2009. http://news.bbc .co.uk/2/hi/africa/8349020.stm.

BBC News. "Clashes at Côte d'Ivoire Army Camp." October 25, 2000. http://news .bbc.co.uk/2/hi/africa/988935.stm.

BBC News. "Côte d'Ivoire: Amnesty Warns Over Rights Abuses." February 22, 2011. http://www.bbc.co.uk/news/world-africa-12540968.

BBC News. "Côte d'Ivoire: Army and Ex-Rebels 'Breach Ceasefire.'" February 24, 2011. http://www.bbc.co.uk/news/world-africa-12569372.

BBC News. "Côte d'Ivoire: AU Panel of Leaders to Seek Way Forward." January 29, 2011. http://www.bbc.co.uk/news/world-africa-12314022.

BBC News. "Côte d'Ivoire Bars Opposition Leader." October 6, 2000. http://news .bbc.co.uk/2/hi/africa/960415.stm.

BBC News. "Côte d'Ivoire: Besieged Gbagbo 'in Basement' of Residence." April 5, 2011. http://www.bbc.co.uk/news/world-africa-12967610.

BBC News. "Côte d'Ivoire Cocoa Farmers Protest at EU Sanctions." February 17, 2011. http://www.bbc.co.uk/news/business-12497524.

BBC News. "Côte d'Ivoire: Gbagbo 'Expels UK and Canada Envoys.'" January 7, 2011. http://www.bbc.co.uk/news/world-africa-12132835.

BBC News. "Côte d'Ivoire Government Takes Control of Foreign Banks." February 17, 2011. http://www.bbc.co.uk/news/business-12500544.

BBC News. "Côte d'Ivoire: Odinga Makes Fresh AU Mediation Attempt." January 17, 2011. http://www.bbc.co.uk/news/world-africa-12204139.

BBC News. "Côte d'Ivoire: Rebels Take Western Town Zouan-Hounien." February 25, 2011. http://www.bbc.co.uk/news/world-africa-12582014.

BBC News. "Côte d'Ivoire Reins In Soldiers." October 30, 2000. http://news.bbc.co.uk/2/hi/africa/998144.stm.

BBC News. "Côte d'Ivoire's Former First Lady Simone Gbagbo Jailed." March 10, 2015. http://www.bbc.com/news/world-africa-31809073.

BBC News. "Côte d'Ivoire's Laurent Gbagbo Son Michel Calls for Peace." August 8, 2013. https://www.bbc.com/news/world-africa-23612701.

BBC News. "Did Sierra Leone Get War Crimes Justice?" November 6, 2009. http://news.bbc.co.uk/2/hi/8345618.stm.

BBC News. "France Attacks Ivoirian Airbase." November 6, 2004. http://news.bbc.co.uk/2/hi/africa/3988769.stm.

BBC News. "Heavy Gunfire in Ivoirian City." September 19, 2002. http://news.bbc.co.uk/2/hi/africa/2267971.stm.

BBC News. "Ghana President Questions Côte d'Ivoire Military Option." January 7, 2011. http://www.bbc.co.uk/news/world-africa-12136353.

BBC News. "ICC Drops Uhuru Kenyatta Charges for Kenya Ethnic Violence." December 5, 2014. http://www.bbc.com/news/world-africa-30347019.

BBC News. "Ivoirian Peace Deal Provokes Fury." February 1, 2003. http://news.bbc.co.uk/2/hi/africa/2715779.stm.

BBC News. "Ivoirian Rebels Stick to Peace Deal." February 4, 2003. http://news.bbc.co.uk/2/hi/africa/2724805.stm.

BBC News. "Ivoirian Rival Ouattara Tells Gbagbo to Leave." December 12, 2010. http://www.bbc.co.uk/news/world-africa-11977920.

BBC News. "Ivory Coast Policemen Die in Clashes in Abidjan." January 12, 2011. http://www.bbc.co.uk/news/world-africa-12170838.

BBC News. "Ivory Coast Set for Presidential Election Run-Off." November 4, 2010. http://www.bbc.co.uk/news/world-africa-11681134.

BBC News. "Ivory Coast to Compensate Civil Conflict Victims." May 6, 2015. http://www.bbc.com/news/world-africa-32606494.

BBC News. "Ivory Coast Unity Cabinet Possible, Says UN Ambassador." January 11, 2011. http://www.bbc.co.uk/news/world-africa-12157810.

BBC News. "Liberia Hails $1.2bn Debt Pardon by Paris Club." September 17, 2010. http://www.bbc.co.uk/news/business-11341667.

BBC News. "On This Day, April 27, 1961: Sierra Leone Wins Independence." April 27, 2005. http://news.bbc.co.uk/onthisday/hi/dates/stories/april/27/newsid_2502000/2502411.stm.

BBC News. "Ouattara's Men Waiting to March on Abidjan, Côte d'Ivoire." March 21, 2011. http://www.bbc.co.uk/news/world-africa-12804613.

BBC News. "PM Signals New Ivoirian Stand-Off." November 8, 2006. http://news.bbc.co.uk/2/hi/africa/6130248.stm.

BBC News. "Thabo Mbeki Begins Côte d'Ivoire Mediation Mission." December 5, 2010. http://www.bbc.co.uk/news/world-africa-11920739.

BBC News. "US Cancels Liberia's $391m Debt." February 13, 2007. http://news.bbc.co.uk/2/hi/business/6358665.stm.

BBC News. "US Pulls Out of Liberia." September 30, 2003. http://news.bbc.co.uk/2/hi/africa/3150650.stm.

BBC News. "World: Africa Sierra Leone Rebels Reject Peace Offer." June 23, 1999. http://news.bbc.co.uk/2/hi/africa/376323.stm.

Bebler, Anton, ed. *Military Rule in Africa: Dahomey, Ghana, Sierra Leone, and Mali.* Santa Barbara, CA: Praeger, 1973.

Beck, Ulrich. *What Is Globalization?* Translated by P. Camiller. Malden, MA: Polity, 2000.

Beevers, Michael D. "Natural Resource Reforms in Postwar Liberia and Sierra Leone: Contradictions and Tensions." In *Post-Conflict Institutional Design: Peacebuilding and Democracy in Africa,* edited by Abu Bakarr Bah. London: Zed, 2020.

Bennett, David. *Multicultural States: Rethinking Difference and Identity.* New York: Routledge, 1998.

Bhowmick, Nilanjana. "India Pledges $5bn to Help African States Meet the MDGs." *The Guardian,* May 25, 2011. http://www.guardian.co.uk/global-development/poverty-matters/2011/may/25/india-pledges-5bn-to-help-african-states-meet-mdgs.

Bienen, Henry. "Populist Military Regimes in West Africa." *Armed Forces & Society* 11, no. 3 (1985): 357–377.

Birdsall, Nancy, Stijn Claessens, and Ishac Diwan. "Policy Selectivity Forgone: Debt and Donor Behavior in Africa." *World Bank Economic Review* 17, no. 3 (2003): 409–435.

Blair, Robert. *Peacekeeping, Policing, and the Rule of Law after Civil War.* Cambridge, UK: Cambridge University Press, 2020.

Blood, Hilary. "History of Sierra Leone." *African Affairs* 62, no. 246 (1963): 76.

Boahen, A. Adu. *Africa Under Colonial Domination: 1880–1935.* Paris: UNESCO and Heinemann Educational Books, 1985.

Bøås, Morten. "Liberia and Sierra Leone—Dead Ringers? The Logic of Neopatrimonial Rule." *Third World Quarterly* 22, no. 5 (2001): 697–723.

Bøås, Morten, and Kevin C. Dunn, eds. *African Guerillas: Raging Against the Machine.* Boulder, CO: Lynn Rienner, 2007.

Bogaards, Matthijs. "Ethnic Party Bans and Institutional Engineering in Nigeria." *Democratization* 17, no. 4 (2010): 730–749.

Bogetic, Zelijko, John Noer, and Carlos Espina. "Côte d'Ivoire: From Success to Failure: A Story of Growth, Specialization, and the Terms of Trade." World Bank Policy Research Working Paper 4414, 2007.

Bonneuil, Christophe. "Development as Experiment: Science and Statebuilding in Late Colonial and Postcolonial Africa, 1930–1970." *Osiris* 15, no. 1 (2000): 258–281.

Boutros-Ghali, Boutros. "An Agenda for Peace Preventive Diplomacy, Peacemaking and Peace-Keeping." *International Relations* 11, no. 3 (1992).

Bratton, Michael. "Second Elections in Africa." *Journal of Democracy* 9, no. 3 (1998): 51–66.

Bratton, Michael, and Nicolas Van de Walle. *Democratic Experiments in Africa: Regime Transitions in Comparative Perspective*. New York: Cambridge University Press, 1997.

Bratton, Michael, and Nicolas Van de Walle. "Neopatrimonial Regimes and Political Transitions in Africa." *World Politics* 46, no. 4 (1994): 453–489.

Bratton, Michael, and Robert B. Mattes. "Support for Democracy in Africa: Intrinsic or Instrumental?" *British Journal of Political Science* 31, no. 3 (2001): 447–474.

Bräutigam, Deborah. "Chinese Development Aid in Africa: What, Where, Why, and How Much?" In *Rising China: Global Challenges and Opportunities*, edited by Jane Golley and Ligang Song. Canberra: Australian National University Press, 2011.

Bräutigam, Deborah. *The Dragon's Gift: The Real Story of China in Africa*. Oxford: Oxford University Press, 2009.

Bräutigam, Deborah A., and Stephen Knack. "Foreign Aid, Institutions, and Governance in Sub-Saharan Africa." *Economic Development and Cultural Change* 52, no. 2 (2004): 255–285.

Bremmer, Ian, and Ray Taras. *Nation and Politics in the Soviet Successor States*. New York: Cambridge University Press, 1993.

Brender, Valerie. *"No Money, No Justice": Police Corruption and Abuse in Liberia*. New York: Human Rights Watch, 2013.

British Army. "Overseas Deployment: Africa." 2010. https://www.medal-medaille.com/sold/product_info.php?products_id=8542. British Council. "Justice Sector Development Programme." Accessed November 2, 2023. http://www.britishcouncil.org/partner/track-record/justice-sector-development-programme.

Brown, David. "On the Category 'Civilised' in Liberia and Elsewhere." *Journal of Modern African Studies* 20, no. 2 (1982): 287–303.

Brown, George William. *The Economic History of Liberia*. Gainesville, FL: Associated Publishers, 1941.

Brubaker, Rogers. *Citizenship and Nationhood in France and Germany*. Cambridge, MA: Harvard University Press, 1992.

Bryant, Antony. "The Grounded Theory Method." In *Reviewing Qualitative Research in the Social Sciencs*, edited by Audrey A. Trainer and Elizabeth Graue. New York and London: Routledge, 2013. 120–136.

Bryman, Alan. *Social Research Methods*. Oxford: Oxford University Press, 2016.

Bryman, Alan, and Bob Burgess, eds. *Analyzing Qualitative Data* London and New York: Routledge, 2002.

Bull, Hedley. *The Anarchical Society: A Study of Order in World Politics.* New York: Columbia University Press, 1977.

Burayidi, Michael A. *Multiculturalism in a Cross-National Perspective.* Lanham, MD: University of America Press, 1997.

Burnside, Craig, and David Dollar. "Aid, Policies and Growth." *American Economic Review* 90, no. 4 (2000): 847–868.

Busia, Kofi Abrefa. *Africa in Search of Democracy.* Santa Barbara, CA: Praeger, 1967.

Buzan, Barry. "From International System to International Society: Structural Realism and Regime Theory Meet the English School." *International Organization* 47, no. 3 (1993): 327–352.

Cabinet du Premier Ministre, République de Côte d'Ivoire. "Communique du Porte-Parole du Premier Ministre (01/050308)." March 6, 2008.

Calderisi, Robert. *The Trouble with Africa: Why Foreign Aid Isn't Working.* New York: Palgrave-MacMillan, 2006.

Caplan, Richard. "International Authority and Statebuilding: The Case of Bosnia and Herzegovina." *Global Governance* 10, no. 1 (2004): 53–65.

Carothers, Thomas. "The 'Sequencing' Fallacy." *Journal of Democracy* 18 (2007): 12–27.

Center on International Cooperation. *Annual Review of Global Peace Operations 2008.* Boulder, CO: Lynne Rienner, 2008.

Center on International Cooperation. *Annual Review of Global Peace Operations 2010.* Boulder, CO: Lynne Rienner, 2010.

Center on International Cooperation. *Annual Review of Global Peace Operations 2012.* Boulder, CO: Lynne Rienner, 2012.

Chabal, Patrick. "The Quest for Good Government and Development in Africa: Is NEPAD the Answer?" *International Affairs* 78, no. 3 (2002): 447–462.

Chabal, Patrick, and Jean-Pascal Daloz. *Africa Works: Disorder as Political Instrument.* Bloomington: Indiana University Press, 1999.

Chafer, Tony. *The End of Empire in French West Africa: France's Successful Decolonization?* Gordonsville, VA: Berg, 2002.

Chandler, David. "Peacebuilding as Statebuilding." In *Peacebuilding: The Twenty Years' Crisis, 1997–2017,* edited by David Chandler, 69–94. London: Palgrave Macmillan, 2017.

Charley, Joseph P. C., and Freida I. M'Cormack. *Becoming and Remaining a 'Force for Good'—Reforming the Police in Post-conflict Sierra Leone.* Brighton, UK: Institute of Development Studies, 2011.

Cheeseman, Nic. *Democracy in Africa: Successes, Failures, and the Struggle for Political Reform.* Cambridge, UK: Cambridge University Press, 2015.

Chelpi, Magali L. B. *Militarized Youths in Western Côte d'Ivoire: Local Processes of Mobilization, Demobilization, and Related Humanitarian Interventions (2002–2007).* Leiden, NL: African Studies Centre, 2011.

Cheru, Fantu. *The Silent Revolution in Africa: Debt, Development and Democracy.* London: Zed, 1989.

Chesterman, Simon. *You, the People: The United Nations, Transitional Administration, and Statebuilding.* New York: Oxford University Press, 2005.

China-Africa Development Fund. "China-Africa Development Fund." Accessed October 17, 2023. http://en.cadfund.com.

China Development Bank. "CAD Fund." Accessed January 12, 2024. http://en .cadfund.com/.

Chirot, Daniel. "The Debacle in Côte d'Ivoire." *Journal of Democracy* 17, no. 2 (2006): 63–77.

Choi, Y. J., SRSG, and UNOCI. "Statement of the Certification of the Result of the Second Round of the Presidential Election Held on 28 November 2010." United Nations, December 3, 2010.

Clapham, Christopher S. "The Global-Local Politics of State Decay." In *When States Fail: Causes and Consequences*, edited by Robert Rotberg. Princeton, NJ: Princeton University Press, 2004.

Clapham, Christopher S. *Africa and the International System: The Politics of State Survival.* New York: Cambridge University Press, 2002.

Clapham, Christopher S., ed. *African Guerrillas.* Bloomington: Indiana University Press, 1998.

Clapham, Christopher S. *Private Patronage and Public Power: Political Clientelism in the Modern State.* London: Pinter, 1982.

Clough, Michael. *Free at Last? U.S. Policy Toward Africa and the End of the Cold War.* New York: Council on Foreign Relations Press, 1992.

CNN. "Thousands Cheer U.S. Troops in Liberia." *CNN World*, August 14, 2003. http://edition.cnn.com/2003/WORLD/africa/08/14/us.liberia/index.html.

Cohen, Anthony P. *The Symbolic Construction of Community.* London: Tavistock, 1985.

Cohen, Roberta, and Francis Mading Deng. *Masses in Flight: The Global Crisis of Internal Displacement.* Washington, DC: Brookings Institution, 1998.

Coleman, James S. "Nationalism in Tropical Africa." *American Political Science Review* 48, no. 2 (1954): 404–426.

Coleman, James S. *Nigeria: Background to Nationalism.* Berkeley: University of California Press, 1958.

Collier, Paul. "Aid 'Dependency': A Critique." *Journal of African Economies* 8, no. 4 (1999): 528–545.

Collier, Paul, and Anke Hoeffler. "Greed and Grievance in Civil War." *Oxford Economic Papers* 56, no. 4 (2004): 563–595.

Collier, Paul, and Anke Hoeffler. "On the Incidence of Civil War in Africa." *Journal of Conflict Resolution* 46, no. 1 (2002): 13–28.

Collier, Paul, and Anke Hoeffler. "Resource Rents, Governance, and Conflict." *Journal of Conflict Resolution* 49, no. 4 (2005): 625–633.

Collier, Paul, and Anthony J. Venables. "Rethinking Trade Preferences: How Africa Can Diversify its Exports." *World Economy* 30, no. 8 (2007): 1326–1345.

Colombant, Nico, and Guillaume Michel. "Gbagbo Speech Divides Ivoirians." *Voice of America*, October 31, 2009. https://www.voanews.com/a/a-13-2006-12-20-voa26/319336.html.

Colvin, Christopher J. "'Brothers and Sisters, Do Not Be Afraid of Me': Trauma, History and the Therapeutic Imagination in the New South Africa." In *Contested Pasts: The Politics of Memory*, edited by Katharine Hodgkin and Susannah Radstone. New York: Routledge, 2003.

Commission Electorale Indépendante de Côte d'Ivoire. "CEI." Accessed October 14, 2023. http://www.ceici.org/elections/ci/index.php.

Commission for Africa. "Our Common Interest: Report of the Commission for Africa." Council on Foreign Relations, 2005.

Commission for Africa. "Still Our Common Interest: Commission for Africa Report." Council on Foreign Relations, 2010.

Commission on Human Security. *Human Security Now.* New York: United Nations Publications, 2003.

Commonwealth Heads of Government. "The Edinburgh Communiqué." Commonwealth Secretariat, London, 1998.

Comte, Auguste. *Auguste Comte and Positivism: The Essential Writings.* New Brunswick, NJ: Transaction, 1975.

Conciliation Resources. "The Liberian Peace Process 1990–1996." *Accord: An International Review of Peace Initiatives* 1, no. 1 (1996).

Conklin, Alice L. *A Mission to Civilize: The Republican Idea of Empire in France and Africa.* Palo Alto, CA: Stanford University Press, 1997.

Conteh-Morgan, Earl, and Shireen Kadivar. "Ethnopolitical Violence in the Liberian Civil War." *Journal of Conflict Studies* 15, no 1 (1995): 30–44.

Conway, Patrick. "IMF Lending Programs: Participation and Impact." *Journal of Development Economics* 45, no. 2 (1994): 365–391.

Cooper, Andrew Fenton, and Agata Antkiewicz, eds. *Emerging Powers in Global Governance: Lessons From the Heiligendamm Process.* Waterloo Ontario: Wilfrid Laurier University Press, 2008.

Cooper, Frederick. "Africa and the World Economy." *African Studies Review* 24, no. 2–3 (1981): 1–86.

Cooper, Frederick. *Decolonization and African Society: The Labor Question in French and British Africa.* New York: Cambridge University Press, 1996.

Corey, Allison, and Sandra F. Joireman. "Retributive Justice: The Gacaca Courts in Rwanda." *African Affairs* 103, no. 410 (2004): 73–89.

Coulibaly, Loucoumane, and Ange Aboa. "Ivory Coast Opposition Says Third Term for Ouattara Would Destabilise Country." Reuters, August 7, 2020. https://www.reuters.com/article/us-ivorycoast-politics/ivory-coast-opposition-says-third-term-for-ouattara-would-destabilise-country-idUSKCN2531QD.

Council of Ministers. Decisions Adopted by the Sixty-Sixth Ordinary Session of the Council of Ministers. Organization of African Unity, Harare, ZW, May 28–31, 1997.

Crawford, Neta. *Argument and Change in World Politics: Ethics, Decolonization, and Humanitarian Intervention*. Cambridge: University Press Cambridge, 2002.

Crook, Richard C. "Patrimonialism, Administrative Effectiveness and Economic Development in Côte d'Ivoire." *African Affairs* 88, no. 351 (1989): 205–228.

Crook, Richard C. "Politics, the Cocoa Crisis, and Administration in Côte d'Ivoire." *Journal of Modern African Studies* 28, no. 4 (1990): 649–669.

Crowder, Michael. "Indirect Rule: French and British Style." *Journal of the International Africa Institute* 34, no. 3 (1964): 197–205.

Crowder, Michael. *West Africa Under Colonial Rule*. Evanston, IL: Northwestern University Press, 1968.

Crowder, Michael, and Obara Ikime. *West African Chiefs: Their Changing Status Under Colonial Rule and Independence*. New York: Africana Publishing, 1970.

Cruise O'Brien, Donal B. "A Lost Generation? Youth Identity and State Decay in West Africa." In *Postcolonial Identities in Africa*, edited by Richard Werbner and Terence Ranger. London: Zed, 1996.

Cupitt, Don. *After God: The Future of Religion*. New York: Basic Books, 1997.

Dahl, Robert. *Polyarchy: Participation and Opposition*. New Haven, CT: Yale University Press, 1971.

Daley, Patricia. "Population Displacement and the Humanitarian Aid Regime: The Experience of Refugees in East Africa." In *Mobile Africa: Changing Patterns of Movement in Africa and Beyond*, edited by Mirjam de Bruijn, Rijk Adrianus van Dijk, and Dick Foeken. Leiden, NL: Brill, 2001.

Daniel, Donald C. F., Patricia Taft, and Sharon Wiharta. *Peace Operations: Trends, Progress, and Prospects*. Washington, DC: Georgetown University Press, 2007.

Daou, Awa Faye. "Sierra Leone: An Election without Violence." *ISS Today*, February 27, 2013. Institute for Security Studies. https://issafrica.org/iss-today/sierra-leone-an-election-without-violence.

Davidson, Basil. *The Black Man's Burden: Africa and the Curse of the Nation-State*. New York: Times Press, 1993.

Dawisha, Karen, and Bruce Parrott. *Russia and the New States of Eurasia: The Politics of Upheaval*. New York: Cambridge University Press, 1994.

Death, Carl. "An Introduction to Africa and the World." In *The African Affairs Reader: Key Texts in Politics, Development, and International Relations*, edited by Nic Cheeseman, Lindsay Whitfield, and Carl Death. Oxford: Oxford University Press, 2017.

Decalo, Samuel. "The Process, Prospects, and Constraints of Democratization in Africa." *African Affairs* 91, no. 362 (1992): 7–35.

Delacroix, Jacques, and Charles C. Ragin. "Structural Blockage: A Cross-National Study of Economic Dependency, State Efficacy, and Underdevelopment." *American Journal of Sociology* 86, no. 6 (1981): 1311–1347.

Delanty, Gerard, and Krishan Kumar. *The SAGE Handbook of Nations and Nationalism*. Thousand Oaks, CA: Sage, 2006.

Denney, Lisa. *Justice and Security Reform: Development Agencies and Informal Institutions in Sierra Leone*. New York: Routledge, 2014.

Denney, Lisa. "Reducing Poverty with Teargas and Batons: The Security–Development Nexus in Sierra Leone." *African Affairs* 110, no. 439 (2011): 275–294.

Den Tuinder, Bastiaan A. *Côte d'Ivoire, the Challenge of Success: Report of a Mission Sent to the Ivory Coast by the World Bank*. Baltimore, MD: Johns Hopkins University Press, 1978.

Department for International Development. "Justice Sector Development Programme (GB-1-104594)." Accessed January 9, 2024. https://www.britishcouncil .org/partner/track-record/justice-sector-development-programme.

Devex. "Germany Cancels Liberia's Debts." *Newswire Newsletter*, February 15, 2007. https://www.devex.com/news/germany-cancels-liberia-s-debts-50223.

de Waal, Alex. "Mission without End? Peacekeeping in the African Political Market Place." *International Affairs* 85, no. 1 (2009): 99–113.

Diamond, Larry. *Class, Ethnicity and Democracy in Nigeria: The Failure of the First Republic*. Syracuse, NY: Syracuse University Press, 1988.

Diamond, Larry. "Class Formation in the Swollen African State." *Journal of Modern African Studies* 25, no. 4 (1987): 567–596.

Diehl, Paul F., Daniel Druckman, and James Wall. "International Peacekeeping and Conflict Resolution: A Taxonomic Analysis with Implications." *Journal of Conflict Resolution* 42, no. 1 (1998): 33–55.

Diène, Doudou. *Report of the Independent Expert on the Situation of Human Rights in Côte d'Ivoire*. United Nations, Geneva, June 24, 2013.

Dobbins, James F., John G. McGinn, Keith Crane, Seth G. Jones, Rollie Lal, Andrew Rathmell, Rachel M. Swanger, and Anga R. Timilsina. *America's Role in Nation-Building: From Germany to Iraq*. Santa Monica, CA: RAND, 2003.

Dorman, Andrew. *Blair's Successful War: British Military Intervention in Sierra Leone*. Burlington, VT: Ashgate, 2009.

Dowyaro, E. T. "ECOMOG Operations in West Africa: Principles and Praxis." In *Monograph 44: Boundaries of Peace Support Operations*. Pretoria, ZA: Institute for Security Studies, 2000.

Doyle, Mark. "No Rush to Military Intervention in Côte d'Ivoire." *BBC News*, December 31, 2010. http://www.bbc.co.uk/news/world-africa-12096437.

Dozon, Jean-Pierre. "La Côte d'Ivoire entre démocratie, nationalisme et ethnonationalisme." *Politique Africaine* 78, no. 2 (2000): 45–62.

Duffield, Mark. *Global Governance and the New Wars: The Merging of Development and Security*. London: Zed, 2014.

Dunn, D. Elwood. *Liberia and the United States During the Cold War: Limits of Reciprocity*. New York: Palgrave-Macmillan, 2009.

Dunning, Thad. "Conditioning the Effects of Aid: Cold War Politics, Donor
    Credibility, and Democracy in Africa." *International Organization* 58, no. 2 (2004):
    409–423.

Du Pisani, Jacobus A., and Kwang-Su Kim. "Establishing the Truth about the
    Apartheid Past: Historians and the South African Truth and Reconciliation
    Commission." *African Studies Quarterly* 8, no. 1 (2004): 77–95.

Durkheim, Emile. *Emile Durkheim: Selected Writings*. Cambridge, UK: Cambridge
    University Press, 1972.

Easterly, William. "What Did Structural Adjustment Adjust? The Association of
    Policies and Growth with Repeated IMF and World Bank Adjustment Loans."
    Journal of Development Economics 76, no. 1 (2005): 1–22.

Ebo, Adedeji. "The Challenges and Lessons of Security Sector Reform in Post-
    conflict Sierra Leone: Analysis." *Conflict, Security & Development* 6, no. 4 (2006):
    481–501.

Economic Community of West African States (ECOWAS). "Final Communiqué."
    Ministers of Foreign Affairs meeting, Conakry, GN, June 26, 1997.

Elbadawi, E., and N. Sambanis. "Why Are There So Many Civil Wars in Africa?
    Understanding and Preventing Violent Conflict." *Journal of African Economies* 9,
    no. 3 (2000): 244–269.

Elkins, Zachary, and John Sides. "Can Institutions Build Unity in Multiethnic
    States?" *American Political Science Review* 101, no. 4 (2007): 693–708.

Elliott, Jennifer A. *An Introduction to Sustainable Development*. New York: Routledge,
    2006.

Ellis, Stephen. "Liberia 1989–1994: A Study of Ethnic and Spiritual Violence." *African
    Affairs* 94, no. 375 (1995): 165–197.

Ellis, Stephen. *The Mask of Anarchy: The Destruction of Liberia and the Religious
    Dimension of an African Civil War*. New York: New York University Press, 1999.

Elster, Jon, Claus Offe, and Ulrich K. Preuss. *Instiutional Design in Post-Communist
    Societies: Rebuilding the Ship at Sea*. New York: Cambridge University Press, 1998.

Eluwa, G. I. C. "Background to the Emergence of the National Congress of British
    West Africa." *African Studies Review* 14, no. 2 (1971): 205–218.

Ero, Comfort. "ECOWAS and the Subregional Peacekeeping in Liberia." *Journal of
    Humanitarian Assistance*, 2, no 4 (1995).

Europa Publications. *Africa South of the Sahara*. London: Psychology Press, 2004.

Europa Publications. *The Europa World Year Book 2004*, vol. 1. London: Routledge,
    2004.

European Union. Generalised Scheme of Preferences (GSP). Accessed December 20,
    2023. https://trade.ec.europa.eu/access-to-markets/en/content/generalised
    -scheme-preferences-gsp.

European Union. Proposal for a Regulation of the European Parliament and of the
    Council: Applying a Scheme of Generalized Tariff Preferences. United Nations,
    Brussels, October 5, 2011.

Evans, Peter B., Dietrich Rueschemeyer, and Theda Skocpol, eds. *Bringing the State Back In.* Cambridge, UK: Cambridge University Press, 1985.

Evenson, Elizabeth M. "Truth and Justice in Sierra Leone: Coordination between Commission and Court." *Columbia Law Review* (2004): 730–767.

Extractive Industries Transparency Initiative. "EITI Implementation." Accessed January 12, 2024. https://eiti.org/.

Fambul Tok. "Home Page." Accessed January 12, 2024. http://www.fambultok.org.

Fanon, Frantz. *Toward the African Revolution: Political Essays.* New York: New Grove, 1988.

Fassbender, Bardo. *The United Nations Charter as the Constitution of the International Community.* Leiden, NL: Matinus Nijhoff, 2009.

Fauré, Yves. "Democracy and Realism: Reflections on the Case of Côte d'Ivoire." *Africa: Journal of the International African Institute* 63, no. 3 (1993): 313–329.

Fearon, James D. "International Financial Institutions and Economic Policy Reform in Sub-Saharan Africa." *Journal of Modern African Studies* 26, no. 1 (1988): 113–137.

Ferguson, James. *Global Shadows: Africa in the Neoliberal World Order.* Durham, NC: Duke University Press, 2006.

Fessy, Thomas. "Côte d'Ivoire: Life Inside Ouattara's Hotel." *BBC News*, December 23, 2010. http://www.bbc.co.uk/news/world-africa-12068131.

Fierens, Jacques. "*Gacaca* Courts: Between Fantasy and Reality." *Journal of International Criminal Justice* 3, no. 4 (2005): 896–919.

Finer, Samuel E. "The One-Party Regimes in Africa: Reconsiderations." *Government and Opposition* 2, no. 4 (1967): 491–509.

Finnemore, Martha. *National Interests in International Society.* Ithaca, NY: Cornell University Press, 1996.

Firmin-Sellers, Kathryn. "Institutions, Context, and Outcomes: Explaining French and British Rule in West Africa." *Comparative Politics*, 32, no. 3 (2000): 253–272.

Fisher, Humphrey J. "Elections and Coups in Sierra Leone, 1967." *Journal of Modern African Studies* 7, no. 4 (1969): 611–636.

Forde, Daryll, and Phyllis Mary Kaberry. *West African Kingdoms in the Nineteenth Century.* New York: Oxford University Press, 1967.

Foreign Policy. "Special Report: 2010 Failed States Index—Interactive Map and Rankings." 2010. Accessed January 12, 2024. https://foreignpolicy.com/2010/06/16/2010-failed-states-index-interactive-map-and-rankings/.

Forst, Rainer. "The Basic Right to Justification: Towards a Constructivist Concept of Human Rights." *Constellations: An International Journal of Critical and Democratic Theory* 6, no. 1 (1999): 35–60.

Foulkes, Imogen. "Côte d'Ivoire: UN Warns of Forgotten Humanitarian Crisis." *BBC News*, March 22, 2011. http://www.bbc.co.uk/news/world-africa-12827243.

Fraenkel, Merran. *Tribe and Class in Monrovia.* London: Oxford University Press, 1964.

Francis, David J. "Torturous Path to Peace: The Lomé Accord and Postwar Peacebuilding." *Sierra Leone Security Dialogue* 31, no. 3 (2000): 357–373.

Franck, Thomas M. "Legitimacy in the International System." *American Journal of International Law* 82, no. 4 (1988): 705–759.

Frazer, Elizabeth. *The Problems of Communitarian Politics Unity and Conflict*. Oxford: University Press, 2000.

Fukuyama, Francis. "Building Democracy After Conflict: Stateness First." *Journal of Democracy* 16, no. 1 (2005): 84–88.

Fukuyama, Francis. "The Imperative of Statebuilding." *Journal of Democracy* 15, no. 2 (2004): 17–31.

Fukuyama, Francis. *Statebuilding: Governance and World Order in the 21st Century*. Ithaca, NY: Cornell University Press, 2004.

Gaanderse, Miranda, and Kristen Valasek, eds. *The Security Sector and Gender in West Africa: A Survey of Police, Defense, Justice and Penal Services in ECOWAS States*. Geneva: DCAF, 2011.

Gann, Lewis H., and Peter Duignan, eds. *Colonialism in Africa, 1870–1960*. London: Cambridge University Press, 1975.

Gberie, Lansana. *A Dirty War in West Africa: The RUF and the Destruction of Sierra Leone*. Bloomington: University of Indiana Press, 2005.

Gberie, Lansana. "The Special Court for Sierra Leone Rests—for Good." *Africa Renewal*, April 2014. http://www.un.org/africarenewal/magazine/april-2014 /special-court-sierra-leone-rests-%E2%80%93-good.

Gberie, Lansana. "Truth and Justice on Trial in Liberia." *African Affairs* 107, no. 428 (2008): 455–465.

Gbla, Osman. "Security Sector Reform under International Tutelage in Sierra Leone," *International Peacekeeping* 13, no. 1 (2006): 78–93.

Geertz, Clifford. *Old Societies and New States: The Quest for Modernity in Asia and Africa*. Ontario: Free Press of Glencoe, 1963.

Gegout, Catherine, *Why Europe Intervenes in Africa: Security, Prestige, and the Legacy of Colonialism*. Hurst, 2017.

Gellar, Sheldon. *Statebuilding and Nation-Building in West Africa*. Bloomington: International Development Research Center, Indiana University, 1972.

Geschiere, Peter. *The Perils of Belonging: Autochthony, Citizenship, and Exclusion in Africa and Europe*. Chicago: University of Chicago Press, 2009.

Ghani, Ashraf, and Clare Lockhart. *Fixing Failed States: A Framework for Rebuilding a Fractured World*. Oxford: Oxford University Press, 2008.

Giddens, Anthony. *The Nation-State and Violence: Volume Two of a Contemporary Critique of Historical Materialism*. Cambridge: Polity, 1996.

Giddings, Bob, Bill Hopwood, and Geoff O'Brien. "Environment, Economy, and Society: Fitting them Together into Sustainable Development." *Sustainable Development* 10, no. 4 (2002): 187–196.

Gilchrist, Alison. *A Well-Connected Community: A Net Working Approach to Community Development*. Bristol, UK: Policy, 2004.

Glaser, Barney G., and Anselm L. Strauss. *The Discovery of Grounded Theory: Strategies for Qualitative Research*. New Brunswick, NJ: AldineTransaction, 1967.

Goldstein, Andrea, Nicolas Pinaud, Helmut Reisen, and Xiaobao Chen. "The Rise of China and India: What's in it for Africa?" Organization for Economic Cooperation and Development Centre, 2006.

Goodin, Robert E. *The Theory of Institutional Design*. New York: Cambridge University Press, 1996.

Goody, Jack. "Feudalism in Africa?" *Journal of African History* 4, no. 1 (1963): 1–18.

Goulding, Marrack. "The United Nations and Conflict in Africa since the Cold War." *African Affairs* 98, no. 391 (1999): 155–166.

Gouvernement de Côte d'Ivoire. "Conseil des Ministres: L'election presidentielle fixee au 29 novembre 2009," May 14, 2009. https://www.gouv.ci/_actualite-article.php?d=1&recordID=690&p=51.

Government of Sierra Leone. Human Rights Commission of Sierra Leone Act of 2004, August 20, 2004.

Grier, Robin M. "Colonial Legacies and Economic Growth." *Public Choice* 98, no. 3-4 (1999): 317–335.

Gros, Jean-Germain. "Towards a Taxonomy of Failed States in the New World Order: Decaying Somalia, Liberia, Rwanda and Haiti." *Third World Quarterly* 17, no. 3 (1996): 455–471.

Gross, Feliks. *Citizenship and Ethnicity: the Growth and Development of a Democratic Multiethnic Institution*. Oxford: Greenwood, 1999.

Group of 77. *Declaration of the South Summit*. Group of 77 South Summit, Havana, CU, April 10–14, 2000.

Guéhenno, Jean-Marie. *The End of the Nation-State*. Translated by Victoria Elliott. Minneapolis: University of Minnesota Press, 1995.

Hale, William, and Eberard Kienle, eds. *After the Cold War: Security and Democracy in Africa and Asia*. London and New York: I. B. Tauris, 1998.

Hamber, Brandon, and Richard A. Wilson. "Symbolic Closure Through Memory, Reparation and Revenge in Post-Conflict Societies." *Journal of Human Rights* 1, no. 1 (2002): 35–53.

Hameiri, Shahar. "Capacity and its Fallacies: International Statebuilding as State Transformation." *Millenium: Journal of International Studies* 38, no. 1 (2009): 55–81.

Handel, Michael I. *Weak States in the International System*. London: Frank Cass, 1990.

Hansen, Thomas Blom, and Finn Stepputat, eds. *States of Imagination: Ethnographic Explorations of the Postcolonial State*. Durham, NC: Duke University Press, 2001.

Harbeson, John Willis, and Donald S. Rothchild, eds. *Africa in World Politics: Post-Cold War Challenges*. Boulder, CO: Westview, 1995.

Hargreaves, John D. *Prelude to the Partition of West Africa*. New York: Macmillan, 1963.

Hargreaves, John D. *West Africa: The Former French States*. Englewood Cliffs, NJ: Prentice-Hall, 1967.

Harris, David. "From Warlord to Democratic President: How Charles Taylor Won the 1997 Liberian Elections." *Journal of Modern African Studies* 37, no. 3 (1999): 431–455.

Harrison, Graham. *The World Bank and Africa: The Construction of Governance States.* New York: Routledge, 2004.

Harrold, Peter, Malathi Jayawickrama, and Deepak Bhattasali. *Practical Lessons for Africa from East Asia in Industrial and Trade Policies.* Washington, DC: World Bank, 1996.

Harsch, Ernest. "Accumulators and Democrats: Challenging State Corruption in Africa." *Journal of Modern African Studies* 31, no. 1 (1993): 31–48.

Havard, Jean-François. "Tuer les 'Pères des Indépendances?' Comparaison de Deux Générations Politiques Post-Indépendances au Sénégal et en Côte d'Ivoire." *Revue Internationale de Politique Comparée* 16, no. 2 (2009): 315–331.

Hecht, Robert M. "The Ivory Coast Economic 'Miracle': What Benefits for Peasant Farmers?" *Journal of Modern African Studies* 21, no.1 (2008): 25–53.

Hegre, Håvard. "Toward a Democratic Civil Peace? Democracy, Political Change, and Civil War, 1816–1992." *American Political Science Review* 95, no.1 (2002): 33–48.

Heller, Peter S. "Pity the Finance Minister: Issues in Managing a Substantial Scaling Up of Aid Flows." International Monetary Fund Working Paper 05/180, 2005.

Hensel, Howard M. *Sovereignty and the Global Community: The Quest for Order in the International System.* Aldershot, Hants, England and Burlington, VT: Ashgate, 2004.

Herder, Johann G. *Reflections on the Philosophy of the History of Man.* Chicago: University of Chicago Press, 1968.

Hirsch, John. *Sierra Leone: Diamonds and the Struggle for Democracy.* Boulder, CO: Lynne Rienner, 2001.

Hobsbawm, Eric. *On History.* London: Weidenfeld and Nicolson, 1997.

Hodgkin, Thomas. *Nationalism in Colonial Africa.* New York: New York University Press, 1957.

Hodgkin, Thomas, and Ruth Schachter. *French-Speaking West Africa in Transition.* New York: Carnegie Endowment for International Peace, 1961.

Hoerder, Dirk, Christiane Harzig, and Adrian Shubert. *The Historical Practice of Diversity: Transcultural Interactions from the Early Modern Mediterranean to the Postcolonial World.* New York: Berghahn, 2003.

Hoffman, Danny. "The Civilian Target in Sierra Leone and Liberia: Political Power, Military Strategy, and Humanitarian Intervention." *African Affairs* 103, no. 411 (2004): 211–226.

Hoffmann, Stanley, Robert C. Johansen, James T. Sterba, and Raimo Vayrynen. *The Ethics and Politics of Humanitarian Intervention.* Notre Dame, IN: University of Notre Dame Press, 1996.

Holmes, Stephen. "Constitutionalism, Democracy, and State Decay." In *Deliberative Democracy and Human Rights*, edited by Harold Hongju Koh and Ronald C. Slye. New Haven, CT: Yale University Press, 1999.

Holsoe, Svend E. "A Study of the Relations Between Settlers and Indigenous Peoples in Western Liberia, 1821–1847." *African Historical Studies* 4, no. 2 (1971): 331–362.

Holzgrefe, J. L., and Robert Owen Keohane. *Humanitarian Intervention: Ethical, Legal, and Political Dilemmas.* New York: Cambridge University Press, 2008.

Hope, Kempe R., and Bornwell C. Chikulo, eds. *Corruption and Development in Africa: Lessons From Country Case-Studies.* New York: Palgrave, 2000.

Hopkins, Antony G. *An Economic History of West Africa.* New York: Longman, 1973.

Hopwood, Bill, Mary Mellor, and Geoff O'Brien. "Sustainable Development: Mapping Different Approaches." *Sustainable Development* 13, no. 1 (2005): 38–52.

Horowitz, Donald L. *Ethnic Groups in Conflict.* Berkeley: University of California Press, 1985.

Huang, Reyko. *The Wartime Origins of Democratization: Civil War, Rebel Governance, and Political Regimes.* Cambridge, UK: Cambridge University Press, 2016.

Human Rights Commission of Sierra Leone. "Vision, Mission and Core Values." Accessed December 22, 2024. https://www.hrc-sl.org/Mission_Vision.aspx.

Ihonvbere, Julius O. "Are Things Falling Apart? The Military and the Crisis of Democratization in Nigeria." *Journal of Modern African Studies* 34, no. 2 (1996): 193–225.

Ikegami, Eiko. *The Taming of the Samurai: Honorific Individualism and the Making of Modern Japan.* Cambridge, MA: Harvard College, 1995.

Ikelegbe, Augustine. "Civil Society, Oil and Conflict in the Niger Delta Region of Nigeria: Ramifications of Civil Society for a Regional Resource Struggle." *Journal of Modern African Studies* 39, no. 3 (2001): 437–469.

Institute for Economics and Peace. "Positive Peace Report 2019: Analysing the Factors that Sustain Peace," October 2019. https://www.economicsandpeace.org /wp-content/uploads/2020/08/PPR-2019-web.pdf.

International Center for Transitional Justice. "Ignoring Cries for Justice, South Africa Fails Victims of Apartheid-era Crimes." January 7, 2013. https://www.ictj .org/news/ignoring-cries-justice-south-africa-fails-victims-apartheid-era-crimes.

International Commission on Intervention and State Sovereignty "The Responsibility to Protect: Report of the International Commission on Intervention and State Sovereignty." International Development Research Centre, 2001.

International Criminal Court. "Registry." Accessed January 12, 2024. https://www .icc-cpi.int/about/registry/default.

International Criminal Court. "Rome Statute of the International Criminal Court: Article 11," International Criminal Court, 1998,

International Crisis Group. "Côte d'Ivoire: Les demi-mesures ne suffiront pas." *International Crisis Group Africa* 33 (2005).

International Crisis Group. "Côte d'Ivoire: The War Is Not Yet Over." *International Crisis Group Africa* 72 (2003).

International Monetary Fund. "Communiqué of the Interim Committee of the Board of Governors of the International Monetary Fund." Press release no. 96/49, 1996.

International Monetary Fund. *Côte d'Ivoire: Poverty Reduction Strategy Paper.* Country report no. 09/156, 2009.

International Monetary Fund. "Côte d'Ivoire Reaches Decision Point Under the Enhanced HIPC Debt Relief Initiative." Press release no. 09/104, 2009.

International Monetary Fund. "Debt Relief Under Heavily Indebted Poor Countries (HIPC) Initiative," 2011. Accessed November 2, 2023. http://www.imf.org /external/np/exr/facts/hipc.htm.

International Monetary Fund. "The Extended Credit Facility," 2012. Accessed November 2, 2023. http://www.imf.org/external/np/exr/facts/ecf.htm.

International Monetary Fund. "Good Governance: The IMF's Role." Washington, DC, 1997.

International Monetary Fund. "IMF and World Bank Support Sierra Leone's Completion Point under the Enhanced HIPC Initiative and Approve Debt Relief under the Multilateral Debt Relief Initiative." Press release no. 06/286, 2006.

International Monetary Fund. "IMF Approves in Principle US$169 Million Three-Year PRGF Arrangement for Sierra Leone." Press release no. 01/39, 2001.

International Monetary Fund. "IMF Executive Board Completes Sixth and Final Review Under Sierra Leone's PRGF Arrangement and Approves US$20.8 Million Disbursement." Press release no. 05/130, 2005.

International Monetary Fund. *International Financial Statistical Yearbook, 1994.* International Financial Statistics, 1994.

International Monetary Fund. *International Financial Statistics Yearbook, 2011.* International Financial Statistics, July 19, 2011.

International Monetary Fund. *Liberia: Poverty Reduction Strategy Paper.* Country report no. 08/219, 2008.

International Monetary Fund. Sierra Leone: Poverty Reduction Strategy Paper. June 10, 2005 (stock no. 1SLEEA2005002). https://www.imf.org/en/Publications/CR /Issues/2016/12/31/Sierra-Leone-Poverty-Reduction-Strategy-Paper-18313.

International Monetary Fund. "The Multilateral Debt Relief Initiative," 2012. Accessed January 12, 2024. http://www.imf.org/external/np/exr/facts/mdri .htm.

International Trade Centre. "Programme for Building African Capacity for Trade: PACT II: Programme Logical Framework." June 2009.

International Trade Centre. "Programme for Building African Capacity for Trade: PACT II: Programme Summary." March 2009. https://www.intracen.org /uploadedFiles/intracenorg/Content/About_ITC/Where_are_we_working /Multi-country_programmes/Pact_II/PACT%20II%20Programme %20Summary-June09.pdfInternational Trade Centre. "Regional Trade for Global

Gains: Programme for Building African Capacity for Trade." Accessed March 29, 2010.

International Trade Centre. "Women Access! Export Success: The Voice For African Businesswomen." Accessed January 12, 2024. https://intracen.org/news-and -events/news/women-access-export-success-the-voice-of-african-business -women.

Jackson, Robert H., and Carl G. Rosberg. *Personal Rule in Black Africa: Prince, Autocrat, Prophet, Tyrant.* Berkeley: University of California Press, 1982.

Jackson, Robert H., and Carl G. Rosberg. "Why Africa's Weak States Persist: The Empirical and the Juridical in Statehood." *World Politics* 35, no.1 (1982): 1–24.

Jalloh, Alusine, and Toyin Falola. *The United States and West Africa: Interactions and Relations.* Rochester, NY: University of Rochester Press, 2008.

Jalloh, Charles Chernor. "Special Court for Sierra Leone: Achieving Justice?" *Michigan Journal of International Law* 32, no. 3 (2011): 395–460.

Jalloh, Charles C., and Alhagi Marong. "Ending Impunity: The Case for War Crimes Trials in Liberia." *African Journal of Legal Studies* 1, no. 2 (2005): 53–79.

James, Alan. *Sovereign Statehood: The Basis of International Society.* East Melbourne, AU: Allen and Unwin, 1986.

James, John. "Cocoa Farmers: A Mirror to Côte d'Ivoire's Divisions." *BBC News,* November 25, 2010. http://www.bbc.co.uk/news/mobile/world-africa-11832982.

Jennings, Ray Salvatore. "The Road Ahead: Lessons in Nation Building from Japan, Germany, and Afghanistan for Postwar Iraq." *Peaceworks* 49, United States Institute of Peace (April 2003).

Jensen, Nathan, and Leonard Wantchekon. "Resource, Wealth, and Political Regimes in Africa." *Comparative Political Studies* 37, no. 7 (2004): 816–841.

Jessop, Bob. "The State and Statebuilding." In *The Oxford Handbook of Political Institutions,* edited by R. A. W. Rhodes, Sarah A. Binder, and Bert A. Rockman. Oxford: Oxford University Press, 2006.

Johansen, Robert. "Limits and Opportunities in Humanitarian Intervention." In *The Ethics and Politics of Humanitarian Intervention,* edited by Stanley Hoffman, Robert C. Johansen, James P. Sterba, and Raimo Väyrynen. Notre Dame, IN: University of Notre Dame Press, 1996.

Johnston, Harry. *Liberia Vol. 1.* London: Hutchinson, 1906.

Jones, Brian. "Graduation—The End and Beginning of a Journey." Foreign and Commonwealth Office, October 8, 2013. http://blogs.fco.gov.uk/ukinsierraleone /2013/10/08/graduation-the-end-and-beginning-of-a-journey/.

Jones, Bruce D. *Peacemaking in Rwanda: The Dynamics of Failure.* Boulder, CO: Lynn Rienner, 2001.

Jones, Sue. "The Analysis of Depth Interviews." In *Applied Qualitative Research,* edited by Robert Walker. Aldershot: Gower, 1985.

Jordan, Tim. "Community, Everyday and Space." In *Understanding Everyday Life,* edited by Tony Bennett and Diane Watsons. Oxford: Wiley-Blackwell, 2002.

Joseph, Richard A. "Class, State, and Prebendal Politics in Nigeria." *Commonwealth & Comparative Politics* 21, no. 3 (1983): 21–38.

Kabia, John. *Humanitarian Intervention and Conflict Resolution in West Africa: From ECOMOG to ECOMIL*. Burlington, VT: Ashgate, 2009.

Kaldor, Mary. *New and Old Wars: Organized Violence in a Global Era*. Stanford, CA: Stanford University Press, 2007.

Kandeh, Jimmy D. "Politicization of Ethnic Identities in Sierra Leone." *African Studies Review* 35, no. 1 (1992): 81–99.

Kandeh, Jimmy D. "What Does the 'Militariat' Do When It Rules? Military Regimes: The Gambia, Liberia and Sierra Leone." *Review of African Political Economy* 23, no. 69 (1996): 387–404.

Kanya-Forstner, A. S. *The Conquest of Western Sudan: A Study in French Military Imperialism*. New York: Cambridge, 1969.

Karnga, Abayomi Wilfrid. *History of Liberia*. Liverpool: D. H. Tyte, 1926.

Kayode-Fayemi, J. "Governing Insecurity in Post-Conflict States: The Case of Sierra Leone and Liberia." In *Reform and Reconstruction of the Security Sector*, edited by Alan Bryden and Heiner Hänggi. New Brunswick, NJ: Transaction, 2004.

Keen, David. *Conflict and Collusion in Sierra Leone*. Oxford: James Currey, 2005.

Kelsall, Tim. "Truth, Lies, Ritual: Preliminary Reflections on the Truth and Reconciliation Commission in Sierra Leone." *Human Rights Quarterly* 27, no. 2 (2005): 361–391.

Kemp, Kenneth W., and Charles Hudlin. "Civil Supremacy over the Military: Its Nature and Limits." *Armed Forces and Society* 19, no. 1 (1992): 7–26.

Keohane, Robert Owen, ed. *Power and Governance in a Partially Globalized World*. London: Routledge, 2002.

Keohane, Robert Owen. *International Institutions and State Power: Essays in International Relations Theory*. Boulder, CO: Westview, 1989.

Kerr, Rachel, and Jessica Lincoln. *The Special Court for Sierra Leone: Outreach, Legacy and Impact (Final Report)*. War Crimes Research Group, King's College, London, 2008.

Khadiagala, Gilbert M. *Meddlers or Mediators? African Interveners in Civil Conflicts in Eastern Africa*. Leiden, NL: Martinus Nijhoff, 2007.

Khobe, Mitikishe M. "The Evolution and Conduct of ECOMOG Operations in West Africa." In *Monograph 44: Boundaries of Peace Support Operations*. Pretoria, ZA: Institute for Security Studies, 2000.

Kieh, George Klay. *The First Liberian Civil War: The Crises of Underdevelopment*. New York: Peter Lang, 2008.

Kiely, Ray. "Neoliberalism Revised? A Critical Account of the World Bank Concepts of Good Governance and Market Friendly Intervention." *Capital & Class* 22, no. 1 (1998): 63–88.

Kilson, Martin L. "Authoritarian and Single-Party Tendencies in African Politics." *World Politics* 15, no. 2 (1963): 262–294.

King, Gary, Robert O. Keohane, and Sidney Verba. *Designing Social Inquiry: Scientific Inference in Qualitative Research*. Princeton, NJ: Princeton University Press, 1994.

Klein, Martin A. *Slavery and Colonial Rule in French West Africa*. New York: Cambridge University Press, 1998.

Klinghoffer, Arthur J. *Soviet Perspectives on African Socialism*. Rutherford, NJ: Dickinson University Press, 1969.

Klugman, Jeni. *Human Development Report 2009: Overcoming Barriers—Human Mobility and Development*. United Nations Development Programme, 2009.

Kondeh, Al-Hassan K. "Formulating Sierre Leone's Defence White Paper." In *Security System Transformation in Sierra Leone, 1997–2007*, edited by Paul Jackson and Peter Albrecht. London: International Alert, 2008.

Koné, Amadou K. *Houphouët-Boigny et la Crise Ivoirienne*. Paris: Karthala, 2003.

Kpundeh, Sahr J. "The Fight Against Corruption in Sierra Leone." In *Curbing Corruption: Toward a Model for Building National Integrity*, edited by Rick Stapenhurst and Sahr J. Kpundeh. Washington, DC: World Bank, 1999.

Kumar, Krishna, ed. *Rebuilding Societies After Civil War: Critical Roles for International Assistance*. Boulder, CO: Lynne Rienner, 1997.

Laitin, David. "Somalia: Civil War and International Intervention." In *Civil Wars, Insecurity, and Intervention*, edited by Barbara F. Walter and Jack Snyder. New York: Columbia University Press, 1999.

Land, Isaac, and Andrew Schocket. "New Approaches to the Founding of the Sierra Leone Colony, 1786–1808." *Journal of Colonialism and Colonial History* 9, no. 3 (2008).

Langer, Arnim. "Horizontal Inequalities and Violent Group Mobilization in Côte d'Ivoire." *Oxford Development Series* 33, no. 1 (2005): 25–45.

Langley, J. Ayodele. *Pan-Africanism and Nationalism in West Africa, 1900–1945: A Study in Ideology and Social Classes*. Gloucestershire, UK: Clarendon, 1973.

Leonard, David K., and Scott Straus. *Africa's Stalled Development: International Causes and Cures*. Boulder, CO: Lynne Rienner, 2003.

Levinson, David. *Ethnic Groups Worldwide: A Ready Reference Handbook*. Phoenix: Oryx, 1998.

Leys, Collin. "The 'Overdeveloped' Post Colonial State: A Re-evaluation." *Review of African Political Economy* 3, no. 5 (1976): 39–48.

Liberia. Comprehensive Peace Agreement Between the Government of Liberia and the Liberians United for Reconciliation and Democracy (LURD) and the Movement for Democracy in Liberia (MODEL) and Political Parties. Accra, August 18, 2003. https://www.usip.org/publications/2003/08/peace-agreements -liberia.

Liberia. Cotonou Agreement, 25 July 1993, https://www.refworld.org/docid /3ae6b5796.html.

Library of Congress. "Maps of Liberia, 1830–1870." Accessed October 28, 2023. https:// www.loc.gov/collections/maps-of-liberia-1830-to-1870/about-this-collection/.

Linton, Suzannah. "Cambodia, East Timor and Sierra Leone: Experiments in International Justice." *Criminal Law Forum* 12, no. 2 (2001): 185–246.

Linz, Juan J. "Statebuilding and Nation Building." *European Review* 1, no. 4 (1993): 355–369.

Linz, Juan J., and Alfred Stepan. *Problems of Democratic Transition and Consolidation: Southern Europe, South America, and Post-Communist Europe*. Baltimore, MD: Johns Hopkins University Press, 1996.

Lipschutz, Ronnie D. "Reconstructing World Politics: The Emergence of Global Civil Society." *Millenium: Journal of International Studies* 21, no. 3 (1992): 389–420.

Lipset, Seymour Martin. "Some Social Requisites of Democracy: Economic Development and Political Legitimacy." *American Political Science Review* 53, no. 1 (1959): 69–105.

Lubeck, Paul M. *The African Bourgeoisie: Capitalist Development in Nigeria, Kenya, and the Côte d'Ivoire*. Boulder, CO: Lynne Rienner, 1987.

Luke, David F., and Stephen P. Riley. "The Politics of Economic Decline in Sierra Leone." *Journal of Modern African Studies* 27, no. 1 (1989): 133–141.

Lustick, Ian S., Dan Miodownik, and Roy J. Eidelson. "Secessionism in Multicultural States: Does Sharing Power Prevent or Encourage It?" *American Political Science Review* 98, no. 2 (2004): 209–229.

MacFarlane, S. Neil, and Yuen Foong-Khong. *Human Security and the UN: A Critical History*. Bloomington: Indiana University Press, 2006.

MacQueen, Norrie. *United Nations Peacekeeping in Africa Since 1960*. London: Longman, 2002.

Macrae, Joanna, ed. "The New Humanitarianisms: A Review of Trends in Global Humanitarian Action." *Humanitarian Policy Group, Overseas Development Institute* 11 (2002).

Madhav, Joshi, Jason Michael Quinn, and Patrick M. Regan. "Annualized implementation data on comprehensive intrastate peace accords, 1989–2012." Journal of Peace Research 52(4) (2015): 551-562.

Magee, James S. "What Role for ECA? Or Pan-Africanism Revisited." *Journal of Modern African Studies* 9, no.1 (2008): 73–89.

Mahoney, James. *Colonialism and Postcolonial Development: Spanish America in Comparative Perspective*. Cambridge, UK: Cambridge University Press, 2010.

Mahoney, James. "Comparative-Historical Methodology." *Annual Review of Sociology* 30, no.1 (2004): 81–101

Malan, Mark. "Security and Military Reform." In *Monograph 80: Sierra Leone: Building the Road to Recovery*. Pretoria, ZA: Institute for Security Studies, 2003.

Malan, Mark. *Security Sector Reform in Liberia: Mixed Results from Humble Beginnings*. Carlisle, PA: US Army Strategic Studies Institute, 2008.

Malan, Mark, Phenyo Rakate, and Angela McIntyre. *Monograph 68: Peacekeeping in Sierra Leone: UNAMSIL Hits the Home Straight*. Pretoria, ZA: Institute for Security Studies, 2002.

Malinowski, Bronislaw. *A Scientific Theory of Culture and Other Essays*. Chapel Hill: UNC Press, 2015.

Mamdani, Mahmood. "Amnesty or Impunity? A Preliminary Critique of the Report of the Truth and Reconciliation Commission of South Africa (TRC)." *Diacritics* 32, no. 3 (2002): 32–59.

Mamdani, Mahmood. *Citizen and Subject: Contemporary African and the Legacy of Late Colonialism*. Princeton, NJ: Princeton University Press, 1996.

Management Systems International. Accessed December 31, 2008. http://www .msiworldwide.com.

Mandela, Nelson. *Long Walk to Freedom: The Autobiography of Nelson Mandela*. Boston: Little Brown, 1994.

Marais, Hein. *South Africa: Limits to Change: The Political Economy of Transition*. New York: Zed, 2001.

Marshall, Thomas Humphrey. *Citizenship and Social Class and Other Essays*. Cambridge, UK: Cambridge University Press, 1950.

Marshall, Thomas Humphrey. *Class, Citizenship, and Social Development*. New York: Greenwood, 1964.

Marshall-Fratani, Ruth. "The War of 'Who is Who': Autochthony, Nationalism, and Citizenship in the Ivoirian Crisis." *African Studies Review* 49, no. 2 (2006): 9–44.

Marte, Fred. *Political Cycles in International Relations: The Cold War and Africa, 1945–1990*. Amsterdam: Paul Publishing Consortium, 1994.

Mayotte, Judy. "Civil War in Sudan: The Paradox of Human Rights and National Sovereignty." *Journal of International Affairs* 47, no. 2 (1994): 497–524.

Mayson, Dew Tuan-Wleh, and Amos Sawyer. "Labour in Liberia." *Review of African Political Economy* 14, no. 14 (1979): 3–15.

Mazrui, Ali A. *The African Condition: A Political Diagnosis*. Cambridge, UK: Cambridge University Press, 1980.

Mbaku, John M. "African Elections in 2015: A Snapshot for Côte d'Ivoire, Tanzania, Burkina Faso and Sudan." In *Foresight Africa: Top Priorities for the Continent in 2015*, edited by Africa Growth Initiative. Washington, DC: Brookings Institution, 2015.

Mbaku, John M. *Corruption in Africa: Causes, Consequences, and Cleanups*. Lanham, MD: Lexington, 2007.

Mbembe, Achille. *On the Postcolony*. Berkeley: University of California Press, 2001.

McGowan, Patrick J. "Economic Dependence and Economic Performance in Black Africa." *Journal of Modern African Studies* 14, no. 1 (1976): 25–40.

McPherson, John Hanson Thomas. *History of Liberia*. Whitefish, MT: Kessinger, 2004.

Médard, J. F. "Patrimonialism, Neo-Patrimonialism, and the Study of the Postcoloniaal State in Sub-Saharan Africa." In *Political Corruption: Concepts and Contexts*, edited by Arnold J. Heidenheimer and Michael Johnston. New Brunswick, NJ: Transaction, 2009.

Medie, Peace A. *Global Norms and Local Action: The Campaigns to End Violence against Women in Africa.* New York: Oxford University Press, 2020.

Mehler, Andreas. "Peace and Power Sharing in Africa: A Not so Obvious Relationship." *African Affairs* 108, no. 432 (2009): 453–473.

Mehta, Pratap Bhanu. "From State Sovereignty to Human Security (via Institutions?)." *Humanitarian Intervention* 47 (2006): 257–285.

Meierhenrich, Jens. "Forming States After Failure." In *When States Fail: Causes and Consequences*, edited by Robert I. Rotberg. Princeton, NJ: Princeton University Press: 2004.

Meyer, John W., John Boli, George M. Thomas, and Francisco O. Ramirez. "World Society and the Nation-State." *American Journal of Sociology* 103, no. 1 (1997): 144–181.

Mgbeoji, Ikechi. *Collective Insecurity: The Liberian Crisis, Unilateralism, and Global Order.* Vancouver: University of British Columbia Press, 2003.

Mieth, Friederike, "Bringing Justice and Enforcing Peace? An Ethnographic Perspective on the Impact of the Special Court for Sierra Leone." *International Journal of Conflict and Violence* 7, no. 1 (2013): 10–12.

Migdal, Joel S. *Strong Societies and Weak States: State-Society Relations and State Capabilities in the Third World.* Princeton, NJ: Princeton University Press, 1988.

Miles, Matthew B., and A. Michael Huberman. *Qualitative Data Analysis: An Expanded Sourcebook.* Thousand Oaks: Sage, 1994.

Miller, Scott L. "History on the Cheap: Using the Online Archive to Make Historicists out of Undergrads." *Pedagogy* 5, no. 1 (2005): 97–101.

Milliken, Jennifer. *State Failure, Collapse and Reconstruction.* Malden, MA: Blackwell, 2003.

Mills, Kurt, and Richard Norton. "Refugees and Security in the Great Lakes Region of Africa." *Civil Wars* 5, no. 1 (2002): 1–26.

Mo Ibrahim Foundation. "The Ibrahim Index, 2011." Accessed October 17, 2023. https://mo.ibrahim.foundation/iiag.

Mo Ibrahim Foundation. "Ibrahim Prize for Achievement in African Leadership." Accessed October 17, 2023. https://mo.ibrahim.foundation/prize.

Montana, Ismael. *The Abolition of Slavery in Ottoman Tunisia.* Tampa: University Press of Florida, 2013.

Moore, Barrington. *Social Origins of Dictatorship and Democracy: Lord and Peasant in the Making of the Modern World.* Boston, MA: Beacon, 1966.

Moran, Mary H. *Liberia: The Violence of Democracy.* Philadelphia: University of Pennsylvania Press, 2006.

Morris Jr., Sahr. "Sierra Leone: U.S$15 Million Economic Reform Package." allAfrica, May 22, 2009. https://allafrica.com/stories/200905220668.html.

Moss, Todd, Gunilla Pettersson, and Nicolas Van de Walle. "An Aid-Institutions Paradox? A Review Essay on Aid Dependency and Statebuilding in Sub-Saharan Africa." Mario Einaudi Center for International Studies, 2005.

Moyo, Dambisa. *Dead Aid: Why Aid Is Not Working and How There Is a Better Way for Africa*. New York: Farrar, Straus and Giroux, 2010.

Muekalia, Domingos Jardo. "Africa and China's Strategic Partnership." *African Security Review* 3, no. 1 (2004): 5–11.

Munene, Macharia, J. D. Olewe Nyunya, and Korwa Gombe Adar. *The United States and Africa: From Independence to the End of the Cold War*. Nairobi: East African Educational Publishers, 1995.

Murison, Katherine. *Africa South of the Sahara*. London: Europa Publications, 2004.

Musah, Abdel-Fatau. "A Country Under Siege: State Decay and Corporate Military Intervention in Sierra Leone." In *Mercenaries: An African Security Dilemma*, edited by Abdel-Fatau Musah and J. Kayode-Fayemi. Sterling, VA: Pluto, 2000.

Mutwol, Julius. *Peace Agreements and Civil Wars in Africa: Insurgent Motivations, State Responses and Third Party Peacemaking in Liberia, Rwanda, and Sierra Leone*. Amherst, NY: Cambria, 2009.

Nagel, Joane, and Susan Olzak. "Ethnic Mobilization in New and Old States: An Extension of the Competition Model." *Social Problems* 30, no. 2 (1982): 127–143.

Nandjui, Pierre. *Houphouët-Boigny: l'homme de la France en Afrique*. Paris: L'Harmattan, 1995.

Nardin, Terry. "The Moral Basis of Humanitarian Intervention." *Ethics and International Affairs* 16, no. 1 (2002): 57–70.

Nation Master. "Economy > GDP > Per capita: Countries Compared." Accessed October 23, 2023. http://www.nationmaster.com/graph/eco_gdp_percap -economy-gdp-per-capita&date='964.

Ndegwa, Stephen N. *The Two Faces of Civil Society: NGOs and Politics in Africa*. West Hartford, CT: Kumarian, 1996.

N'Diaye, Boubacar. *The Challenge of Institutionalizing Civilian Control: Botswana, Côte d'Ivoire*. Lanham, MD: Lexington, 2001.

N'Diaye, Boubacar. "The Military in the Politics of West Africa." *Journal of Political and Military Sociology* 28, no. 2 (Winter 2000): 187–190.

N'Diaye, Boubacar, Abdoulaye Saine, and Matturin Houngnikpo. *Not Yet Democracy: West Africa's Slow Farewell to Authoritarianism*. Durham, NC: Carolina Academic Press, 2005.

New Dawn. "Liberia: Disabled Press for Reparation from Government." allAfrica, April 17, 2013. https://allafrica.com/stories/201304170838.html.

New Dawn. "Liberia: Police Boss Marc Amblard Sacked." allAfrica, November 28, 2011. http://allafrica.com/stories/201111280821.html.

New Humanitarian. "Côte d'Ivoire: All Sides Pledge Commitment to Peace Process Again, but Will Anything Change?" December 7, 2004. https://www .thenewhumanitarian.org/news/2004/12/07/all-sides-pledge-commitment -peace-process-again-will-anything-change.

New Humanitarian. "Côte d'Ivoire: ECOWAS Approves Beefed-Up ECOMICI Contingent." April 8, 2003. https://www.thenewhumanitarian.org/news/2003/04/08 /ecowas-approves-beefed-ecomici-contingent.

New Humanitarian. "Paving the Way for Justice in Côte d'Ivoire." July 22, 2011. http://www.irinnews.org/report/93307/analysis-paving-the-way-for-justice -in-c%C3%B4te-d-ivoire.

New Humanitarian. "War-Wounded Get Micro-Grants." November 12, 2009. http:// www.irinnews.org/report/87007/sierra-leone-war-wounded-get-micro-grants.

New Partnership for Africa's Development. "African Peer Review Mechanism (APRM)." http://www.nepad.org.

New Partnership for Africa's Development. "African Union Development Agency (AUDA-NEPAD)." December 17, 2024. http://www.nepad.org/.

New Partnership for Africa's Development. "Economic and Corporate Governance: Overview." http://www.nepad.org.

New Partnership for Africa's Development. "NEPAD: A Programme of the African Union." http://www.nepad.org.

New York Times. "World Briefing: Africa—Sierra Leone: U.N. Prosecutor Demands Body." May 14, 2003. http://www.nytimes.com/2003/05/14/world/world-briefing -africa-sierra-leone-un-prosecutor-demands-body.html?src=pm.

Niane, Djibril Tamsir, and Joseph Ki-Zerbo. *Africa from the Twelfth to the Sixteenth Century*. Oxford: James Currey, 1998.

Nkrumah, Kwame. *Neo-Colonialism: The Last Stage of Imperialism*. London: Thomas Nelson, 1965.

Non-Aligned Movement. "Declaration of the Group of 77 South Summit held in Havana from 10 to 14 April 2000." https://www.g77.org/summit/Declaration _G77Summit.htm.

Novosseloff, Alexandra. "The Many Lives of a Peacekeeping Mission: The Un Operation In Côte D'ivoire." New York: International Peace Institute, June 2018. https://www.ipinst.org/wp-content/uploads/2018/06/1806_Many-Lives-of-a -Peacekeeping-Mission.pdf.

Noy, Chaim. "Sampling Knowledge: The Hermeneutics of Snowball Sampling in Qualitative Research." *International Journal of Social Research Methodology* 11, no. 4 (2008): 327–344.

Nwajiaku, Kathryn. "The National Conferences in Benin and Togo Revisited." *Journal of Modern African Studies* 32, no. 3 (1994): 429–447.

Nwankpa, Michael. "Understanding the Local-Global Dichotomy and Drivers of the Boko Haram Insurgency." *African Conflict and Peacebuilding Review* 10, no. 2 (2020): 43–64.

Nwankwo, Basil O. *Institutional Design and Functionality of African Democracies: A Comparative Analysis of Nigeria and Uganda*. Berlin: Tenea, 2003.

Nyerere, Julius. *Freedom and Unity: Uhuru na umoja; A Selection from Writings and Speeches, 1952–65*. New York: Oxford University Press, 1967.

Nyerere, Julius. *Ujamaa: Essays on Socialism*. New York: Oxford University Press, 1968.

Nyong'o, Peter Anyang'. "Africa: The Failure of One-Party Rule." *Journal of Democracy* 3, no. 1 (1992): 90–96.

Nzongola-Ntalaja, Georges. *The Congo from Leopold to Kabila: A People's History.* London: Zed, 2002.

Obadare, Ebenezer, and Wale Adebanwi, eds. *Governance and The Crisis of Rule in Africa: Leadership in Transformation.* New York: Palgrave-Macmillan, 2016.

Obasanjo, Olusegun. "Nigeria, Africa and the World in the Next Millennium: Statement by President Olusegun Obasanjo." General Debate of the 54th Session of the United Nations General Assembly, 1999.

Obeng, Samuel. *Selected Speeches of Kwame Nkrumah.* Ghana: Afram, 1997.

O'Brien, Patricia. "Statement by Ms. Patricia O'Brien Under-Secretary-General for Legal Affairs, The Legal Counsel." Office of Legal Affairs, United Nations, New York, September 23, 2009.

Office for the Coordination of Humanitarian Affairs (OCHA), Reliefweb, "Linas-Marcoussis Agreement: Cote d'Ivoire," January 23, 2003. https://reliefweb.int /report/c%C3%B4te-divoire/linas-marcoussis-agreement-cote-divoire.

Office of the United Nations High Commissioner for Human Rights. "Lomé Declaration of July 2000 on the Framework for an OAU Response to Unconstitutional Changes of Government (AHG/Decl.5 [XXXVI])." Accessed November 3, 2023. https://www2.ohchr.org/english/law/compilation _democracy/lomedec.htm.

Office of the United States Trade Representative. "Generalized System of Preference (GSP)." Accessed February 9, 2021. https://ustr.gov/issue-areas /trade-development/preference-programs/generalized-system-preference-gsp.

Ogunbadejo, Oye. "Soviet Policies in Africa." *African Affairs* 17, no. 316 (1980): 239–244.

Olarreaga, Marcelo, and Çaglar Özden. "AGOA and Apparel: Who Capturers the Tariff Rent in the Presence of Preferential Market Access." *World Economy* 28, no. 1 (2005): 63–77.

Olivier de Sardan, Jean-Pierre. "A Moral Economy of Corruption in Africa?" *Journal of Modern African Studies* 37, no. 1 (1999): 25–52.

Olonisakin, Funmi. "Nigeria, ECOMOG, and the Sierra Leone Crisis." In *Between Democracy and Terror: The Sierra Leone Civil War,* edited by Ibrahim Abdullah. Dakar, SN: Codresia, 2004.

Olonisakin, Funmi. *Peacekeeping in Sierra Leone: The Story of UNAMSIL.* Boulder, CO: Lynne Rienner, 2008.

Omeje, Kenneth. "The State, Conflict & Evolving Politics in the Niger Delta, Nigeria," *Review of African Political Economy* 31, no. 101 (2004): 425–440.

Omotola, J. Shola. "From Political Mercenarism to Militias: The Political Origin of Niger Delta Militias." *Journal of Alternative Perspective in the Social Sciences* (2009): 91–124.

Onimode, Bade, ed. *The IMF, the World Bank and the African Debt: The Social and Political Perspectives.* London: Zed, 1989.

Oomen, Barbara. "Donor-Driven Justice and Its Discontents: The Case of Rwanda." *Development and Change* 36, no. 5 (2005): 887–910.

Organization of African Unity/African Union. "Declaration on the Principles of Governing Democratic Elections in Africa AHG/Decl. 1 (XXXVIII)." Durban, ZA, 2002.

Ottaway, Marina. "Rebuilding State Institutions in Collapsed States." *Development and Change* 33, no. 5 (2002): 1001–1023.

Otto, Dianne. "Subalternity and International Law: The Problems of Global Community and the Incommensurability of Difference." *Social & Legal Studies* 5, no. 3 (1996): 337–364.

Oyebade, Adebayo, and Abiodun Alao. *Africa after the Cold War: The Changing Perspectives on Security.* Trenton: African World Press, 1998.

Paris, Roland. *At War's End: Building Peace after Civil Conflict.* Cambridge, UK: Cambridge University Press, 2004.

Parley, Winston P. "LNP, Much Expected." *New Dawn,* June 10, 2011.

Peters, Krijn. *War and the Crisis of Youth in Sierra Leone.* Cambridge, UK: Cambridge University Press, 2011.

Pick, Susan, and Jenna T. Sirkin. *Breaking the Poverty Cycle: The Human Basis for Sustainable Development.* New York: Oxford University Press, 2010.

Pieterse, Jan Nederveen. "Deconstructing/Reconstructing Ethnicity." *Nations and Nationalism* 3, no. 3 (1997): 365–395.

Pieterse, Jan Nederveen. "Sociology of Humanitarian Intervention: Bosnia, Rwanda and Somalia Compared." *International Political Science Review* 18, no. 1 (1997): 71–93.

Poggi, Gianfranco. *The State: Its Nature, Development, and Prospects.* Palo Alto, CA: Stanford University Press, 1990.

Pomy, Matthew. "African Union Urges Members to Stand Against ICC Trials of Presidents." *The Jurist,* February 1, 2014. https://www.jurist.org/news/2014/02/african-union-urges-members-to-stand-against-icc-trials-of-presidents.

Power, Christopher, Andrew Lewis, Helen Petrie, Katie Green, Julian Richards, Mark Eramian, Brittany Chan, Ekta Walia, Isaac Sijaranamual, and Maarten de Rijke. "Improving Archaeologists' Online Archive Experiences through User-Centred Design." *Journal on Computing and Cultural Heritage* 10, no. 1 (2017): 1–20.

Power, Timothy J., and Mark J. Gasiorowski. "Institutional Design and Democratic Consolidation in the Third World." *Comparative Political Studies* 30, no. 2 (1997): 123–155.

Présidence de la République de Côte d'Ivoire. Constitution De 2000. La Deuxieme Constitution. Loi N°2000-513 DU 1 er AOÛT 2000 Portant Constitution De La Côte D'ivoire. August 1, 2000. https://www.presidence.ci/constitution-de-2000/.

Press, Robert M. "Sierra Leone's Peaceful Resistance to Authoritarian Rule." *African Conflict and Peacebuilding Review* 2, no. 1 (2012): 31–57.

Prunier, Gérard. *The Rwanda Crisis: History of a Genocide.* New York: Columbia University Press, 1997.

Przeworski, Adam. *Democracy and the Market: Political and Economic Reforms in Eastern Europe and Latin America.* Cambridge, UK: Cambridge University Press, 1991.

Puddington, Arch. *Freedom in the World 2012: The Arab Uprisings and Their Global Repercussions*. Washington, DC: Freedom Publications, 2012.

Ra'anan, Uri. "The Nation-State Fallacy." In *Conflict and Peacemaking in Multiethnic Societies*, edited by Joseph V. Montville. Lexington, MA: Lexington, 1990.

Radio France Internationale. "Côte d'Ivoire: la liste des membres de la Commission vérité et réconciliation est publiée." June 9, 2011. http://www.rfi.fr/afrique /20110905-cote-ivoire-liste-membres-commission-verite-reconciliation-est -publiee/ 06–09-2011.

Ragin, Charles C., and Lisa M. Amoroso. *Constructing Social Research: The Unity and Diversity of Method*. Thousand Oaks, CA: Pine Forge, 2011.

Rajan, Raghuram G., and Arvind Subramanian. "What Undermines Aid's Impact on Growth?" National Bureau of Economic Research Working Paper 11657, 2005.

Randall, Vicky, and Lars Svåsand. "Political Parties and Democratic Consolidation in Africa." *Democratization* 9, no. 3 (2002): 30–52.

Rapley, John. *Ivoirien Capitalism: African Entrepreneurs in Côte d'Ivoire*. Boulder, CO: Lynne Reiner, 1993.

Rashid, Ishmail. "Subaltern Reactions, Lumpen, Students and the Left." *Africa Development* 22, no. 3–4 (1997): 19–43.

Rauber, Andreas, Andreas Aschenbrenner, and Oliver Witvoet. "Austrian Online Archive Processing: Analyzing Archives of the World Wide Web." *International Conference on Theory and Practice of Digital Libraries*. Berlin: Springer, 2002.

Reece, Katherine E. *West African Kingdoms: Empires of Gold and Trade*. Vero Beach, FL: Rourke, 2005.

Reno, William. "African Weak States and Commercial Alliances." *African Affairs* 96, no. 383 (1997): 165–185.

Reno, William. "Anti-corruption Efforts in Liberia: Are They Aimed at the Right Targets?" *International Peacekeeping* 15, no. 3 (2008): 387–404.

Reno, William. *Corruption and State Politics in Sierra Leone*. New York: Cambridge University Press, 2008.

Reno, William. "Reinvention of an African Patrimonial State: Charles Taylor's Liberia." *Third World Quarterly* 16, no. 1 (1995): 109–120.

République de Côte d'Ivoire, Loi n° 61–416 du 14 Décembre 1961 Portant Code de la Nationalité Ivoirienne, modifiée par la loi n° 72–852 du 21 décembre 1972.

Republic of Côte d'Ivoire, Constitution of 2000. Accessed January 10, 2024. https:// www.constituteproject.org/constitution/Cote_DIvoire_2000.

Republic of Côte d'Ivoire. "Foire aux Questions." *Audience Foraines*, November 2007. http://www.audiencesforaines.gouv.ci/foire.php.

Republic of Côte d'Ivoire. Office of the President of the Republic. Ordonnance N° 2011-167 Du 13 Juillet 2011 Portant Creation, Attributions, Organisation Et Fonctionnement De La Commission Dialogue, Verite Et Reconciliation. July 13, 2011.

Republic of Côte d'Ivoire. "Pretoria Agreement on the Peace Process in the Côte d'Ivoire." Pretoria, ZA, 2005.

Republic of Côte d'Ivoire. Remise du rapport de la CDVR: Allocution de SEM Alassane Ouattara. December 15, 2014. https://www.icc-cpi.int/sites/default/files /RelatedRecords/CR2015_04388.PDF.

Republic of Côte d'Ivoire. Remise du rapport final de la CDVR: Charles Konan Banny Recommande Des Journées Nationales De La Mémoire Et Du Pardon. December 15, 2015. https://www.gouv.ci/_actualite-article.php?d=1&recordID=5153&p=296.

Republic of Liberia. "Agreement on Ceasefire and Cessation of Hostilities between the Government of the Republic of Liberia and Liberians United for Reconciliation and Democracy and the Movement for Democracy in Liberia." United States Institute of Peace, June 17, 2003. https://www.usip.org/sites/default/files/file /resources/collections/peace_agreements/liberia_ceasefire_06172003.pdf.

Republic of Sierra Leone. "Abidjan Peace Accord." Sierra Leone Web, November 30, 1996. http://www.sierra-leone.org/abidjanaccord.html.

Republic of Sierra Leone. "Abuja Ceasefire Agreement." Sierra Leone Web, November 10, 2000. http://www.sierra-leone.org/ceasefire1100.html.

Republic of Sierra Leone. Agenda for Change: Second Poverty Reduction Strategy Paper (PRSP II), 2008-2012, Freetown, June 2008, https://www.undp.org/sites/g /files/zskgke326/files/2022-05/agenda_for_change.pdf.

Republic of Sierra Leone. Interim Poverty Reduction Strategy Paper. Freetown, June 2001, https://www.imf.org/external/np/prsp/2001/sle/01/063101.pdf.

Republic of Sierra Leone. "Lomé Peace Agreement." Sierra Leone Web, June 3, 1999. http://www.sierra-leone.org/lomeaccord.html.

Republic of Sierra Leone. Ministry of Finance. Accessed November 3, 2023. https:// mof.gov.sl.

Republic of South Africa. Office of the President. National Unity and Reconciliation Act (no. 34 of 1995, July 26, 1995). http://www.justice.gov.za/legislation/acts/1995 -034.pdf.

Republic of South Africa. Truth and Reconciliation Commission. "Welcome to the Official Truth and Reconciliation Commission Website." Accessed October 20, 2023. https://www.justice.gov.za/trc.

République de Côte d'Ivoire. "Accord Accra II (Ghana) sur la Crise en Côte d'Ivoire." Accra, GH, March 7, 2003.

République de Côte d'Ivoire. "Institut National de la Statistique." Accessed November 3, 2023. http://www.ins.ci/stats/data/DEMOGRAP.html.

Residual Court of Sierra Leone. "Mandate of the Residual Special Court for Sierra Leone." Residual Court of Sierra Leone. Accessed February 25, 2021. https://rscsl .org/the-rscsl/mandate-of-the-residual-special-court-for-sierra-leone/.

Resnick, Danielle, and Nicolas Van de Walle, eds. *Democratic Trajectories in Africa: Unravelling the Impact of Foreign Aid*. Oxford: Oxford University Press, 2013.

Reuters. "Curfew in Sierra Leone Town after Rioting, Shooting over Ebola Case." October 21, 2014. https://www.reuters.com/article/us-health-ebola -leone/curfew-in-sierra-leone-town-after-rioting-shooting-over-ebola-case -idUSKCN0IA2AY20141021.

Reuters. "The Military Mission in Sierra Leone." May 30, 2007. https://www.medal-medaille.com/sold/product_info.php?products_id=8542.

Richards, Paul. "The Political Economy of Internal Conflict in Sierra Leone." Netherlands Institute of International Relations, Clingendael Conflict Research Unit, 2003.

Richards, Paul. "To Fight or to Farm? Agrarian Dimensions of the Mano River Conflicts (Liberia and Sierra Leone)." *African Affairs* 104, no. 417 (2005): 571–590.

Riddell, J. Barry. "Things Fall Apart Again: Structural Adjustment Programmes in Sub-Saharan Africa." *Journal of Modern African Studies* 30, no. 1 (1992): 53–68.

Riddell, Roger. *Aid in the 21st Century.* ODS Discussion Paper Series 6. United Nations, New York, 1996.

Riley, Stephen P. "The Democratic Transition in Africa: An End to the One-Party State?" *Conflict Studies* 245 (1991): 1–37.

Riley, Steve, and Max Sesay. "Sierra Leone: The Coming Anarchy?" *Review of African Political Economy* 22, no. 63 (1995): 121–126.

Rivkin, Arnold. *Nation-Building in Africa: Problems and Prospects.* Piscataway, NJ: Rutgers University Press, 1969.

Roberts, Adam. "The Road to Hell: A Critique of Humanitarian Intervention." *Harvard International Review* 16, no.1 (1993): 10–13.

Rodney, Walter. "How Europe Underdeveloped Africa." In *Beyond Borders: Thinking Critically About Global Issues*, edited by Paula S. Rothenberg. New York: Worth, 2006.

Ross, Michael. "How Do Natural Resources Influence Civil War? Evidence from Thirteen Cases." *International Organization* 58, no. 1 (2004): 35–68.

Ross, Michael L. "What Do We Know about Natural Resources and Civil War?" *Journal of Peace Research* 41 (2004): 337–356.

Rotberg, Robert I. "Failed States, Collapsed States, Weak States: Causes and Indicators." In *State Failure and State Weakness in a Time of Terror*, edited by Robert I. Rotberg. Washington, DC: Brookings Institution, 2003.

Rotberg, Robert I. "The Failure and Collapse of Nation-States: Breakdown, Prevention, and Repair." In *When States Fail: Causes and Consequences*, edited by Robert I. Rotberg. Princeton, NJ: Princeton University Press, 2004.

Ruggie, John Gerard. "Territoriality and Beyond: Problematizing Modernity in International Relations." *International Organization* 47, no.1 (1993): 139–174.

Sachs, Jeffrey, and John W. McArthur. "Moyo's Confused Attack on Aid for Africa." *HuffPost*, May 27, 2009. http://www.huffingtonpost.com/jeffrey-sachs/moyos-confused-attack-on_b_208222.html.

Sachs, Jeffrey D., and Andrew M. Warner. "Sources of Slow Growth in African Economies." *Journal of African Economies* 6, no. 3 (1997): 335–376.

Saha, Santosh C., ed. *The Politics of Ethnicity and National Identity.* New York: Peter Lang, 2007.

Saldaña, Johnny. "Coding and Analysis Strategies." *The Oxford Handbook of Qualitative Research.* New York: Oxford University Press, 2014.

Sandbrook, Richard. *The Politics of African Economic Stagnation.* New York: Cambridge University Press, 1986.

Sandbrook, Richard. "The State and Economic Stagnation in Tropical Africa." *World Development* 14, no. 3 (1986): 319–332.

Sangmpam, S. N. "Neither Soft nor Dead: The African State Is Alive and Well." *African Studies Review* 36, no. 2 (1993): 73–94.

Sankoh, Foday Saybana. "Footpaths to Democracy: Toward a New Sierra Leone." Revolutionary United Front Manifesto, 1995.

Santiso, Carlos. "Good Governance and Aid Effectiveness: The World Bank and Conditionality." *Georgetown Public Policy Review* 7, no. 1 (2001): 1–22.

SAPA-AFP. "Ouattara Camp Urges Ivoirians to Help Take Government Sites." *Times Live, Africa,* December 14, 2010. https://www.timeslive.co.za/news/africa /2010-12-14-ouattara-camp-urges-Ivoirians-to-help-take-government-sites/.

Sarkin, Jeremy. "The Tension Between Justice and Reconciliation in Rwanda: Politics, Human Rights, Due Process and the Role of the *Gacaca* Courts in Dealing with the Genocide." *Journal of African Law* 45, no. 2 (2001): 143–172.

Saul, John S. "The State in Post-Colonial Societies: Tanzania." *Socialist Register* 11 (1974): 349–371.

Savage, Sanusi, and Paul K. Kargbo. "Sierra Leone Conflict Victims Receive Reparations." International Organization for Migration, October 4, 2013. https:// www.iom.int/news/sierra-leone-conflict-victims-receive-reparations.

Sawyer, Amos. "Proprietary Authority and Local Administration in Liberia." In *The Failure of the Centralized State: Institiutions and Self-Governance in Africa,* edited by James Wunsch and Dele Oluwu. Boulder, CO: Westview, 1990.

Sawyer, Amos. "Violent Conflicts and Governance Challenges in West Africa: The Case of the Mano River Basin Area." *Journal of Modern African Studies* 42, no. 3 (2004): 437–363.

Sawyer, Edward. "Remove or Reform? A Case for (Restructuring) Chiefdom Governance in Post-conflict Sierra Leone." *African Affairs* 107, no. 428 (2008): 387–403.

Schachter, Ruth. "Single-Party Systems in West Africa." *American Political Science Review* 55, no. 2 (1961): 294–307.

Scharf, Michael P. "The Special Court for Sierra Leone." *American Society of International Law: Insights* 5, no. 14 (2000).

Schümer, Tanja. *New Humanitarianism: Britain and Sierra Leone, 1997–2003.* New York: Palgrave Macmillan, 2008.

Schumpeter, Joseph A. *Capitalism, Socialism, and Democracy.* New York: Harper, 1942.

Schwab, Peter. "Cold War on the Horn of Africa." *African Affairs* 77, no. 306 (1978): 6–20.

Search for Common Ground. "Funders and Donors." Search for Common Ground. Accessed December 31, 2008. http://www.sfcg.org/sfcg/sfcg_ funders.html.

Search for Common Ground. "Our Mission and Vision." Accessed December 31, 2008. http://www.sfgc.org/sfcg/sfc g_mission.html.

Sesay, Amadu, Charles Ukeje, Osman Gbla, and Olawale Ismail. *Post War Regimes and State Reconstruction in Liberia and Sierra Leone*. Dakar, SN: Codresia, 2009.

Sesay, Max. "'Bringing Peace to Liberia.'" In *The Liberian Peace Process 1990–1996*, edited by J. Armon and A. Carl. London: Conciliation Resources, 1996.

Sesay, Max. "Security and State-Society Crises in Sierra Leone and Liberia." In *Globalization, Human Security, and the African Experience*, edited by Caroline Thomas and Peter Wilkin. Boulder, CO: Lynne Rienner, 1999.

Sesay, Terence. "Liberia Supreme Court: TRC Ban on Politicians Unconstitutional." *African Press International*, January 27, 2011. https://africanpress.wordpress.com/2011/01/27/liberia-supreme-court-trc-ban-on-politicians-unconstitutional.

Seton-Watson, Hugh. *Nations and States: An Enquiry into the Origins of Nations and the Politics of Nationalism*. New York: Routledge, 2019.

Shaw, Rosalind. "Memory Frictions: Localizing the Truth and Reconciliation Commission in Sierra Leone." *International Journal of Transitional Justice* 1, no. 2 (2007): 183–207.

Shaw, Rosalind. *Rethinking Truth and Reconciliation Commissions: Lessons from Sierra Leone (Special Report No. 130)*. Washington, DC: United States Institute of Peace, 2005.

Shearn, Rick. "In Sierra Leone—IMATT to ISAT." *Sierra Express Media*, March 29, 2013. https://sierraexpressmedia.com/?p=54524.

Shillington, Kevin, ed. *Encyclopedia of African History Volume 1: A-G*. New York: Taylor and Francis, 2005.

Shout-Africa. "Liberia's US$194.1 Million Debt Cancelled by Japan." Shout-Africa, March 11, 2011. http://www.shout-africa.com/news/liberia%E2%80%99s-us194-1-millin-debt-cancelled-by-japan/.

Sibthorpe, A. B. C. *The History of Sierra Leone*. London: Frank Cass, 1970.

Sierra Leone Police. *Annual Crime Management Statistical Report for January-December, 2012* Freetwon, Sierra Leone.

Skinner, Elliott P. *Beyond Constructive Engagement: United States Foreign Policy Toward Africa*. New York: Paragon House, 1986.

Skocpol, Theda. *States and Social Revolutions: A Comparative Analysis of France, Russia, and China*. Cambridge, UK: Cambridge University Press, 1979.

Skocpol, Theda, and Margaret Somers. "The Uses of Comparative History in Macrosocial Inquiry." *Comparative Studies in Society and History* 22, no. 2 (1980): 174–197.

Skowronek, Stephen. *Building a New American State: The Expansion of National Administrative Capacities, 1877–1920*. New York: Cambridge University Press, 1982.

Smith, Anthony D. *Nationalism and Modernism: A Critical Survey of Recent Theories of Nations and Nationalism*. London: Routledge, 1998.

Smith, Anthony D., ed. *Nationalist Movements*. London: Macmillan, 1976.

Smith, Gerald H. "The Dichotomy of Politics and Corruption in a Neopatrimonial State: Evidence from Sierra Leone, 1968–1993." *A Journal of Opinion* 25, no. 1 (1997): 58–62.

Smith, Robert A. *The American Foreign Policy in Liberia: 1822–1971*. Granite Bay, CA: Providence, 1972.

Soro, Guillaume, and Serge Daniel. *Pourquoi je Suis Devenu un Rebelle: La Côte d'Ivoire au Bord du Gouffre; Entretiens avec Serge Daniel*. Paris: Hachette Littératures, 2005.

Spears, Ian. "Africa: The Limits of Power-Sharing." *Journal of Democracy* 13, no. 3 (July 2002): 123–136.

Spears, Ian. *Believers, Skeptics and Failure in Conflict Resolution*. London: Palgrave, 2019.

Spitzer, Leo. *The Creoles of Sierra Leone: Responses to Colonialism, 1870–1945*. Madison: University of Wisconsin Press, 1974.

Spruyt, Hendrik. "The End of the Empire and the Extension of the Westphalian System: The Normative Basis of the Modern State Order." *International Studies Review* 2, no. 2 (2000): 65–92.

Straus, Scott. "'It's Sheer Horror Here': Patterns of Violence during the First Four Months of Côte d'Ivoire's Post-electoral Crisis." *African Affairs* 110, no. 440 (2011): 481–489.

Straus, Scott. *The Order of Genocide: Race, Power, and War in Rwanda*. Ithaca, NY: Cornell University Press, 2013.

Strayer, Joseph R. *On the Medieval Origins of the Modern State*. Princeton, NJ: Princeton University Press, 1970.

Suberu, Rotimi. *Federalism and Ethnic Conflict in Nigeria*. Washington, DC: United States Institute of Peace, 2001.

Sunwabe Jr., Charles K. "We the Victims: Why Liberians Must Demand a War Crimes Tribunal for the Prosecution of Crimes Against Humanity." *The Perspective*, January 25, 2013.

Szeftel, Morris. "Clientelism, Corruption & Catastrophe." *Review of African Political Economy* 27, no. 85 (2000): 427–441.

Tadesse, Bedassa, and Bichaka Fayissa. "The Impact of African Growth and Opportunity Act (AGOA) on U.S. Imports from Sub-Saharan Africa (SSA)." *Journal of International Development* 20, no. 7 (2008): 920–941.

Tally, Bill, and Lauren B. Goldenberg. "Fostering Historical Thinking with Digitized Primary Sources." *Journal of Research on Technology in Education* 38, no. 1 (2005): 1–21.

Tamba. "Liberia Won't Pay Reparations to Civil War Victims." *Africa Review*. September 17, 2010.

Taori, Kamal. *Sustainable Human Development: Issues and Challenges*. New Delhi, IN: Concept, 2000.

Taylor, Charles. *Multiculturalism: Examining the Politics of Recognition*. Princeton, NJ: Princeton University Press, 1994.

Taylor, Wayne Chatfield. *Firestone Operations in Liberia*. Washington, DC: National Planning Association, 1956.

Thomas, Abdul R. "Dr Sylvia Blyden Arrested as US Government Signs Multi-Million Dollar Grant Aid with President Bio." *Sierra Leone Telegraph*, December

16, 2020. https://www.thesierraleonetelegraph.com/dr-sylvia-blyden-arrested-as-us-government-signs-multi-million-dollar-grant-aid-with-president-bio.

Thomas, Abdul R. "The Palo Conteh Treason Trial—Lesson Learnt." *Sierra Leone Telegraph*, July 5, 2020. https://www.thesierraleonetelegraph.com/the-palo-conteh-treason-trial-lesson-learnt.

Thomas, Abdul R. "President Bio Throws Insults at Britain, USA, Germany, Ireland and the EU over Rigged Election Results." *Sierra Leone Telegraph*, July 5, 2023. https://www.thesierraleonetelegraph.com/president-bio-throws-insults-at-britain-usa-germany-ireland-and-the-eu-over-rigged-election-results/.

Thomas, Abdul Rashid. "All Change in Freetown as UN closes office and IMATT becomes ISAT." *Sierra Leone Telegraph*, March 29, 2013. https://www.thesierraleonetelegraph.com/3724.

Thomas, Caroline. "Global Governance, Development and Human Security: Exploring the Links." *Third World Quarterly* 22, no. 2 (2001): 159–175.

Thomas, Dominic Richard David. *Nation-Building, Propaganda, and Literature in Francophone Africa*. Bloomington: Indiana University Press, 2002.

Thompsell, Angela. "A Brief History of The African Country of Liberia." ThoughtCo., September 9, 2020. https://www.thoughtco.com/brief-history-of-liberia-4019127#.

Thompson, Bankole. *The Constitutional History and Law of Sierra Leone (1961–1995)*. Lanham, MD: University Press of America, 1997.

Thompson, Bankole, and Gary Potter. "Governmental Corruption in Africa: Sierra Leone as a Case Study." *Crime, Law, and Social Change* 28, no. 2 (1997): 137–154.

Thompson, Virginia McLean, and Richard Adloff. *French West Africa*. Stanford, CA: Stanford University Press, 1957.

Thornhill Capital. "China's Policy Bank: China Development Bank—The Muscle behind China's Global Expansion." April 1, 2013. http://thornhillcapital.info/featured-articles/chinas-policy-bank-china-development-bank-the-muscle-behind-chinas-global-expansion.

Tice, Robert D. "Administrative Structure, Ethnicity and Nation-Building in the Côte d'Ivoire." *Journal of Modern African Studies* 12, no. 2 (1974): 211–229.

Tilly, Charles. *Big Structures, Large Processes, Huge Comparisons*. New York: Russell Sage Foundation, 2006.

Tilly, Charles. *From Mobilization to Revolution*. Reading, MA: Addison-Wesley, 1978.

Tilly, Charles. "Reflections on the History of European State-Making." In *The Formation of National States in Western Europe*, edited by Charles Tilly and Gabriel Ardant. Princeton, NJ: Princeton University Press, 1975.

Tilly, Charles. "War Making and State Making as Organized Crime." In *Bringing the State Back In*, edited by Peter Evans, Dietrich Rueschemeyer, and Theda Skocpol. Cambridge, UK: Cambridge University Press, 1985.

Tilly, Charles, and Gabriel Ardant. *The Formation of National States in Western Europe*. Princeton, NJ: Princeton University Press, 1975.

Totten, Samuel, and Eric Markusen. *Genocide in Darfur: Investigating the Atrocities in the Sudan*. New York: Routledge, 2006.

Toungara, Jeanne Maddox. "The Apotheosis of Côte d'Ivoire's Nana Houphouët-Boigny." *Journal of Modern African Studies* 28, no. 1 (1990): 23–54.

Toungara, Jeanne Maddox. "Francophone Africa in Flux: Ethnicity and Political Crisis in Côte d'Ivoire." *Journal of Democracy* 12, no. 3 (2001): 63–72.

Toyin, Falola, ed. *Africa: African History Before 1885*. Durham, NC: Academic Press, 2000.

Toyin, Falola. *The Power of African Cultures*. Rochester, NY: University of Rochester Press, 2008.

Truth and Reconciliation Commission of Liberia. "Final Report." Accessed November 3, 2023. https://web.archive.org/web/20170515044651/http://trcofliberia.org/reports/final-report.

Truth and Reconciliation Commission of Sierra Leone. *Witness to Truth: Report of the Sierra Leone Truth & Reconciliation Commission*, vol. 1, 2, 3A, and 3B (2004). Accessed November 3, 2023. https://www.sierraleonetrc.org/index.php/view-the-final-report.

Truth and Reconciliation Commission of South Africa. "Reparation & Rehabilitation Committee Transcripts, Policies & Articles." Accessed October 20, 2023. http://www.justice.gov.za/trc/reparations/index.htm.

Tuck, Christopher. "Every Car or Moving Object Gone: The ECOMOG Intervention in Liberia." *African Studies Quarterly* 4, no. 1 (2000): 1–16.

Tucker, Robert C., ed. *The Marx-Engels Reader*. New York: W. W. Norton, 1978.

Turay, Aruna. "In Sierra Leone, NaCSA Certifies Female War Victims." *Awareness Times*, March 17, 2011.

Ukeje, Charles. "Rethinking Africa's Security in the Age of Uncertain Globalisation: NEPAD and Human Security in the 21st Century." Paper submitted to the 11th CODESRIA General Assembly, Maputo, MZ, 2005.

United Nations. Agreement Between the United Nations and the Government of Sierra Leone on the Establishment of a Special Court for Sierra Leone. Freetown, SL, April 12, 2002.

United Nations. "Explorer." Accessed October 23, 2023. http://data.un.org/Explorer.aspx.United Nations. "Millennium Development Goals Indicators." http://unstats.un.org/unsd/mdg/Data.aspx.

United Nations. "Infant Mortality Rate." Accessed October 23, 2023. http://data.un.org/Data.aspx?q=infant+mortality&d=WHO&f=MEASURE_CODE%3aimr.

United Nations. "Life Expectancy." Accessed October 23, 2023. http://data.un.org/Data.aspx?q=life+expectancy&d=PopDiv&f=variableID%3a68.

United Nations. *The Millennium Development Goals Report: 2010*. 2010.

United Nations, "Mission in Liberia," accessed December 20, 2023. https://unmil.unmissions.org/.

United Nations. "Official List of MDG Indicators." United Nations Statistics Division, January 15, 2008. https://www.developmentgoals.org/About_the_goals.html.

United Nations. "Per Capita GDP at Current Prices—US Dollars." UN Data: A
    World of Information. Accessed October 12, 2023. http://data.un.org/Data
    .aspx?q=GDP+per+capita&d=SNAAMA&f=grID%3a101%3bcurrID%3aUSD
    %3bpcFlag%3a1.
United Nations. "Political and Peacebuilding Affairs: Elections." Accessed October
    17, 2023. https://dppa.un.org/en/elections.
United Nations. "Population Using Improved Drinking-Water Sources (%)."
    Accessed October 23, 2023. http://data.un.org/Data.aspx?q=drinking+water&d
    =WHO&f=MEASURE_CODE%3aWHS5_122.
United Nations. "Report of the Visit of the Peacebuilding Commission to Sierra
    Leone." February 15–20, 2013. https://www.un.org/peacebuilding/content
    /report-visit-peacebuilding-commission-sierra-leone.
United Nations. *Report of the World Commission on Environment and Development:
    Our Common Future.* UN Digital Library, 1987. Accessed November 3, 2023.
    https://digitallibrary.un.org/record/139811?ln=en.
United Nations. UN Data: A World of Information. Accessed October 12, 2023.
    http://data.un.org/Data.aspx?q=GDP+per+capita&d=SNAAMA&f=grID
    %3a101%3bcurrID%3aUSD%3bpcFlag%3a1.
United Nations. "UNMIL: Fact Sheet." Accessed October 14, 2023. https://
    peacekeeping.un.org/en/mission/unmil.
United Nations. "UN Peace-Building: An Orientation." New York, 2010.
United Nations. "We Can End Poverty: Millennium Development Goals and
    Beyond 2015." Accessed October 17, 2023. https://www.un.org/millenniumgoals.
United Nations. "World Economic and Social Survey 2010: Retooling Global
    Development 2010." Department of Economic and Social Affairs, 2010.
United Nations Commission on Human Rights. Resolution 1989/51. New York,
    March 7, 1989.
United Nations Conference on Trade and Development. *Economic Development in
    Africa: Doubling Aid: Making the 'Big Push' Work.* Geneva, 2006.
United Nations Country Team. *United Nations Development Assistance Framework
    (UNDAF) Sierra Leone 2004–2007.* Freetown, SL, 2003.
United Nations Development Fund for Women. *Women, Peace and Security:
    UNIFEM Supporting Implementation of Security Council Resolution 1325.* New York,
    2004.
United Nations Development Group. *Human Development Reports,* 1991, 1993, 2002,
    2004, 2009. Accessed October 23, 2023. http://hdr.undp.org/en/reports.
United Nations Development Group "UNDG Guidance Note to United Nations
    Country Teams on the PRSP." Final version, November 8, 2001. http://www.undg
    .org/index.cfm?P=16.
United Nations Development Program. *UNDP and Electoral Assistance: Ten Years of
    Experience.* New York, November 15, 2015. https://www.undp.org/content/undp
    /en/home/librarypage/democratic-governance/electoral_systemsandprocesses
    /undp-and-electoral-assistance-10-years-of-experience.html.

United Nations Development Programme. *Guidelines on SGBV Case Management: A Reference Handbook for the FSU.* Freetown, SL. Accessed May 10, 2022. http://www.sl.undp.org/content/dam/sierraleone/docs/focusareadocs/undp_sle _SGBVCaseManagementGuidelines.pdf.

United Nations Development Programme. *Human Development Report 1990.* Oxford: Oxford University Press, 1990.

United Nations Development Programme. *Human Development Report 1996.* Oxford: Oxford University Press, 1996.

United Nations Economic Commission for Africa. Progress in Intra-African Trade (E/ECA/CTRC/7/5). Addis Ababa, May 16, 2011.

United Nations Educational, Scientific and Cultural Organization. "Data Browser." Institute for Statistics. Accessed October 23, 2023. http://stats.uis.unesco.org/.

United Nations Educational, Scientific and Cultural Organization. "Professional Development and Access to Technical Resources." Liberia Media Centre (with support from members of Partnership for Media and Conflict Prevention in West Africa). Project PDC/51 LIR/01.

United Nations General Assembly. *Enhancing the Effectiveness of the Principle of Periodic and Genuine Elections—Report of the Secretary-General* (A/49/675). November 17, 1994.

United Nations Mission in Sierra Leone. "UNAMSIL: A Success Story in Peacekeeping." United Nations Department of Public Information: Peace and Security Section, December 2005. Accessed November 3, 2023. https://peacekeeping.un.org/mission/past/unamsil/Overview.pdf.

United Nations General Assembly. *Enhancing the Effectiveness of the Principle of Periodic and Genuine Elections* [1991] UNGA 197; A/RES/46/137 (17 December 1991). http://www.worldlii.org/int/other/UNGA/1991/197.pdf.

United Nations General Assembly. *Humanitarian Assistance and Rehabilitation for Countries and Regions—Report of the Secretary-General.* August 24, 2004.

United Nations General Assembly. International Covenant on Civil and Political Rights (Resolution 2200A [XXI]). December 16, 1996.

United Nations General Assembly. Resolution 44/146. December 15, 1989.

United Nations General Assembly. Resolution 45/150. December 18, 1990.

United Nations General Assembly. Resolution 46/137. December 17, 1991.

United Nations General Assembly. United Nations Millennium Declaration (Resolution 55/2). September 8, 2000.

United Nations General Assembly. Universal Declaration of Human Rights (Resolution 3/217A). December 10, 1948.

United Nations High Commission for Refugees. *REFWORLD: Cotonou Agreement,* July 25,1993, https://www.refworld.org/docid/3ae6b5796.html.

United Nations High Commissioner for Refugees. *Statistical Yearbook 2003: Trends in Displacement, Protection and Solutions.* Geneva, 2005.

United Nations Industrial Development Organization and United Nations Conference on Trade and Development. *Economic Development Report 2011:*

Fostering Industrial Development in Africa in the New Global Environment. New York, 2011.

United Nations in Liberia. *United Nations Development Assistance Framework (UNDAF) Liberia 2008–2012*. Monrovia, LR, 2007.

United Nations Millennium Development Goals. "Employment-to-Population Ratio, Both Sexes, Percentage." http://mdgs.un.org/unsd/mdg/SeriesDetail .aspx?srid=758.

United Nations Operation in Côte d'Ivoire. Côte d'Ivoire presidential elections October 31, 2010." October 25, 2010.

United Nations Peacekeeping. "After Action Report MINUCI Use of Pre-Mandate Commitment Authority for Rapid Deployment." Report 1, June 5, 2003.

United Nations Peacekeeping, "MINUCI: Background." Accessed October 14, 2023. https://peacekeeping.un.org/en/mission/past/minuci/background.html.

United Nations Peacekeeping. "Past Peace Operations." Accessed October 14, 2023. https://peacekeeping.un.org/en/past-peacekeeping-operations.

United Nations Peacekeeping. "United Nations Mission in Liberia." Accessed October 12, 2023. https://unmil.unmissions.org.

United Nations Peacekeeping. "UNMIL: Background." Accessed October 14, 2023. https://unmil.unmissions.org/background.

United Nations Peacekeeping. "UNMIL: DDR." Accessed October 14, 2023. https:// unmil.unmissions.org/disarmament-demobilization-and-reintegration-ddr.

United Nations Population Fund. "Worldwide Offices." Accessed November 4, 2023. http://www.unfpa.org/public/countries.

United Nations Secretary-General. "Statement Attributable to the Spokesperson for the Secretary-General on the Presidential Election in Côte d'Ivoire." December 3, 2010. https://www.un.org/sg/en/content/sg/statement/2010-12-03 /statement-attributable-spokesperson-secretary-general-presidential.

United Nations Security Council. "Accra III Agreement on Côte d'Ivoire." July 30, 2004.

United Nations Security Council. "Concerned at Delay Plans in Côte d'Ivoire Elections, Security Council, in Presidential Statement, Urges Parties to Work for Poll by Spring 2009." November 7, 2008.

United Nations Security Council. "Direct Dialogue: Ouagadougou Political Agreement." (S/2007/144) March 4, 2007. https://peaceaccords.nd.edu/wp -content/accords/Ouagadougou_Political_Agreement_OPA.pdf.

United Nations Security Council. *Final Report of the Group of Experts on Côte d'Ivoire Pursuant to Paragraph 19 of Security Council Resolution 2101 (2013)*. April 14, 2014.

United Nations Security Council. *First Report of the Secretary-General on the United Nations Operation in Côte d'Ivoire (S/2004/443)*. June 2, 2004.

United Nations Security Council. *Fourth Report of the Secretary-General on the United Nations Mission in Sierra Leone*. May 19, 2000.

United Nations Security Council. Linas-Marcoussis Agreement. January 27, 2003.

United Nations Security Council. *Nineteenth Progress Report of the Secretary-General on the United Nations Operation in Côte d'Ivoire.* January 8, 2009.

United Nations Security Council. *Ninth Report of the Secretary-General on the United Nations Mission in Sierra Leone.* March 14, 2001.

United Nations Security Council. *Report of the Secretary-General on Côte d'Ivoire.* March 26, 2003.

United Nations Security Council. Resolution 866. September 22, 1993.

United Nations Security Council. Resolution 1020. November 10, 1995.

United Nations Security Council. Resolution 1132. October 8, 1997.

United Nations Security Council. Resolution 1181. July 13, 1998.

United Nations Security Council. Resolution 1289. February 7, 2000.

United Nations Security Council. Resolution 1346. March 30, 2001.

United Nations Security Council. Resolution 1479 (2003). May 13, 2003.

United Nations Security Council. Resolution 1509 (2003). September 19, 2003.

United Nations Security Council. Resolution 1528 (2004). February 27, 2004.

United Nations Security Council. Resolution 1572. November 15, 2004.

United Nations Security Council. Resolution 1609. June 24, 2005.

United Nations Security Council. Resolution 1638. November 11, 2005.

United Nations Security Council. Resolution 1721. November 1, 2006.

United Nations Security Council. Resolution 1739. January 10, 2007.

United Nations Security Council. Resolution 1765. July 16, 2007.

United Nations Security Council. Resolution 1967. January 19, 2011.

United Nations Security Council. "Security Council Establishes UN Integrated Office in Sierra Leone to Further Address Root Causes of Conflict." August 31, 2005.

United Nations Security Council. "Security Council Extends Ivory Coast Mission Until 24 June, With Intention to Renew for Further 7 Months." June 3, 2005.

United Nations Security Council. *Security Council Extends Operation in Ivory Coast until 15 January 2008, Unanimously Adopting Resolution 1765 (2007).* July 16, 2007.

United Nations Security Council. *Seventh Report of the Secretary-General on the United Nations Observer Mission in Sierra Leone.* July 30, 1999.

United Nations Security Council. *Thirty-Fourth Report of the Secretary-General on the United Nations Operation in Côte d'Ivoire.* May 15, 2014.

United Nations Security Council. *Twelfth Progress Report of the Secretary-General on the United Nations Operation in Côte d'Ivoire.* March 8, 2007.

United Nations Security Council. *Twentieth Progress Report of the Secretary-General on the United Nations Operation in Liberia.* February 17, 2010.

United Nations Security Council. *Twenty-Eighth Progress Report of the Secretary-General on the United Nations Operation in Liberia.* August 15, 2014.

United Nations Security Council. *Twenty-First Progress Report of the Secretary-General on the United Nations Operation in Liberia.* August 11, 2010.

United Nations Statistics Division. "Department of Economic and Social Affairs: Statistics." Accessed January 13, 2024. https://unstats.un.org/.

United States Agency for International Development. "Côte d'Ivoire Radio Stations Promote Healing and Disclosure." July 2015. https://2012-2017.usaid.gov/results -data/success-stories/local-radio-stations-du%C3%A9kou%C3%A9-promote -reconciliation.

United States Agency for International Development. "Data Sheet." Accessed December 31, 2008. http://www.usaid.gov/policy/budget/cbj2006/afr/pdf/sl636 -002.pdf.

United States Agency for International Development. "Office of Transition Initiatives CITI Program in Côte d'Ivoire." Accessed October 1, 2020. https:// www.usaid.gov/stabilization-and-transitions/closed-programs/cote-divoire.

United States Congress. H.R. 434. Trade and Development Act of 2000. 106th Congress (2000).

United States Department of State. "U.S. Relations with Liberia." August 2, 2019. https://www.state.gov/u-s-relations-with-liberia/.

United States Embassy in Côte d'Ivoire. "Closing OTI and its Côte d'Ivoire Transition Initiatives (CITI) Program." March 29, 2016. https://ci.usembassy.gov /closing-of-the-office-of-transition-initiatives-oti-and-its-cote-divoire-transition -initiatives-citi-program/.

United States Institute of Peace. *Truth Commission: South Africa.* December 1, 1995. http://www.usip.org/publications/truth-commission-south-africa.

Uvin, Peter. "Difficult Choices in the New Post-Conflict Agenda: The International Community in Rwanda after the Genocide." *Third World Quarterly* 22, no. 2 (2001): 177–189.

Uvin, Peter, and Charles Mironko. "Western and Local Approaches to Justice in Rwanda." *Global Governance* 9, no. 2 (2003): 219–231.

Van de Walle, Nicolas. *African Economies and the Politics of Permanent Crisis, 1979– 1999.* Cambridge, MA: Cambridge University Press, 2001.

Van de Walle, Nicolas. "Africa's Range of Regimes." *Journal of Democracy* 13, no. 2 (2002): 66–80.

Van Veen, Erwin. *"Global Developments in State Failure.* A Brief Analysis of the Failed States 2005—2010." Accessed December 29, 2023. The Hague, Holland: Netherlands Institute of International Relation, March 2011. https://www .clingendael.org/sites/default/files/2016-02/20110304_cru_publicatie _evanveen.pdf.

Von Kemedi, Dimieari. "The Changing Predatory Styles of International Oil Companies in Nigeria." *Review of African Political Economy* 30, no. 95 (2003): 134–139.

Wai, Zubairu. "Rethinking War and Violence in Sierra Leone: The RUF and the Nature and Condition of Insurgency Violence," *African Conflict & Peacebuilding Review* 13, no. 1 (2023): 44–76.

Walker, Connor. "National-Building or Nation-Destroying?" *World Politics* 24, no. 3 (1972): 319–355.

Wallerstein, Immanuel M. *The Capitalist World-Economy*. Cambridge, UK: Cambridge University Press, 1979.

Wallerstein, Immanuel M. *Historical Capitalism: with Capitalist Civilization*. London: Verso Trade, 2011.

Wallerstein, Immanuel M. *Modern World System: Capitalist Agriculture and the Origins of the European World Economy in the Sixteenth Century*. New York: Academic Press, 1974.

Wallerstein, Immanuel M. "The Rise and Future Demise of the World Capitalist System: Concepts for Comparative Analysis." *Comparative Studies in Society and History* 16, no. 4 (1974): 387–415.

Wallerstein, Immanuel M. *World Systems Analysis: An Introduction*. Durham, NC: Duke University Press, 2004.

Wallis, William, and Tom Burgis. "Africa-China Trade: Continent Drives a Harder Bargain." *Financial Times*, June 14, 2010. http://www.ft.com/intl/cms/de832bb2 -7500-11df-aed7-00144feabdco.pdf.

Waltz, Kenneth N. "The Emerging Structure of International Politics." *International Security* 18, no. 2 (1993): 44–79.

Weber, Max. *Max Weber: Essays in Sociology*. Translated and edited by H. H. Gerth and C. Wright Mills. New York: Routledge, 2009.

Weiskel, Timothy C. *French Colonial Rule and the Baule Peoples: Resistance and Collaboration, 1889–1911*. Gloucestershire: Clarendon, 1980.

Weiss, Thomas G. "The Sunset of Humanitarian Intervention? The Responsibility to Protect the in a Unipolar Era." *Security Dialogue* 35, no. 2 (2004): 135–153.

Weiss, Thomas George. *Humanitarian Intervention: Ideas in Action*. Cambridge, UK: Polity, 2007.

Welsh, Paul. "Côte d'Ivoire: Who Are the Rebels?" *BBC News*, January 15, 2003. http://news.bbc.co.uk/2/hi/africa/2662655.stm.

White, Howard, ed. *Aid and Macro-Economic Performance: Theory, Empirical Evidence and Four Country Cases*. Basingstoke, UK: Palgrave Macmillan, 1998.

Widner, Jennifer A. "Single Party States and Agricultural Policies: The Cases of Ivory Coast and Kenya." *Comparative Politics* 26, no. 2 (1994): 127–147.

Widner, Jennifer A. "Two Leadership Styles and Patterns of Political Liberalization." *African Studies Review* 37, no. 1 (1994): 151–174.

Wiley, Edwin, Albert Bushnell Hart, and Irving Everett Rines, eds. *Lectures on the Growth and Development of the United State, Vol. 6*. Washington, DC: American Educational Alliance, 1915.

Williams, David, and Tom Young. "Governance, the World Bank and Liberal Theory." *Political Studies* 42, no. 1 (1994): 84–100.

Williams, Gabriel I. H. *Liberia: The Heart of Darkness: Accounts of Liberia's Civil War and its Destabilizing Effects in West Africa*. Bloomington, IN: Trafford, 2002.

Wilmsen, Ewin N., and Patrick McAllister. *The Politics of Difference: Ethnic Premises in a World of Power*. Chicago: University of Chicago Press, 1996.

Wilson, Richard. *The Politics of Truth and Reconciliation in South Africa: Legitimizing the Post-apartheid State.* Cambridge, UK: Cambridge University Press, 2001.

Wiseman, John A. *Democracy and Political Change in Sub-Saharan Africa.* London: Routledge, 1995.

Wiseman, John A. *The New Struggle for Democracy in Africa.* Aldershot, UK: Avebury, 1996.

Woods, Dwayne. "Elites, Ethnicity, and 'Home Town' Associations in the Côte d'Ivoire: An Historical Analysis of State Society Links." *Africa* 64, no.4 (1994): 465–483.

Woods, Dwayne. "The Tragedy of the Cocoa Pod: Rent-Seeking, Land and Ethnic Conflict in Côte d'Ivoire." *Journal of Modern African Studies* 41, no. 4 (2003): 641–655.

Woods, Larry J., and Timothy R. Reese. *Military Interventions in Sierra Leone: Lessons from a Failed State.* Seattle, WA: CreateSpace, 2008.

World Bank. *Côte d'Ivoire—Country Partnership Strategy for the Period FY10-FY13 (Report no. 53666-CI).* April 1, 2010.

World Bank. *Emergency Project Paper for an IDA Grant in the Amount of SDR6.7 Million (US$11.0 Million Equivalent) to the Republic of Liberia for an Economic Governance and Institutional Reform Project (Report no. 42836-LR).* April 29, 2008.

World Bank. *Financing Agreement (Economic Governance and Recovery Grant) between Republic of Côte d'Ivoire and International Development Association (H3500-CI).* April 1, 2008.

World Bank. "Financing Agreement (Integrated Public Financial Management Reform Project) between REPUBLIC OF SIERRA LEONE and INTERNATIONAL DEVELOPMENT ASSOCIATION." October 19, 2009. Accessed January 25, 2011. http://www-wds.worldbank.org/external/default/WDSContentServer /WDSP/AFR/2010/06/09/F02928C642C280C9852576660068E22F/2_0 /Rendered/PDF/IPFMRP0FA101Conf.1.pdf.

World Bank. "IMF and World Bank Announce More Than US$4 Billion in Debt Relief for Côte d'Ivoire." June 26, 2012. https://www.worldbank.org/en/news /press-release/2012/06/26/imf-world-bank-announce-more-than-4-billion -debt-relief-cote-divoire.

World Bank. *International Development Association Program Document for a Proposed Credit in the Amount of SDR 33.3 Million (US$50 Million Equivalent) to the Republic of Côte d'Ivoire for the First Poverty Reduction Support Credit (PRSC-1) (Report No. 67854-CI).* July 25, 2013.

World Bank. *International Development Association Program Document for the Second Economic Governance and Recovery Grant in the Amount of SDR 96.4 Million (US$150 Million Equivalent) to the Republic of Côte d'Ivoire (Report no. 46167-CI).* March 4, 2009.

World Bank. *International Development Association Project Appraisal Document on a Proposed Credit in the Amount of SDR 1.4 Million (US$2.0 Million Equivalent) to the Republic of Liberia for a Public Sector Modernization Project (Report no. 83735-LR).* January 15, 2014.

World Bank. *International Development Association Project Appraisal Document on a Proposed Credit in the Amount of SDR 3.20 Million (US$5 Million Equivalent) to the Republic of Liberia for an Integrated Public Financial Management Reform Project (Report no. 64363-LR).* November 18, 2011.

World Bank. *Liberia—Joint Country Assistance Strategy for the Period FY09-FY11 (Report no. 47928-LR).* March 31, 2009.

World Bank. "Liberia Qualifies for Complete Debt Relief under HIPC Initiative." June 29, 2010. https://www.worldbank.org/en/news/feature/2010/06/29 /liberia-qualifies-for-complete-debt-relief-under-hipc-initiative.

World Bank. *Mining Technical Assistance Project: Environmental and Social Management Framework (Report no. E2691).* September 24, 2009.

World Bank. *Project Appraisal Document on a Proposed Credit in the Amount of SDR 7.9 Million (US$12 Million Equivalent) to the Republic of Sierra Leone for the Public Financial Management & Consolidated Project.* October 31, 2013.

World Bank. *Project Information Document (PID) Concept Stage (Report no. AB3782).* March 28, 2008.

World Bank. *Project Paper on a Proposed Additional Credit in the Amount of SDR 4.5 Million (US$7 Million Equivalent) to the Republic of Liberia for an Economic Governance and Institutional Reform Project (Report no. 58891-LR).* March 14, 2001.

World Bank. *Project Paper on a Proposed Additional Grant and Proposed Restructuring of Original Project in the Amount of SDR 2.6 Million (US$4.0 Million Equivalent) to the Republic of Sierra Leone for an Extractive Industries Technical Assistance Project (Report no. 59466-SL).* March 29, 2011.

World Bank. *Restructuring Paper on a Proposed Project Restructuring of LR-Public Financial Management—IFMIS—Project Grant: Main Report (Report no. 66453, vol. 1).* January 4, 2012.

World Bank. *Sierra Leone—Country Assistance Strategy for the Period FY2006-2009 (Report no. 31793-SL).* May 5, 2005.

World Bank. *Sierra Leone—Joint Country Assistance Strategy for the Period FY10-FY13 (Report no. 52297-SL).* March 4, 2010.

World Bank. "World Bank Approves US$150 Million Grant to Support Côte d'Ivoire's Economic Recovery and Governance Program." World Bank press release no. 2009/269/AFR, March 31, 2009.

World Bank. "World Bank Country and Lending Groups: Country Classification." Accessed October 30, 2023. http://data.worldbank.org/about/country -classifications?print&book_recurse.

World Bank. World Bank Open Data. Accessed October 23, 2023. https://data .worldbank.org.

World Bank. *World Development Report* (1978, 1979, 1989, 2000/2001, and 2005). Accessed October 12, 2023. https://openknowledge.worldbank.org/handle /10986/2124.

World Elections. "Category Archives: Côte d'Ivoire—African Review 2011." Accessed October 14, 2023. http://welections.wordpress.com/category/cote -divoire/.

World Trade Organization and Organization for Economic Co-Operation and Development. *Aid for Trade and LDCs: Starting to Show Results*, 2011. Accessed November 4, 2023. https://www.oecd.org/aidfortrade/48294296.pdf.

World Trade Organization. Ministerial Declaration (WT/MIN[01]/DEC/1). Doha, QA, November 14, 2001.

World Vision International. "Structure and Funding." Monrovia, CA: World Vision International, 2007 Accessed December 31, 2008. http://www.wvi.org/wvi /wviweb.nsf/maindocs/39F905AE21E265C1882573750075074B?opendocument.

World Vision International. "Who We Are." Monrovia, CA: World Vision International, 2008. Accessed December 31, 2008. http://www.wvi.org/wvi /wviweb.nsf/maindocs/3F50B250D66B7629882573640063F21?opendocument.

Wreh, Tuan. *The Love of Liberty: The Rule of President William V. S. Tubman in Liberia, 1944–1971*. New York: Universe Books, 1976.

Yeros, Paris, ed. *Ethnicity and Nationalism in Africa: Constructivist Reflections and Contemporary Politics*. New York: Macmillan, 1999.

Young, Crawford. *The African Colonial State in Comparative Perspective*. New Haven, CT: Yale University, 1995.

Young, Crawford. "The End of the Post-Colonial State in Africa? Reflections on Changing African Political Dynamics." *African Affairs* 103, no. 410 (2004): 23–49.

Young, Michael, and Peter Willmott. *Family and Kinship in East London*. Harmondsworth, UK: Penguin, 1957.

Zack-Williams, Alfred B. "Sierra Leone: The Political Economy of Civil War, 1991–98." *Third World Quarterly* 20, no. 1 (1999): 143–162.

Zartman, I. William, ed. *Collapsed States: The Disintegration and Restoration of Legitimate Authority*. Boulder, CO: Lynne Rienner, 1995.

Zartman, I. William, and Christopher L. Delgado, eds. *The Political Economy of Côte d'Ivoire*. New York: Praeger, 1984.

Zejly, Ahmed, and Gilbert Galibaka. *Appraisal Report: The National Good Governance and Capacity Building Programme (PNBGRC) Republic of Côte d'Ivoire*. African Development Fund, West Region, October 2001.

Znaniecki, Florian. *Modern Nationalities: A Sociological Study*. Urbana: University of Illinois Press, 1952.

Zolberg, Aristide R. "The Military Decade in Africa." *World Politics* 25, no. 2 (1973): 309–321.

Zolberg, Aristide R. *One-Party Government in the Ivory Coast*. Princeton, NJ: Princeton University Press, 1964.

Zolberg, Aristide R. "The Structure of Political Conflict in the New States of Tropical Africa." *American Political Science Review* 62, no.1 (1968): 70–87.

INDEX

ABU BAKARR BAH is Presidential Research Professor of Sociology and Department Chair at Northern Illinois University (USA). He is also Founding Editor of *African Conflict & Peacebuilding Review*, African Editor for *Critical Sociology*, and Founding Director of the Institute for Research and Policy Integration in Africa. Bah is author of *Breakdown and Reconstitution: Democracy, the Nation-State, and Ethnicity in Nigeria* and numerous articles published in top journals such as *African Affairs* and *Critical Sociology* and an invited speaker at over forty major institutions around the world.

NIKOLAS EMMANUEL is Professor of Political Science in the Graduate School of International Peace Studies at Soka University (Japan). He is also an External Research Collaborator with the Centre for Global Criminology at the University of Copenhagen. Nikolas has been an invited speaker at major institutions such as Cornell University, ETH Zurich, the University of Tokyo, and the Kofi Annan Peacekeeping Training Center.

For Indiana University Press

Tony Brewer, Artist and Book Designer
Dan Crissman, Editorial Director and Acquisitions Editor
Gary Dunham, Acquisitions Editor and Director
Anna Francis, Assistant Acquisitions Editor
Anna Garnai, Editorial Assistant
Brenna Hosman, Production Coordinator
Katie Huggins, Production Manager
Dave Hulsey, Associate Director and Director of Sales and Marketing
Nancy Lightfoot, Project Manager/Editor
Bethany Mowry, Acquisitions Editor
Dan Pyle, Online Publishing Manager
Michael Regoli, Director of Publishing Operations
Stephen Williams, Assistant Director of Marketing
Jennifer Witzke, Senior Artist and Book Designer